FIGURE IT OUT

Getting from Information to Understanding

by

STEPHEN P. ANDERSON
and KARL FAST

foreword by Christina Wodtke

TWO WAVES
BOOKS

TWO WAVES BOOKS
NEW YORK, NEW YORK, USA

"We all think. But we rarely think about *how* we think. Stephen and Karl dissect how we naturally make sense of the world, using not only our minds, but also our bodies and our surroundings. They break down the process into its different constituent parts and lay out the mental operations, physical behaviors, strategies, and activities we all use on a day-to-day basis. By revealing and describing these processes in a structured way, they provide the reader with a rich and actionable toolkit for sharpening their thinking and extending their capabilities for understanding and reasoning."

—Eva-Lotta Lamm,
designer and visual thinker

"The challenge of making sense of the oceans of information brought to us by digital technology is the truly significant task of our era. Not since Pinker's 1997 tome has anyone addressed this important arena with the breadth and clarity it deserves. We will never create machines that understand their world until we can wrap our heads around the more daunting question of how humans understand it. This book brings us a step closer to that day."

—Alan Cooper,
author of *About Face* and *The Inmates Are Running the Asylum*

"Designers need to help users make sense of an increasingly complex world. Karl Fast and Stephen P. Anderson have laid out an invaluable toolkit to design for understanding."

—Julie Dirksen,
author, *Design for How People Learn*

Figure It Out
Getting from Information to Understanding
By Stephen P. Anderson and Karl Fast

Two Waves Books
an Imprint of Rosenfeld Media, LLC
125 Maiden Lane, Suite 209
New York, New York
10038 USA

On the Web: twowavesbooks.com
Please send errors to: errata@twowavesbooks.com

Publisher: Louis Rosenfeld
Managing Editor: Marta Justak
Sketch-Note Illustrations: Eva-Lotta Lamm
Figures: Stephen P. Anderson
Interior Layout Tech: Danielle Foster
Cover and Interior Design: The Heads of State
Indexer: Marilyn Augst
Proofreader: Sue Boshers

Printed and bound in the United States of America

Stephen P. Anderson

For my boys: Gabriel, Liam, Elijah, and Jonas
Read this book carefully, and you'll understand
how the world works.
—Dad

Karl Fast

For my students—keep asking good questions.

Contents

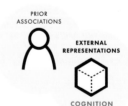

Part 4. How We Understand Through Interactions   241

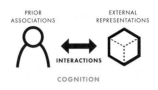

Part 5. Coordinating for Understanding   289

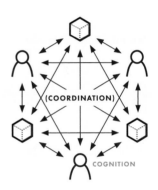

Part 6. Tools and Technologies for Understanding   337

Foreword

There comes a time in every professional's life when they wish to make a model.

This may sound silly at first glance, but as you dig into a body of work by any prolific thinker, you'll see attempts to organize that knowledge in order to clarify the problem they are studying.

Darwin drew rambling tree diagrams as he contemplated the origin of the species. Zaha Hadid sketched, but you would expect that from an architect. Grant Achatz and Michel Bras, renowned chefs, both made simple models of their complex dishes. Marie Curie and J. K. Rowling did, too.

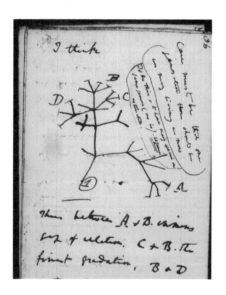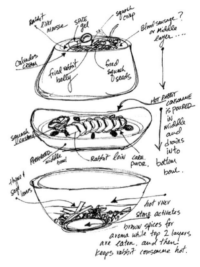

Sometimes a thinker will attempt to represent a model with words, a "dancing about architecture"[1] attempt. When people say that all teams need three things: someone who knows about business, someone who understands the customer, and someone who understands how to make things, you are hearing

---

1. "Writing about music is like dancing about architecture." Martin Mull

about a model. You might picture it in your head as a Venn diagram or a three-legged stool, because it is a model.

Some thinkers will tentatively draw something—helped along by the proliferation of tools, such as PowerPoint's SmartArt. Steve Blank, the "father of modern entrepreneurship," made this diagram to explain how one finds customers. The ideas are good, but the execution leaves something to be desired.

Of course, academic papers are full of terrible charts and diagrams.

I was in the thick of this problem when I started running workshops on social software design. I knew what I wanted people to consider when they added social features, such as forums or commenting. But I couldn't make a model, which was shocking to me, because I am an art school graduate. Yet drawing is not the same as modeling. I took Karl and Stephen's workshop on "Design for Understanding" in 2014. Karl was the academic who knew why things worked, Stephen was the design expert who knew how to make things that worked, and I was the lucky ignoramus who got to ride along (after all, ignorance is curable.)

The last few years have been filled with discussions, in the real world and online, as we pieced together the mysteries of why some things are good and some things are not, why things are the way they are. And I was the lucky one who got to read the book you are now holding in its many stages, from fumbling in the dark to shining a light on the problem. Through my conversations with Karl and Stephen, I learned that we don't think with just our brain, we think with our bodies and our environment as well.

This journey to understand how we think has paid off for me. It helped me understand why some teams fall apart and some don't, so I could write my book on teams. It gave me a way to teach students at Stanford to design more effectively and think more clearly. You are at the start of your journey, and as the cliché goes, I envy you.

This book is full of ideas, big and small, theoretical and practical. When you are done, you will not only speak a new language, but you'll be able to dream in it. And best of all, there are plenty of pictures to help you understand. Pictures are not just for children—they are for anyone who wants to engage more of their mind.

I agree with Alice: "What is the use of a book," thought Alice, "without pictures or conversation?" (Lewis Carroll, *Alice's Adventures in Wonderland*).

Figure It Out is both, and it is a supremely useful book.

—Christina Wodtke, author of *Radical Focus* and
The Team That Managed Itself and lecturer in HCI at Stanford University

Introduction

by Stephen P. Anderson

I love making complex topics and challenges more approachable. Throughout my career, from my earliest days as a high school teacher to the many design and leadership roles I've enjoyed over the years, I've earned a reputation for seeing and communicating how all the pieces and parts of a thing might fit together into a cohesive whole. This has spanned everything from creating "site maps" for websites to facilitating strategy sessions that made sure everyone's voice was heard in forming a unified vision. But my own need to make sense of things has been more than a job—it's a way of living for me, one that shows up in nearly everything I do, both professional and personal. Often, I was asked "how" I do what I do. I suppose that's how this book began, as a way to work out for myself how—exactly—I make sense of things. I wanted to understand, well … understanding!

My early answers were only part of a much bigger picture.

As a designer, what I've commonly produced to "solve" these problems of understanding has involved some kind of visual representation. Concept models. Posters. Sketches. Graphs. Visual artifacts of all kinds. I knew going in that some portion of this book would deal with how to craft these kinds of visual explanations. But more critically, I wanted to learn *why* exactly visuals are so effective. I also knew there was more to it. Just as visuals are powerful for understanding, so, too, is the right metaphor or a good story that people can latch onto. I also knew that all these things only work because of the associations they activate in the brain. It's not about the story that's shared or the picture we see—it's about how these things change our perceptions. All these topics would become the first half of this book.

But there are more pieces to the "understanding" puzzle.

Consider what happens when you're in a workshop, moving sticky notes around on the wall. Or when you rearrange scrabble tiles, to help you see more word possibilities. It's not just about seeing things—it's also about *interacting* with these things, to change your own understanding. This was the world that my co-author Karl Fast opened my eyes to, introducing me to concepts such as "epistemic interactions" and the notion of "small data" problems. Following an introduction at a conference, it became clear that we each had been circling this "understanding" topic for many years, but came at it from different perspectives. Where I tend to fall back on personal examples and ideas based on experiences, Karl brought an academic perspective, grounded in rigor and research. One thing led to another, and we concluded this book would be better if written by both of us.

Of course, while writing this book, my activities at work began to change—I found myself doing more training and facilitation. Where public speaking and presentations emphasize communicating an idea, workshops are an altogether different challenge. While the pictures, the stories, and the interactions still have their place, I developed an appreciation for what skilled facilitators do: they hold space for reflection, and they know how to ask the exact question that lets others figure things out for themselves. I began replacing the lecture heavy bits of my own workshops with more experiential learning activities, where people could sort out for themselves some difficult concept. Through it all, I developed my ability to explain as well as to facilitate understanding.

That, essentially, is the arc of this book.

As with the process that produced what you now hold in your hands, this book is very much a journey, with each subsequent chapter building on the one before it.

And when you arrive at the end of this book, you will be able to answer this question: *How might we help ourselves and others make sense of confusing information?*

To be clear, the problem is not that we have "too much information," as we so often hear. Rather, it's that we don't know what to do with the information we do have. Email. Tweets. Newspapers. Podcasts. Data. Knowledge. Content. Statistics. Technology has made it easier, faster, and cheaper to do much with information: create, publish, share, organize, search, consume. But this ready access to information doesn't promise understanding. We're given information, but not in a form that makes sense to us.

Simply passing on all this information for others to figure out leads to things like incomprehensible tax policies, business models that can't easily be explained, and facts and figures on global issues that have divided rather than united us around possible solutions. Information alone is not the answer. It's what we *do* with the information that matters. In nearly all areas of life, we lack the tools, skills, and literacy needed to cope in a world of endless information.

At a fundamental level, this is *why* Karl and I wrote this book, to change the conversation from discussions of "information overload" and "big data" (and even "data visualization") to the question these discussions ultimately beg: *How do we make sense of it all?* In short, how do we work with information as a resource, as a "thing" we can adapt, modify, and transform to meet our needs.

The Book, in Brief

Let's look at the structure of this book and what you can expect:

Part 1, "A Focus on Understanding," clears the way for the rest of the book. We'll start small by clarifying *what* we mean when we talk about problems of understanding. From incomprehensible privacy policies to confusing medical explanations, you'll see how we typically respond when things are confusing. You'll also become aware of just how often we're given information, but not in a form that makes sense to us.

Then we'll explore *where* understanding happens with a historical survey of cognitive science, one that begins with the cognitive revolution in the 1950s and ends with how a new revolution—embodied cognition—changes how we approach problems of understanding.

With that foundation in place, the remainder of the book will turn to our central question: *How does understanding take place?*

Part 2, "How We Understand by Associations," opens with a brief look at how the brain—as a perceptual organ—uses prior associations to make sense of new information. Given how fundamental this is to our topic of understanding, we've devoted three chapters to the many ways these associations show up—from stories we tell ourselves, to the metaphors we use, to how a specific word choice can alter how we think. This is followed with a cautionary chapter on the dangers and limits of associative thinking.

Part 3, "How We Understand with External Representations," investigates how we create external representations to extend our thinking into the world using tools, maps, drawings, and spaces. We dedicate a chapter to our sense of vision, and a chapter to the topic of color, before turning to the ways we use space to hold and convey meaning.

Part 4, "How We Understand Through Interactions," explores how interactions are not the *result* of thinking (our brain telling our hands to grab something), but an integral *part of* thinking. We then identify the different kinds of interactions we use to create understanding from information.

Part 5, "Coordinating for Understanding," examines the coordination of these activities, first challenging us to see a system of cognitive resources, before considering how we might coordinate small and large groups of people for understanding.

Part 6, "Tools and Technologies for Understanding," concludes with a look at tools and technologies used to facilitate understanding. First, we'll take a critical look at those things *currently* available to us. Then we'll drive all this newfound knowledge into the future and explain how new technologies won't radically reconfigure everything written about in this book, but will instead enable us to do everything we've been doing, but even more powerfully.

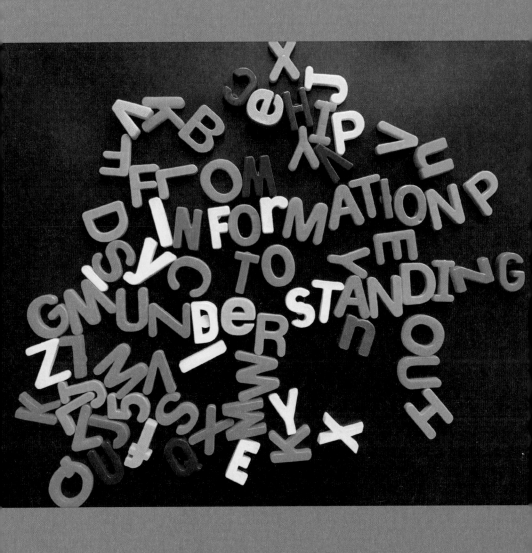

COGNITION

1

A Focus on Understanding

From incomprehensible privacy policies to confusing medical explanations, we are often given information, but not understanding. But we can create—or at least reduce the cost of—understanding. By treating information as a resource, as raw material rather than a finished product, we give ourselves permission to adapt, modify, and transform it into a shape that aids understanding and makes us better thinkers.

Of course, this leads us to ask *"where* does understanding happen?" It's a simple enough question, but one whose answer has broad implications for how we approach all problems of understanding.

We'll explore how different schools of thought have answered this question, before sharing our own perspective on cognition, a perspective that allows us to make substantial headway on a wide range of messy, complex, real-world problems of understanding. In short, we'll argue that thinking is spread across the brain, the body, and anything in the world.

This is critical, because we don't just think. We create tools and technologies to help us think better, understand more, and solve bigger problems. Our ability to understand is limited when we try to do everything in our head, especially when we have lots of information and when the challenges are daunting. But when we spread the cost of understanding into the world, we open up incredible possibilities for understanding. We increase our capacity for understanding when cognition is seen as something that happens in and through the world.

1

From Information to Understanding

Cram them full of noncombustible data, chock them so damned full of "facts" they feel stuffed, but absolutely "brilliant" with information. Then they'll feel they're thinking, they'll get a sense of motion without moving.

—RAY BRADBURY, *FAHRENHEIT 451*

We all want to understand. None of us wants the information in our lives to leave us confused or ignorant or frustrated, though it often does. What we want is for information to inform, for that is the fundamental job of *inform*_ation—a job that includes making us smarter, educated, and more knowing, not to mention entertained. Life is unimaginable without information, and although we have gobs of it, the goal is not having it, but using it to some end. We want information to help us solve problems, make decisions, create insights, reveal truths, and set us on a better path. Information should add to our lives, not subtract, though when we lack understanding that is just what it does.

When we consider the arc of civilization, humanity has been relentless in developing more powerful information technologies—from clay tablets to sticky notes and smartphones—along with more effective ways to share this information, organize it, and search for it. This relentlessness has only intensified as we have built a global digital infrastructure. This effort has rendered information both abundant and cheap, and, as a result, it has been injected into the whole fabric of life. We have seemingly infinite information at our fingertips, often literally, no matter where we are or what we are doing. You will even find Wi-Fi at Mount Everest, and the first climber to tweet from the summit did so in 2011. We use information for grand challenges, such as climate change or curing cancer, or small ones, such as staying in touch with friends or digging up obscure baseball stats. But in every facet of life, whether our need is ambitious or trivial, information fails us unless we also understand it.

Even as authors of a book on understanding, we are not immune to the challenges posed by so much information. We, too, often find ourselves with piles of information and a paucity of understanding. At the same time, we have, both of us, built careers by making information more understandable. We have created websites, mobile apps, concept models, data visualizations, navigation systems, organization schemes, university courses, strategy sessions, and endless presentations. We have learned, often the hard way, that simply giving people information, or making it easier to find, is just a halfway measure. Providing information is merely the start. The whole job includes figuring out how to fit the pieces into a cohesive, useful, understandable whole in much the same way that a recipe and the freshest of ingredients does not make a meal. Understanding, like dinner, doesn't happen by magic, and in this book we aim to provide a full-spectrum picture of how we, as human beings, go about making sense of the information in our lives.

Living with Diabetes

When information is everywhere, so, too, is understanding problems. Allow me (Stephen) to share a personal example.

My son was diagnosed with Type 1 diabetes just before his fourth birthday. Previously known as *juvenile diabetes*, Type 1 diabetes is when your pancreas—for reasons unknown—stops producing insulin, a hormone we all need in order to live. Without insulin, your body has no way to convert sugar from carbohydrates into energy and no way to maintain healthy blood sugar levels. It is a life-changing disease.

When we got the diagnosis, my wife and I knew it meant big changes for our family. We knew that living with diabetes meant insulin shots. What we didn't know, but quickly learned, was the sheer number of activities that diabetics must do to maintain their health. One activity is *finger pokes*, where you draw a small sample of blood to test blood sugar levels. If you're diabetic, you do this about a dozen times a day to make sure that your blood sugar levels are within a safe zone—not too high and not too low.

Type 1 diabetics also have to *count carbohydrates* on absolutely everything they eat. Setting aside social graces, most of us begin eating right away when a meal is served. Diabetics have no such luxury. Instead, they have to calculate how many carbs they think they're going to consume, before eating. This is even more troublesome in restaurants, where access to nutritional information is nearly impossible, and where predicting their appetite is difficult. *Will I want a dessert later or not?*

And the reason diabetics count carbohydrates? So they can *inject the right amount of insulin.* These are the needle shots you so often see associated with diabetes. While healthy bodies are great at producing and regulating the amount of insulin to produce for all the carbs people consume, Type 1 diabetics must do so artificially, including the math needed to balance things out. Give themselves too much insulin, and they have a "low," quickly leading to a diabetic coma. Not enough insulin, and they have high blood sugar, which causes long-term complications, including loss of limbs, eyesight, and failing organs.

All of this is a lot to learn and a lot to take in as a parent of a diabetic child. For the child, it's a whole new way of living that—until a cure is found—overshadows everything else. My wife and I were fortunate in that our hospital had a superb training program to prepare parents and children for this new life, this "new normal" that you quickly adjust to.

During the three-day "retraining" process, the hospital gave us a lot of useful information. They helped us process what to expect. And they gave us plenty of paperwork.

Among the many forms we were given, mostly of a legal/compliance nature, special attention was given to the form in Figure 1.1.

This is *the* sheet that you put on your refrigerator, the "one-pager" that is meant to organize everything you'll do in a day. It is the checklist of all the things that you need to know: *When to give your child insulin. When to test blood sugar levels. How many carbs they can eat. How many units of insulin to give.* All the information you need to know is in this form.

This form is also *broken.*

Endocrinology Center Diabetes Management Instructions	DOB	0	Page 1 of 2

Time of Day

H = Humalog   N = NPH

9am Test blood glucose
Take insulin injection: Rapid acting(_H_) _2_ units Long acting(_NPH_) _4_ units
Eat breakfast ....grams carbohydrates _40-45g_

_____ Eat mid morning snack ....grams carbohydrates_____

12pm Take blood glucose
Take insulin injection (if needed): Rapid acting(_H_) _per sliding scale_ units
Eat lunch ....grams carbohydrates _40-45g_

4pm Eat mid-afternoon snack ....grams carbohydrates _15-20_

6pm Test blood glucose
Take insulin injection: Rapid acting(_H_) _I_ units Long acting(_____)____units
Eat dinner.....................................grams carbohydrates _60-65g_
_55-60 g_

8pm Test blood glucose
Take insulin injection: Long acting(_NPH_) _1.5_ units
Eat bedtime snack ....grams carbohydrates _15-20_ + protein

3am Overnight blood glucose testing (If needed) x _2 days_

Supplemental/Correction Insulin Guidelines
Use rapid acting insulin only. Use only at mealtimes or before bedtime snack.

For blood glucose below	_300_		, do not add extra insulin		
For blood glucose from	_301_	to _400_	add _1/2_	units _Humalog_	insulin
For blood glucose from		to	add	units	insulin
For blood glucose from		to	add	units	insulin
For blood glucose over	_401_		add _/_	units _Humalog_	insulin

- Do not vary the scheduled times by more than one hour; Keep 2 hours between meals and snacks
- Test for urinary ketones: (a) when blood glucose is over 250

FIGURE 1.1 The diabetes management aid provided to families as a daily checklist for monitoring blood sugar, tracking carbohydrates, injecting insulin, and so forth.

This form is so very confusing that nurses routinely spend 30 minutes explaining it. Moreover, a couple areas on this form are outright dangerous—if misunderstood, you could harm your child by giving them too much insulin.

After the nurse left the room, my wife looked at me and said, "You've got to fix this." What you see in Figure 1.2 is my makeover of this chart.

As dramatically different as this version is, I want to highlight something: I did not *add* any information, nor did I *remove* any information. All that has changed is *how* the information is presented.

My goals were simple:

1. **I wanted to create something that my son—at only four years of age—could look at and get a sense of what he was supposed to do.** I wanted him to manage this disease from an early age. I needed him to understand what was expected of him.

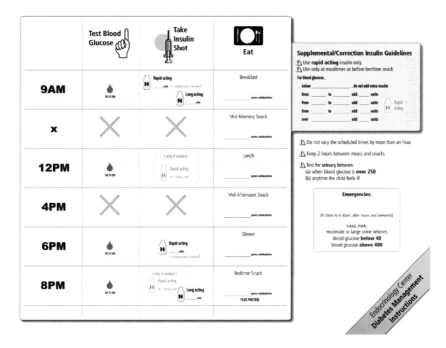

FIGURE 1.2 This version of the diabetes chart has the same information as the one provided by the hospital. All that has changed is the visual design.

2. **I wanted to give us, as parents, a sense of control.** My wife and I *needed* to create something like this. Of course, we needed to understand what was expected of us. But on a deeper level, we needed something we could control. As parents, you've done everything right, fed your child the right foods, avoided the things that might harm a child. And yet, something like this happens, for no explicable reason. We felt powerless. Creating this chart was one way for us to assert some level of control over a small piece of the diagnosis.

Now, what about the after version? From a graphic design perspective, there is plenty to critique. The icons are inconsistent. There are some padding and alignment imperfections. Color schemes are *meh*. I could have fixed this with more time. But winning a graphic design award was not my goal. My goal was to make the information *understandable* and fixating on small tweaks wouldn't make it much more understandable. This kind of transformation is largely functional, not aesthetic. Moreover, it's something we can all do, or should be able to do, by the time you're finished with this book.

If you can organize a closet or sort spices in a kitchen cabinet, you can do what I've done here. At the core, all I did was identify and align "like" information. If you look closely at the before version, you can see three kinds of activities listed (finger pokes, insulin shots, and eating), as well as the times for each; this information was—in the before version—listed, but not shown. By introducing a column for each of the three types of activities, then mapping those columns against the time of day, resulting in a grid layout, we could see more clearly when to do which activity. (This also allowed us to be explicit about when we should *not* do an activity as well, as indicated by the × shape.) This chart was largely about using space to hold meaning, something that we'll explore in detail.

Beyond this sorting and alignment exercise, I added images to reinforce the literal things being referenced with words: the column headers had corresponding images (finger for finger pokes, needle for taking shots, a food tray for eating). Where finger pokes were involved, I grabbed a "drop of blood" icon (courtesy of a Google image search). And when it was time to give my son a shot, I reinforced the language of which type of insulin by adding illustrations of "H" or "N" vials of insulin. Where something was optional ("only if needed"), I used opacity to fade that back into the background, a type of visual encoding that we'll also discuss.

Understanding Is Created

It is a truism and a time-worn cliché that we have more information—and more access to information—than at any other point in history. Yet all this information doesn't get us especially far if we can't make sense of it. At the same time, we tend to assume that information should come in an understandable shape. When it does not—when we are given information but not understanding—we are likely to blame the information-industrial complex for failing us. This is why the diabetes chart example is so irksome. Medical professionals provided accurate and reliable information in a critical situation, yet also left my wife and me feeling uncertain and powerless and fearful of doing harm to our child. While the hospital's training program was superb, my family needed more from that chart, a great deal more, given the pivotal role it would play in our lives.

But consider this story from another angle. While we should have been given a more understandable chart, should we *also* expect all information to be this way? Should every bit of information that comes our way be instantly and immediately understandable? Is it reasonable, or even possible, to be given understanding anytime we are given information? There are many situations, such as health and public safety, when information should be unambiguous. This has led to standardizing the meaning of everything from traffic lights to symbols on radioactive material. But even when the information before us is clear and comprehensible, the path to understanding may still require us to engage with it. Quite often, we need to *create* understanding.

Suppose that you wanted to knit a pair of socks, and we gave you the best book ever written on the subject, the best instructional videos ever produced, and a few hours with a world-class knitting instructor. Furthermore, let's consider what would happen if you divided the process into two stages. In the first stage, you would absorb the information from these three world-class sources—reading, watching, listening closely, and taking it all in. Once you'd gone through and studied all the information, then, and only then, would you move to the second stage: sitting down and starting to knit. Such an approach seems silly and doomed, no matter how clear the information is or how wonderful the instruction. You would still need to act. You would need to pick up the needles and start knitting, ask questions, review the examples, make mistakes, and keep going. This would be true even for experienced knitters. The understanding comes *through* doing, not just taking in information.

Even the revised diabetes chart, despite the improvements, didn't eliminate the need for finger pokes and counting carbohydrates. By making the chart more understandable, it became easier to monitor blood sugar levels and manage insulin, while also reducing the chance of making a mistake. But the chart was still just a part, albeit a central part, of living with diabetes.

Or take privacy policies as another example. How often, in the course of a month, do you agree to an app's "Terms of Service"? Or what about your bank's annual privacy notice, or the last employee agreement you signed? How often do you read all the terms and conditions? And if you have, did you *understand* the binding legal terms you agreed to? The phrase "I have read, understand, and agree to the terms …" has been called the biggest lie on the Internet.[1] We have all committed this lie and for good reason. Terms of service documents are dozens of pages long and written in legalese. They can

---

1. https://tosdr.org/

only be understood with significant effort. In one study, researchers asked people to sign up for early access to a new social networking site. The site didn't exist, but it had a convincing home page and a sign-up process based on the design of Facebook, LinkedIn, and other social networking sites. The privacy policy and terms of service were modified from actual LinkedIn documents.[2] The privacy policy told users that, if asked, the site would share any user data requested with the government, including the NSA and other intelligence agencies. Some 97% of people accepted the policy. The terms of service document was more brazen. It required all users to "immediately assign their first-born" child to the company, including unborn children through the year 2050, and that accepting the terms meant said children automatically became company property—"No exceptions." Of the 543 people who signed up, 93% agreed to the terms. Too long—should've read it.

Think of these legal documents, or the knitting tutorials, or any other information, as a jigsaw puzzle (see Figure 1.3). All of the raw information we might need is there—pieces of the puzzle—waiting to be assembled into something coherent. With some effort, it is *possible* to understand the content of these documents in their original form. In some cases, it's simply a matter of fitting the pieces together. In other cases, it means *transforming* the information into

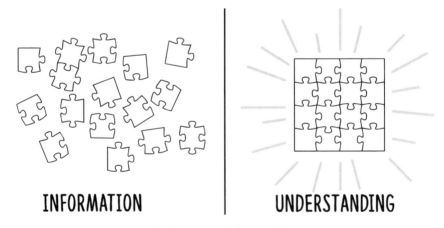

INFORMATION   UNDERSTANDING

FIGURE 1.3 Making sense of information is like assembling pieces of a jigsaw puzzle.

2. Obar, Jonathan A., and Anne Oeldorf-Hirsch. 2018. "The Biggest Lie on the Internet: Ignoring the Privacy Policies and Terms of Service Policies of Social Networking Services." *Information, Communication & Society* 23 (1): 128–47. https://doi.org/10.1080/1369118x.2018.1486870

some new form that makes sense, adapting the information to yourself, your situation, your particular needs—precisely what Stephen did with the diabetes chart. The legalese of privacy policies makes this difficult, even mind-numbingly so, but it can be done. Such documents should be more understandable since they have legal implications. Yet we should also acknowledge their complexity and accept that understanding them will never be as simple as interpreting the red, yellow, and green of a traffic light.

We have grown so used to "problems of understanding" (as we'll call them) that it can be hard to even see them as problems. Like fish unaware of the water in which they swim, we often go through life, accustomed to or unaware of these problems of understanding. We do not always realize the ways in which we can solve this puzzle and create understanding. We joke about incomprehensible privacy policies. We expect medical explanations to be confusing. We're frustrated by confusing parking signs. But all these things, and more, can be understood and, more precisely, can be *made* understandable.

Information Is a Resource

We tend to think of information as an object, some *thing*, however ephemeral, that was created to inform: a newspaper story, a podcast episode, an airline ticket, a restaurant menu, a privacy policy, or a street sign telling us if, when, and where we can park. In this book, we will take a somewhat different view. We will treat information as a *resource*—more like wheat than bread. Wheat is a resource from which we can make bread, or the crust for a cherry pie, or paper mâché. By treating information as a resource, as raw material rather than a finished product, we give ourselves permission to transform it into a shape that aids understanding and makes us better thinkers.

"Information must be that which leads to understanding," wrote the designer Richard Saul Wurman in the late 1980s, an era that was, even then, concerned about information overload.[3] Information that failed to inform was merely data, he argued, but as data, it became a malleable material through which

---

3. People have long worried about information overload. The term was coined by Bertram Gross, a political science professor, in 1964 and popularized by the futurist Alvin Toffler in the 1970s. But the fear that we will become overwhelmed by information, utterly unable to cope, predates the modern world much farther than you might think. The Harvard historian Ann Blair has traced these worries back more than 2,300 years. Blair, Ann. 2011. *Too Much to Know: Managing Scholarly Information Before the Modern Age*. New Haven, CT: Yale University Press.

understanding could be created. "What constitutes information to one person may be data to another," Wurman explained, and "if it doesn't make sense to you, it doesn't qualify for the appellation."[4]

In this book, we will also take the perspective that information is understandable in relation to people and their needs. This means that information may be perfectly understandable to some people and, at the same time, perfect gobbledy-gook to others. But unlike Wurman and many others, we will avoid fretting over the distinction between information and data (as well as how information and data relate to knowledge and wisdom).[5] For our purposes, there is simply information. And how understandable some information is depends on who is using it and what they need it for. The privacy policy *is* information to lawyers and judges since they are trained to read and write documents in that style. For the rest of us, it is also information; it's just information in a form that befuddles us. Even so, information can be made understandable, or at least more understandable, and in the coming pages, we will explore the ways that this happens as we adapt, modify, and transform information to our needs.

To be sure, it's infuriating when we need information to be clear and it isn't. We should expect more from the information in our lives, especially when it comes from experts and professionals. But we should also remember that nobody can predict, or control, how information will be used. This does not absolve those who produce information as a shoddy, disorganized, and baffling mess. The diabetes chart should not endanger. The terms of service should not obfuscate. But we should neither abdicate, nor overlook, how understanding also depends on what we, as we seek to understand, bring to the table. When we have information, we always do *something* as we figure it out.

Consider this very book. As authors, we want to be understood. We wrote and rewrote the manuscript (ad nauseam, it often seemed) to hone our ideas and clarify our prose. Yet we also knew it would never be perfectly understandable and, more importantly, we knew that you, the reader, would do things to create your own understanding. You might mark interesting passages, perhaps

4. Wurman, Richard Saul. 1989. In *Information Anxiety*, 38. New York: Doubleday.
5. For more on this topic, see: Badia, Antonio. 2014. "Data, Information, Knowledge: An Information Science Analysis." *Journal of the Association for Information Science and Technology* 65 (6): 1279–87. https://doi.org/10.1002/asi.23043; Rowley, Jennifer. 2007. "The Wisdom Hierarchy: Representations of the DIKW Hierarchy." *Journal of Information Science* 33 (2): 163–80. https://doi.org/10.1177/0165551506070706

with a pencil or a sticky note. You might write in the margins to say "don't quite get it" or "Huh?!" or "great example!"[6] You will, almost for sure, use a bookmark instead of remembering the current page in your head. We hope you'll discuss the book with friends and colleagues, perhaps as part of a book club. And if you are a designer, or anyone whose work requires producing information in any form, we hope you will do all this, and more, as you wrestle with applying the concepts to your understanding projects. We wrote this book to give you information and understanding, but these pages cannot do that well if you just scan your eyes over the words. Understanding information demands more from you than consumption.

Understanding often means adjusting the balance between the information you have and the understanding you need. In some cases, this balance should be strongly tipped toward writers, graphic designers, podcasters, filmmakers, and anyone who creates information, even if it's just a lunch menu or a yard sale poster. When you create information, you should always strive to make it understandable.

Yet this always comes with a cost, whether that cost is time and effort or learning new tools and developing better skills. It often means establishing a process for testing information with the intended audience, evaluating how well it is understood, and iterating until it reaches an acceptable level of understanding. This book, for example, was reviewed by many people (to whom we are wildly grateful) and from that we retooled much of the manuscript, followed by more reviews, editing, and revisions.

This balance also tips the other way. Understanding doesn't happen like Neo in *The Matrix*; we don't plug a cable into our brain and suddenly know Ju Jitsu. We do things all the time to create understanding, whether it's making notes in the margins of a book, rearranging sticky notes to find a meaningful pattern, or a child asking their teacher to walk them through the steps of long division. We often need to rebalance the information in our lives, making it support our goals, align it with our abilities, and adapt it to our needs.

Information is cheap; understanding is expensive. Much of the cost rests with the people who created the information. But not all, if only because they

---

6. If you're averse to marking up this book, we suggest you reconsider. Writing in the margins has been, for centuries, a favored practice of important writers and scholars, not to mention everyday readers. Making a mess of it will help you better understand it. For a history of how and why people mark up their books, we recommend: Jackson, Heather J. 2010. *Marginalia: Readers Writing in Books*. New Haven, CT: Yale University Press.

can't control how the information will be used. Some of the cost lies with the reader, the watcher, the listener—with us, with the person who has this information and wants to understand. We all figure things out, all the time, and in this book we will explore the many ways we create understanding from the information in our lives.

Figuring It Out

If access to information led directly to understanding, then we would illustrate the relationship as follows in Figure 1.4.

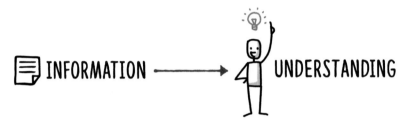

FIGURE 1.4 Access to information is sufficient where there is a simple mapping between information and understanding.

Sometimes, of course, straightforward access to information is all that's required. When we ask narrow questions with specific answers—*Who wrote Fahrenheit 451?* or *What time will my train arrive?* or *How do you pronounce Cynefin?*—the information we get back, whether it comes from a book, or an app, or a person, is sufficient. There's a simple mapping between information asked for and understanding.

But life is filled with questions that don't have simple answers. *Should I buy a solar roof? What will the changes to the tax laws mean for me? How is imitation learning different from supervised learning?* The formulation of access = understanding breaks down as our information needs increase in scope and complexity. For anything more than a narrow question, understanding takes effort. There is *always* a cost involved, always trade-offs to be made. Someone or something must analyze and synthesize and transform the information at hand into something that will lead to understanding. Someone or something must transform the many different strands of information into something that leads to understanding. Thus, our illustration might look more like Figure 1.5.

FIGURE 1.5 Information is so abundant in the modern world that we routinely need to create understanding by weaving together multiple strands. Understanding is often messy and complex and comes at a cost.

When there are many strands, the cost of understanding goes up. The cost depends on various factors: how large and complex the topic is; the prior knowledge of the people trying to understand; the availability and power of relevant tools; our confidence that we have the right information; and much more. In one sense, this book is about how we can manage, shift, or reduce the cost of understanding. How then, do we manage this cost? And who does the bulk of this work?

If we return to our privacy policy example, the cost of understanding is traditionally addressed in one of several ways. Assuming we care enough about the topic, we will either:

- **Call an expert:** A legal professional could bear that cost for us, as they've been trained to make sense of the information (granted, this option brings with it a different kind of cost!). If we're lucky, we might have a friend who is also an expert and willing to help us.

- **Figure things out on our own:** Given the time and motivation, we could make sense of all the legalese. While some people will undertake this effort, most people give up, concluding that "I'm not smart enough."

Of course, many more of us opt for a third "nonunderstanding" option; we conclude that the cost of understanding is not worthwhile. Given the cost (money or time) of the two options above, we give up or trust things will work out, hoping we haven't agreed to anything of consequence (like our first-born child).

Generally speaking, these two (or three) responses summarize how we respond when most things get confusing. Are there other ways to manage the cost of understanding?

When it comes to those obfuscating privacy policies, another approach is to distill the documents into something that is concise and easy to grasp. This is the approach taken by the group *Terms of Service; Didn't Read* (ToS;DR). It's a nonprofit group, staffed by volunteers, who read terms of service documents and convert them into a list of bullet points (Figure 1.6). Each item is given a thumbs-up (your rights are protected), thumbs-down (your rights are not protected), or a star (neutral). Each service also receives an overall rating, from Class A (terms that treat you fairly and respect your rights) all the way down to Class E (the terms raise serious concerns).

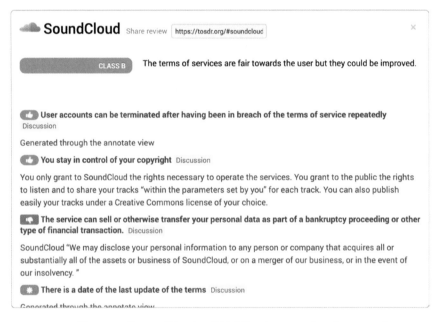

FIGURE 1.6 The group Terms of Service; Didn't Read converts lengthy terms of service documents into a series of bullet points, rating each item and classifying the service as a whole.

ToS;DR does to privacy policies what I did for the diabetes chart: transforms something complex into something simple. But where I neither added nor removed any information, ToS;DR removes almost everything. They have to do that since the original documents are overwhelming. They carefully work through all the gory details, identify the essential details, convert them into plain English, and assemble the result into a clear and readable list. They distill and translate, taking on, as volunteers, the bulk of the understanding. They do the hard work, making your life easier.

Projects such as *Polisis* take a different approach to the same problem. They use machine learning to scan and summarize legal contracts, displaying information back to users in a consistent, visual representation (see Figure 1.7). Where ToS;Dr relies on humans, Polisis relies on algorithms.

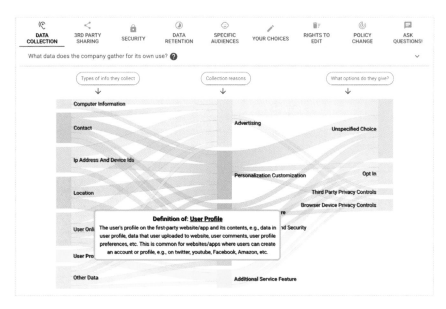

FIGURE 1.7 Polisis uses machine learning to translate policy documents into a visual form.

Polisis produces an interactive, visual summary of a specific contract. Notice the difference between these two approaches: ToS;DR shifts the cost of understanding by doing work for us, then asking us to trust their conclusion. Polisis shifts the cost of understanding by making the document easier for us to figure out—there's still work to be done. With Polisis, there is no easy recommendation, but rather clarity. From their project's web page: "You don't have to read the full privacy with all the legal jargon to understand what you are signing up for." Polisis makes the information understandable, empowering you to make a more informed choice; it's a tool that *facilitates* understanding. It's probably not as easy to understand as the lists provided by ToS;DR, but it provides more detailed information about what information is collected and why.

This kind of solution excites us, not necessarily for the use of technology, but for how this technology taps into natural human abilities. As you'll soon see, we learn through interactions. Our sense of vision is powerful. Humans are great at spotting patterns. We value learning that is active and self-directed. But, we're getting ahead of ourselves …

When we begin to view information as a resource, we open our eyes to not only the many problems of understanding, but also the many ways we might transform information to create understanding.

Who takes the time or effort to facilitate understanding? When should we delegate this work to other people, or algorithms, and when should we do it for ourselves? If we do take this on, *how* might we create our own understanding? What role does technology play in how we understand? These are central themes of this book. We hope that after reading this, you will be fully aware of when something is an understanding problem and what can be done about it, whether that means fixing things yourself, or being able to articulate what needs to change so that understanding can take place.

A Distributed System of Resources

Whether we are making sense of something for ourselves, or others, the questions are the same: How does understanding happen? And—more fundamentally—*where* does understanding take place?

Think of cognition as a distributed system of resources, resources that include mental perceptions but also much more. Where understanding takes place depends upon what resources we use.

Here is a brief explanation:

In some cases, what you think is in your head, based on *prior associations*. If you multiply 32 by 11 in your head, the cognitive work happens—in that moment—in your brain.

But where does the cognitive work happen when you use pencil and paper? Not in your brain and not in the pencil either. It happens everywhere, spread across brain, hand, pencil, and graphite symbols etched on the page. In this case, we introduce *interactions* with *external representations*.

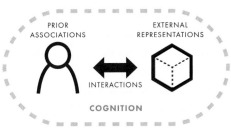

When we introduce more resources into the mix, things get more interesting. Now, what we think of as cognition is spread through a collection of people, resources, tools, interactions, and so on.

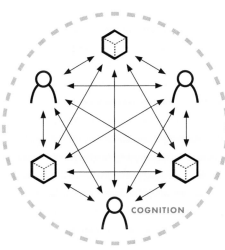

To say that cognition is distributed across people and things doesn't mean we're talking about a new kind of cognition. It's about seeing how all forms of cognitive activity—remembering, planning, reasoning, deciding, analyzing—depend on the ways people use their available resources. Moreover, these cognitive resources can include everything from neurons and whiteboards to laptops and airspeed indicators. Figuring it out is the art of bringing all this to bear.

This shift in perspective, away from just objects and representations and interactions and toward distributed cognitive systems, is vital for taking on complex understanding problems. This also requires *coordination*, whether this is simply coordinating the cognitive resources at your desk or the resources at play within a globally distributed team of people.

So *where* understanding takes place really depends upon the complexity of the topic you're trying to understand. A relatively simple problem—with sufficient prior associations—might actually be solved "in your head," as the expression goes. But it's more likely the case that you will need to employ or engage with other cognitive resources in the environment, be these other people, tools, time, and so on.

In sum, *where* understanding happens depends upon the nature of the problem, while *how* depends upon:

- Prior associations
- External representations
- Interactions
- Coordination

This is how we've come to understand understanding, and how we've chosen to structure this book.

Human Understanding

You'll notice in all this, our focus is not so much on the tools and technologies, as much as the human at the center of things. For example, we could talk about *interaction* in terms of *interface controls*—sliders and checkboxes and such, but these things change. What hasn't changed in thousands of years are the fundamental ways in which humans interact with information. Sorting, chunking, annotating, and so on, these are not new concepts. Whether it's saving an Instagram photo with a heart, or leaving a mark on a cave wall, the fundamental interaction pattern—annotation—is the same.

Accordingly, this is not a "how to" book, but rather a "how to think about it" book. Bridging theory from cognitive sciences with plenty of practical examples, you'll learn how to think about the ways humans can play with and explore difficult concepts. This will apply both in the here and now and into the future. While technologies and modalities change, the humans at the center change very slowly, over millennia not milliseconds. By knowing how we—as human creatures—get a sense of information, you'll be prepared for most problems of understanding.

2

Understanding as a Function of the Brain, Body, and Environment

I hear and I forget, I see and I remember, I do and I understand.

—CONFUCIUS

In the waning years of the nineteenth century, George Stratton, a graduate student who became one of his generation's pre-eminent psychologists, conducted a simple yet curious experiment on his eyes. What would happen, he wondered, if the world appeared upside down? Glasses aim to correct vision. Stratton crafted glasses to distort his vision by inverting the world so that up became down, left became right. In one of his experiments, he wore the glasses for eight consecutive days. When he took them off, which was rarely, and mostly to sleep, he immediately put on a blindfold. In total, Stratton spent almost 90 hours peering at the world through his distorting lenses. The rest of the time he lived in darkness, as though blind.

Stratton's experience began exactly as you would expect. He was clumsy and bumbled around. He experienced dizziness, headaches, and what he called a "nervous depression." Ordinary tasks, such as pouring a glass of milk, had to be "cautiously worked out," and he found "all but the simplest movements extremely fatiguing."[1] He was less disoriented by the second day. His vision slowly adjusted and after the eight days, when the experiment concluded, the world appeared to him as normal.

This is known as the *Stratton effect*, and it's a marvelous example of the brain's adaptability. Stratton became so well adjusted to his topsy-turvy lenses that when he finally took them off, he faced the same problem: the world appeared to be flipped. Once again, he stumbled, grew dizzy, and used his left hand to reach for items to his right. And once again, his visual system adapted. A few days after removing the glasses, his vision was just as before.

Stratton's curious experiment has been repeated many times with lenses that distort the world in different ways and with similar results. People experience nausea and clumsiness, slowly adapt, and if they wear the glasses long enough, the world stops looking weird. Hubert Dolezal, for example, attached inverted lenses to a football helmet during a five-week visit to a small village in Greece. Once he overcame the initial awkwardness, Dolezal adapted so well that he was able to bike, swim, and read.[2] Hundreds of similar experiments have been conducted over the years, including dozens of long-term experiments in Japan, where people have worn the glasses for as long as 21 days.[3]

That people can adapt to such a bizarre visual experience is surprising. Hence the hundreds of studies to explore the phenomenon. More surprising is that if the person remains stationary, they do not adapt. If they don't walk, or they are handed objects instead of reaching for them, their brain doesn't reconfigure itself to this new way of seeing.[4] Furthermore, when people take off the

1. Stratton, George M. 1897. "Vision Without Inversion of the Retinal Image." *Psychological Review* 4 (4): 341–60. https://doi.org/10.1037/h0075482
2. Dolezal, Hubert. 2005. *Living in a World Transformed: Perceptual and Performatory Adaptation to Visual Distortion.* West Caldwell, NJ: Blackburn Press.
3. Yoshimura, H. 1996. "A Historical Review of Long-Term Visual-Transposition Research in Japan." *Psychological Research* 59 (1): 16–32. https://doi.org/10.1007/bf00419831
4. For a summary of findings from this period, see: Welch, R B. 1974. "Research on Adaptation to Rearranged Vision: 1966–1974." *Perception* 3 (4): 367–92. https://doi.org/10.1068/p030367. For a discussion of these studies in a broader cognitive context, and the importance of motion for how the mind works, see: Tversky, Barbara. 2019. In *Mind in Motion: How Action Shapes Thought*, 17–18. New York: Basic Books.

glasses in these stationary studies, they readapt immediately, without any dizziness or other adverse symptoms.

Our brain is astonishing. Our perceptual abilities are magnificent, especially our visual perception. But our bodies matter, too, often more than we realize. Action changes the brain and how we interpret information in the world. Yet the modern story of the brain is largely about what happens in our head. We are told the brain is a kind of biological supercomputer. That three-pound lump of squishy goo, nestled in our skull, is the engine that drives our ability to think, reason, decide, plan, and make sense of the world around us. That's the standard story and so, as a result, we tend to view the world as *out there* (beyond the head) and understanding is *in here* (inside the head). Although the brain remains supremely important, there is more to the story, as the Stratton effect suggests.

The Stratton effect brings to mind an aphorism, often attributed to Confucius, sometimes as just an old Chinese proverb, that goes "I hear and I forget, I see and I remember, I do and I understand." It's a reminder of the connection between doing and understanding, and how acting in the world shapes our ability to make sense of it. In the pages that follow, we will see how the science of mind is evolving in a direction that echoes Confucius, though, of course, as always with science, it's somewhat more complicated than something you can print on a t-shirt. Our purpose in this chapter is to wrap our arms around this new science of mind and, from that, develop a foundation for how the information in our world can help us become better thinkers. Let's start there, with a question: How does the mind work?

Behaviorism and the Cognitive Revolution

Since the days of Socrates and Plato, and almost certainly before then, human beings have wondered how we think, understand, and gain knowledge about the world we inhabit. The modern quest for a theory of mind began with the emergence of cognitive science in the late 1950s. Back then, the dominant theory was behaviorism, which viewed the brain as a black box—a biological device whose inner workings could never be directly observed. Because there was no way to see an idea, or a thought, or anything that happened in the head, behaviorists were taught "to eschew such topics as mind, thinking, or imagination and such concepts as plans, desires, or intentions."[5] What happened in the brain was mysterious and unknowable and, therefore, off limits.

Not everyone was convinced. Some researchers believed that clever experiments could be devised that would explain the machinery of mind, at least in part. Early experiments were promising, many more were undertaken, and the cognitive revolution was underway. By the 1990s, cognitive science had convincingly demolished the central premise of behaviorism: the machinery of mind *was* knowable. Harvard psychologist Steven Pinker summarized the cognitive turn this way: "Behaviorists insisted that all talk about mental events was sterile speculation … Exactly the opposite turned out to be true."[6]

Cognitive science came to see the mind as an elaborate biological apparatus for processing information. It starts with your senses, which perceive information from the world and send signals to your brain. When you stub your toe, for example, information passes from the nerve ending, through the spinal cord, and up to your brain. When the stoplight turns green, your eyes perceive this change and send the information along the optic nerve. Your brain takes these signals and converts them into symbols. Cognitive scientists call these symbols *mental representations*, which is simply a scientific phrase that means thoughts or ideas. The brain processes these representations, transforming them into other representations, and the whole operation is what we call *cognition*. Originally known as the information-processing theory, today it is often called the *computational theory of mind*.

Thus, cognitive science is based on two fundamental concepts: mental representation and mental computation. The term *computation*, however, requires some qualification. To say the mind does computation does not mean the neurons in your brain work just like the silicon transistors in your laptop. Rather, it means that we can explain how brains and computers operate using many of the same principles, even though the details are vastly different. Pinker provides a useful analogy: "To explain how birds fly, we invoke principles of lift and drag and fluid mechanics that also explain how airplanes fly. That does not commit us to an airplane metaphor for birds, complete with jet engines and complimentary beverage service."[7] This view of the mind does, however, hinge on the conviction that brains do perform computation, in some way, on mental representations.

5. Gardner, Howard. 1987. In *The Mind's New Science: A History of the Cognitive Revolution*, 11. New York: Basic Books.
6. Pinker, Steven. 1997. In *How the Mind Works*, 84. New York: W.W. Norton.
7. Pinker, Steven. 1997. In *How the Mind Works*, 26–27. New York: W.W. Norton.

The Computational Theory of Mind

The computational theory of mind has a straightforward model of cognition built around four parts: the external world, perception, cognition, and action. These form a loop, as shown in Figure 2.1. Under this model, we perceive information from the world through our senses, which our brain converts into mental representations. This is followed by cognition proper (mental computation on mental representations), which, in turn, leads to acting on the world. Then the cycle begins anew with more perception, cognition, action, and so forth.

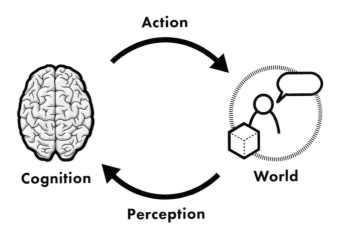

FIGURE 2.1 The basic structure of human cognition according to the computational theory of mind. Although grossly simplified, it captures the essential features of the standard model.

The most notable features of this model are that it's *sequential*—first one thing, then another—and that cognition happens *in the head*. Perception serves as the input to cognition, and the output is action on the world. The starring role in the cognitive drama goes to brain-based processes (i.e., mental computation). Anything that happens outside the skull is secondary, merely part of the supporting cast.

This brain-centered view of human thinking forms the foundation for many models of human cognition. One of the most influential models is the Model Human Processor, which was developed in the early 1980s as the cognitive revolution was in full swing. This model divides the mind into three main parts: perception (for converting sensory input into mental representations), cognition (for mental computation and memory), and motor control (for moving the body).[8] In other words, perception is input, cognition happens in the brain, and action is output, just like the diagram in Figure 2.1.

Other cognitive models share a similar structure. Consider EPIC, which was developed to model how human beings interact with computers.[9] Like the Model Human Processor, EPIC is also based on input and output mechanisms (see Figure 2.2). It describes the human body in terms so comically detached from everyday life that you can almost see the lab coats and pocket protectors.

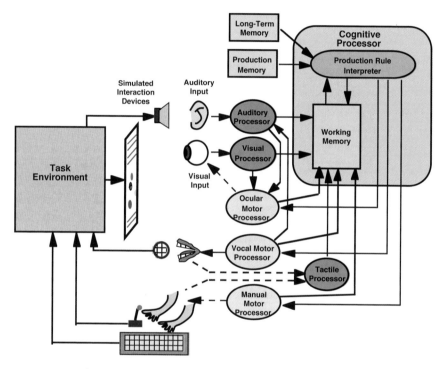

FIGURE 2.2 The EPIC model of cognition: note how the terminology describes parts of the body in terms of inputs, outputs, and processing information. The model also omits many parts of the body—legs and feet being the most obvious.

8. Card, Stuart K., Thomas P. Moran, and Allen Newell. 1983. *The Psychology of Human-Computer Interaction*. Hillsdale, NJ: Lawrence Erlbaum Associates.
9. Kieras, Davis E., and Davis E. Meyer. 1997. "An Overview of the EPIC Architecture for Cognition and Performance with Application to Human-Computer Interaction." *Human–Computer Interaction* 12 (4): 391–438. https://doi.org/10.1207/s15327051hci1204_4

It features an "auditory processor" instead of ears, a "vocal motor processor" instead of a mouth, and an "ocular motor processor" instead of eyes. Hands are called *manual motor processors* and, in an oversight that reflects a world before smartphones, the modeled human has no feet.

Where the Body Meets the Mind

These models are obviously incomplete. They may be accurate as far as they go, but they could go farther. They should include hands, as well as feet, not as mere "motor processors," but in a deeper way, and for a simpler reason—we had bodies long before we had computers, or calculators, or even language. Our evolutionary past is rooted in a spatial experience of the world. We move through the world and pick things up and turn our heads. To be alive is to be in motion. So it's not unreasonable to suspect that cognitive models which ignore, or downplay, the relationship between body and mind are missing something—something vital.

What might this mean for how we understand information? In the Stratton effect, moving the body was needed for the brain to resolve the distortions created by the upside-down lenses. That finding provides us with a clue. Another clue comes from basketball. A group of Italian researchers recorded professional basketball players shooting free throws, and then asked people to watch the video and predict if the ball would go through the hoop or not.[10] They asked three groups of people to watch the videos: professional basketball players (expert players), professional basketball coaches and reporters (expert watchers), and students with no experience playing basketball (novice watchers). The researchers stopped the video at different stages of the shot, from when the player was preparing to shoot, to just before the ball reached the hoop. At each stage, people were asked to make their prediction.

As you would expect, predictions got better the closer the ball was to the basket. And as you would also expect, the farther the ball was from the basket, the worse the predictions were, especially for novice watchers. The interesting finding was that expert players, who had the most experience shooting baskets, were surprisingly accurate when making predictions *before* the

10. Aglioti, Salvatore M., Paola Cesari, Michela Romani, and Cosimo Urgesi. 2008. "Action Anticipation and Motor Resonance in Elite Basketball Players." *Nature Neuroscience* 11 (9): 1109–16. https://doi.org/10.1038/nn.2182

ball was released. When the video was stopped just before the ball left the shooter's hand, expert players were right as much as 60 percent of the time. Shooting free throws again and again, over many years, changed the player's ability to interpret, make sense of, and extrapolate from visual information. Here, too, as with the Stratton effect, we have a case where action shapes our ability to understand information.

Let's consider an example from something unlike basketball, something where we don't expect the body to play any role at all in how we understand information: politics. Dutch researchers wondered if the spatial metaphor of politics—left-wing and right-wing—was more than just a metaphor.[11] They gave volunteers a series of generic political statements, such as "rules regarding road safety should be tightened" and "the number of available rental homes should increase gradually." The volunteers were asked to associate each statement with one of the ten political parties in the Dutch House of Representatives, some on the left and others on the right. The twist? They did this standing on a Wii balance board. Before answering the questions, each volunteer went through a process to level the board, but unbeknownst to them, the calibration process tilted the board slightly, yet undetectably, to one side. When the board was tilted left, people were more likely to rate statements such as "more money should become available to caregivers" as a left-wing position, but if the board tilted right they rated it as more right-wing. The effect wasn't enormous, but it was measurable and consistent and statistically significant across all the statements, even when the researchers accounted for pre-existing political opinions and affiliations.

In the basketball study, prior physical experience improved the ability to make predictions from visual information. In the balance board study, the finding was that *physical* states of the body could influence *conceptual* states of the mind. We don't perceive information from the world in a clean, unbiased way. Instead, our perceptions are modified and transformed by and through our bodies. This kind of finding has popped up on all kinds of studies. For example, researchers have also found that coffee can influence how you feel about other people. When volunteers were asked to judge another person's warmth and friendliness, their rating depended on coffee. When people in the study

11. Dijkstra, Katinka, Anita Eerland, Josjan Zijlmans, and Lysanne S. Post. 2012. "How Body Balance Influences Political Party Evaluations: A Wii Balance Board Study." *Frontiers in Psychology* 3: 536. https://doi.org/10.3389/fpsyg.2012.00536

held a cup of hot coffee, they judged other people to be warmer: more generous, more caring, and friendlier. When the cup was full of iced coffee, they rated people as cooler and less welcoming.[12]

The clothes you wear can make a difference, too. In one experiment, people who wore lab coats paid more attention to their work and made about half as many mistakes when compared with people who wore their own clothes.[13] Lab coats are worn by scientists, doctors, and lab technicians—people who cannot afford to be sloppy or lazy in the work. Just wearing a lab coat was enough to make people more attentive. We often wear clothing for the effect it will have on others. Consider how the uniforms of police, judges, and priests serve as useful cues on how to behave. We wear uniforms because they have an outward effect, one directed at the people around us. Yet here we have studies showing that clothes, balance boards, and steaming cups of coffee have *inward-facing* consequences, too, not only for how we *feel*, but also for how we *think*.

Or step away from the lab and reflect on situations from everyday life. Why, for example, do we pick up and rotate pieces of a jigsaw puzzle, testing them in various holes? If perception is merely input, and the brain is so impressive, why don't we just look at the pieces, rotate them in our brain, and then plop them into place? When making pancake batter, why do we mutter aloud while counting out the four cups of flour? Why do we often use paper and pencil, or a calculator, even for modest math problems? Or what about this one: Why do we talk with our hands even when we're on the phone and nobody is there to see our hands waving about? Again and again, close examination of everyday behavior reveals that we consistently interact with the world in seemingly superfluous ways. Why not just pause, perceive, ponder, and *then* act? We are not—as a brain-centric model would suggest—"thinking, *then* doing." Rather, we are "thinking *through* doing."

The assumptions of behaviorism meant that, eventually, it was forced to give way to the computational theory of mind. Now the assumptions of the computational theory are, in turn, leading to a new way of understanding how the mind works.

12. Williams, L. E., and J. A. Bargh. 2008. "Experiencing Physical Warmth Promotes Interpersonal Warmth." *Science* 322 (5901): 606–7. https://doi.org/10.1126/science.1162548
13. Adam, Hajo, and Adam D. Galinsky. 2012. "Enclothed Cognition." *Journal of Experimental Social Psychology* 48 (4): 918–25. https://doi.org/10.1016/j.jesp.2012.02.008

The Embodied Mind

Taken together, the studies just mentioned, and thousands more, are the basis for a new view of the mind called *embodied cognition*. Evidence for this view, which is commonly referred to as just *embodiment*, has been building for decades and is considered "the most exciting idea in cognitive science right now."[14]

Embodiment proposes a theory of mind that, at its most broad and blunt, says simply this: *Descartes was wrong*. René Descartes, you may recall, was a 17th century French philosopher who introduced the idea of mind-body dualism, distilled most famously in his dictum, *Ego cogito, ergo sum* (I think, therefore I am). Everything in the world was made of physical matter, Descartes observed, but the mind was different. You can't ever point to something and say "that is a mind." As a result, Descartes reasoned, the body was made of flesh and blood and was part of the world, but the mind was not.[15] With this proposition, Descartes changed the course of Western philosophical and scientific thought.

Embodiment is a counterargument to four centuries of mind-body dualism. It contends that we cannot explain the human experience if we have cleaved mind from body, perception from cognition, and action from understanding. We must stitch together what Descartes pulled apart. The psychologist Arthur Glenberg summarizes the embodiment perspective this way: "All approaches to embodiment agree that behavior is produced by more than a disembodied Cartesian mind manipulating symbols according to rules. In other words, embodiment is in strong contrast to cognitive psychology as developed in the 1960s, 1970s, and 1980s."[16] The computational theory of mind has produced decades of solid science. The embodied theory of mind says, hold on, that isn't the whole story.

14. Wilson, Andrew D., and Sabrina Golonka. 2013. "Embodied Cognition Is Not What You Think It Is." *Frontiers in Psychology* 4: 58. https://doi.org/10.3389/fpsyg.2013.00058
15. For a thorough discussion of embodiment and how it challenges Descartes, and the bulk of Western philosophy, see: Lakoff, George, and Mark Johnson. 1999. *Philosophy in the Flesh: The Embodied Mind and Its Challenge to Western Thought*. New York: Basic Books.
16. Glenberg, Arthur M. 2010. "Embodiment as a Unifying Perspective for Psychology." *Wiley Interdisciplinary Reviews: Cognitive Science* 1 (4): 586–96. https://doi.org/10.1002/wcs.55

From Brainbound Minds to Extended Minds

To reconcile these two views, let's turn to the cognitive philosopher Andy Clark, who has proposed two opposing models of human thought.[17] One model, based on the computational theory, equates the mind with the brain and puts cognition—every last bit of it—in the head. Clark calls this the *brainbound* model. If this model is correct, it means that the body exists exclusively for sensory perception (i.e., information inputs), with motor movements (i.e., action outputs) playing no role in cognition itself. It also means that cognition depends entirely on neural activity. If that's the case, we should, in theory, be able to pop the top off a human skull, scoop out the brain, dump it into a cognition tank hooked up to ocular and auditory processors and say, "Voila, there it is, a thinking, intelligent, conscious being."[18]

When you read an article about the mind that features an image of the brain, you're probably dealing with the brainbound model. It is the culturally dominant conception of the mind, one exemplified by the computer scientist and futurist Ray Kurzweil. Kurzweil envisioned a day when our brains could be uploaded to the cloud, and we would exist as conscious creatures made of pure information.[19] While this view has many proponents, it's worth noting that even neuroscience has been coming around to the idea that what the brain does is intimately connected to the messy reality of our biology. The neuroscientist Alan Jasanoff summed up the "fundamental lesson of neuroscience" this way: "The brain cannot be all there is."[20] The more science learns, the more questions arise about the brainbound model.

Because of this, Clark proposed an alternative model called the *extended* mind.[21] In this model, neural processes don't handle each and every cognitive task. Some will happen in the head, while others might happen in the world. The basis for this idea is that we evolved in a physical world, which also

17. Clark, Andy. 2008. *Supersizing the Mind: Embodiment, Action, and Cognitive Extension.* Oxford: Oxford University Press.
18. The brain-in-a-vat is a famous thought experiment proposed by the philosopher Harry Putnam. See: Putnam, Hilary. 1981. *Reason, Truth and History.* Cambridge: Cambridge University Press.
19. Kurzweil, Ray. 2012. *How to Create a Mind: The Secret of Human Thought Revealed.* London: Duckworth Overlook.
20. Jasanoff, Alan. 2018. In *Biological Mind: How Brain, Body, and Environment Collaborate to Make Us Who We Are*, 220. New York: Basic Books.
21. Clark, Andy, and David J. Chalmers. 1998. "The Extended Mind." *Analysis* 58 (1): 7–19. https://doi.org/10.1093/analys/58.1.7

means we evolved cognitive tooling that relies on our brains *and* our bodies *and* anything in the world. Sometimes that means thinking happens entirely in the head with mental representations. Other times it means the cognitive act depends on information outside the head—*external* representations—and interactions with other worldly resources. When the mind is extended, to use Clark's vivid wordage, "Cognition leaks out into the world."[22]

We can draw a line between these two models (see Figure 2.3). On one side is brainbound, with mind and brain co-located in the skull and the body serving only as input and output. On the other side is extended, with cognition spread across brain, body, and anything in the world: whiteboards, smartphones, sticky notes, maps, notebooks, and even other people. The extended model doesn't dismiss what the brain does. But neither is it biased toward electrical signals whizzing through squishy gray tissue.

"Brainbound"	**"The Extended Mind"**

Thinking happens in the brain, only.	Thinking is spread across brain, body, and anything in the world.

FIGURE 2.3 Contrasting models of human cognition. Brainbound locates all of cognition in the brain. Extended spreads it across brain, body, and the world.

A key difference between these two models is how much they depend on neurons. Brainbound assumes neuronal hegemony: thinking is restricted to what neurons do. Extended argues for neural frugality: thinking can happen with neurons, but it doesn't have to. Sometimes our thinking happens outside the

---

22. Clark (2008), pp. xxviii.

head because it can be faster, or easier, or just plain better to do the work out there.[23] This isn't the brain being lazy. Instead, it's more like the busy executive who effectively delegates certain tasks to the people around her rather than doing all the work herself.

Mental Representations and the Big Divide

The question before us then is twofold. First, how does this most exciting idea change our view of how the mind works? And second, what does it mean for how we create understanding from information?

We've long understood that Starbucks and Calvin Klein use marketing to influence *what* we think. But it is surprising, and intriguing when science finds that a cappuccino or a lab coat can influence *how* we think. The temperature of our morning coffee can make the grumpy bus driver seem friendlier? Wearing a long white jacket can help us focus on a task? It sounds a bit crazy.[24] In one sense, it's not that controversial: *of course,* the outside world influences what happens in our head. Imagine taking a calculus test, not in a classroom, but outside, on a glorious day, at the beach. Who wouldn't find it hard to concentrate when you could be lounging or surfing or reading a great book. But embodiment is making a much deeper claim: our ability to think *depends* on the world outside our head. We can never fully escape how the way we interact with our environment shapes our cognitive powers.

Embodiment is far from settled science. Just how far to take this idea is a matter of much debate and even more research. It is helpful to think of embodiment, not as a singular theory, but as an umbrella term that includes many different challenges to the computational theory of mind. You will find Clark's extended mind under this umbrella, along with ecological psychology, distributed cognition, enactivism, activity theory, and something

---

23. Clark, Andy. 2012. "Do Thrifty Brains Make Better Minds?" *The New York Times.* January 15, 2012. https://opinionator.blogs.nytimes.com/2012/01/15/do-thrifty-brains-make-better-minds/
24. It is worth being skeptical about these studies. While they do show a measurable effect in the lab, that doesn't mean the effect is especially large or long-lasting. It only provides another piece of evidence for a deep connection between our bodies and how we understand information. If the effect was large, and permanent, it would have enormous implications. Think of the balance board study. It might mean that an app could change how you vote, simply by how often it makes you swipe left or right. That does seem crazy.

called *radical embodied cognition*, to name just a few. Although they each have various intellectual roots, and the distinctions between them are often fuzzy, they all share a belief that no robust theory of mind can come from studying neurons alone.

There is one topic, however, where there is a notable disagreement. Do mental representations exist or not? This is the big dividing line. Some groups under the embodiment umbrella, most notably radical embodied cognition, posit that we don't need mental representations. To those who stand under this part of the embodiment umbrella, symbols in the brain are as mythical as unicorns. Since even the most advanced brain scanning technology has failed to observe even a single mental representation, this idea has an obvious allure. Experiments with creatures ranging from robots and crickets to children and baseball players have provided intriguing evidence for this position.[25] Even so, explaining the mind without mental representations is so difficult that Anthony Chemero opened his book *Radical Embodied Cognitive Science* with the following qualifier: "One of the things I try to make clear is that it is actually very difficult to reject internal representations, and that radical embodied cognitive science must be more radical than most of its proponents realize."[26]

The debate over mental representations means we can, and should, expand our brainbound vs. extended framework. Our revised diagram, shown in Figure 2.4, puts brainbound at one end of a spectrum (cognition is all about symbols in the head), radical at the other (cognition involves no mental representations whatsoever), and extended somewhere in the middle. Exactly where in the middle is not easy to say. It depends on where one stands under the embodiment umbrella. That middle area covers a lot of different ideas. The later chapters in this book, for example, often draw from distributed cognition, but for our purposes, it's sufficient to overlook these differences since this is the region that accepts mental representations as part of an embodied view of the mind.

25. See: Wilson & Golonka (2013).
26. Chemero, Anthony. 2011. *Radical Embodied Cognitive Science*. Cambridge: MIT Press.

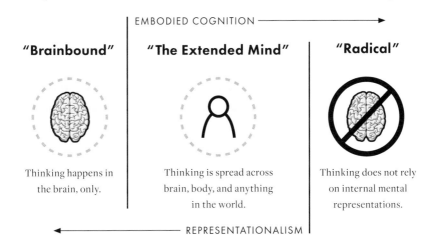

EMBODIED COGNITION

"Brainbound"   **"The Extended Mind"**   **"Radical"**

Thinking happens in the brain, only.

Thinking is spread across brain, body, and anything in the world.

Thinking does not rely on internal mental representations.

REPRESENTATIONALISM

FIGURE 2.4 A spectrum of perspectives on the nature of human cognition.

What Is the Truth About Embodiment?

What is the truth about embodiment? Don't ask the scientists because nobody knows. Not really. This is how science works. Hypotheses are put forth, experiments are designed, evidence is collected, debates rage, and scientific knowledge slowly moves forward. For decades, the evidence has been building in favor of an embodied view of mind. But here's the thing: the rock-bottom truth doesn't matter. Not for our purposes, at least.

The embodiment debate stems from a simple yet eternal question: How does the mind *really* work? Yet where scientists are looking for truth, the rest of us seek something else. All we require is a perspective on cognition that allows us to make substantial headway on a wide range of messy, complex, real-world problems of understanding. We need better ways to recognize how people solve problems, create meaning, and make decisions. That is precisely the focus of subsequent chapters in this book. Debating the existence of mental representations is part of building theories, but largely irrelevant for creating more understandable information. Where scholars want scientific truth, we need analytic utility: a way to examine problems of understanding so that we can create better ways of thinking. In short, we're more interested in *utility* than in truth.

Taking embodiment seriously means there is much to be gained by shifting our position away from the brainbound view and toward the radical one. That means recognizing that our default view is the brainbound model and the limitations it imposes. But it doesn't mean we have to also become radicalized. Representations and how we transform them, whether in our head or in the world, are a useful way of looking at problems of understanding. In fact, much of this book is about how we can create understanding by moving representations out of the head, putting them into the world, and using technologies to manipulate them. As authors, we like the way Andy Clark puts it: Some problems seem to be "representation hungry."[27]

Seeing the World Through a New Lens

How does this extended view of cognition help us see the world and the way people make sense of information, in a new way? What does it provide over the standard brainbound model? For now, let's consider a single, illustrative example. Imagine you're in a kickoff meeting for a new project. First, let's consider the usual way these meetings proceed …

The Brainbound View

More than likely, one person is leading the meeting. This person has prepared a PowerPoint deck chock-full of information. Attendees are expected to listen and then ask questions. Some take notes on their laptops, or maybe on paper. Everyone expects a copy of the presentation to review later, which excuses (although no one would admit this) the partial attention given to the presenter. And, as you'd expect, half of these people will spend much of the meeting discretely dealing with emails or otherwise being distracted.

The entire meeting is structured around an information transmission model: *I have information. You should pay attention and file this away.* Understanding depends on how well information is communicated and how carefully people pay attention. We might easily imagine some future technology, let's call it *PowerPoint Plus*, where you could attach a cable from your laptop to your brain and download the slides directly. Given how these meetings work, this sounds

27. Clark, Andy, and Josefa Toribio. 1994. "Doing Without Representing?" *Synthese* 101 (3): 401–31. https://doi.org/10.1007/bf01063896

appealing: skip the boring stuff and download the information straight into your brain. The brainbound model says this is at least a theory.

The Extended View

Here's an alternative way that we might design this meeting through our lens of understanding.

People are themselves viewed as part of a distributed system of cognitive resources—we believe each person in attendance brings with them a set of experiences and perspectives that are probably vital to the meeting topic. In addition to the people in attendance, the whiteboard, the markers, the sticky notes—even the height of the table—are all viewed as potential resources to be designed. The leader views their role as more of a facilitator than speaker, more as a cognitive enabler than an information transmitter. This means that attention is managed through active learning and sharing. Care is taken to create a psychologically safe environment. Rather than marching people through a bullet-laden deck, a single problem statement is handed to all, with an opening challenge to explore options and share ideas. If there was background knowledge, it was distributed ahead of time for folks to read. Knowledge is curated rather than transmitted. Ideas are drawn together, on the board, with markers or sticky notes handed to people to make their ideas visible, or to show how their idea fits into or contradicts what someone else has rendered. The meeting moves fluidly between moments of standing and sitting, depending upon the activity, as the facilitator knows there's a correlation between the body and thinking. The facilitator is also careful to frame and reframe the problem in many different ways (and encourages others to do the same), challenging how this problem is viewed. In short, people are *actively working and learning together*, to make sense of the project ahead (see Figure 2.5).

There's a lot to unpack in this second scenario. It illustrates many of the *principles* that run throughout our work, principles that guide how we work and think and create understanding with information. These principles might be stated as follows:

- Attend to every association
- Make learning active
- See learning as a communal activity
- Make concepts tangible

FIGURE 2.5 Two very different kinds of meetings—one originating with a brain-bound view of cognition, the other with an extended view of cognition.

- Make concepts visible
- Design the environment
- Explore multiple frames
- Use the whole body
- Make it safe to share

Although this is an incomplete list, we provide it to show how all this theoretical discourse might be applied in a daily activity. Our concerns are practical rather than theoretical—we're more interested in utility than truth. First, how do people understand information, especially when they have a lot of it? And second, how can we make information more understandable? Understanding the underlying theories of cognition provides us with a chance to radically reframe how we approach all problems of understanding.

Becoming Smarter

In the beginning, the web was all text, no video, not even pictures. That changed in 1993 when Marc Andreesen and a colleague, Eric Bina, released Mosaic, the first graphical web browser. This was the moment when "several million [people] noticed the web might be better than sex."[28] Mosaic led to Netscape, which attracted people to the web in droves and paved the way for everything from Wi-Fi and smartphones to social media and ebooks. We are all familiar with this evolution: more powerful technologies that allow us to do more powerful things with information.

This chapter has followed another evolution, one not widely known outside of graduate seminars and scientific journals: a new science of mind that gives us a different perspective on how we understand information. This book aims to stitch these two parallel evolutions together. In doing so, we echo the words of the cognitive scientist Don Norman, who wrote "The power of the unaided mind is highly overrated. Without external aids, memory, thought, and reasoning are all constrained."[29] Precisely.

28. Metcalfe, Bob. 1995. "Microsoft and Netscape Open Some New Fronts in Escalating Web Wars." *Infoworld*, Vol. 17, Issue 34. August 21, 1995.
29. Norman, Donald A. 1993. In *Things That Make Us Smart: Defending Human Attributes in the Age of the Machine*, 43. Reading, MA: Addison-Wesley.

We don't just think. We create tools and technologies to help us think *better*, understand *more*, and solve *bigger* problems. Norman reminds us that our ability to understand is limited when we try to do everything in our head, especially when we have lots of information and when the challenges are daunting, say cancer, sustainable energy, or space travel. We need to appreciate the complex interplay between prior associations, things we bring into and manipulate in the world, and how we figure things out by collaborating and cooperating with others.

If we treat sensemaking as brainbound, the cost of understanding will be expensive, perhaps too costly. This is not to say we should never rely on what the brain can do. But when we spread the cost of understanding into the world, we open up incredible possibilities for understanding. Think of the tools that extend our physical abilities, the telescopes that let us see deep into space, or the group of people who, only by working together, could push a car up a hill. In the same way that tools or groups enhance our physical abilities, so, too, can we extend our cognitive abilities. By moving expensive operations into the world, we adjust the cost structure. By creating a map or sharing ideas, by playing with a data visualization or a deck of flashcards, by simply being allowed to point at something, we can reduce time, complexity, and errors. We increase our capacity for understanding when cognition is seen as something that happens in and through the world.

Once we grok these ideas, we have the context for all that follows.

The Blind Man and the Stick (Redrawing the Boundaries of Cognition)

The anthropologist Gregory Bateson was an early advocate for the idea that we can only understand the mind by accounting for the person *plus* the environment. After decades of research that spanned everything from anthropology and semiotics to cybernetics and schizophrenia, Bateson concluded that boundaries were the essential question for understanding the complexity and messiness of human experience. Broadly speaking, that's what embodiment does: redraws the boundaries of cognition.

To comprehend the consequences, Bateson proposed a simple thought experiment:

> Suppose I am a blind man, and I use a stick. I go tap, tap, tap. Where do *I* start? Is my mental system bounded at the handle of the stick? Is it bounded by my skin? Does it start halfway up the stick? Does it start at the tip of the stick? But these are nonsense questions … If what you are trying to explain is a given piece of behavior … you will need the street, the stick, the man; the street, the stick, and so on, round and round.[30]

The blind man, in Bateson's metaphor, uses the stick to navigate the world. It provides spatial understanding. But we can make all kinds of "sticks" for all kinds of people to help them figure out all kinds of problems. Today's stick is the smartphone, so we can rephrase Bateson as follows:

> Suppose I am a person, and I use a smartphone. I go tap, tap, tap. Where do *I* start? Is my mental system bounded at the surface of the phone? Is it bounded by my skin? Does it start halfway into the glass? But these are nonsense questions … you need the world, the phone, the person, the world, the phone, and so on, round and round.

If you have ever designed an app, or a website, or anything for a screen, the impulse is to start by arranging menus, images, buttons, and other widgets on a smooth pixelated surface. This decision means that understanding is hugely dependent on one place, the screen, and while not irrevocable, adjusting "where" understanding actually happens—in and through the world, the person, the phone, and so on—requires conscious effort.

This is what we mean when we say that "understanding is about a system of resources distributed across the environment and then dynamically assembled to perform the activity and achieve a goal." This is also a good, quick example for how these two evolutions, the evolution of technology and the evolution of our understanding of the mind, converge to unlock new possibilities.

---

30. Bateson, Gregory. 1987. "Form, Substance, and Difference." In *Steps to an Ecology of Mind: Collected Essays in Anthropology, Psychiatry, Evolution, and Epistemology*, 465. Northvale, NJ: Aronson.

PRIOR
ASSOCIATIONS

COGNITION

2

How We Understand by Associations

Based on sensory input from our body and the environment, we recall prior associations. What we "think" may or may not be what was intended. Whether we're having a conversation, reading words on a page, making inferences based on someone's body language, even being affected by something as subtle as the temperature or a faint smell—all of these sensations influence the associations that come to mind, and what we ultimately think. For this reason, we say: "Associations among concepts *is* thinking."

To improve understanding at this level requires some basic knowledge about the brain as a perceptual organ and how much of what we call "thought" is really a tangled web of prior associations, associations that are activated by everything from stories to pictures to even the slightest turn of a phrase. The bulk of this section is dedicated to the many ways these associations are activated, followed by a cautionary note on the dangers and limits of associative thinking.

3

Understanding Is Fundamentally About Associations Between Concepts

Neo: *This—This isn't real?*
Morpheus: *What is real? How do you define real? If you're talking about what you feel, taste, smell, or see, then real is simply electrical signals interpreted by your brain.*

—*THE MATRIX, 1999*

I'm in a room, standing in front of five other people. For the last several minutes, I've been trying—unsuccessfully—to explain this new idea. It is a bit of a novel idea, but that shouldn't be a problem. I've got a clear explanation. My explanation uses plain language. I even draw a visual model so people can see what I'm describing. Still, no one "gets" it. Then I say: *"It's kind of like …"* Eyes light up. Heads nod. Now, everyone *understands*.

What just happened?

We've all been in this situation, or one like it. Pitching a startup idea. Defending a design. Advocating a particular political position. Sorting out a big-picture concept. Explaining the business model. Drafting technical schemas. Explaining that niche interest we know so much about ...

By calling to mind an already familiar concept, we make it easier for others to understand what we're talking about. Sometimes it's explicit: "It's like Pinterest for Teachers" (a product pitch) or "Think Pocahontas on an alien planet" (the movie *Avatar*). Other times it's more subtle, as with the engineering team that talks about bad decisions building up "technical *debt*." And other times it's allegorical, from the parables told by Jesus to an astrophysicist describing "the Goldilocks Zone" necessary for life on other planets.

But this runs deeper than the associations we try to evoke in others. We *all*—whether we're consciously aware of it or not—make sense of any new information by likening it to some other familiar concept. To understand, we link the unknown to what is already known.

Douglas Hofstadter, an American professor of cognitive science, writes "The human ability to make analogies lies at the root of all our concepts ... analogy is the fuel and fire of thinking."[1] These analogies are invaluable, not only for communicating with others, but also for *our own* understanding. Again, *whether we're aware of it or not*, we all think in concepts and patterns. Sure, we can point to the consultant who uses a picture of an iceberg to explain what is seen and (more critically) unseen by the business—the concept is familiar. But it's more than simple, explicit *"A is to B as C is to D"* analogies. If we look at research from George Lakoff and Mark Johnson,[2] we see how many concepts are so deeply embedded in our language, culture, and thought processes that the underlying associations go unobserved. Consider the spatial associations embedded in phrases like "Cheer *up*!" or "You seem *down* in the dumps." We use this language without pausing to consider why "up is good" and "down is bad." And yet, if we look at how the unwatered plant droops over or how our shoulders sag and our posture droops when we're "upset"—we have clues to a set of associations rooted in biology and widespread throughout our thought processes. We can go even deeper and suggest that all thinking is conceptual in nature. Take a word like "jazzercise," ideas like "Republican" or "Democrat," or phrases like "The Paris of the Middle East"—we take for granted the layers

---

1. Hofstadter, Douglas R., and Emmanuel Sander. 2013. *Surfaces and Essences: Analogy as the Fuel and Fire of Thinking*. New York: Basic Books.
2. Lakoff, George, and Mark Johnson. 1981. *Metaphors We Live By*. Chicago: University of Chicago Press.

of concepts and associations that have accumulated, often over many decades, to give meaning to these words; imagine explaining these phrases to someone transported from even just a few centuries ago! Even the way we *express* a single word can evoke a wildly different set of concepts. Consider some different ways we might utter a simple word like *please*: Puh-LEASE. (please). Please! Pleeeeeaaze? In this case, it is more than the word that is uttered; we've built up a set of prior associations—based on tone of voice—that also contribute to the message we understand.

Becoming aware of the conceptual systems that govern our own and others' understanding is a powerful tool for understanding. This section is about the variety of ways that we might trigger, use with intent, and be aware of these pre-existing conceptual associations to help us and others understand new information.

But first, why care? How much of a difference can a simple association really make on understanding and subsequent decisions? To show how being aware of these associations can affect understanding—and decision-making—let's explore our relationship with technology. Let's take a critical look at the literal concepts we use to orient ourselves with something that is an abstraction.

Technology: Person, Place, or Tool?

As a designer working with technology, one of the fundamental frames I (Stephen) struggle with is how to think about the "things" I help make. Are the digital apps and sites I've designed more like:

- **People** with whom we interact?
- **Places** where we do stuff?
- **Tools** that extend our abilities?
- **Something else**, altogether?

Steve Krug, author of the book *Don't Make Me Think*, suggests that technology should function like a butler, a ***person*** with whom we converse and ask to do stuff for us. When we say "Let's check with Google" or "Ask Siri," we're thinking of these services like a butler. This "technology as person" frame is the one I (Stephen) opted for in my first book *Seductive Interaction Design* where I asked "How do we get people to fall in love with our applications?" By looking at first-time user experiences through the lens of dating, I was able to highlight all the opportunities we have to make our software more humane, desirable, and—to be honest—a little less geeky! This technology-as-person association also expands to many other areas, from personal robotic vacuums such as the Neato and Roomba to the sentient, sometimes frightening, AIs portrayed in movies like *Iron Man, 2001,* or *Ex Machina.*

But now consider how we view something like Facebook or even the internet as a whole: our frame shifts to that of a ***place*** we visit. As author and consultant Jorge Arango comments: "We 'go' online. We meet with our friends 'in' Facebook. We visit 'home' pages. We log 'in' to our bank. If we change our mind, we can always 'go back.' These metaphors suggest that we subconsciously think of these experiences spatially."[3]

This frame shifts once more when we turn our attention to mobile devices, which by their physical proximity seem more like personal ***tools***, extending our limited capabilities. We don't talk with our phone—it's not a person with whom we converse. We use our phone to talk to others; it's a device we use to do things, a tool that extends our capabilities. Notebooks let us hold onto thoughts. Robotic arms let us lift more than we could otherwise. Shoes let us run farther. Mobile apps let us do more and better. But even this "mobile device as tool" frame isn't that straightforward. If we use our phones to visit the places above, don't they become *portals to places* in addition to being *tools*?

These shifting associations suggest that we as humans don't have a consistent frame for thinking about technologies. We're all trying to use tangible terms to make sense of something fundamentally intangible. But person, place, or tool … something else … Why should all this matter?

The Effect of These Different Frames for Technology

Where this choice of technology frame shows up is certainly in detailed labeling decisions, such as when a product team building software must decide whether to label something as "My Stuff" or "Your Stuff"—the best answer depends upon this fundamental framing question, and broader brand, experience, and perhaps even legal considerations. If it's "my stuff," then this thing is a tool and an extension of myself—like *my* files in *my* file folder. If it's "your stuff," then there's an actor or person with whom I interact, that I hand stuff over to hold things for me.

3. Arango, Jorge. 2015. " …For Everybody." Jorge Arango, April 24, 2015. https://jarango.com /2015/04/24/for-everybody/

What about hardware products? When the Neato robotic vacuum gets stuck, the error message asks us to "Please remove stuff from *my* path" or "Help *me*," invoking the frame of a subservient cleaning bot that needs help from time to time. Even the sounds on these robots are meant to suggest something juvenile and prone to making errors—all an intentional frame designed to help us be more forgiving of what is still an early stage technology with plenty of kinks to be worked out.

If we take a broad, rational view of information technology, this person, place, or tool concept is how we understand something that is neither person, place, nor tool. In his article "The Post-Mac Interface," designer Adam Baker comments: "Metaphors in user interface are like sets in theatre. They convince us to believe that the thing we're looking at is like something else."[4] But software is bits and bytes that can be anything. Indeed, while the desktop metaphor was a big leap forward and useful to make personal computers accessible to a generation—linking the unknown to what is already known—we're now stuck trying to move beyond a metaphor that holds us back, often in subtle or invisible ways. Consider how difficult it's been for most people to switch from a folder-based system to a more robust tagging and keyword-based system. It's hard to set aside one frame and view something in a wholly different way.

Or consider the underlying conceptual shift embedded into something like Google Docs. Behind the document editor as a "writing tool," is a more fundamental shift to writing as a shared, collaborative activity (technology as platform). While most of us have rationally made this transition, consider how often we're still caught off guard when we see other people—in real time— editing a document that we're also working on. This shift from solitary tools to a shared collaborative activity is a fundamental one that we're seeing across multiple domains. But these shifts take a long time before they feel natural. What more could we do if we didn't have to bridge these concepts from one generation to the next, or one major invention to the next?

Okay, maybe you're thinking "Software labels. Robot sounds. Desktop metaphors. Our concepts for approaching technology aren't that huge of a deal, right?" Let's make this personal. Let's extend this out to a critical conversation that is happening right now and will have serious legal implications for decades to come.

---

4. Baker, Adam. 2016. "The Post-Mac Interface." Medium. November 16, 2016.
     https://medium.com/@twomonthsoff/the-post-mac-interface-1031b94df77b

Technology Framing and Human Rights

At the level of public policy, our choice of frame can affect legislation dictating our rights as citizens. If we view our mobile phone as a butler who relays messages for us, then intercepting messages is akin to surveillance, and we have legal precedents for this. We can treat this technology like we do wiretapping. But what if, as human rights activist Aral Balkan suggests, our mobile devices are extensions of ourselves? In a rather impassioned plea, Balkan questions the nature of our relationship with technology (while also presenting the same questions we posed in Chapter 2 about *Where does thinking happen?*).

> What if, when I write down a thought on my phone to remember it later, what I am actually doing is extending my mind, and thereby extending myself using the phone.
>
> Today, we are all cyborgs. This is not to say that we implant ourselves with technology, but that we extend our biological capabilities using technology. We are shared beings; with parts of ourselves spread across and augmented by our everyday things.
>
> Perhaps it is time to extend the boundaries of the self to include the technologies by which we extend our selves.
>
> My iPhone is not like a safe (that I can be ordered to open) any more than my brain is like a safe.[5]

Our phones as extensions of ourselves? This may sound a bit far-fetched, but is it really? How quickly does the conversation change if our mobile devices move from our hands and wrists to permanent, updatable implants in the brain? We already see technology heading in this direction. If we view these devices as intimate extensions of ourselves and our mind, then the conversation shifts into radically different places. Do we want a society where corporations and city-states have legal rights to peer into our minds and access our most intimate thoughts?

Notice how simply shifting or substituting the underlying conceptual metaphor, from that of a tool to that of personal augmentation, allows our own thinking to change: we see things differently. That is the point of this short, dystopian journey: To understand how associations shape understanding, and how we can be *intentional* with our use—or avoidance—of such associations.

---

5. Balkan, Aral. 2016. "The Nature of the Self in the Digital Age." Aral Balkan, March 3, 2016. https://ar.al/notes/the-nature-of-the-self-in-the-digital-age/

Associations Among Concepts Is Thinking

In truth, the message of this section is a simple one: *Associations among concepts **is** thinking.* That's it. We could stop here, ending with some practical takeaways. However, this simple message manifests in so many different ways that it's worthwhile to hold up example after example, until the profundity of this message sinks in. Indeed, it took me (Stephen) some years, bouncing between a number of communities—linguistics, advertising, behavioral economics, speechwriting, semiotics, storytelling, and more—before this simple truth became so clear. *Associations among concepts **is** thinking.* This is the universal common denominator that sits quietly behind so many of the conclusions reached by these different communities. As with the previous technology example, it's how we frame something, yes. But it's also everything else that might trigger a concept: a sight, a smell, sounds. Specific word choices. Invoking a familiar narrative. Using an aggressive shape. Using an illustrative picture. All these things trigger concepts, that in turn shape our understanding. Consider how (and for what purpose) the following professions try to shape our thoughts and beliefs:

- Politicians craft the words they use and the clothes they wear, to influence voters.
- Retailers spend billions on packaging and retail build-outs to increase sales.
- Marketers use product placement in movies and celebrity endorsements to alter how people think of products.
- Magicians lead us to believe the unbelievable (and delight us in the process) by exploiting our cognitive weaknesses.
- The hospitality industry influences our emotions through scents, lighting, space planning, decor, and delighters; a good hotel is more than just about a place to sleep.
- Photographers, through photo cropping, depth of field, blurs, composition, and other photographic details, shape our experience of their story.
- Graphic designers choose typefaces, shapes, and colors to create a desired feeling.

All of the conclusions we reach, the beliefs we form, the perceptions we believe to be reality, what someone comes to believe is truth, all of this is based on a whole constellation of sensory inputs.

To really understand what is going on here, and what is common to all of the diverse examples cited, we need to turn our attention to the brain; this is not to exalt a "brainbound" model of reasoning (we don't take that stance), but to understand the role that the brain plays in understanding. We can go on saying things like "Associations among concepts is thinking" and even offer tips like "Be careful with the words you choose" or "Consider the frame you're trying to evoke," but understanding *why* this is the case—neurologically—is the foundation for all that follows.

The Brain as a Perceptual Organ

Essentially, the brain is an associative pattern-matching organ, whose job is to predict patterns like those we've previously encountered. These predictions—what we think of as *thought*—are based on existing concepts, each formed through prior associations. Throughout our lives, we become attuned to perceptual information in the ambient environment and the accompanying possibilities for action. This perceptual information comes to us through various sensations—smells, sights, sounds, increased blood flow, and so on—all of which are transformed into electrical and chemical signals in the brain, that match (or don't match) with our existing concepts. We build concepts upon concepts, starting from the most basic ability to recognize faces within days of being born to the ability to exclaim "a virus wiped out my PC"—a phrase that would be meaningless to someone who didn't grow up with the modern social constructs that make this phrase meaningful.

What we think at any given moment is a construction based on a lifetime of personal, social, bodily, and environmental experiences.

For an overly simplistic analogy of what all this looks like (but sufficient for our purposes), imagine a cardboard box full of tangled Christmas lights. Each of the tiny bulbs represents a single neuron. If you were to count them, your box might contain about 300 lights. (For reference, your brain has around 86 billion neurons!) Now, imagine that at any given moment, a number of these tiny lights, among the tangled mass of unlit lights, are flickering on and off. These are the neurons being activated, constructing a simulation based on various sensations. Whether you are looking "back" at a memory, making sense in the moment, or imagining future plans, your brain is activating these neurons—turning on a pattern of lights in your box—such that they collectively bring to mind prior concepts. When we mention a perceptual pattern, it's not at all like retrieving a file from the file cabinet. Rather, it's like activating this constellation of lights—your neurons—that fire together in that moment to create your present simulation.

Understanding cognition in this way helps you see how unrelated information—such as when magicians misdirect your attention or marketers anchor with higher prices—influences what your brain perceives; these sensations affect which lights get activated. Understanding thought in this way also helps you understand the malleability of memories; if you recognize that every time you "dig up" a memory, you are simply reactivating a bunch of these lights (activating neurons), you can see how memories would change with time. It's easy to understand how some neurons may no longer activate while new ones have been added to and become part of the memory. This also helps to explain how multiple people can witness the same event yet walk away with different accounts—present circumstances (a triggering event) recall different concepts for different people.

When we talk about designing for understanding, and more specifically attending to every association (whether it's a story, a drawing, or something else), we're ultimately concerned with the concepts and prior associations that this activates for an individual. We just asked you to imagine a box of Christmas lights. We could have also included, in this book, an illustration of that box. Either way, *you* brought that concept to mind. That's the takeaway.

But let's unpack this a bit more. Below are three things you should know about the brain as a perceptual organ. When we talk about shifting the cost of understanding, it's easy to focus on outward things—the stories we tell, the maps we make, how we interact with things—but to really get what's going on, let's first turn inward, to understand the changes facilitated by these outward things.

Understanding Is Dependent on Sensory Information

Everything we know, we know because of incoming sensory information. An infant, before she can even see clearly, learns through tactile and auditory sensations. A toddler, by accidentally touching a hot stove, learns that very hot things can be harmful. From an evolutionary perspective, foul smells signal danger, while avoiding stinky foods is probably a good survival mechanism. Our understanding of the world is due to the input provided by the world that comes in through our bodies.

This then forms the basis for the many cases that show how altering sensory information affects perceptions. For example, research has shown that weight has an influence on how you perceive drinks—a whiskey served in a heavier glass is perceived as a more premium beverage. If we turn to car design, with something as simple as a brake lever, sensations such as grip *force*, lever *position*, sound *pressure*, and the *noise* of a brake lever are all coordinated to shape our perceptions of performance.[6]

The takeaway for those of us who want to design information environments: *When we manipulate sensory information, we alter perceptions.*

While some of our senses are far more efficient and discerning than other senses (such as vision for humans), it is ultimately the combination of this incoming sensory information that the brain uses to make sense of reality. We understand and learn with all of our senses—and the more senses you engage simultaneously, the more likely someone will be able to understand and recall that information. (This is critical to understanding why whole-body learning or having tangible interactions aids in understanding.) Understanding is based on available sensory information.

Your Brain Constructs (an Experience of) Reality

Using the incoming sensory information (deemed relevant and worth giving attention to), your brain constructs an experience of reality. The brain tries to make sense of this relevant, incoming information. While we'd like to believe we're rational beings, good at objectively evaluating things, study after study has shown otherwise. With only the incoming sensory information to go off of, prior concepts to refer to, and the need to reconcile things quickly, our brains can reach some rather curious conclusions. Take this humorous newspaper cover shown in Figure 3.1 as an example.

We see a photo that, while intended to go with the headline, does so in an unintended way. The headline "Violent crime duo caught on video" suggests that the two whimsical characters are the crime duo being referred to. This is humorous precisely because our brain is trying to force a connection where none was intended.

6. Haverkamp, Michael. 2013. *Synesthetic Design: Handbook for a Multisensory Approach*. Basel, Switzerland: Birkhäuser.

FIGURE 3.1 The humor of the newspaper front page comes from our brain trying to reconcile the headline "Violent crime duo caught on video" with the photo of two whimsical children's characters.

This *juxtaposition* of image and headline is what fuels mediums like comedy, comic books, and film. Comics and graphic novels rely on the brain to fill in the gap between multiple panels. In film, edits and cuts ask the brain to piece scenes together into a cohesive story. To test how powerful this can be, grab any two or three photos from a magazine, put them together, and your brain will begin to construct a story that links these randomly grabbed objects together (see Figure 3.2).

FIGURE 3.2 Three images—a spilled wine glass, a cat looking up, and a person unlocking a door—grabbed at random. What story do you construct after looking at these three images?

Withholding or adding sensory information then determines what "pieces" the brain has to work with and reconcile. As with working a puzzle, the brain tries to "make sense" of things by identifying a sensible pattern.

Stated another way: The brain is an *associative, pattern-matching* organ. But the associations aren't based solely on the incoming, external stimuli. The brain also brings to mind prior experiences that help fast-forward the pattern-matching process.

Perception Is a Process of Active Construction

While we've focused so far on the brain making sense of *incoming* sensory information, the real pattern matching happens in the matching of this "new" information with prior experiences. The brain is always asking "Have I seen this, or something like this, before?"

RECOGNIZING LETTERS

To understand this pattern-matching function of the brain, let's take something simple, like a letter from the alphabet. In Figure 3.3 we see the letter "A" set in various typefaces.

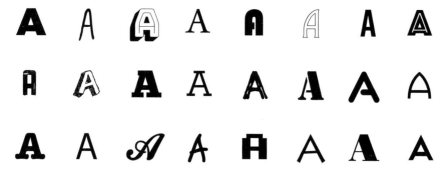

FIGURE 3.3 Typographical variations of the letter A. Consider why you can recognize all these forms, even forms you've never seen, as the letter A.

Assuming you are an English reader, it's doubtful you have any difficulty recognizing all these shapes as the letter A. Some of these exact letterforms may even be new to you, but you likely had no difficulty figuring out what the shape is—the letter A. But have you considered why it's so easy to recognize all these shapes as the letter A? Seems like a silly question, and yet … There was probably a time in early childhood when, having just mastered recognizing block letters, you were introduced to cursive letters, and it felt like you were starting all over. But soon, you mastered this new form. And now you can probably recognize the letters of the alphabet in nearly any typeface—including new type styles you've never seen before. This human ability to recognize approximate patterns (vs. exact matches) is something we're good at.

But this example doesn't really show off the matching part of pattern-matching. Let's consider some things that require more of us.

RECOGNIZING SHAPES AND COLORS

In an exploration of brand identity and our ability to recognize popular logos, designer Graham Smith reduced dozens of popular logos to simple circles and colors.[7] See how many of these "unevolved brands" you recognize in Figure 3.4.

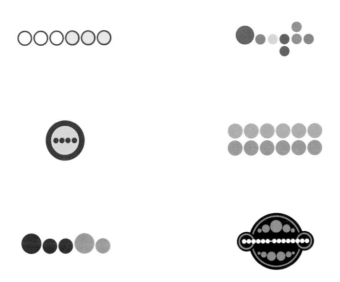

FIGURE 3.4 Six logos reduced to circles and base colors. We recognize most or all of these abstractions because they call to mind prior associations with a similar, previous encounter.

7. Smith, Graham. 2019. "Unevolved Brands: Brand Logo Simplification Project by The Logo Smith." The Logo Smith. November 18, 2019. https://imjustcreative.com/unevolved-brands/2019/10/02

Chances are you do recognize most or all of these logos. Here's something interesting. Suppose that you don't recognize one of these logos. This might occur because either you've never encountered it before, which means there's no pattern to match with, or you're not able to recall the pattern at this moment. For this latter case, close this book. Go do something else. Come back, and you may recognize that logo when there's a different set of associations bouncing around in your brain.

Here's a similar abstraction of characters from four popular cartoon or children's TV shows.[8] See how many of these you can identify in Figure 3.5.

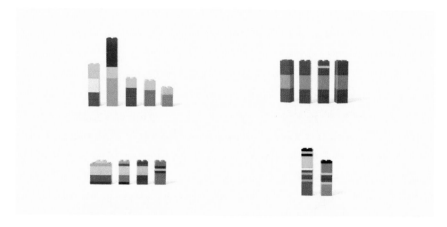

FIGURE 3.5 An abstraction of characters from four popular cartoon or children's TV shows. We recognize these because of the brain's associative pattern-matching abilities. If you do not recognize one or more of these, it's because you can't recall seeing a similar pattern.

The real question for both of these examples: How is it that you're able to recognize these logos and cartoon references? After all, these are nothing more than shapes and colors.

This is the brain's associative pattern matching at work. Assuming that you've seen this pattern before, or something like it, you are thus able to make a match. Let's focus on this "seen it before" aspect, as here's where things get really interesting.

8. "Lego: The Simpsons." March 1, 2012. www.adsoftheworld.com/media/print /lego_the_simpsons

SEEING WHAT WE EXPECT TO SEE

In the vase shown in Figure 3.6, what do you see?

FIGURE 3.6 An optical illusion by artist Sandro Del-Prete.[9] Based on prior experiences and current expectations, viewers see either a depiction of dolphins or two lovers.

9. Del-Prete, Sandro. 1987. *Message of Love from the Dolphins* (*Message d'Amour des Dauphins*). www.sandrodelprete.com/index.php/dolphins.html

Most adults will see two lovers. Yet, show this same image to young children, and they see the dolphins. (Go ahead, look for them!) While a fun optical illusion, this (like most optical illusions) reveals something about how we perceive things. This is a great example of how the brain matches based on *prior* experiences and expectations. For most adults, we're far more likely to see lovers than we are dolphins—this concept is likely on our minds more often! Children, who aren't accustomed to seeing two adults together in this sexual way, are more likely to see the image they are familiar with, dolphins (assuming they've read about or seen dolphins). In short: *We see what we've seen before (and also what we expect to see).*

There's far more to the brain and perceptions than what we've covered here, but the three points we've called out are sufficient for our purpose, which is to understand the role the brain plays as a pattern-matching and prediction organ. Understanding this gives depth to the examples that follow in the next several chapters.

To recap: *associations among concepts is thinking.* The brain is a perceptual organ, looking to make associations. Let's return then to the observable world, to look at how these perceptions are activated by stories and pictures and other things we can point to.

How We'll Explore Everyday Associations

To the extent that we use (or intentionally choose to avoid) certain associations, we affect understanding—understanding for ourselves and for others. Accordingly, it's critical to consider how these conceptual associations slip into nearly every part of our daily interactions. Once we become aware of how associations show up, we can become more fluent at using, challenging, and avoiding associative thinking. That's the goal.

To kick off our *investigation* into associations (notice the detective concept we're activating with that specific word choice), we'll begin primarily with examples based in language and then turn our attention to the associations invoked by what we see. While there is no clean way to structure this exploration, we have chosen to examine how associations are activated in the following ways.

First, Chapter 4, "Everyday Associations: Metaphors, Priming, Anchoring, and Narrative," will examine what we commonly hear, read, or say:

- Metaphors (which touches on emotionally laden phrases, decision framing, and subversive language)
- Priming and anchoring
- Narratives (briefly, with a subsection on simulation)

Then Chapter 5, "Everyday Associations: Aesthetics and Explicit Visual Metaphors," will look at associations activated by what we see:

- Aesthetics (both visual and nonvisual)
- Explicit visual metaphors

Finally, Chapter 6, "Closing Thoughts and Cautionary Notes About Associations," will explore first principles and other considerations that should accompany any discussion of associative thinking.

4

Everyday Associations: Metaphors, Priming, Anchoring, and Narrative

C is for COOKIE.

—COOKIE MONSTER, *SESAME STREET*

Countless books and articles are dedicated to topics such as the power of stories, how skilled orators should choose their phrasing, or how we're irrational creatures susceptible to cognitive biases. But most of these commentaries stop at the level of "what to do" or "what happens" with little discussion as to *why*. A more fundamental way to assess these things is through the lens of prior associations: To what extent do these things we most commonly hear or read (or say) activate prior associations, and in doing so, shape understanding? By applying more intention to the concepts and associations we activate, we can help shift and reduce the cost of understanding. Keep this in mind as we explore how written and oral language affects our understanding.

How Metaphors Shape Associations

I (Stephen) still recall how late-night comedian David Letterman described the Mach3 razor (back when triple blades were a new thing):

> "It's like shaving with the back of a spoon."

Perhaps this was paid placement? Regardless, this was, for me at least, a powerfully persuasive and memorable statement. Nine simple words said more to me than a 30-second commercial or full-page ad would ever communicate. But more than the words, it was what the words evoked. I don't know of anyone who loves to shave their face. It's not fun. It burns. We get cuts. But running the back of a spoon across my face … That's … Delightful. Smooth. Perhaps cold. Not at all unsettling. Fine razor cuts and itchy skin were the farthest things from my mind when I heard Letterman describe this razor like the back of a spoon. And now my brain had formed an emotionally charged connection: I understood the (purported) feeling of this innovative new razor by way of some other, quite pleasant association.

> "Reach for the stars."

> "We'll beat the competition."

> "It's like shaving with the back of a spoon."

From the poetry of advertising to the well-crafted political speech, a careful choice of words can win hearts and change minds. It can be an *explicit* association—like shaving with a spoon—or something more suggestive.

Consider what is now a near-ubiquitous phrase in software development: *technical debt* (or *tech debt* for short). This metaphor was coined by Ward Cunningham to explain the refactoring work that programmers so often must contend with. It's one thing to argue that cutting corners—to deliver results more quickly in the near term—will cost more in the long run. It's quite another thing to link that rational argument with something we all know and *feel* emotionally: the dangers of going into *financial* debt. Whether we're in debt or not, it's commonly known that debt is a dangerous thing. You shouldn't knowingly enter into debt unless you have a plan to get out of debt and you're fully aware of what it will cost you. This phrase *technical debt* is so powerful, we've seen it picked up by other product groups to draw attention to analogous situations: *design debt, product debt, conceptual debt.*

A very subtle association can certainly change how people think and feel about something. Spoons. Debt. But can these associations change behavior?

Metaphors and Crime: Is Crime a Virus or a Beast?

Researchers Paul H. Thibodeau and Lera Boroditsky have investigated the role of metaphors in reasoning.[1] In a study from 2011 (and repeated again in 2015), students were asked to read one of two reports about crime in a city and then suggest solutions for the problem. These reports were nearly identical, citing the same statistical data, except for one small detail: the metaphor used to describe the crime. In the first report, crime was characterized as a "wild beast preying on the city" and "lurking in neighborhoods." In the second report, crime was described as a "virus infecting the city" and "plaguing" neighborhoods. The researchers wanted to investigate if changing the metaphorical framing would influence whether students chose solutions that were more enforcement-oriented (prison, street patrols) or social-reform-oriented (education, economic reform). Would this *beast or virus* framing make a difference in the selection of policy responses? While sifting through the data from these studies was complicated and highlighted a broader issue with shifting cultural norms, the research did conclude that framing crime as a *beast* made people more likely to prefer enforcement-oriented solutions than if crime had been framed as a *virus*. The research also stated that "people who read that crime was a virus were more likely to endorse the proposal to 'develop neighborhood watch programs and do more community outreach,' than people who read that crime was a beast."

In this case, the metaphors used to describe crime did seem to influence people's reasoning about crime and the selection of correlative solutions.

> *Far from being mere rhetorical flourishes, metaphors have profound influences on how we conceptualize and act with respect to important societal issues. We find that exposure to even a single metaphor can induce substantial differences in opinion about how to solve social problems.*
>
> **—PAUL H. THIBODEAU AND LERA BORODITSKY**

---

1. Thibodeau, Paul H., and Lera Boroditsky. 2011. "Metaphors We Think With: The Role of Metaphor in Reasoning." *PLoS ONE* 6 (2). https://doi.org/10.1371/journal.pone.0016782; Thibodeau, Paul H., and Lera Boroditsky. 2015. "Measuring Effects of Metaphor in a Dynamic Opinion Landscape." Opion. *PLoS ONE* 10 (7). https://doi.org/10.1371/journal.pone.0133939

Decision Framing and Cognitive Bias

While research into metaphors and linguistic framing is ongoing (at least one study has offered up alternative explanations other than metaphorical framing[2]), similar studies going back to the 1970s also seem to support this general correlation between things as stated and our reasoning. In studies on "decision framing," behavioral economists have found that the identical question, asked in different ways, leads to completely different responses.

For example, would you prefer a condom that was "95% effective" or one that had a "5% failure" rate? What about "80% lean" ground beef versus "20% fat" ground beef?[3]

Rationally, these are identical options. But in repeated studies, most people chose the first option, or the one that either avoided loss or framed things in the positive. The conclusion of behavioral economists such as Amos Tversky and Daniel Kahneman was that the choices we make are influenced by the way these options are framed.

In what is now an oft-cited study from behavioral economics,[4] participants were asked to choose between two alternative programs to combat the outbreak of a disease expected to kill 600 people. The first group of respondents was presented with this outbreak situation, with two options to choose from, both framed in terms of lives *saved*; the second group of respondents was presented with the identical situation and the same two options, but these options were framed in terms of lives *lost*. What Tversky and Kahneman found was that "choices involving gains were often risk averse and choices involving losses were often risk taking." While respondents from both groups were asked essentially the same question, answers were nearly reversed between groups. To the extent that framing something triggered a human bias (*risk aversion* or *risk taking* in this study), we can conclude that framing—generally—has a powerful effect on the choices we make.

2. Steen, Gerard J., W. Gudrun Reijnierse, and Christian Burgers. 2014. "When Do Natural Language Metaphors Influence Reasoning? A Follow-Up Study to Thibodeau and Boroditsky (2013)." *PLoS ONE* 9 (12). https://doi.org/10.1371/journal.pone.0113536
3. Specific examples from "Framing Effect—Biases & Heuristics." n.d. The Decision Lab. https://thedecisionlab.com/biases/framing-effect/
4. Tversky, A., and D. Kahneman. 1981. "The Framing of Decisions and the Psychology of Choice." *Science* 211 (4481): 453–58. https://doi.org/10.1126/science.7455683

One of the more humorous studies into decision framing came from researchers at the University of Nottingham Centre for Decision Research and Experimental Economics, who posed an interesting question: Would other experimental economists—those professionals who researched these types of topics—be prone to the same framing effects? Using a "natural field experiment" (participants were not aware they were part of a study), researchers used registrations for the 2006 Economic Science Association conference as part of their experiment. As part of the registration process, attendees—the unwitting research participants—were sent an email reminder concerning a fee for late registration. In what is known in web analytics as an A/B test, participants were sent one of two possible emails, each using a different frame. One email warned attendees of a *penalty* of $50 for registering after the first deadline. The other email communicated a *discount* of $50 for registering before the first deadline. What were the results? Curiously, 93% of the junior researchers responded to the *late fee* messaging compared to 67% who responded to the *discount* messaging.[5] These results—that things framed in the negative received more engagement—were consistent with other studies.

Of course, many of these studies beg more investigation. With the conference signup, the study points also showed there was no effect for senior researchers. And with the "disease outbreak" study, critics have pointed out that the phrasing might suggest different—rather than identical—outcomes. That disclaimer aside, the effects of framing are well researched and generally agreed upon. In our view, none of this undercuts the broader point we're trying to make, that behind all of these studies sits a common thread: how we think and reason about things is based on associations between concepts. Framing, as with metaphors, is an example of this cognitive process in action.

The Economic Engine, Sick Patient, or …?

Understanding the power of language to shape how we think, it's no surprise that an economist and author like Paul Krugman might lash out against the metaphors used to characterize the economy. In "Block That Metaphor," a 2010 Op-Ed piece for *The New York Times*, Krugman called out phrases like

5. Gächter, Simon, Henrik Orzen, Elke Renner, and Chris Starmer. 2009. "Are Experimental Economists Prone to Framing Effects? A Natural Field Experiment." *Journal of Economic Behavior & Organization* 70 (3): 443–46. https://doi.org/10.1016/j.jebo.2007.11.003

"jump-start the economy" and "a fragile recovery time to strengthen." From the column:

> America's economy isn't a stalled car, nor is it an invalid who will soon return to health if he gets a bit more rest. Our problems are longer-term than either metaphor implies.
>
> And bad metaphors make for bad policy. The idea that the economic engine is going to catch or the patient rise from his sickbed any day now encourages policy makers to settle for sloppy, short-term measures when the economy really needs well-designed, sustained support.[6]

To be fair, whether a metaphor is bad or good might depend upon hindsight and a clear definition of what is good. But we do know that metaphors have a profound effect on how we understand a topic. Simply changing *how* we describe a problem changes how people respond. We absolutely should be aware of the metaphors that affect our reasoning, for both their benefits and their limitations. These are ways of thinking that allow us to see a thing in a different way—for better or worse.

Can Merely Suggesting a Concept Frame a Decision?

While the examples listed previously might also get cited as *direct semantic* or *affective priming* (something we'll discuss next), we're presenting these as metaphors, since they liken one thing to another. But what if there is no clear parallel? What if there's no explicit correlation made between the focus topic and the metaphor brought to mind? Studies seem to suggest similar outcomes when the framing is unrelated to the decision being made. That is, simply having a particular concept suggested and in memory may influence an unrelated decision. In a 2009 study on this topic, psychologists Mark Landau, Daniel Sullivan, and Jeff Greenberg proposed that "metaphor is a mechanism by which motivational states in one conceptual domain can influence attitudes in a superficially unrelated domain."[7]

---

6. Krugman, Paul. 2010 "Block Those Metaphors." Opinion. *The New York Times*. www.nytimes.com /2010/12/13/opinion/13krugman.html

7. Landau, Mark J., Daniel Sullivan, and Jeff Greenberg. 2009. "Evidence That Self-Relevant Motives and Metaphoric Framing Interact to Influence Political and Social Attitudes." *Psychological Science* 20 (11): 1421–27. https://doi.org/10.1111/j.1467-9280.2009.02462.x

In this study, participants were split into groups, and each group was asked to read an article about airborne bacteria. One group's article described airborne bacteria as ubiquitous and harmful, while the other described airborne bacteria as ubiquitous and harmless. This article seeded an idea, that of airborne bacteria as either harmful or harmless.

Next, participants were asked to read one of two articles about U.S. domestic issues *other than* immigration. One of these articles contained a number of "country as body" metaphorical expressions: "After the Civil War, the United States experienced an unprecedented growth spurt, and is scurrying to create new laws that will give it a chance to digest the millions of innovations." The other version of this article contained no such metaphors. "After the Civil War, the United States experienced an unprecedented period of innovation, and efforts are now underway to create new laws to control the millions of innovations."

Finally, subjects completed a questionnaire about immigration and the minimum wage. As expected, subjects who read about the harmful effects of bacterial contamination along with an article that employed the country as body metaphor were more likely to hold negative attitudes regarding immigration.

Application: Choosing Our Words Carefully

If studies show that metaphors do seem to shape our thinking, shouldn't we be more cautious—and intentional—about the associations we evoke? This is the takeaway: we should learn to be aware of and wary of words we commonly use. Why do we talk about our "target" audience—is it healthy to think about customers as prey to be hunted? How does this influence how we later think about and treat these customers? Or what about this statement, usually from well-meaning teachers: "It's time to stop playing and get back to work." Implied in this statement is that learning isn't fun or that play isn't learning. Is that a message we want to reinforce? From the work of folks such as game designer Raph Koster[8] to an expert on the topic of play such as Stuart Brown, M.D., the conclusion is the same: we know that playing is learning and learning is play. Look at students engaged with a subject or making things, and you'll see students caught up in the flow state associated with play. Serious question: How much authentic learning can take place when learning is framed as labor?

8. Koster, Raph. 2014. *A Theory of Fun for Game Design*. Sebastopol, CA: OReilly.

More subtle (and perhaps more controversial), consider how we talk about public education. Aren't phrases like "learning standards" and "raising the bar" rooted in a business or factory-like view of teaching? Is this a realistic analogy, given that student attendance is compulsory, and schools cannot simply choose to hire or fire students, as with employees? How do we reconcile treating students like workers in a factory with all we now know about learning differences, special needs, personalized learning, and the like?

Or consider phrases like "I won the argument" or "He backed down." Why do we tend to view conflict as a fight, where one person must beat the other person? What if we viewed conflicts as a puzzle to be solved, and doing so required sorting out the experiences and beliefs that have led to the conflicting conclusions?

So yes, metaphors can trigger emotions; they also shape how we reason about something, and perhaps even affect the decisions we make. But how does this help us figure things out?

Changing the metaphor changes our thinking. And when we change our thinking, we see new possibilities. Metaphors can reduce the cost of understanding by bridging what we do know with something we don't yet know. But this reduced cost in understanding comes at a price: this metaphor will only work to a point, and then it limits our understanding. This is only *a* way to view a topic. The lesson? Use metaphors with care. The tricky part is how embedded these metaphors are in our language (and in our thoughts). But view this as a challenge[9] from us, to be vigilant and intentional with the words we choose, and the frames they invoke.

How Priming and Anchoring Influence Associations

Metaphors are one form of conceptual associations. What about something that isn't quite so decipherable? Something less … narrative. Might simply suggesting a word, a phrase, or a number affect our reasoning abilities? To answer this question, let's consider *priming* and *anchoring*, two closely related but different ideas that have been well studied by behavioral economists.

---

9. Yes, we're aware that "challenge" is itself a metaphor! Pick another, if you like.

Priming

Suppose we're talking about food and what you had for lunch yesterday. Then we ask you to fill in the "missing" letter in this word: SO_P. Go ahead. What's the word? Chances are you'd say "SOUP." If, however, we're talking about hygiene, showers, and topics of cleanliness, and we ask you the same question, you're more likely to complete the word as "SOAP." Simple studies like this one are numerous.[10] A specific suggestion influences what comes to mind. This is priming.

Priming is "the use of background factors to put someone in a psychological state that affects their actions without their conscious knowledge." Magicians frequently use priming to "read people's minds" when in reality they are planting ideas—often without our conscious awareness. Unlike metaphors, where we might stop and call out the metaphor being invoked, or use a word that conjures up a metaphor, priming is more subconscious, likely to go unnoticed by the person being "primed." Like a metaphor, it's still triggering a prior association; however, it's not explicit, more likely to be suggestive than correlative, and probably separated by a bit of time (often minutes). (For our broader point, these distinctions are less important—these are all different forms of an associative pattern-matching process.)

As with our SO_P example, the most common examples of priming are rather directed, that is, we can trace back our primed actions to one or more background factors. A *specific* suggestion then influences what comes to mind. This makes sense. But research into priming has veered into even more interesting directions.

Priming and Subtle Suggestions

In a study dubbed "The Florida Effect,"[11] rather than make a specific suggestion, leading to an easy correlation (EAT —> SOUP / WASH —> SOAP), we saw something more fascinating. First, research participants were primed to recall an idea that was never explicitly stated (but was itself suggested by other words). Second, we saw priming affect physical behaviors.

---

10. Example from Kahneman, Daniel. 2015. *Thinking, Fast and Slow*. New York: Farrar, Straus and Giroux.
11. Bargh, John A., Mark Chen, and Lara Burrows. 1996. "Automaticity of Social Behavior: Direct Effects of Trait Construct and Stereotype Activation on Action." *Journal of Personality and Social Psychology* 71 (2): 230–44. https://doi.org/10.1037/0022-3514.71.2.230

Broken into two parts, the study first asked subjects to arrange words into sentences. For the control group, the words given to them were random and neutral—to not suggest any specific ideas. The test group was given words such as *Florida, forgetful, bald, gray,* and *wrinkly*—all words that we might associate with the elderly. That's the first part of the study—priming subjects with words that might suggest old age. The second part of the study was where things got interesting. After they finished arranging the words, the subjects were sent to do another experiment in an office down the hall. Of course, this short walk was the real experiment—researchers were timing their walk. The results? "Participants for whom an elderly stereotype was primed walked more slowly down the hallway when leaving the experiment than did control participants." Apparently, unconscious thinking about old age influenced physical actions. When subjects were questioned afterward, none of them recalled noticing a theme in the words they arranged, and they insisted that nothing in that first experiment could have influenced their stride. And yet ...

Focus on the *conceptual* associations.

This connection between the mind and body—that what we think and do are linked—is a fascinating one, that seems to work both ways. When we explored the mind-body connection in Chapter 2, we mentioned the "warm cup" study, one of several studies exploring links between physiological and affective associations. Similar studies seem to suggest this same correlation between bodily states and concepts brought to mind. Perhaps you've heard that placing a pencil in your mouth for three minutes leads to a happier state? The idea here being that forcing your mouth into a smile actually triggers the associated feelings of happiness and can actually "hack" your brains to be happier. Or maybe you've seen the TED talk about "power poses," that reclining in a chair, and putting your hands behind your head before an interview can lead to more confidence.[12] On a purely anecdotal note, I (Stephen) have found chewing gum just before an important social event (client pitch, social conversation) leads to increased feelings of confidence and helps counter my introverted tendencies. While the science of this mind-body connection is still emerging (and tenuous, at times!), the connection is well-acknowledged by a number of professions that focus on the body, from yoga, theater, and dance instruction to the sports coach who has the athletic team practicing visualization techniques.

12. Popularized by Amy Cuddy. Listed here as an example, although the scientific validity has been challenged. See Caution Note.

Anchoring

Whereas priming suggests a concept that somehow correlates with present or future concepts, anchoring need not exhibit such a correlation. With anchoring, introducing an irrelevant number biases your judgment. Adding a completely arbitrary factor—say the last two digits of your Social Security number—affects an unrelated piece of information, say the estimated value of a bottle of wine or a trackball mouse. In fact, this is precisely what Professor Dan Ariely and others did in a classroom experiment.[14]

---

13. Doyen, Stéphane, Olivier Klein, Cora-Lise Pichon, and Axel Cleeremans. 2012. "Behavioral Priming: It's All in the Mind, but Whose Mind?" *PLoS ONE* 7 (1). https://doi.org/10.1371/journal .pone.0029081
14. Ariely, Dan, George F. Loewenstein, and Drazen Prelec. 2005. "Tom Sawyer and the Construction of Value." *SSRN Electronic Journal.* https://doi.org/10.2139/ssrn.774970

After being shown an array of objects—wines of different values, computer equipment, books, boxes of chocolate—students were asked to do several things.

- First, translate the last two digits of their Social Security numbers into a dollar amount. For example, if the last two digits of your SSN were 37, then you would write this as a dollar amount: $37.

- Next, students wrote this dollar amount next to each object, and were asked if they would pay this amount for each object. Yes or no. Students were reminded that this was a completely arbitrary number and should have no correlation with the actual price value of the object.

- Finally, students were asked to write the maximum amount they *would* be willing to pay for each object.

Here is where things got interesting. The assessed value of these objects showed a strong correlation with the last two digits of the students' SSNs. Students with Social Security numbers in the lowest 20%, priced (on average) a bottle of '98 Côtes du Rhône wine at U.S. $8.64; students on the other end of the bell curve, the 20% with the highest Social Security numbers priced (on average) the same bottle at U.S. $27.91.

While completely arbitrary, the number written down appears to influence, or "anchor," the value attribution. This is the basic idea of price anchoring, that when asked to make a numerical estimate where we have little information to go on, we're often biased by some initial starting number. This happens in everything from auctions to retail price settings. If a retailer prices an object at a high dollar amount, then any discount off that amount will seem to be a good deal. Conversely, this same fixed amount might seem like too much, if the initial anchor were set much lower.

In his book *Predictably Irrational*, Ariely comments on this price anchoring research, stating:

> Social Security numbers were the anchor in this experiment only because we requested them. We could have just as well asked for the current temperature or the manufacturer's suggested retail price. Any question, in fact, would have created the anchor. Does that seem rational? Of course not.

While we're focused here on one popular study, *anchoring* is a well-studied phenomenon, with research going back to at least the 1950s by researchers such as Muzafer Sherif.

On their own, these studies were remarkable. In the context of this chapter, though, anchoring should be less remarkable: it's simply an association. By suggesting a detail—even a detail that may have little or nothing to do with the subject—we introduce extra information into our conscious (or unconscious) mind. This detail becomes part of the web of related associations that our brain has to sort out, in a never-ending job as a perceptual organ. The brain doesn't necessarily care that information is unrelated—it's all information to reconcile into a sensible pattern, if there is one. In economic terms, we might describe this as *arbitrary coherence*, where the brain attempts to maintain a decision consistent with previous decisions (coherence), even if the initial decision was arbitrary.

While the majority of studies investigate anchoring with numeric values, there are exceptions, studies that explore other—non-numeric—forms of anchoring. In a study of "cross-modality" anchoring, researchers wanted to push the boundary conditions for anchoring, to assess at what point a piece of irrelevant information would no longer influence an individual's judgments.

With this study, students were given a survey with a series of unrelated questions, one per page. Among the decoy questions was an activity that required students to draw a series of either short or long lines. Later, one of the questions would ask students an estimation question, such as the length of the Mississippi River or the average temperature in Honolulu in July. The results? Researchers found a strong correlation between being primed with drawing long or short lines and the river length or temperature estimates, concluding that the "boundaries of anchoring effects might be much wider than previously thought." Anchoring might work not just with irrelevant numbers, but also irrelevant shapes, sounds, temperatures, weights, and so on.

In their conclusion, researchers speculated on other ways that anchoring might be manifest:

> Students filling out class evaluation forms might have lower evaluations of the class if the forms are completed with golf pencils rather than regular pencils. The fact that the taller candidate won 80% of the presidential election contests between 1904 and 1980 (Gillis, 1982) could be due partly to the fact that their heights biased people's estimates of their positive qualities. Waiting in a long line to get tickets at the theater may bias people to then think that the cost of theater popcorn is not exorbitant. This is

hardly an exhaustive list; clearly, there are many far-reaching applications and implications of these findings.[15]

Of course, our interest in all this is to show how we reason and think via associations—even with irrelevant associations. While there are worthwhile distinctions between anchoring bias, priming effects, decision framing, and other named effects, these distinctions seem to blur into each other, coalescing around this more fundamental idea of associations.

Let's turn them to another form of associative thinking, also triggered through words and language, but one that is much more robust, developed, and explicit—that of narratives.

How Narratives Shape Associations

"Let me tell you a story …"

Stories are perhaps the most powerful driver of human behaviors. From the inspiring vision cast by a U.S. President ("I believe that this nation should commit itself to achieving the goal, before this decade is out, of landing a man on the moon and returning him safely to the Earth.") to the deep, personal narratives we construct that govern our beliefs and behaviors, stories are potent things. In the midst of an otherwise boring speech, the speaker will begin to tell a story, and we can't help but listen. If I start sharing details of my family vacation to London or begin gossiping about that coworker who tried to get me fired—I've got your attention. Quite literally. Our brains cannot help but devote attention to stories.

But why? What is it about stories that grabs our attention? From a neuroscience perspective, if all thoughts are simply a jumble of neurons firing and wiring together, what is it about *narrative* associations that is so much stronger, compared to other kinds of associations? Stories seem like a much more complicated, sustained web of associations. How does this fit with the "associated concepts" narrative we're presenting? Figure this out, and you've unlocked one of the most potent tools for drawing people into a space where everyone is engaged in the process of understanding.

15. Oppenheimer, Daniel M., Robyn A. Leboeuf, and Noel T. Brewer. 2008. "Anchors Aweigh: A Demonstration of Cross-Modality Anchoring and Magnitude Priming." *Cognition* 106 (1): 13–26. https://doi.org/10.1016/j.cognition.2006.12.008

While investigations into the science of narrative are still at the early stages, there are at least three explanations for why stories are so powerful (none of which invalidates the others). The explanations are as follows:

- We need stories for survival.
- Stories captivate our brain in ways that facts do not.
- Stories are critical to forming social bonds.

Let's look at each of these in more detail.

Explanation #1: We Need Stories for Survival

Stories are a safe way to explore the dangers that might kill us.

The most popular hypothesis is that stories are—from an evolutionary biology perspective—vital to survival. Before the written word, we used myths, stories, and fables to contain simple ideas and warnings that should keep us safe, whether from physical harm or straying from a moral path. And before oral stories, it was the accumulation of certain kinds of narrative associations that quite literally kept us alive. Lisa Cron, author of *Wired for Story*, suggests that "Story was more crucial to our evolution than our opposable thumbs because all opposable thumbs did is let us hang on. It was story that told us what to hang on to."[16]

What stories let us do—in a safe way—is to step out of our *present* circumstances and explore *possible* outcomes. For ancient ancestors on the savanna, this might have been a physical survival story about what happens when we eat this red berry or ignore that rustling in the bushes. The ability to pass on this cause-and-effect knowledge would quite literally have meant the difference between life and death. In modern times, these same underlying narrative patterns are now hardwired into our subconscious, but they are more likely to influence the ability to navigate social situations. *Do I see myself as a victim of circumstances, or the hero facing adversity? Is someone out to get me? Will that leader save or betray me?* Whether we are aware of it or not, we all create these narratives to make sense of present circumstances and to project possible outcomes. The problem is when these primitive narratives ("us vs.

---

16. Cron, Lisa. 2012. *Wired for Story: The Writers Guide to Using Brain Science to Hook Readers from the First Sentence*. Berkeley: Ten Speed Press.

them," "I have to get tough," "it's a conspiracy") are misdirected and lead to faulty conclusions.

THE RISK WITH STORIES

Exposing narratives has been the focus for many branches of psychology—helping patients recognize the beliefs and "scripts" that drive behaviors. Exercises to help people separate facts from feelings are used by counselors and coaches alike. Work in the field of behavioral economics has highlighted the differences between our natural inclination to make emotional decisions and our more recently evolved ability to think in rational terms. As much as we like to think of ourselves as rational creatures, our ability to reason is a relatively recent addition to the evolution of our brains. This ability to think rationally and project ourselves into the future or into the past sits atop a more powerful and primitive set of instincts and inclinations.

Biologically, this means we are an accumulation of stories, cognitive biases, and heuristics, which while helpful to make quick decisions, also makes it difficult to be objective and rational about things. To be clear, the completely rational person is a myth. Spock from *Star Trek* isn't a reality. We need emotions to make decisions; otherwise, we become paralyzed by analysis. We need stories to navigate reality. These are the patterns and conceptual wrappers that give quick meaning to things as they unfold. But we also need to develop our ability to recognize these emotions, biases, heuristics, and beliefs, and see them for what they are—useful, albeit fictional, shortcuts for understanding. Someone *might* be out to get you fired; more likely, it's all in your head. You might think you've failed at something, but a reality check with outside observers would prove otherwise. Simply recognizing that "story provides context for the facts," and that you can spin many stories from the same set of facts, helps us to be more thoughtful about such things.

WHAT'S GREAT ABOUT STORIES

What's great about stories, whether fictional or not, is how they inspire. By invoking a basic narrative, we are challenged to do more than we believe is possible, to work together for greater purpose, or to be the best version of ourselves. Want to change how someone thinks about something? You must first change how they *feel* about it. Stories change how people feel. This is as true of a compelling speech as it is a moving film. We're certain there's at least one fictional book that changed you in some way. Personally, I (Stephen) was inspired by the compassion shown to and by Jean Valjean in Victor Hugo's book *Les Misérables*. And after reading Cory Doctorow's book *Little Brother*, I was moved from being merely *concerned* about data privacy to actually taking efforts to protect and defend what are basic human rights. Compared to factual accounts, fictional stories have far more influence on changing attitudes and behaviors. It's not just the explicit narrative so easily discussed. We also experience quiet, personal shifts in narrative: challenging one person to "assume good intent" where there is a conflict with another person, may be enough to change the underlying narrative, confront the source of negative feelings, and in so doing, open the doors for healing.

Whether for harm or for good, it's important to recognize stories for what they are: ways to assess a situation, in order to predict possible outcomes. Through fiction, we can run through simulations of what might be, whether it's fiction of our own invention or the fiction we pay to enjoy as entertainment. Stories are hardwired—biologically—to this deeper need for survival. So, this "stories as survival mechanism" is the popular "story" (see what we did there!), but is there more? Let's delve a bit into the neuroscience behind narrative.

Explanation #2: Stories Engage More Parts of the Brain

As you'd expect, a number of fMRI studies have looked at brain activity in response to different kinds of narratives. What these studies reveal is that stories engage more parts of the brain. If we state facts in neutral terms, only a few areas of the brain—those typically associated with language processing—light up. When we wrap the facts in a narrative and use evocative words, many more parts of the brain light up.[17]

Accordingly, the more active the brain is (that is, the more parts of the brain being activated), the more we are engaged in the moment and likely to find that thing memorable. And if the story is at all emotional, we're even more likely to recall these events later. This goes a long way toward explaining why narratives get our attention. I can state a fact, that "snakes are venomous," but if instead I describe how "a snakebite is like fire coursing through your veins,

17. Paul, Annie Murphy. 2012. "Your Brain on Fiction." Opinion. *The New York Times*. March 17, 2012. www.nytimes.com/2012/03/18/opinion/sunday/the-neuroscience-of-your-brain-on-fiction.html

and I should know, because once upon a time, while visiting my aunt in New York we took a trip to the Statue of Liberty, where...." Your brain can't help but pay attention. The story and the metaphors invoke all of these associated sensory images. Sticking to the facts of a thing means fewer areas of the brain are active, while engaging *more* areas of the brain seems to correlate—the current belief—with attention. This alone is a reason to include stories in a book about understanding: to the extent that a narrative can grab and hold a person's attention, and then help them—by association—make complex information accessible (via the lens of the narrative), that is powerful. This should also lend some scientific credence to the writer's mantra of "show, don't tell."

FACT OR FICTION, IT DOESN'T MATTER

So then, stories arouse attention by invoking more areas of the brain. Got it. Here's where things get really interesting. Whether we are *in the moment*, or watching a movie, the same specific regions of our brain light up in these fMRI studies. I could be walking in the rain, or simply reading about a walk in the rain—it doesn't make a difference; the very same areas of the brain are stimulated. The degree of intensity is less with these imagined situations, but researchers observe the same neural changes whether you read about something or actually do that something.

This has been noted in studies involving smell, texture, motor movement, and more. Most of the studies focus on single words; more recent studies have had subjects read passages from a story. In these cases, someone may read about eating breakfast, or actually eat breakfast—the same areas of the brain are activated. The studies conclude that "readers understand a story by simulating the events in the story world and updating their simulation when features of that world change."[18]

Where this is more interesting is when *people* are involved. There seems to be a significant overlap between the regions of the brain associated with narrative comprehension and the regions associated with social cognition.[19] In a quantitative meta-analysis of neuroimaging studies pertaining to *theory of mind* (the ability to infer the mental states of others), Raymond Mar,

18. Speer, Nicole K., Jeremy R. Reynolds, Khena M. Swallow, and Jeffrey M. Zacks. 2009. "Reading Stories Activates Neural Representations of Visual and Motor Experiences." *Psychological Science* 20 (8): 989–99. https://doi.org/10.1111/j.1467-9280.2009.02397.x
19. Mar, Raymond A. 2011. "The Neural Bases of Social Cognition and Story Comprehension." *Annual Review of Psychology* 62 (1): 103–34. https://doi.org/10.1146/annurev-psych-120709-145406

a psychologist at York University in Canada, found that the core networks involved with trying to figure out the thoughts and feelings of others were also activated by stories.

This might lead us to conclude, as did *The New York Times* article "Your Brain on Fiction," that:

> There is evidence that just as the brain responds to depictions of smells and textures and movements as if they were the real thing, so it treats the interactions among fictional characters as something like real-life social encounters.[20]

Given this information, when an expert on stories such as Lisa Cron remarks (in her TEDx talk) that "You're not just reading about Jane Eyre. You Are Jane Eyre …," she's right, cognitively speaking. If we conclude that it is a thin line between a lived experience and being present in a story, then all stories become worthy of serious consideration. This only strengthens the notion that stories shape who we are. And they're a powerful way to manage the cost of understanding, whether used as a lens to view some information, or used to develop the social bonds needed to bring people together, to figure something out.

Seeming to support this assertion, research led by Dr. Keith Oatley, a professor emeritus of the University of Toronto Department of Applied Psychology and Human Development, has found that reading fiction increases empathy.[21] Through fictional stories, we improve our ability to understand other people, empathize with them, and imagine ourselves in another's situation. If we connect what we see with regions of the brain lighting up during reading, with the previous comments on narratives as a survival mechanism, then reading fiction allows us to safely explore different kinds of social interactions. Research in this direction quickly veers back to discussions of *theory of mind*, which, to offer up a more precise explanation, is "the ability to attribute mental states—beliefs, intents, desires, emotions, knowledge, etc.—to oneself, and to others, and to understand that others have beliefs, desires, intentions, and

---

20. Paul (2012).
21. Mar, Raymond A., Keith Oatley, and Jordan B. Peterson. 2009. "Exploring the Link Between Reading Fiction and Empathy: Ruling Out Individual Differences and Examining Outcomes." *Communications* 34 (4): 407-428. https://doi.org/10.1515/comm.2009.025; Mar, Raymond A., Keith Oatley, Jacob Hirsh, Jennifer Dela Paz, and Jordan B. Peterson. 2006. "Bookworms Versus Nerds: Exposure to Fiction Versus Non-Fiction, Divergent Associations with Social Ability, and the Simulation of Fictional Social Worlds." *Journal of Research in Personality* 40 (5): 694–712. https://doi.org/10.1016/j.jrp.2005.08.002

perspectives that are different from one's own." Theory of mind is, as you'd expect, critical to everyday human social interactions.

Which is a nice transition to the more recent argument for why stories are so powerful: *It's all about the characters.*

Explanation #3: Stories Are Critical to Social Bonds

The most recent research into narratives has focused on a neurochemical called *oxytocin*, associated with feelings of trust. When we are trusted or shown a kindness, the brain produces oxytocin. This signals "it is safe to approach others." Accordingly, oxytocin is critical to cooperation in groups.

So what does this have to do with narratives? While we can dwell on different kinds of narratives, conflicts, plot twists, and so on, it seems what the brain cares most about are characters, especially our hero. We are wired to pay attention to the thoughts and feelings of the protagonist.

According to Paul J. Zak, Ph.D., who has led much of the research into this topic:

> It seems that once we are attentive and emotionally engaged, our brains go into mimic mode and mirror the behaviors that the characters in the story are doing or might do. As social creatures we are biased toward engaging with others, and effective stories motivate us to help others …
>
> To the brain, good stories are good stories, whether first-person or third-person, on topics happy or sad, as long as they get us to care about their characters.[22]

In reading, or sometimes watching, these stories, we quite literally identify with the characters. We experience an empathy that is every bit as real as what we experience when interacting with others.

Stories and Understanding

So what do we do with all this? What role do stories and narrative play in our broader purpose—understanding?

---

22. Zak, Paul J. 2015. "Why Inspiring Stories Make Us React: The Neuroscience of Narrative." Dana Foundation. www.dana.org/article/why-inspiring-stories-make-us-react-the-neuroscience -of-narrative/

As social creatures, the pull toward narrative associations is a powerful—perhaps inescapable—one. What we've believed for years, that science is starting to explain, is that narratives are powerful vehicles for discovering or transferring critical information in a compelling way. If our goal is understanding, then knowing how and why stories work can help in this respect. We can use narrative with intention, to create empathy, or to bridge the unknown with known. We've seen this for years with inspiring speakers, leaders, teachers, and many other professions where stories are critical vehicles for passing on information. With incredibly difficult and contentious topics, we've seen great orators who—rather than argue about facts and details—seek only to change your overarching frame. Succeed at changing someone's frame of reference—or at least get them to open up to another way of seeing things differently—and the individual is left to sort out the details. But it's not just the literal stories.

SIMULATIONS

For our purposes, there's another form of story, *simulations*, a form that falls at the intersection of everything we're discussing. From the domain of learning and development, we know that simulations are arguably the most powerful way to convey understanding.

Through video games, immersive fiction, simulations, scenarios, and similar narrative or character-driven media, we have an incredibly effective way to educate, to figure things out. This effectiveness is due in part to the benefits of narrative, but also due to the cognitive benefits of interactions (a topic we'll revisit in much more detail in Part 4, "How We Understand Through Interactions"). Of course, this approach does require more upfront design and construction, but if our goal is effective education and understanding, these kinds of narrative experiences tend to be ranked as most effective, just behind actual "hands-on" experience.

For examples of the power of a good narrative simulation, we only need to look at projects such as *Spent* or *The Uber Game*. With *Spent*, you're given a straightforward challenge: make $1,000 last for one month. In attempting to do so, you experience what it's like to live in poverty, complete with difficult choices and unexpected events that make getting to the next paycheck an ordeal.[23] It's a difficult "game" that creates empathy for people living in poverty (and aims to raise awareness and funds in the process).

23. http://playspent.org/

Similar to *Spent*, *The Uber Game*, is a news game created by the *Financial Times* based on interviews with dozens of Uber drivers (see Figure 4.1). As a complement to the regular news article about life as an Uber driver, this game lets you experience being an Uber driver for a week.[24]

FIGURE 4.1 *The Uber Game* lets players experience what it's like to be an Uber driver for a week, through a series of choices—and outcomes—all based on interviews with dozens of Uber drivers.

Through a series of scripted scenarios—all based upon actual data and investigative reporting—you gain empathy for ride-sharing drivers, while being given a safe way to explore the potential financial upsides, coupled with the oft-overlooked costs to health, social, and other areas of life. As with most video games, simulations let you learn through trial and error, learning from failed attempts. You can replay the game, again and again, until you start to see patterns and ways of being more successful.

What both of these games do is let you step into another person's shoes. Depending on how the game is tweaked, you'll certainly feel some amount of empathy, but also an understanding of the difficult decisions and the probable outcomes of those decisions.

Think about what these games represent as learning challenges. Assuming the facts built into these experiences are sound and somewhat unbiased, people

24. "The Uber Game: Can You Make It in the Gig Economy?" n.d. *Financial Times*. https://ig.ft.com /uber-game

get to experience—first-hand—a compelling, instructional narrative. If we're the ones bearing the cost of understanding (the creators of this simulation), this is a powerful way to *transfer* understanding to another person. But let's pause for a second. What if we're the players in someone else's game, or what if the research is flawed or biased? What we still end up with is a shared story around which we can discuss assumptions and errors. Rather than vague, ideological disagreements, or unchecked assumptions, we have a storyline complete with tactics and decisions, ready to be assessed and critiqued. As a cognitive artifact, shouldn't this lead to more critical and constructive dialogue? Even with something like watching a movie, it's not uncommon for people to use the fictional narrative as the vehicle by which to debate or discuss the choices and consequences made by a character.

What we're circling here with simulations is an interesting space between stories and games, which most certainly fits with our theme of "getting from information to understanding." As with the Polisis representation for legal documents (from Chapter 1, "From Information to Understanding"), these simulations fit into the overlap of everything we've written about throughout this book—prior associations, external representations, interactions, and coordination.

With simulations and narrative games, we see a growing format for understanding that captivates players with an emotionally engaging narrative, but lets them also be in the story, learning directly from their actions. It's like a supercharged version of *Choose-Your-Own-Adventure* books—supercharged through technology, able to support more complicated, even nonlinear narratives. As with video games, by playing and replaying through a scenario, players discover what advances and doesn't advance the game (at least according to the rules established by the game's creators). The difference is, rather than focus on gathering loot or amassing kills, these games offer different kinds of rewards. Yes, it can be instructional on a topic, but with the rise of indie publishers, we've seen games that create empathy through experiential narratives (*Gone Home*), offer meta-stories that leave players changed (*Spec Ops*), or place them into difficult, moral situations (*Papers, Please*).

Note, these are different from games that offer facts about a topic, teach physics lessons, hand us clever puzzles to solve, or build in abstract lessons about economics or cooperation. Here, gameplay is wholly integrated with the content of the game. We learn through play. By turning complex issues into a game, complete with win (or end) conditions, players now have a feedback loop on decisions made.

All this sounds an awful lot like learning, as if we're creating spaces in which to interact and play with information.

OTHER APPLICATIONS OF NARRATIVE

Of course, the application of narratives isn't limited to simulations or speeches.

One thing that struck me (Stephen), from all the academic research into narrative, is just how much we focus on people. If the most compelling parts of a book or movie are character-driven, if according to the research it's *people*—more than any other element of a story—that captivate our attention, then how might we add or introduce characters to our topic?

The software and design worlds have done this for years in the form of personas, a tool intended to foster empathy for users of products, especially where access to actual users is limited. But it need not be this literal. We've seen the periodic table of elements brought to life by making each and every element a character. Some of the bestselling business books—such as Patrick Lencioni's *The Five Dysfunctions of a Team*—illustrate their lessons through a long, extended fable, with a brief bit of commentary at the end.

Moreover, if the content we are seeking to understand concerns the complexities of social life, shouldn't we embrace—rather than obscure—these kinds of narrative associations?

What We Hear, Read, and Say

The goal here is to become aware of how associations show up in everyday activities, so we can become more fluent at using, challenging, and avoiding associative thinking. So far, we've looked primarily at how associations are activated by things we hear, read, and say. Key ideas we covered were:

- Metaphors and stories frame how we reason about things.
- Priming and anchoring work at an unconscious level to activate prior associations.
- Stories are powerful because they tap into a need for survival, engage more senses, and are critical for building social bonds.
- Technology-driven simulations are a new and exciting form of narrative.
- All these associations affect reasoning, behaviors, and decision-making.

Next, let's consider how associations are activated by what we see.

5

Everyday Associations: Aesthetics and Explicit Visual Metaphors

Woody: Okay. Calm down, guys. Let's just keep this in perspective.
Mr. Potato Head: Perspective? This place is perfect.
Rex: Woody, it's nice! See? The door has a rainbow on it.

—TOY STORY 3

Up to this point, our attention has primarily been on concepts suggested by language. But remember: it's not about the words read or heard, it's the associated *concepts*. (We'll repeat this a few more times before the chapter is through!) Language is one way of eliciting an idea. We can say "It's *like* an iceberg." We can also draw a sketch of an iceberg. In both instances, what is critical is that the *idea* of an iceberg is brought to mind. In this chapter, we'll look at how concepts are activated by what is *seen*, first through the subtlety of shapes, forms, weight, motion, and other kinds of aesthetics; then through the explicit use of visual metaphors.

How Aesthetics Trigger Associations

For a classic example of the associations we make between shapes and sounds, let's look at the Bouba-Kiki effect. This is a study that's been repeated for nearly a century across cultures and age groups (even toddlers have been included in versions of this study), with near universal agreement. Essentially, people are presented with two shapes and told that one is "bouba" and the other "kiki." See if you can identity which shape goes with which word in Figure 5.1.

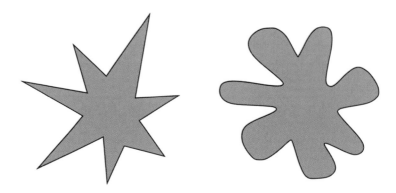

FIGURE 5.1 The Bouba-Kiki effect demonstrates a correlation between sounds and shapes. Viewers are presented with two distinct shapes and asked to identify which shape is "bouba" and which shape is "kiki."

If you concluded that the sharp-looking shape is kiki and the roundish one is bouba, then you've reached the same conclusion that nearly all people reach. But why? Why do we pair the shapes with these nonsensical words? Why do 95–98% of people polled consistently arrive at the same conclusion? The answer suggests something about the evolution of language—that naming things isn't completely arbitrary. If we consider the shape of our mouths, and how our tongues are placed when we pronounce each word, we see the similarities. Bouba sounds like a rounded object, and even your mouth forms a circular shape when pronouncing this word. In contrast, kiki requires you to make a "sharp" movement of the tongue on your palate. The words sound like their shapes and vice versa. Researchers Vilayanur S. Ramachandran and Edward M. Hubbard have examined these similarities from a neuroscience perspective, speculating about the nature of nonarbitrary connections that might exist between the sensory and motor areas of the brain. In their 2001 paper on the Bouba-Kiki effect, they remarked "These rules [of metaphor production] are a result of strong anatomical constraints that permit certain types of cross-activation, but not others."[1]

Of course, the Bouba-Kiki effect is an extreme example, cherry-picked to open up this chapter. However, if we place this simple example in the context of arguments made by George Lakoff and Mark Johnson—that much of our thought is based in primary, *embodied* interactions—you start to see the pattern: associations, whether observable in nature or shared by a culture group, are fundamental to all cognition.

But let's stick with these aesthetic associations.

A "Thick" Relationship

Below is an image of three faces, each connected by a line. What do you notice about the relationship between each pair of people? What leads you to this conclusion?

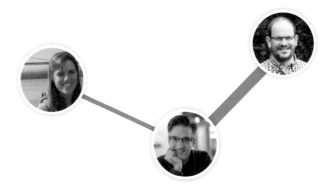

What we see are avatars each connected by a single line, and this line is either thin or thick. What do these lines say about the relationships?

In workshops where we've posed this question, the response was always the same: the thick line suggested a stronger relationship between two people; the thin line, a weaker relationship. But why is this? What if we directed you to the legend and told you something else, that the thin line was actually the strongest connection? It "wouldn't make sense" was what we heard every time. But why? This is where we like to direct the conversation. Perhaps it's

1. Ramachandran, Vilayanur S., and Edward M. Hubbard. 2001. "Synaesthesia: A Window into Perception, Thought and Language." *Journal of Consciousness Studies* 8 (12): 3–34.

something more fundamental that we've all experienced: thread is easy to rip apart, but wind these single threads into string or rope (making thicker strands), and it becomes much harder, if impossible, to tear apart. The same is true of trees: a twig is easy to break, but trunks and limbs, forget about it. Ripping a single sheet of paper (thin) is easy, but a book (thick) will slow down a bullet. *Thin is weak. Thick is strong.* Through a lifetime of interactions with the world, we become attuned to this perceptual association. It follows then that the thick line is the strong connection. Anything else violates the natural patterns we've accumulated. Whether we encounter this thick/thin concept via pixels on a screen or climbing a tree outdoors, we expect the same rules to apply. Meaning comes from the suggested associations, whether those associations are intended or not.

Associations and Transference of Meaning

Consider the "buttons" we use on websites and apps. If we turn our attention to things like why "rounded corners on buttons seem friendly," or "things that look like a button get higher click-through rates," it all begins to make sense. These are associations, forged from deep attunement to perceptual information via our lived experience in the natural world. Why are rounded corners on buttons perceived as friendly? Soft, round things in the real world don't cut us; sharp things do. Why would the outline around a label or icon increase click-through rates? It looks more like something we can push. At the core of our button discussions is a simple cognitive test: *I can/cannot associate this with something I've previously interacted with.* With rounded button corners, we can argue for an association rooted in nature, that soft, rounded things are perceived as being friendly because there are no sharp jags or edges to cut us. In the second example where adding an outline creates more click-throughs, it's a thoroughly invented (rather than natural) association. We associate the outline with a button, but the concept of a physical button was something we learned from interacting with physical buttons. Would the association even make sense if we traveled back in time to a pre-button century? It wouldn't, at least not until people were introduced to a button and could begin forming associations between what is seen and the possibilities for action. Of course, aesthetics include everything that appeals to the senses—not just what we *see*, but also what we hear, smell, taste, and feel. Aesthetics are concerned with anything perceived via the senses. In what other ways do we form aesthetic associations?

Heavy Suggests Value/Glass Suggests Transparency

A BMW owner might comment on how the doors on their car feel heavy. The doors are not, in fact, any heavier than other cars. But they feel heavier, as the hinges have been "tuned" to offer greater resistance. Why do this? Engineers have found that "a heavier feel helps impart a feeling of weightiness, importance, and value."

Apple also uses similar embodied ideas in the design of Apple stores. In a 2014 *Wired* interview, designer Michael Hendrix commented that

> High tables make you lean forward toward the devices, giving them the brunt of our attention and expectation. The ubiquitous glass lends a feeling of transparency, which in turn makes us aware of everything in the store. It helps the whole place feel open, inviting, and user-friendly.[2]

This idea that much of our thought is rooted in conceptual metaphors, based on physiology, sums up much of the work from George Lakoff and Mark Johnson. We've mentioned their names now, a few times, but this seemed like the best place to unpack a bit more of what they've brought to the conversation.

Over several decades, Lakoff has argued that metaphors are primarily a conceptual construction, central to the development of thought. And where do these metaphors come from? From our sensorimotor interactions with the world via our bodies. From the opening of their book *Philosophy in the Flesh*:[3]

> The mind is inherently embodied.
>
> Thought is mostly unconscious.
>
> Abstract concepts are largely metaphorical.

Building on these three ideas, Lakoff and Johnson go on to argue for a view of reason that begins with an understanding of the body.

> The very structure of reason itself comes from the details of our embodiment. The same neural and cognitive mechanisms that allow us to perceive and move around also create our conceptual systems and modes of reason. Thus, to understand

2. Kuang, Cliff. 2014. "6 Ideas That Define Design in 2014." *Wired*. Conde Nast. October 7, 2014. www.wired.com/2014/10/6-ideas-define-design-2014/
3. Lakoff, George, and Mark Johnson. 1999. *Philosophy in the Flesh: The Embodied Mind and Its Challenge to Western Thought*. New York: Basic Books.

reason we must understand the details of our visual system, our motor system, and the general mechanisms of neural binding.

To put this into perspective, consider bodies other than that of human creatures. We speak of left- and right-wing politics, but how much of this is rooted in our human biology, having developed two hands? Lakoff and Johnson might argue that if snakes and squid developed democratic governments, they would organize their political discourse in completely different ways because they have no hands. The external world shapes our conceptual structures, so having a different body and living in a different environment results in a different conceptual understanding of the world. François Chollet, a software engineer and AI researcher, summarizes this point rather eloquently: "The intelligence of an octopus is specialized in the problem of being an octopus. The intelligence of a human is specialized in the problem of being human … A human baby brain properly grafted in an octopus body would most likely fail to adequately take control of its unique sensorimotor space, and would quickly die off."[4]

For human creatures then, we have a physical basis for deep conceptual metaphors about everything from spatial relationships such as "Control is UP" (as indicated by phrases such "I have control *over* him," "I am *on top of* the situation," "He's at the *height* of his power," or "He ranks *above* me in strength") to emotion and temperature associations such as "Affection is warmth" (which seems to fit with the "warm cup" study we referenced in Chapter 2, "Understanding as a Function of the Brain, Body, and Environment").

Bringing This on Stage

While the limits of this kind of metaphorical thinking have been challenged—some concepts are inconsistent, many concepts don't seem to follow a basic primary—this does fit with our broader focus on *associations*. We're not concerned with whether these associations are based on a common set of physiological primaries, shared across all cultures, or whether these associations are learned and layered upon through interactions with the world. Whatever the theoretical source, we are, each of us, an accumulated set of associations. *Associations among concepts **is** thinking.* Exploring how this simple statement manifests in dozens of different examples is the point of this section.

4. Chollet, François. 2017. "The Implausibility of Intelligence Explosion." Medium. November 27, 2017. https://medium.com/@francois.chollet/the-impossibility-of-intelligence-explosion-5be4a9eda6ec

Let's bring this to life with a familiar activity: public speaking. As a frequent speaker and trainer, I (Stephen) am very aware of the "meta-messages" signaled by things beyond the content of a presentation. Below are just a few of the cross-sensory associations I try to be conscious and intentional about:

- In building slides for a public presentation, if I have a big idea I'm building up to, I might use the "anvil" animation built into Apple Keynote, where a phrase or object falls in from the top of the screen, stirs up some dust, and has a very small, tight bounce. This isn't about an anvil, but about the effects of dropping something very heavy. I'm using this animation to convey this is a "weighty" idea.

- The typefaces I choose follow their own logic, both for clarity and tone and voice. While I'll use a strong modern sans-serif typeface for the bulk of what I share, I'll also mix in a handwritten font for outbursts, exclamations, stating what's likely on the audience's minds, or proposing my own volatile ideas. This choice to present something with a handwritten typeface (versus a more formal typeface) is an intentional one, and meant to buffer criticism. Why? We have a higher tolerance for ideas scribbled down quickly, as compared to things more polished, where we expect more rigor and reflection. Using the handwritten typeface suggests this idea is less considered or meant to reflect a *reaction*.

- On stage, I'm conscientious about how I stand and what it suggests. A trainer I worked with commented on my tendencies to assume either the "hostage pose" (hands clasped behind my back) or the "fig leaf" (hands clasped together in front of me). While I've historically found these to be a comfortable resting stance, he pointed out how they might suggest nervousness and reflect a lack of confidence.

- It's not just how I stand, but where I stand and also how I get there— do I move quickly, or with slow deliberation? How does this mirror the content being presented, and what might these movements communicate on some unconscious level? If I'm presenting two opposing ideas, I might move my body from one side of the stage to the other as I present each position. When explaining a progression of ideas, I might move— slowly—from one side of the stage to the other, as I present each stage in the progression. In these ways, my body language echoes the points I'm trying to make.

Basic Shapes, Motion, and Meaning

The shapes we use, the movements we make—these will on some level evoke a fairly predictable set of ideas and emotions. Whether through nature or nurture, these kinds of associations are fairly widespread, inescapable, and—without deliberation—may remain an unseen but powerful force. The goal then is to be aware of and attend to associations. Things are always more than they seem, at least objectively. It's human nature to look for patterns, force associations, and infer meaning, even where no meaning was intended.

Ascribing meaning to even the simplest of shapes and motions was tested back in the 1940s with a simple, animated film dubbed the *Heider-Simmel Illusion*. In this brief (only 90 seconds) film, three simple shapes, of varying size, move into and out of a box, appearing at times to chase each other (see Figure 5.2).

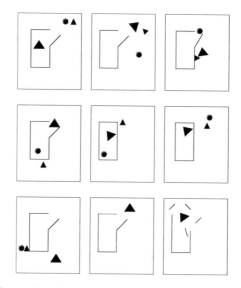

FIGURE 5.2 Keyframes from the *Heider-Simmel Illusion*, where viewers construct rich narratives based on simple shapes and movement.

This has been used in museums, where patrons are asked to narrate the story depicted by these shapes. It's nothing more than a set of shapes moving randomly throughout the scene, and yet we—in our perpetual attempt to pattern match—look for the pattern, the story of what's going on.

For a more instructional tour of how basic graphic design decisions evoke meaning, *Picture This: How Pictures Work* by Molly Bang is an amazing little book that explores the evocative power of various design elements: shape, scale, color, depth, diagonal lines, balance, and so on. See Figure 5.3. Using the tale of *Little Red Riding Hood*, the author guides the reader through various graphic design decisions we could—if we were the illustrators—make along the way, always with a focus on the effect of these various elements and combinations on desired emotions. This little book is a wonderful introduction to graphic design, by letting the reader experience the effects of different visual possibilities on a familiar story.

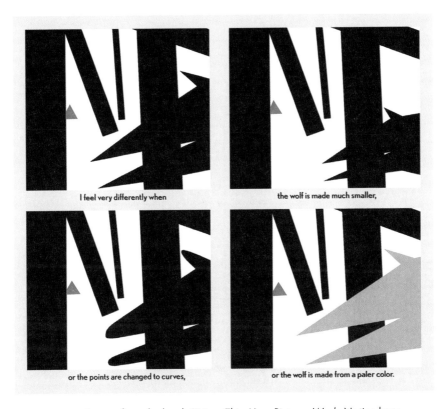

FIGURE 5.3 A page from the book *Picture This: How Pictures Work*. Notice how different graphic design choices affect what we perceive and feel.

While projects like the *Heider-Simmel Illusion* and *Picture This: How Pictures Work* make clear just how much we—as viewers—bring to these pictorial representations, these are primers. We can marvel at the evocative power of simple, flat shapes moving about a screen or printed on a page, but these should help us appreciate the same kind of thoughtful work that goes into physical or industrial design. As with flat shapes, it's the associations we bring that give these things meaning. If we turn to a book like *Watches Tell More Than Time*, author and industrial designer Del Coates provides a brilliant way to assess the objective and subjective qualities of various 3D forms, from automobiles to teacups to watches (see Figure 5.4). In something as simple as a cup, he lays out a structured way to consider the subjective, emotional qualities inherent in the form.

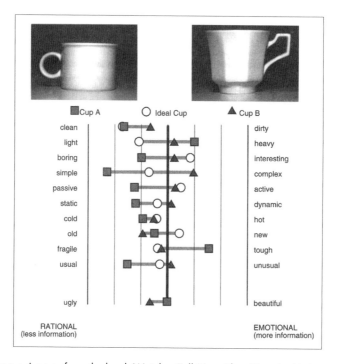

FIGURE 5.4 A page from the book *Watches Tell More Than Time*. In this image, the author uses a list of contrasting attribute pairings to assesses the form of two different cups.

While the ideal form depends on individuals at points throughout history, what's shown here is a way to assess—for the desired associations—what is ideal for that project. It's almost like being shown the invisible DNA of something as "simple" as a teacup. The title of this book (*Watches Tell More Than Time*) is itself worth noting. What Coates presents is a lengthy deconstruction of everyday objects, mostly from his career as an industrial designer, with a focus on exposing the often invisible associations we all bring to things. Watches communicate so much more than time.

The idea of aesthetic associations is also nothing new to advertisers. In 1964, the French philosopher Roland Barthes published his paper "Rhetoric of the Image," which deconstructs an ad for packaged pasta into three messages: the linguistic message, the coded iconic message, and the noncoded iconic message. What we're talking about here are the "coded iconic messages" associated with specific images, that is, those things suggested or associated with the literal objects pictured. In Barthes's example, he discusses how the decision to show beautiful, fresh vegetables (and a box of pasta displaying a brand name) in a mesh grocery bag suggests freshness, plenty, and even "Italianicity" (in the yellow, green, and red of the tomato and peppers). A certain still-life aesthetic is also suggested, as shown in Figure 5.5. All in all, these are very positive brand associations.[5]

FIGURE 5.5 An ad for packaged pasta, from the early 1960s, used to comment on the "coded iconic messages" built into the color choices and imagery.

5. This paragraph is borrowed from Stephen's first book, *Seductive Interaction Design*. Anderson, Stephen P. 2011. *Seductive Interaction Design: Creating Playful, Fun, and Effective User Experiences*. Berkeley: New Riders.

An ad is always more than it claims to be. The message is always more than what is stated. The choice of colors, the cropping of photos, the cuts of a video, the animations used, typefaces selected, the choice of spokesperson—all of these kinds of things contribute to a meta-message that advertisers are keenly aware of and monitor. The power of many ads lies more in what is suggested than what is stated. Connotation matters as much, if not more, than denotation.

But are we now talking about emotions? Isn't this book about figuring things out?

Yes, and … every association called to mind will shape our perceptions and how we reason about things. Every explanation we might offer, every tool for understanding we might create, every sketch we may produce … it's in the details of these things that we invoke associations. We can add a slider control to a web interface, but how easily that slider slides may bring to mind friction and resistance, or something as smooth as glass. We might use squiggly lines when drawing something, never pausing to consider the additional meaning suggested by the squiggly lines. Nothing is as simple and direct as we might think. As with public speaking and the associations I'm keenly aware of when presenting, we should also be hyperaware of the likely associations we're creating—intentionally or not.

Similar to priming and anchoring, attending to aesthetic associations is one of the more nuanced, equally vital, things to consider. The shapes we use, the movements we make, the sounds we add, the temperatures at which things are set—all of these aesthetic details evoke a fairly predictable (or identifiable) set of ideas and emotions. Understand this and attend to these details, and you become a better facilitator of understanding.

Let's turn our attention now to more deliberate, contrived associations, those forced analogies we employ to explain what is difficult to explain.

How Explicit Visual Metaphors Force Associations

We opened the previous chapter with an exploration of metaphors. Let's return to this topic. However, rather than discuss the metaphors suggested by likening something to a "virus" or "engine," let's explore what happens when these metaphors are expressed in a literal way, using a visual image.

Icebergs!

We've mentioned the iceberg model, as it's a common—if overused—metaphor that frequently shows up in business presentations. It's been used to communicate everything from hidden cultural forces that drive visible behaviors to underappreciated processes in the web development process (see Figure 5.6).

FIGURE 5.6 The iceberg model is used to explain an organizational culture, levels of the user experience process, and unseen activities behind social media activities.

The iceberg model elegantly illustrates a simple concept: there are things that are seen, and there are things that are unseen (below the water). It's a compact analogy. If your goal is to communicate "there is more here than meets the eye," an iceberg is a perfectly acceptable (though overused) parallel. Find a good visual metaphor, one that's fairly accurate and extensible, and it can be a powerful thing. To see what can be good—and bad—about using visual metaphors, let's look at more examples.

Metaphors That Create Understanding

Making sense of the healthcare debates in the U.S., has been a daunting task. But thanks to Dan Roam and a simple analogy,[6] we can get a better understanding, or at least orientation. In the mid-2000s, shortly following President Barack Obama's election, the topic of health care entered the mainstream of

---

6. Roam, Dan. 2009. "Healthcare Napkins All." LinkedIn SlideShare. August 16, 2009. www.slideshare.net/danroam/healthcare-napkins-all

public discourse, often leading to heated arguments and polarizing positions. It's a complex topic, made more challenging by tactical disagreements that often mask the deeper issues. To understand what's really going on, especially in conversations, is a challenge. To bring some sanity to these conversations, Roam introduced a wonderfully simple metaphor: the classic children's seesaw (see Figure 5.7).

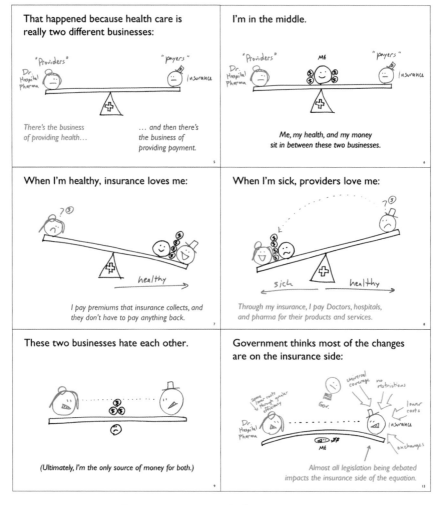

FIGURE 5.7 Excerpts from Dan Roam's "back of the napkin" explanation of fundamental tensions in the U.S. healthcare system.

In a series of "napkin" sketches, something which Dan Roam is famous for, he explained the tensions in U.S. health care, with a broader focus on the system level problem. As patients, we're essentially caught in a tension between the healthcare providers (doctors, physicians, nurses) and the payment providers. We're the fulcrum in this see-saw analogy, with two kinds of providers riding the see-saw. We get caught in the middle of these tensions, which is unfortunate as "[patients are] the only source of money for both." Aside from granting a more complete picture of what's going on, this simple visual also highlighted what has been a persistent frustration: all of the debates and changes are only focused on the health *insurance* side. We're trying to deal with a systemic problem by only addressing half of the equation. A see-saw gave many people a perspective on the broader issues with U.S. health care. Of course, like all associative thinking, this is *a* way to frame the issue—a thoughtful and well-researched frame—but not at all the only one. A different metaphor might lead to a different understanding of the issue. This leads us then to consider the purpose and utility of any metaphor we might choose, and for this, let's consider a metaphor familiar to all of us, the double-helix model of DNA.

Metaphors That Communicate Understanding *and* Stick in Memory

While researchers James Watson, Francis Crick, Rosalind Franklin, and Maurice Wilkins are often credited with "discovering" DNA, it's more accurate to say they were the first scientists to formulate an accurate description—a visual model—of the molecular structure of DNA. Most of us recognize this as that "twisted ladder" thing from science class. But it is this elegant model that has given rise to molecular biology and everything that's followed since—from mapping the human genome to the promise of gene therapy. While we might consider this more of a technical illustration, it is no less a brilliant visual metaphor for making sense of a really complicated subject. This model is the elegant solution to what was—in the early 1950s—a really wicked puzzle: understanding the structure of DNA. What preceded this model were numerous studies and theories, each contributing discrete findings and data, clues to and pieces of this larger puzzle. But none of these findings, on their own, gave the complete picture needed to move things forward. The critical piece of data—an X-ray diffraction photo of DNA—came from Rosalind Franklin[7] and Maurice Wilkins. Named "photograph 51," this photograph showed that DNA crystals form an X shape on X-ray film, a crucial piece of information that led Watson and Crick to revise an earlier triple-helix DNA model to that of a double-helix model (see Figure 5.8). After an intense 18 months of research, things fell into place. Here is Watson's account of that moment when they arrived at the double helix model:

> Using metal scraps from the machine shop, Francis and I built a 3-dimensional model of DNA. This six-foot model incorporated what was already known with my A/T and G/C base pairing scheme and Francis' idea of antiparallel strands. Everything clicked into place beautifully. Upon looking at our model, everyone— including Maurice and Rosalind—agreed that we had the right DNA structure. So, DNA is like a twisted ladder, where the sugar and phosphate are the rails, and the base pairs are the rungs ...[8]

This was a rare case where, as described in a commentary by PBS, "the structure so perfectly fit the experimental data that it was almost immediately accepted."[9]

Part of the enduring strength of this "twisted ladder" metaphor is that it has been both an *accurate* and *memorable* way to understand what is a fairly complicated structure.

1. **The model is incredibly accurate.** Part of the enduring power of this model is that it bears a striking resemblance to the actual structure of a DNA strand. The model itself was arrived at largely by inference, based on the research data and limited imaging options available in 1953. It wouldn't be until decades later—1989—that technology gave us a better picture of what DNA actually looked like. While many visual metaphors are great for orienting us to the unfamiliar, it's rare to find a model that is also a fairly accurate representation of reality. This accuracy is rare with physical things, and will likely never be the case with abstract concepts, which we struggle to know through associations.

---

7. Also, Raymond Gosling, a graduate student working under the supervision of Rosalind Franklin, who captured the photo.
8. This verbiage appears to be adapted from James Watson's account in *The Double Helix*. This text came from "Animation 19: The DNA Molecule Is Shaped Like a Twisted Ladder, CSHL DNA Learning Center." n.d. Cold Spring Harbor Laboratory DNA Learning Center. https://dnalc.cshl .edu/view/16422-Animation-19-The-DNA-molecule-is-shaped-like-a-twisted-ladder-.html
9. "A Science Odyssey: People and Discoveries: Watson and Crick Describe Structure of DNA." n.d. PBS. www.pbs.org/wgbh/aso/databank/entries/do53dn.html

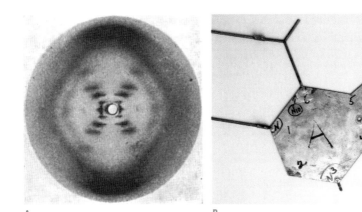

FIGURE 5.8 From top left to right: (A) The X-ray diffraction photo of DNA that came from Rosalind Franklin. (B + C) The three-dimensional model of DNA built by James Watson and Francis Crick using metal scraps. *Credit to A. Barrington Brown © Gonville & Caius College/Science Photo Library*

2. **The model is simple and memorable.** It's a twisted ladder—it's easy to take the concept of a ladder and twist it. While this model may seem remarkably simple in retrospect, the journey certainly included other models and representations that simply didn't hold up to scrutiny. Moreover, because of this simplicity, the DNA model has become an instantly recognizable symbol for life itself, perhaps as familiar as the Coca Cola bottle or a Crucifix.

While this model is generally praised as a boon to science and humanity, it is not without critics. Some have criticized the model for suggesting that—by mapping the entire DNA chain—it is a simple thing to alter the genetic determination of traits, as if life could be reduced to a simple string of instructions, similar to that of a computer program. This is a good cautionary reminder that even with the best of visual metaphors, they are just that—metaphors that in addition to their intended associations will also express other, perhaps unintended, messages.

Metaphors That Suggest Causality: The Three-Legged Stool

In the world of software design, the three-legged stool has become a classic metaphor for representing three areas of concerns that every team must balance (see Figure 5.9). The concept is simple and straightforward: to "support" a great experience, you need three "legs," each representing a different priority:

- What is *feasible* given time, resources, and technology?
- What is *valuable* to our business?
- What is *desirable* to our customers?

It's a perfect metaphor for conveying a simple idea: each of these things is *equally* valuable to the success of the whole. Remove any one leg, and the stool topples over. Give less priority to one leg, and the thing leans in an awkward way. Out of balance, the whole thing becomes useless. The traditional mapping goes something like this: engineers care about what is feasible, designers care about what is desirable to customers, and business people care about what is valuable to the business. In this way, this metaphor is most often used by the underrepresented group, as an argument to be taken more seriously.

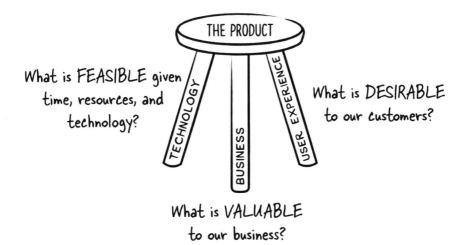

FIGURE 5.9 The three-legged stool as a metaphor for three areas of concerns that every team must balance.

But this metaphor is also problematic.

Someone could suggest we have a four-legged chair, instead of a three-legged stool. How does that change things? Or we might challenge the assumption that equal treatment is the right option in all cases. A big source of tension is when groups try to claim they represent the seat of the stool and have rights to govern the three priorities. Someone else could challenge the metaphor completely and suggest, say … a different model that prioritizes two groups over the third, as with a cart-and-horse metaphor where the two wheels on a cart are pulled by the third, the poor animal yoked to the darn thing.

The frustration I (Stephen) have with this three-legged stool metaphor is one of exclusivity. Switch to an unhealthy environment, where different job families identify with each leg, and this analogy suggests exclusivity, that each group "owns" their focus area, independent of the other two groups. This exclusive thinking is toxic in cross-functional teams.

A slightly better version of the stool comes in the form of a Venn diagram, where there is an overlap of concerns (see Figure 5.10). But still, this visual representation (*not* a metaphor) also has an exclusivity problem: each group still has an area that is theirs, and theirs alone.

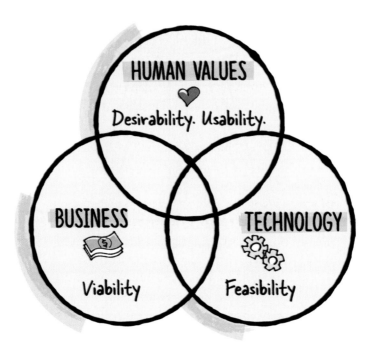

FIGURE 5.10 A Venn diagram illustrating an overlapping set of concerns.

The metaphor I (Stephen) have arrived at is somewhat more inclusive, while also preserving what makes these perspectives unique and valuable. Rather than legs on a stool, or overlapping circles, I liken each of these groups to spotlights lighting up the thing we're all working on, but from a different vantage point (see Figure 5.11).

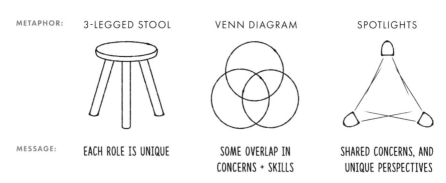

FIGURE 5.11 Three visual models for discussing the unique contributions of engineer, design, and business domains. From left to right, the three-legged stool, the Venn diagram, and the spotlight model.

With this metaphor, we can discuss what is valuable about each perspective, while never claiming ownership or exclusivity. Moreover, we can direct our attention to the shared concerns we all have. And when we place people into this metaphor, we allow for the complexities of human interests and experiences—no one is placed into a narrowly defined box or mold limiting what they should care about.

Upon sharing this metaphor with a design team I worked with, another designer elaborated on the metaphor, suggesting that these spotlights might themselves represent colors, and like older projection TVs, you need all three colors to produce the millions of colors we enjoy (see Figure 5.12). Subtract any one color, and you no longer have a "full-spectrum" picture. All three colors are necessary. You could also riff on this metaphor by suggesting some lights dim or brighten at different moments, depending upon the desired effect. And lighting need not be limited to three-colored gels. As with theater lighting, we could add in more lights for different effects. While far from being an elegant model like that of the double helix, I would say this is a preferable model to that of the three-legged stool.

Which leads us to choosing the *best* or most appropriate metaphor.

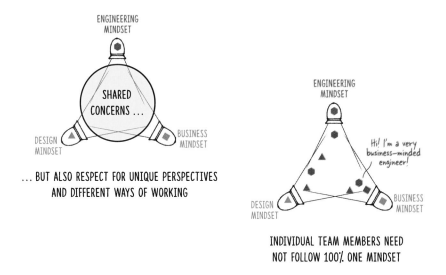

FIGURE 5.12 Illustrating the advantages of the spotlight model.

Choosing the Right Metaphor: Garden or Iceberg?

In organizations throughout the world, culture and culture change is a universal topic of discussion. This topic often comes up when organizations see employee engagement scores drop or when external pressures indicate a need for culture change.

To help facilitate these kinds of situations, consultant Dave Gray (along with Strategyzer) developed the Culture Map,™ a tool that focuses on employee development and aids in building better performing companies.

In its most basic form, the Culture Map is a framework that presents three boxes, each stacked upon each other (see Figure 5.13). These boxes isolate three things to consider about a company culture: Outcomes, Behaviors, and Enablers/Blockers.

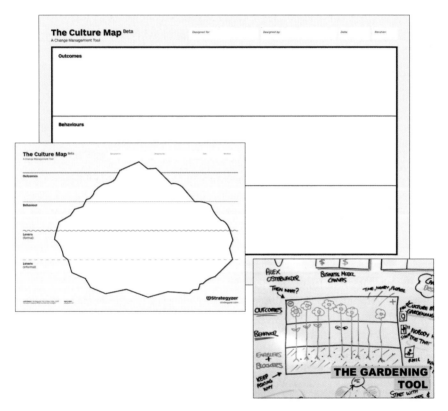

FIGURE 5.13 Three versions in the Culture Map. One, in its basic form, followed by two versions that used metaphors to reinforce key concepts.

You might be asking, what's the metaphor? There is none. At least not in this basic version. What's interesting to note is how this tool has evolved over time, and the metaphors that have been used. Examining these helps us understand how different metaphors lead to different associations.

For a brief time, there was a version that used an iceberg metaphor. This was probably selected to reinforce the "unseen" nature of enablers and blockers. However, a later metaphor dropped the "seen/unseen" message of the iceberg for something more fitting of this as a change management tool: *a garden*.

With the garden analogy, there is still an element of the unseen (roots, soil, fertilizer, and such), but in this garden metaphor, it's the unseen that *drives* behaviors and resulting outcomes—just as good or bad soil contributes to the success of the individual plant. Moreover, by moving to a garden metaphor, you can speak to company-wide changes to the soil, changes that will likely result in better fruits or a better harvest. Where the iceberg metaphor may have been good for illuminating hidden forces, it didn't present these hidden forces as something you could influence or take action upon. In switching to this metaphor, Gray commented:

> Nobody wants to live on an iceberg. They are cold and inhospitable places … But everyone can see a garden as a beautiful thing.
>
> When I describe culture design in this way, it does seem to energize and motivate people. They become engaged when I ask them what they want their garden to be like and ask them to help their management team design it. We start talking about where the weeds are, how the gardeners are doing and what they could do better, how wild or controlled the garden should be, and so on.[10]

So, how do we select a good metaphor?

First and foremost, the metaphor should never be a distraction, visually or conceptually. If we suggest an iceberg, toolbelt, or umbrella, and in doing so the metaphor becomes the focal point, that is likely a failure. Rather, the addition of this association should enrich and energize our understanding of the thing we're seeking to understand. In switching from an iceberg to a garden

---

10. Gray, Dave. 2015. "Culture Mapping and Metaphor." Medium. The XPLANE Collection. September 17, 2015. https://medium.com/the-xplane-collection/culture-mapping-and-metaphor-fc100619d5f

metaphor, we are able to extend the associations in rich and useful ways. Gardening is an excellent and appropriate frame for company culture.

Beyond that, discovering the best metaphor—all things considered—may involve trying on or testing many options. In Gray's case, things evolved. One metaphor that seemed right at one point in time, gave way to a better, more well-rounded metaphor. As with clothing, try an idea out. If it fits, great. If it doesn't, try on a different metaphor. Focus on *intent* and choose a metaphor that aligns closely with your intentions, both functionally and evocatively. Then test the strength of this by exploring all extended associations. If you follow the logical extensions of this metaphor, do these secondary associations also support your message, or would they be unintended?

There is one more bit of advice we can offer: Does it save time to understand?

Mostly Timeless and Universally Recognized

Again, with all of these examples, it's not the visual—the garden drawn in a workshop, the three-legged stool, the iceberg—it's the idea of these things. It is the *concept* that's important. I can draw a three-legged stool, or I can talk about a three-legged stool; if it's a familiar concept, the effect is the same. Though there is power in actually seeing a visual, the success or failure of the visual metaphor is dependent on our recognition of the thing being referenced. While many of us have never seen an iceberg, it's a familiar concept. But, if we were to visit a rural tribe that's never heard about or even seen a photo of an iceberg, the metaphor would mean very little, and the effort required to explain it would defeat the reason for invoking it in the first place. More to the point, different groups and subcultures develop their own sets of familiar metaphors. For this reason, the usefulness of the metaphor must begin with how familiar or widespread a group's understanding of the metaphor is. My simple rule of thumb: the metaphor should *save* you time explaining a concept and answering difficult questions.

Beyond simply choosing a metaphor that maps closely to your problem space, you want to select a metaphor that is universally recognized and (mostly) timeless. Accordingly, I've found that things found in nature are good, as are objects so widespread that everyone will recognize them, from classic toys to familiar architectures to nostalgic objects. In Figure 5.14, there are a few such options to jump-start your exploration. But—never force a metaphor. For every great association, there are a dozen more that should have never been used!

NATURE

icebergs

ripples

beehives

things in orbit

caterpillars

paths/trails

canyon

mountains

tidal waves

apples

avalanche

birds/flocking behaviors

trees/branches/roots

TOYS

wooden blocks

shape sorting

puzzles

piggy bank

game boards

Russian nesting dolls

playing cards

stacking rings

LEGO bricks

FAMILIAR (OR NOSTALGIC) THINGS

meat grinder

funnel

potted plant

hub and spoke

matchbook

cocktail (with layers)

weights (barbell)

scales (for weighing)

pie

toolbelt/toolbox

hourglass

lamp

juggler/juggling

hamburger

city skyline

staircases

lightbulb

Swiss army knife

bricks in a wall

staircase

baseball diamond

revolving door

umbrella

balloon(s)

three-legged stool

cornerstone/arch

pillars/columns

hourglass

railroad tracks

bird's nest with eggs

door/doorframe

FIGURE 5.14 A listing of potentially useful visual metaphors.

Associations Activated by What We See

Once again, the goal of this section is to become aware of how associations show up in everyday activities, so we can become more fluent at using, challenging, or avoiding associative thinking. With this chapter, we've looked primarily at associations activated by things we *see*. These things that are seen can work on an almost unconscious level, as with many aesthetic associations, or they can be more obvious and explicit, as with visual metaphors. But as with the previous chapter, it's not about the things seen, but rather the concepts these things bring to mind. Key ideas are the following:

- Associations, whether observable in nature or shared by a culture group, are fundamental to all cognition.

- Aesthetic associations activate not just what is seen, but anything that appeals to the senses.

- Visual metaphors can be very effective ways to make sense of something, but they must be chosen with care.

CHAPTER

6

Closing Thoughts and Cautionary Notes About Associations

Each of those maps was drawn up by someone who could see in part, but not the whole.

—THE ANCIENT ONE, *DOCTOR STRANGE*

Up to this point, we've discussed associations with a mostly positive or neutral stance, with occasional nods to deeper considerations. And while "associations among concepts *is* thinking," it's precisely because of our natural tendency to find or force patterns, that we also need to be cautious.

Andrea Resmini, teacher and researcher at Jönköping University, once commented that "using analogies is like treading on broken glass: it has to be done carefully."[1] The very thing that makes associations (or "analogies" if you prefer) so powerful is also what makes them dangerous. They shape our thoughts in a *particular* way. Used well, and the unfamiliar becomes familiar. We get quickly *oriented* to the new. But orientation to a topic is not the same as deep understanding. The danger of relying on analogies is that it can lead to faulty reasoning.

---

1. https://andrearesmini.com/

Where this faulty thinking is obvious is with simple—and poor—analogies. If we try to explain what an IP address does by comparing it to your home mailing address, that might work in the moment: "It's the address where things go to on the internet." However, this association quickly falls apart in some meaningful ways when we then get asked about dynamic addresses, domain names, network protocols, and so on. The metaphor isn't extensible and doesn't fit with these other properties.

Where these associations are more dangerous is where they're pervasive *and* unseen.

Let's tour a typical Fortune 500 company.

With software development, the fundamental tension between many business leaders, particularly those who don't have IT backgrounds, and the engineering teams they manage, can be understood by calling out the underlying stories and mindsets. Management processes tend to be based on a deeply-ingrained "manufacturing" mindset—things moving from one stage to another, in a predictable fashion. Along with this mindset come other trappings, such as making plans and setting deadlines. While this might be useful in a more predictable environment, say where the objective is to manufacture thousands of identical widgets and quality means to minimize defects, it doesn't work as well with digital products. The living, dynamic nature of software—working in and through uncertain conditions—is frequently at odds with the "everything should go as planned" manufacturing mindset. This has led teams to seek out better metaphors, such as likening work processes to a team sport, or embracing (more literally) the scientific method upon which things like agile and lean were founded. Recognizing these mindsets—being able to articulate whether a team is more concerned with discovery or delivery—helps people understand the root cause of many conflicts.

At the corporate level, many incumbent businesses fear being disrupted by new entrants in their space. Executives are concerned they'll be the next "Blockbuster," doing more of the same as new, digital companies—the "Netflix-es" of their industry—eat at their business. While this *disruption* story is a good, cautionary tale (and great for spurring action), it's not necessarily a true story for all companies. There are always more details and nuanced circumstances that define reality. The disruption story is a popular one, and might have some usefulness, but that doesn't make it true or relevant in all cases.

At the individual level, we see conflicts and tensions that are themselves governed by these underlying narratives. How many arguments have you seen that weren't over the facts of what happened, but interpretation and belief? Two people may argue about moving a deadline, never recognizing that they're disputing values or acting as players in a narrative about survival, territorial disputes, and competition. Getting the annual bonus or recognition from a peer group becomes more important than broader group accomplishments.

Used well, the choice metaphor, frame, or conceptual association orients and draws us into the unknown. The unfamiliar becomes familiar, through the power of analogy. Used poorly, and we end up with faulty reasoning, flawed assumptions, blind spots, misunderstandings, poor judgment and decision-making—and any number of negative outcomes. By making or adopting associations, we also risk becoming victims of that analogy. In an effort to understand a thing, we may very well fail to see that thing as it truly is.

Given this, we can react in one of several ways:

- We can reject associations and focus on what is essentially known.
- We can be thoughtful about the associations we make and aware of the limits of each.
- We can employ many frames and models to make associations.
- We can—more fundamentally—recognize that most beliefs and categories are social constructs.

First Principles: An Antidote to Thinking by Analogy

Let's start with this first option: to reject all associations. As much as it's possible, let's flush away all stories, analogies, metaphors, and other kinds of associations to focus on the problem space itself and what is inarguably true. This kind of "reasoning from first principles" is a concept well known to physicists and mathematicians: start directly at the level of established laws of physics and do not make assumptions.

In recent years, first principles reasoning has entered mainstream conversations, in large part due to frequent remarks by entrepreneur and visionary Elon Musk.

In an interview with Kevin Rose, Musk commented:

> I think it is important to reason from first principles rather
> than by analogy. The normal way that we conduct our lives
> is we reason by analogy … It's mentally easier to reason by
> analogy than from first principles. First principles is kind of
> a physics way of looking at the world. You boil things down
> to the most fundamental truths … and then reason up from
> there—that takes a lot more mental energy.[2]

In this interview, Musk is criticizing businesses that churn out "slight itera-
tions on a theme," but in doing so he's also advocating for a more rational way of
thinking (one that can be traced back to at least Aristotle, who wrote about pur-
suing first principles as a part of any systemic inquiry[3]). Essentially, we make
too many decisions based on assumptions about "how things are." Or we try
to understand a complex topic such as the economy or immigration by likening
it to something familiar—a game of chess, gardening, the spread of disease. In
these cases, we reason from "how it is" or "kinda like …" associations. And by
thinking in this associative way, we fail to see things as they are and could be.

Reasoning from first principles asks us to start with *what we are sure is true.* By
breaking down a complex structure into its most basic elements, we are able
to identify and challenge these assumptions. Then we can rebuild from there
from the ground up and see if this unlocks new possibilities.

In the case of SpaceX rockets, rather than start with the going price of rockets, Musk asked the team to look at the first principles: "What is a rocket made
of? Aerospace-grade aluminum alloys, plus some titanium, copper, and carbon
fiber." He then asked, "What is the value of those materials on the commodity
market?" In approaching rocket building in this way, the team discovered "the
materials cost of a rocket was around two percent of the typical price—which
is a crazy ratio for a large mechanical product." It was this insight that allowed
SpaceX to produce a much cheaper rocket.

By working with information as a material, in this objective and scientific
way, we gain a deeper understanding of a complex space. Whether your goal
stops at understanding or you want to make something fundamentally new,
this kind of reductionist thinking is crucial. Indeed, most new ventures and

2.   "Episode 20 w/ Elon Musk." n.d. Foundation. http://foundation.bz/20/
3.   Irwin, Terence. 2002. *Aristotles First Principles.* Oxford: Clarendon Press.

new ideas begin by challenging the status quo and a calcified understanding of "how things are."

The Scientific Method and Lateral Thinking

In many ways, first principles thinking resembles the scientific method—we're challenged to apply rigorous skepticism to our observations, recognizing how our biases and beliefs can distort conclusions. Begin with the most basic observations you've tested and agreed to be true and work from there. Of course, you also need stopping rules, lest you go too far down the pile of deeply buried assumptions. When Musk asked his team about the value of the materials on the commodity market, he didn't also ask them to question the existence of commodity markets, or if they should go mine their own materials. But he did challenge them to dig deeper and test widely held assumptions. With the scientific method, we are given a similar challenge to make objective observations and test our hypotheses. And in both approaches, we need to be open to and objective about what is learned, especially when the learnings don't fit with expectations.

To this, we'd add that reasoning from first principles is … creative! Many of the creativity exercises we've encountered over the years share a common theme: exposing *functional fixedness*, our natural tendency to see a thing for its expected use, as opposed to what it could be. We look at a thing, say, a candle, and see it as that thing; what we don't see is a wick, the wax, or a long, flexible cylinder. We create self-imposed limitations by seeing things in the conventional manner in which they are to be used. By reducing a thing to its elemental parts, we are able to see things as they *are* and in doing so, see things as they *could be*. Reductionist thinking is a powerful way to unlock lateral thinking abilities.

Associative Thinking Is Neither Good nor Bad

While there's something noble about rational thought, the reality is that this is not how most people think, at least not naturally. Even Musk admits, "If you tried to reason from first principles all the time, you wouldn't be able to get through your day." We do think via associations and analogies. Present knowledge builds upon prior learnings. We've advanced as a civilization by building upon and remixing what came before us. We build upon prior assumptions, beliefs, and best practices, as well as *challenges to* these assumptions, beliefs, and best practices. And theorists such as Douglas Hofstadter might argue, all thinking is analogical, suggesting there is no such thing as first principles.[4]

The difficulty then is to wield analogies with care, and to know when to shift between analogical thinking and rational discourse. Sometimes we need this reasoned approach; often we don't. We don't need a first principles approach to make toast. But for something complex or complicated, affecting lives, economies, invention, sustainability, viability, and so on—we do need this approach. Moreover, being able to call out when faulty reasoning is being used to advance an ideology—as with most political issues—is vital.

While this entire section on associations has largely been about the *value* of associations and analogies, we've tried throughout and with many of the examples to also raise awareness of potential negative effects of this associative thinking. From thinking of schools as industrial factories to the negative effects of framing immigration, associations are powerful tools, to be wielded with care. We need to be conscious of how much of our thinking is analogical, metaphorical, associative, and learn to master these associations as tools, rather than have them master us.

Associations: A Double-Edged Sword

Let's return to the value of these associations.

If we look at something like a map, a map is useful precisely because it is an abstraction of reality—it doesn't try to represent too many details. It's this abstraction that makes a map valuable. By omitting much of what is known, a map allows us to focus on what is essential, what needs to be understood—whether this is weather patterns, elevation increases, or dangers to be avoided. The same is true of associations.

In a paper from 1933, mathematician Alfred Korzybski remarked that "A map *is not* the territory it represents, but, if correct, it has a *similar structure* to the territory, which accounts for its usefulness."[5] We're interested in the usefulness of associative thinking. Whether through an elaborate story, a visual metaphor, or carefully chosen words, if an association is useful for

---

4. Hofstadter, Douglas R., and Emmanuel Sander. 2013. *Surfaces and Essences: Analogy as the Fuel and Fire of Thinking*. New York: Basic Books.
5. Korzybski, Alfred. 1933. In *Science and Sanity. An Introduction to Non-Aristotelian Systems and General Semantics*, 747–61. The International Non-Aristotelian Library.

understanding, then use it. Just be mindful of the limitations. Just as maps are an abstraction of the landscape, these associations also do not represent all that can—or should—be known about a thing.

A carefully chosen association is one that:

- Is useful for a particular specified bit of information
- Has more properties in common with the source materials
- Has a shared meaning for all involved
- Is explicit about the framing being suggested
- Has considered both functional and evocative associations
- Has considered second-order effects and conclusions of the chosen association

Of course, this kind of judgment and critical thinking is a hard skill to develop. There's an easier way to check our thinking: use *multiple* maps and models.

> *Metaphorical frame offers only a partial view of the problem space. Frames streamline information, necessarily selecting and organizing elements to simplify complex issues. A given metaphor is able to accommodate only some aspects of the problem space and must exclude others. In some cases, such targeted framing may lead to an illusion of simplicity and bad policy decisions, even among experts.*

—PAUL H. THIBODEAU, LERA BORODITSKY,
"NATURAL LANGUAGE METAPHORS COVERTLY INFLUENCE REASONING"[6]

The Benefits of Many Lenses

The simplest antidote to associative and metaphorical thinking? More associations.

Play this out: If every way of looking at something is a simplification, useful for considering one part of the whole, then what happens when you add a second or third orientation? It's only by looking at things through many lenses—different stories, various models, multiple analogies—that we start to appreciate the complexity of a thing and can actually start recognizing which

---

6. Thibodeau, Paul H., and Lera Boroditsky. 2013. "Natural Language Metaphors Covertly Influence Reasoning." *PLoS ONE* 8 (1). https://doi.org/10.1371/journal.pone.0052961

patterns are constant under different conditions. This is true of dynamic models, of stories, of frames, and all manner of associations. This is the value of having many ways to consider a topic.

Think about the people you work with. Many tools exist to label and categorize workers, from personality assessments to analogies to ways to assess performance, some of these being more favorable than others. Let's look at two different analogies—both useful for thinking about individual strengths and weaknesses.

Researcher and advisor Simon Wardley suggests we might think about people as "pioneers," "settlers," or "town planners." As you might infer from these labels, *pioneers* are the ones who come up with all sorts of crazy, untested ideas, the *settlers* are the ones who turn these half-baked ideas into something useful, and the *town planners* are great at making things faster, better, smaller, more economic, and good enough. And all of these people are brilliant and necessary as a product or service evolves from a novel idea to a new product to an eventual commodity. This is a useful way to make sure that people are matched with the right roles.[7]

An expert on rationality, judgment, and strategy, Julia Galef uses a military analogy to categorize people. Her research has identified two different mindsets—the "soldier" and the "scout"—that shape the way we interpret information. In her talk for the Long Now Foundation, she described the soldier mindset as entrenched in their beliefs and more likely to see conflicting information as the "enemy"; by contrast, the "scout" mindset is curious, enjoys learning, and is driven by a desire to find the truth. She argues that "Our capacity for reason evolved to serve two very different purposes that are often at odds with each other. On the one hand, reason helps us figure out what's true; on the other hand, it also helps us defend ideas that are false-but-strategically-useful."[8]

Both of these analogies are useful ways of thinking about people, but they each tell us something different. In one model, we learn the roles we need and perhaps, where to place people. The second model helps us see different mindsets and how we might react to information that challenges our beliefs.

7. Wardley, Simon. 2015. "On Pioneers, Settlers, Town Planners and Theft." *Bits or Pieces?* March 13, 2015. https://blog.gardeviance.org/2015/03/on-pioneers-settlers-town-planners-and.html
8. Galef, Julia. 2018. "Soldiers and Scouts: Why Our Minds Weren't Built for Truth, and How We Can Change That." The Long Now Foundation. September 12, 2018. http://longnow.org/seminars/02018/sep/12/soldiers-and-scouts-why-our-minds-werent-built-truth-and-how-we-can-change/

All models are wrong, but some are useful.

—GEORGE BOX, BRITISH STATISTICIAN

We could explore more analogies.

We could also talk about people as "gardeners" (those who maintain the status quo).

We could fall back on widespread stereotypes such as "scientist, artist, inventor, or performer."

Wardley's characterization is itself a derivative of Robert X. Cringely's description of companies as "Commandos, Infantry, and Police."

What all of these are is *useful* analogies, each allowing us to reflect on a different *dimension* of human complexity.

And none of these models are perfect or right. There are situations under which one person might be a different persona or operate with a different mindset. We might also react in different modes at different times. And that's okay. That's closer to reality.

In his book *The Model Thinker*, author and professor Scott E. Page remarks that "By having this crowd of models, we can see the strengths and limitations of each explanation. We can also delve into their differences and similarities." While Page is writing mostly about mathematical and scientific models, the same comments can be said of our analogical associations, that by having many stories to tell, we can start to see strengths and limitations, differences and similarities.

We can employ many frames and models to make associations.

As part of her design class, bestselling author and Stanford lecturer, Christina Wodtke facilitates an exercise that has students *experience* multiple frames on a given topic. As with most brainstorming sessions, she has students capture and identify research notes—one observation per Post-it Note—around an identified topic, say a recent travel experience. This is, as Wodtke states, "to make your insights modular so we can rearrange them in order to create new insights."[9]

9. Wodtke, Christina. 2016. "Needfinding for Disruptive Innovation." Medium. The Creative Founder. October 6, 2016. https://medium.com/the-creative-founder/needfinding-for-disruptive-innovation-71d8532f2cf3

Using a fast-paced workshop format (disco music is sometimes involved!), as soon as students get their ideas out, they are asked to do an *affinity sort*—arranging Post-its with similar Post-its. This is the first model. Next, students refine this model by re-sorting these Post-it Note clusters based on *frequency*—biggest clusters on top, smallest on the bottom. This helps students identify the top-of-mind themes by how often something was mentioned. At this point, students are exhausted, but Wodtke doesn't let up. Students then rearrange the Post-its into a *timeline*, noting how these observations map to stages of a travel experience. She adds that "this is almost always the first big 'aha' moment." But it doesn't stop with a timeline, the third model. Wodtke continues having students rearranging Post-its into not one more, not two more, but three additional models! In the end, students have looked at the same bits of information through six different lenses, to uncover what people might truly need from a travel experience.

What's the real lesson? It's never about any one model, specifically.

Rather, it's about how we see the information differently, when we're challenged to view something through multiple lenses—time, frequency prioritization, a matrix, and so on. This is the invisible lesson that so many people miss about design thinking exercises. It's not about any particular model or way of sorting things, it's about shifting fluidly between many models and, in doing so, seeing information in a different way. This is what leads to insights and understanding. Wodtke remarks that "time spent upfront getting to know the data results in time savings later (and fewer deadly decisions)."

We can use different models, as Wodtke does, or ask people to consider different narratives. We can ask people to put on different figurative hats, as Edward de Bono teaches with his *Six Thinking Hats*. We can ask people to put on literal hats, as some advertising agencies have done, challenging clients to consider how a strong brand such as Apple, Harley-Davidson, or Disney might uniquely approach the very same problem. These are but a few of the ways we might encourage people to consider many perspectives.

Down the Rabbit Hole of Associations

There's a final, more philosophical consideration: recognizing that most beliefs and categories are social constructs. Just as language and meaning are living things that have—over many decades and centuries—emerged within societies, so too are many of the categories and definitions we accept without questioning. Some of these are valid and useful, such as separating snakes from sticks. Distinguishing between things that are edible and inedible. The 118 identified elements that make up the known universe.[10] But what about other labels we've manufactured, such as gender differences, definitions of race, personality types, or the ideal body type? What about the ways we classify books: fiction, nonfiction, mystery, drama, sci-fi, autobiography, and so on? Or consider how we place students into grade levels and subjects. While these things are commonly shared, popularity doesn't make them absolute, not in a scientific sense. When we talk about information as a resource, we also have to question the information we're working with and from, including ways of thinking about and classifying things, ways that are so widespread that they often go unexamined.

If we hold to the idea that thinking is one concept layered upon another concept, all the way down, then it behooves us to scrutinize the concepts that we base our conclusions upon. Do this, and widely held agreements—and disagreements—start to crumble under scrutiny. I might criticize a company for changing too slowly, while a colleague might believe things are changing just fine. If we examine our prior work experiences, and how I've worked mostly at startups, he for only a few big, established corporations, then we start to get a sense of where we disagree: we have different expectations—*based on our prior experiences*—about what is an appropriate pace of change. Who is "right" no longer matters; we can now have a more fruitful conversation that starts from a place of deeper understanding and appreciation for the subjective experiences that have made each of us who we are. Expectations, definitions, categories, beliefs—these things are the result of our culture and environments, as well as the personal experiences we've accumulated.

And yes, this thinking is a bit like taking "the red pill" that leads us down into the rabbit-hole (to borrow an analogy from the movie *The Matrix*). We're deconstructing what is generally agreed to be "true" among a group of people. But this kind of thinking is important, especially in a book about understanding, as *categorical thinking generates powerful illusions.* This statement comes from a recent *Harvard Business Review* article on "The Dangers of Categorical Thinking."[11] Consistent with everything we've shared here, the authors

10. As of 2019!
11. de Langhe, Bart, and Philip Fernbach. 2019. "The Dangers of Categorical Thinking." *Harvard Business Review*, September–October 2019. https://hbr.org/2019/09/the-dangers-of -categorical-thinking

conclude that "Categories are how we make sense of the world and communicate our ideas to others. But we are such categorization machines that we often see categories where none exist. That warps our view of the world and our decision-making suffers." The goal then is not to abandon categorical thinking—we can't really shift our thinking in this way any more than we can choose to process information like computers (it's not really possible). Instead, we need to learn to recognize when a classification is neither *useful* nor *valid*, that's the challenge.

Earlier, we skipped over the Myers-Briggs personality assessment as a way to classify people. It might be *useful*, in that it has helped people articulate things they couldn't, but it isn't a *valid* assessment. And the usefulness is also suspect to the extent that it forces people into artificial boxes. We mention this to point out how when an association comes in the form of an analogy, we see it as a lens; when the association has the air of science, we tend to accept it as true—but classifying me (Stephen) as INFP is just as much a subjective association as labeling me a "pioneer."

To the extent that a classification is valid and useful, it has value. But, be conscious of these as concepts.

Final Remarks

Throughout this section on associations, we've tried to show that "Associations among concepts *is* thinking." We've looked at *how* humans perceive information, with a brief tour of the brain as a perceptual organ and an extended example of how this thinking affects our reasoning about technology, whether the goal is innovation or setting privacy rights. We then built upon this opening chapter, to demonstrate the many different ways our brain's pattern-matching agenda shows up in daily—if not moment-by-moment—interactions. First, with a chapter on how all this manifests in what we say, hear, and read. Next, with how this manifests in what we see. Again, the focus is never on these activating things, but on the prior associations—concepts—being activated by these things. Finally, we've concluded with some cautionary notes about the usefulness of associative thinking and some additional considerations.

Let's distill all this into some universal observations about associations:

- **(Nearly) all thinking is associative.** While it's easy to spot the obvious metaphorical associations ("iceberg"), associations go all the way down to conceptual ideas (up is good) to more fundamental associations that began perhaps in the womb with spatial orientation.

- **These associations—conscious or not—are thinking.** Working our way back up, we can observe that much of what we consider thinking or learning is layers upon layers of learned associations.

- **Associations vary in *complexity* from "cheer up" to "Goldilocks Zone."** Complicated ideas, once they are chunked and understood, transform into much simpler, compressed units of thought.

- **Associations vary in *explicitness*** from concepts highly embedded in our thought processes (simple aesthetic associations) to overt analogies and visual metaphors.

- **We favor associations that are familiar.** We have a bias for new knowledge that readily maps to existing knowledge; things that fit with our expectations and biases don't challenge us to accommodate new information.

- **Awareness of associations is powerful.** Simply becoming aware of these associations, and how they influence thinking, is profoundly liberating.

- **Shifting among different associations helps us to see things differently.** We need to move fluidly among different associations and narratives if we want to unlock possibilities or gain a richer understanding of a thing.

- **Associations can clarify, but also limit our thinking.** For complex problems, we should think in first principles, avoiding analogies. This objectivity of thought is very challenging for most people.

So where does all this leave us?

First, the primary goal of this section has been to show how "Associations among concepts *is* thinking." Knowing that associations are thinking should lead us to fundamentally reconsider and reframe everything from daily conversations to storytelling.

Second, as we transition to the next several chapters on external representations and interactions, you are well-grounded in what's going on. It's never about the map or the model or the tool alone, or about how we interact with these things—these are part of a system of distributed cognitive resources. The things we create and interact with facilitate changes in the concepts being activated and our own understanding. When it comes to making sense of difficult topics, we reach for the external representations such as sketches, diagrams, charts, and so on. It's critical to understand the role these things play in activating *prior* associations.

Third, consider what this all boils down to: *understanding is essentially pattern recognition.* Let that sink in. There are some cases where the "truth" of something and what we call "understanding" are one and the same. There will be objective "2+2=4" moments of understanding—"Can I park here or not?" being one such example. However, for anything remotely complex, we confuse "truth" and "right" with pattern recognition. It's more likely that the "aha" moment of understanding—what we might describe as a moment of clarity—is, in fact, simply a pattern that feels right to us. This leads us back to a question we posed in the opening chapter: Who creates the understanding? Who creates the patterns? Has someone else created this for you? Have you done this for yourself? Rather than being handed an answer, have you been given tools to play with to reach your own conclusions? Recognizing the active or passive role we play in understanding, and the influence of associations and representations and interactions on our conclusions is vital, if we're to be critical thinkers. Understanding in this sense becomes less about universal truth and more about a *subjective* conclusion that is the most right at that moment, for the individual or the group. What we may conclude—on our own or as a group—as "right" may in reality be familiarity with a pattern. This is a bias we should be aware of and on guard against.

The broad application for all of this is simple: *Be intentional with every association you invoke.* Colors. Type. Words. Metaphors. Stories. Body posture. Movement. Intonation. Everything triggers an association. Everything. Be deliberate about these associations and the web of associations they will trigger in turn.

We want to understand and be understood. To the extent that associations can be used to help us individually see the same thing in different ways, or collectively to look at a thing in the same way, associations are powerful tools for understanding.

FIGURING OUT INSURANCE OPTIONS

I (Stephen), want to close this out with a personal story, a story of how being intentional with associations helped me to understand and explain to others a very complicated topic.

Shortly after I became self-employed around 2009, I needed to explore health insurance options for my family. As you might expect, choosing between healthcare plans—at least in the U.S.—is a bit of a nightmare. The choice is much simpler if you work for a company—someone in HR has already narrowed down the pool of options to three or so. But, if you have no such filter, there are actually dozens of plan options, offered by several providers. Moreover, it's really difficult to make sense of the differences between these plans. In short, I was presented with an overwhelming number of options, all filled with confusing terminology, inconsistent coverage options, varying deductible amounts, and nonsensical groupings. When the broker explaining the information has to apologize for how confusing the paperwork is, that's a bad sign.

Given the exorbitant costs associated with such a critical decision, you end up running these very taxing mental scenarios to determine how much coverage is just enough, without overpaying. It's a difficult choice, fraught with anxiety and compounded by the nearly useless listing of options. Making matters more stressful was my son's diabetes—we had to factor in all of the medical supplies, and whether things like the test strips used to test his blood sugar levels were classified as "durable medical devices" or pharmaceuticals. It was a nightmare.

The biggest challenge though, was how little I knew about how insurance works, in general. I just didn't have a good mental model to orient me to all the confusing jargon.

As you've now seen, one way to make sense of a difficult subject is to change how you see the information. This can include the brute force approach of "trying on" different metaphors. This is what I tried:

CONTINUES ➤

CONTINUED ➤

What if health insurance were like … boiling water. A pinball machine. A carnival. A tree. A ladder. A …

Much of this reasoning led nowhere. Except … I did arrive at one, simple metaphor that helped me to make sense of health insurance options.

Breathing the Blue Sky of Benefits

Think of insurance like an ocean.

Everyone starts off *drowning in a sea of deductibles*. The only question is this: How deep down in the ocean—drowning in deductible payments—do you want to be, before you break free to the surface and can breathe again, finally realizing the *blue sky of benefits* promised to you?

This metaphor communicates so much: drowning is a bad thing—I don't have to explain this. The deeper in the ocean you are, the farther off you'll be from the benefits at the surface. And our bodies can all be at different depths in the ocean, but once we hit the surface, there's no up, just fresh air we can breathe.

Framing things in terms of this simple horizontal line, where the ocean meets sky, and layering specific plan details upon this concept helped me to understand the fundamentals of health insurance (or *all* insurance plans for that matter). With this basic idea in place, we had a *place* (in the sky) to hang our types of benefits, in this case co-payments and co-insurance. In my case with health insurance, benefits came in three broad flavors: office visits (seeing the doctor for a regular checkup), prescription drug coverage, and emergencies and specialists.

Since I was being asked to make a difficult risk calculation, I found it best to list, within each of these classes, personal historical examples within each of these categories: *The time my wife broke her arm, our oldest son's Type 1 diabetes, and associated medicine and supplies. That oral surgery at the dentist.* This listing helped me with the predictive aspects of choosing insurance, assuming history was a predictor of future possibilities.

This exercise ended up as a half-baked concept model, designed solely for my personal needs, and specific to the plans I was being offered. But it's proven to be a useful metaphor. On the second call with the broker, I was able to ask many more pointed and specific questions, having been grounded in the basic jargon of health insurance. What was useless information, I took and turned into something I could understand, through the simple use of a metaphor.

When I invoked the metaphor of an ocean to make sense of my health insurance options, I found that was the appropriate mental scaffolding needed to help me make sense of a complicated set of information (see Figure 6.1). When I shared this with others, it relied upon others recognizing the water analogy, and understanding that drowning is a bad thing (not a far stretch for most of the world!). In doing so, understanding was aided and accelerated due to this pre-existing set of associations.

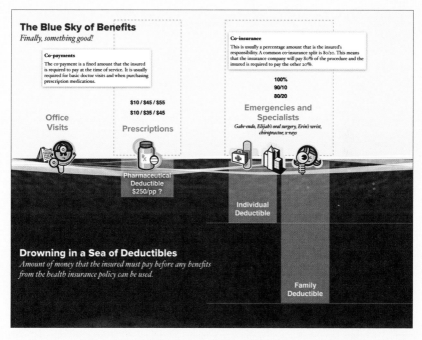

FIGURE 6.1 The author's illustration of health insurance options, using the metaphor of an ocean.

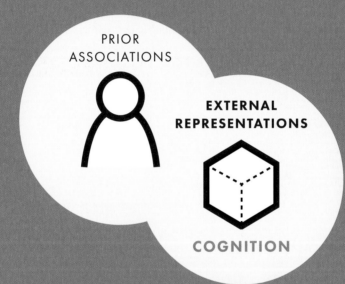

PRIOR
ASSOCIATIONS

EXTERNAL
REPRESENTATIONS

COGNITION

3

How We Understand with External Representations

When thoughts are too complex to hold in memory, or maybe we just need to slow down and reflect on something, we create *external representations*. We bring thoughts into the world. We use the world to hold information. This could be drawing a map in the sand, taking notes, or sketching on a napkin. This could be something more polished like a geographical map, a complex data visualization, or a PowerPoint slide.

This could also be the simple act of stacking bills into piles or lining up ingredients on the kitchen counter, using the arrangement of these things to hold meaning. In all these cases, information is made visible in the world, allowing knowledge to be held in place, reflected upon, and interacted with by one or many people.

In this section, we'll focus on external *visual* representations, with a chapter dedicated to our sense of vision, another devoted to the topic of color, before finally directing our focus to how we use spatial arrangement to hold and convey meaning.

7

Why Our Sense of Vision Trumps All Others

One simply siphons the excess thoughts from one's mind, pours them into the basin, and examines them at one's leisure. It becomes easier to spot patterns and links, you understand, when they are in this form.

—DUMBLEDORE, *HARRY POTTER AND THE GOBLET OF FIRE*

Of all our senses, the most evolved is our sense of vision. Before things even register in our short-term working memory, the brain is able to *quickly* pick out subtle visual differences. Line thickness, curvature, movement, different hues, perceived groupings—researchers have identified about two dozen visual properties that are "pre-attentively" processed, often in less than 200 milliseconds.

Just how fast is this visual processing? At a conference event—after hearing me (Stephen) speak on this very topic—one of my friends decided to test these ideas. As it happens, one of the booth vendors had printed QR codes (those annoying grids of black-and-white squares) on the back of their business cards. But there was a catch: a promotional giveaway was tied into these checkered squares. All the QR codes were identical and would direct you to that vendor's website, except for the one lucky card that had a slightly different QR code. If you were the lucky recipient of this one card, then visiting their website would also alert you that you had won a free tablet device. Or something along these lines. The intention, of course, was that people would, in hopes of winning the tablet, visit the website and in the process learn a bit more about that vendor.

Upon hearing me talk about these "pre-attentive processes" and how quickly our brain notices even the slightest variation in patterns, my friend descended upon that vendor's booth, flipped through the stack of 100 or so cards (as if they were a flipbook), and in seconds was able to find the outlier card. Even scanning dozens of cards a second, each card having 841 black-or-white squares, finding the card with a slightly different arrangement of 841 little squares was a trivial task. He won the tablet. Our brains and our sense of vision are hardwired to quickly spot even the slightest visual difference. Granted, if you add enough visual noise, spotting the differences isn't always easy, as evidenced by numerous "spot the difference" puzzles. Nonetheless, we are biologically wired to notice contrast in our field of vision, whether that's in the form of color, shape, motion, or any of the "visual encodings" we'll identify. It's this ability to spot differences and changes that makes visual representations of information so powerful.

A Superior Sense of Vision

Compared to other senses, the efficiency and fidelity with which our sense of vision can process things is orders of magnitude superior to other senses.

If we apply the frame of computer processing to sensory input, you end with a chart like the one in Figure 7.1, from Tor Nørretranders.[1] In his book on the nature of consciousness, Nørretranders writes that:

> The eye sends at least ten million bits to the brain every second. The skin sends a million bits a second, the ear one hundred thousand, our smell sensors a further one hundred thousand bits a second, our taste buds perhaps a thousand bits a second. All in all, over eleven million bits a second from the world to our sensory mechanisms.

1. Nørretranders, Tor. 1999. *The User Illusion: Cutting Consciousness Down to Size*. New York, NY: Penguin Books.

While Nørretranders' point is about the bandwidth limitations of processing all this sensory input, his visual has been picked up by speakers such as David McCandless, data journalist, as an argument for the power of visual explanations.[2] While the science of such models should be taken with a grain of salt (how do we asses *throughput* of sensory information when this is so entangled with where we direct our attention and the processing of this information?), the broader point is clear: relatively speaking, our sense of vision has more throughput than our other senses. Of all the modalities, our sense of vision—as human creatures—exceeds all others.

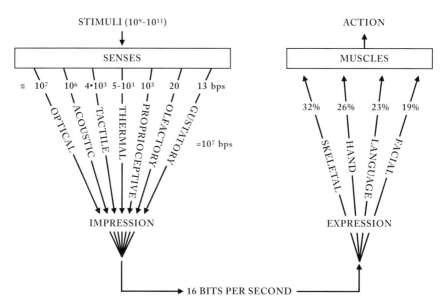

FIGURE 7.1 Image of sensory input speeds from *The User Illusion: Cutting Consciousness Down to Size.*

To appreciate this perspective, consider other (nonhuman) creatures who have developed a different sense that registers fastest for their species. For dogs, it's a sense of smell. For bats, a sense of hearing. Raccoons have a massive number of nerve endings in their hands, which helps to understand how they "see" with their hands. While associations in the brain are based on all incoming sensory information, for human beings it is the eye and the visual

2. McCandless, David. July 2010. "The Beauty of Data Visualization." *TEDGlobal 2010.* www.ted.com/talks/david_mccandless_the_beauty_of_data_visualization

cortex of the brain that provides the highest bandwidth channel into human cognitive centers.

Why is this important? Understanding is about helping the brain to find and recognize patterns. Information that is visually represented can be scanned and patterns can be found far more quickly than through other means. While our brain parses information from all of the senses, it is our sense of vision that has the highest fidelity and the fastest throughput.

When an Infographic Is Worth a 1,000 Words

Given this background knowledge, consider the infographic shown in Figure 7.2. You can see a visual representation of all the missions to Mars[3] (to 2009).

In one poster, we can *quickly* identify a lot information.

- How many missions to Mars have there been?
- What are their names?
- Which countries have been involved?
- When was each launched?
- What is considered to be a success for a mission to Mars? How successful has each mission been?
- What are the planned missions?

Aside from showing this explicit information, this representation could be used to support some interesting conversations. For example, we could discuss the changing economic and political landscape, as reflected by which countries have joined or abandoned their missions to Mars.

Now, consider the alternative: to convey this much information using words alone would require at least a chapter in a textbook, and we probably wouldn't have nearly as clear an understanding of the information. Even if we distilled this information into a spreadsheet, it would still be difficult to spot the main patterns. The strength of this visual is in making it easier to make comparative judgments.

Visuals are powerful because—when used effectively—they ask so little of the person processing the information. We convey a lot of meaning in a compact way. For this reason alone, whether you're creating an infographic or applying

---

3. Christie, Bryan. 2009. "Missions to Mars." https://bryanchristiedesign.com/mission-to-mars

some basic graphic design principles to a spreadsheet, this is far more than "prettying things up"—this is visual communications. This is about smartly and expertly using visuals to convey an idea more effectively.

What then do we need to know about visual processing to represent information effectively?

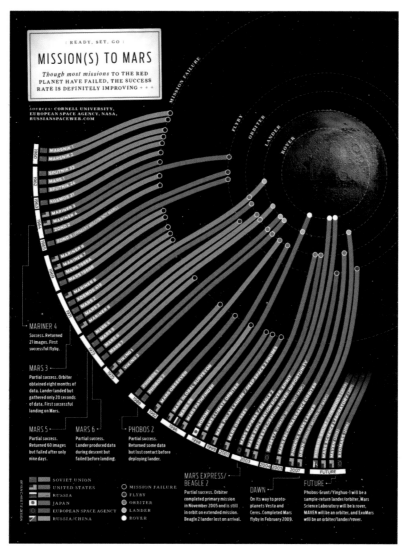

FIGURE 7.2 Infographic illustrating all missions to Mars. *Image courtesy of Bryan Christie Design*

"A Functional Art"[4]

What we'll focus on in this chapter is a scientific perspective on why visual representations are so crucial to understanding. In our experience working with designers, aesthetic design choices are often made because it "feels right" or seems to make sense. Sometimes, these instincts are spot on, whether or not the reasons why can be articulated. Other times, these preferences are just plain wrong and fall apart under scrutiny, as may be the case for less experienced visual designers. Of course, the person skilled at visual communications can make these aesthetic choices *and* speak with authority as to why a certain option should be more effective than the alternatives. Conscious or not, there's a logic to these choices. If you're choosing between using colored sticky notes or differently sized sticky notes to classify things, there's a reasoned approach to guide this choice, an approach that anyone can use. If you're choosing between using iconography or shades of a color to display information, there's a rational way to choose one of these options over another. These can and should be functional choices. Over time, we learn to ask: What works best to convey this kind of information?

We could, of course, talk about the evocative and emotional power of aesthetic choices, or basic graphic design elements such as balance, harmony, rhythm, or color theory. These do factor heavily into how we process and respond to visual displays of information. For our purposes—moving from information to understanding—we'll narrowly focus on the functional qualities of visual and graphic treatments. Let's put a spotlight on the less addressed "grammar" that makes up our visual language.

Understanding Visual Encodings

So, what are the things our eyes notice?

In biological terms, our visual system takes in and transforms light into electro-chemical signals, allowing us to establish contrast by detecting edges and shadows of objects, determine where things are in space, separate the color of an object from the color of ambient light (though even these colors rely somewhat on memories and expectations), detect motion, and handle face and object recognition. Note, this does not work like a camera, capturing

---

4.   Credit to Alberto Cairo for this phrase, also the title of his excellent book on infographics.

an image of what is seen. We don't see what is in front of us. Rather, what is "seen" is an image constructed based on these electro-chemical signals. What we see is our brain's attempt to find patterns in all the firing neurons, many of which happen to be originating with this pair of organs that happen to take in light. This is what optical illusions reveal about how we actually see the world.

In practical terms, we quickly notice things like shape, color, length, things in motion—these are fairly obvious. But we can also extend this visual perception to richer things, such as texture, overlap, and opacity. Collectively, these are all types of visual encodings we pick up on at varying rates of efficiency and for various purposes.

Let's return to our humble sticky note (see Figure 7.3). Many teams use sticky notes to track their progress. But given the amount of information these boards often need to convey (owner, task, status, project it's aligned to, estimation, priority, due date, etc.), teams quickly augment or use the sticky note in more ways, and in doing so begin to create a visual language shared by that team.

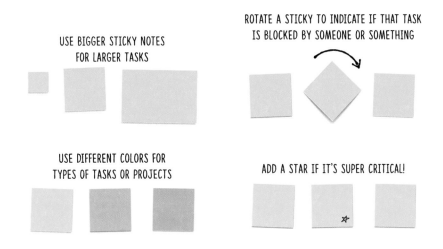

FIGURE 7.3 Different ways that teams use or augment sticky notes to hold and convey meaning. Teams can (a) use differently sized sticky notes for more or less important tasks, (b) rotate a sticky note to indicate a task is blocked, (c) use different colored sticky notes to classify different tasks, or (d) annotate a sticky with a star, if it's especially important.

What then are the specific visual properties that are available to use? What is our palette of colors, so to speak?

For any decision that uses a visual encoding, whether it's how we use sticky notes or design the marker that goes on a digital map, we have several decades of research to inform our decision. Figure 7.4 shows a catalog listing some of the research into each of these different and unique properties.[5]

Table of Visual Attributes (Richard Brath v. Sept 2013)		Information Visualization Researchers									Vision Rsch	Shape Rsch
		Bertin 1967	Cleveland 1985	MacKinlay 1986	MacEachren 1995	Wilkinson 1999	Ware 2000	Mazza 2009	Ilinsky 2012	Chen, Floridi 2013	Preattentive Perception	Brath 2009/2011
Trans-form	Position	X	X	X	X	X	X	X	X	X		
	Length		X	X			X	X	X	X	X	
	Size (Area)	X	X	X	X	X	X	X	X	X	X	
	Orientation	X		X	X	X	X	X	X	X	X	
	Volume		X	X			X					
Shape	Shape	X		X	X	X	X	X	X	X		X
	Angle		X	X						X		X
	Curvature										X	X
	Mark										X	X
	Line Ending							X	X	3	X	X
	Closure									X	X	X
	Local Warp											X
	Edge Type									1,2		X
	Corner Type									3		X
	Icon, glyph, etc									4		
Colour	Brightness	X		X	X	X	X	X	X	X	X	
	Hue	X	X	X	X	X	X	X	X	X	X	
	Saturation			X	X	X	X	X	X	X		
Texture	Granularity	X		X	X	X	X	X	X	X		
	Pattern						X	X	X	X		
	Orientation						X	X				
Relation	Connection			X				X	X	X		
	Containment			X				X	X			
Optics	Blur				X	X					X	
	Transparency				X	X					X	
	Stereo Depth										X	
	Concavity									X	X	
	Light Direction									X	X	
	Shadow									X		
	Partial occlusion									X		
Move-ment	Flicker						X			X	X	
	Speed						X			X	X	
	Direction									X	X	
Misc	Numerosity									X	X	
	Spatial Grouping									X	X	
	Arrangement				X							
	Resolution				X							
	Artistic Effects										X	
	Text Labels							X	X	X		

FIGURE 7.4 A summary of different academic research studies into visual encodings.

From this chart, we can see a number of researchers who have been investigating how our perception is affected by everything from shape to blurring to the presence or removal of text labels. What's great about a list like this is that it pulls together many of the fundamental elements we all use everyday to convey information, whether we are consciously aware of these or not. It's a good start at listing distinct visual properties. But, is there a way to turn this

5. Brath, Richard. "The Table of Visual Attributes (2013)." 2013. Richardbrath. September 28, 2013. https://richardbrath.wordpress.com/2013/09/28/the-table-of-visual-attributes-2013-2/

listing, which is mostly about indexing research, into more of a *how should I use these* cheat sheet?

Figure 7.5 is a synthesis of all that we've since learned about these visual properties, with a special emphasis on being comprehensive, but more critically offering some general guidance as to how to best *use* these visual encodings.

		Representing Categories	Representing Precise Quantitative Perception	Representing General Quantitative Perception	Showing Sequence
Form: Orientation		✓	✓		✓
Form: Line Length			✓		
Form: Line Width		✓		✓	limited
Form: Size / Area				✓	✓
Form: Enclosure		✓			
Form: Shape		✓	limited		
Form: Curvature				✓	
Form: Proximity		✓*		✓*	
Form: Added Marks		✓	limited		
Pattern Density		✓	limited	✓	limited
Line Pattern		✓			
Line Endings		✓			✓
Color: Hue		✓		✓	
Color: Intensity (Saturation, Brightness, Opacity)				✓	✓
Spatial Position: 2-D Position		✓	✓		✓
Motion				limited	✓*
Texture		✓	limited		
Rotation		✓	limited		limited
Perspective				✓	limited
Iconography		✓			✓
Outline or Solid		limited			
Overlay				limited	✓
Overlap		✓		limited	
Join				limited	✓
Aspect Ratio		limited		limited	
Labels		✓	✓	✓	✓
Transformation		✓		limited	✓
Quantity			limited	✓	✓

FIGURE 7.5 A listing of different visual encodings, with a focus on when each should be used to (a) represent categories, (b) represent precise quantitative information, (c) represent general qualitative information, and (d) show sequence. Visit **www.poetpainter.com/visual-encodings.pdf** to download a PDF version of this handout.

Effective Use of Visual Encodings

Knowing the kinds of visual properties we have to play with is useful. Upon seeing a categorical list of these visual properties identified and named in this way, it's easy to get inspired and start thinking of ways we could apply each and every visual treatment. Like the proverbial "kid in a candy store," we get excited by the possibilities, ready to try a bit of everything. But wait. While having a one-page cheat sheet that identifies and names all these visual encodings is exciting, do not miss the critical part: knowing when and where to best use each visual treatment.

To use a kitchen analogy, we need to do more than simply stock our kitchen with a bunch of raw ingredients—spices, fruits, veggies, grains—we need to understand how and when to use each ingredient. What is this good for? What is this not good for? What are good and bad combinations of ingredients? How do these blend together to create something more? Just as with cooking, a couple of visual "ingredients" may suffice, or the recipe may require more. Knowing how to combine your ingredients is crucial.

We could go through each visual encoding one at a time. Overlap. Orientation. Opacity, etc. But most of these things are understood or self-explanatory. What's more effective is to explore these properties by way of their *functions*; we should learn to ask *what is this good and not good for?* Specifically, we want to note if a particular visual encoding is best suited for one of the following:

- Representing precise quantitative information (vs. general qualitative information)
- Showing sequence
- Representing categories

Let's examine each of these functions of visual encodings in more detail.

Representing Precise Quantitative vs. General Qualitative Information

When it comes to assessing precise quantity, certain kinds of perceptual judgments are easier than others. For example, asking how many short line segments will fit onto a longer line is trivial; asking how many little spheres will fit into a big sphere—this proves to be much more challenging.

In Figure 7.6, you can test your own ability at such estimations. (Answers can be found at the end of this chapter.)

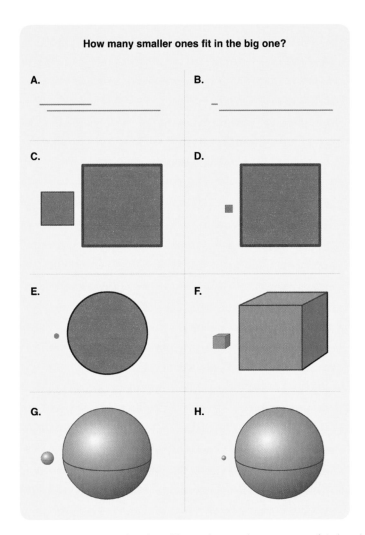

FIGURE 7.6 Estimation game developed by students at the University of Colorado Boulder. For each problem, estimate how many of the smaller objects will fit into the larger object?

What the studies into these topics and interactive simulations highlight are the kinds of visual encodings that lend themselves to displaying precise quantitative information versus those that are better suited for general qualitative assessments. (Note: You can play this online.[6])

6. "Estimation." 2014. PhET. February 20, 2014. https://phet.colorado.edu/en/simulation/legacy/estimation

If we ask you how many little squares fit into a big square, most people can get close enough. But if you're asked to do the same thing with circles (or worse, spheres), it proves to be more challenging.

For precise judgments, our visual perception is better with line lengths and positioning along a scale, versus the use area or volume, especially where there is curvature (such as with circles and spheres) involved.

To demonstrate how the human eye struggles to translate areas into numeric values, try the following exercise. The area of each circle correlates with a specific numeric value. Sort these circles from smallest to largest:

It's not terribly challenging to do this exercise, although your eye probably scanned back and forth across the page, comparing areas a few times, before concluding one circle should be placed before or after another. Now do the same thing with the bar chart below:

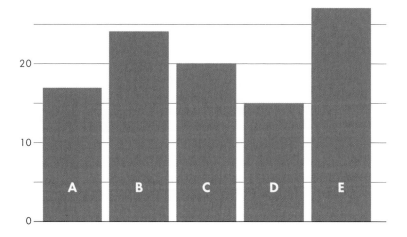

When represented as bars on a scale, it's much easier to pinpoint the different numeric values being represented. Moreover, we're able to compare precise differences with the bar chart in a way we cannot do effectively using the area of a circle.

This is a great illustration for the difference between representing precise quantitative information versus general qualitative information.

With circles, we struggle to estimate and compare area. And it's not just circles. It's hard to make precise judgments based on changes in size, line width, color intensity, or similar properties.

Does this mean we should avoid these kinds of encodings then? No. Not necessarily.

Take a heat map, like the one shown in Figure 7.7. It's also not good for making precise judgments. But it is good for quickly scanning and gaining a *general* sense of things. You might notice that there seem to be more birthdays in July, August, and September. Or that more babies are born on the 14th of February compared to every other day in that month. This kind of representation, which relies on the visual encoding of *color:intensity*, gives us a good relative sense of things.

But, what if we needed to know by how much or to what degree? How many more people have birthdays on February 14th versus December 29th? For this kind of precise information, relying upon our ability to distinguish between 50 shades of tan would prove difficult, if not impossible. For this kind of precision, we might turn again to something like the length of a line or a position along a scale.

And this leads us to the real point: *What is your intent?* By only talking about how quantitative or not a particular visual treatment is, we're presuming that facilitating accurate judgments is the ideal. But what if that's not the goal? It's more important to know when your goal is to show precise, accurate information and when your goal is to show general, relative information. Or maybe your goal is a bit of both (adding numbers to each box in our heatmap would add more precision).

To help determine which visual encodings are best suited for general qualitative versus specific qualitative judgments, we've found value in the visual in Figure 7.8, based on research done by Cleveland and McGill.[7] By arranging different visual encodings on a continuum, we can quickly get a sense of what might be most appropriate for a given situation.

7. Cleveland, W. S., and R. McGill. 1985. "Graphical Perception and Graphical Methods for Analyzing Scientific Data." *Science* 229 (4716): 828–33. https://doi.org/10.1126/science.229.4716.828

HOW POPULAR IS YOUR BIRTHDAY?

Two decades of American birthdays, averaged by month and day.

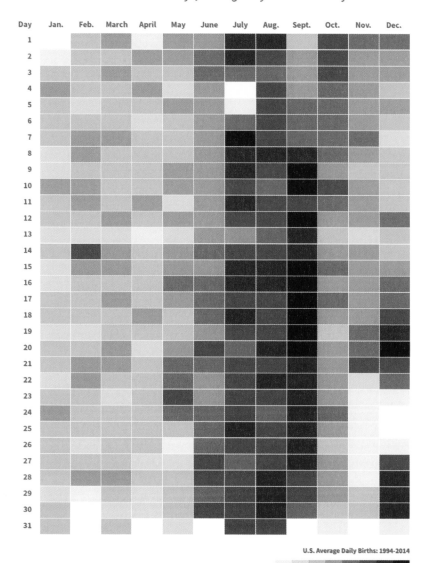

FIGURE 7.7 Relative frequency of different birth dates, represented with a heatmap.[8]

8. Stiles, Matt. 2016. "How Common Is Your Birthday? This Visualization Might Surprise You." *The Daily Viz.* September 17, 2016. http://thedailyviz.com/2016/09/17/how-common-is-your-birthday-dailyviz/

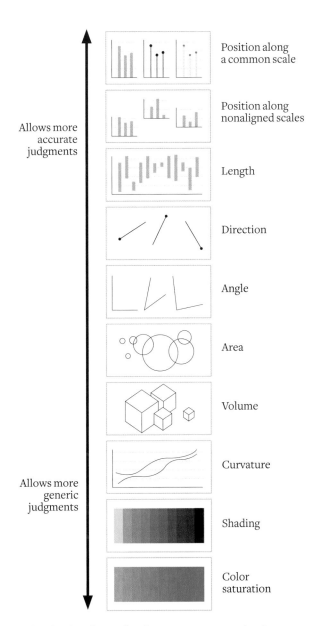

Allows more
accurate
judgments

Allows more
generic
judgments

Position along
a common scale

Position along
nonaligned scales

Length

Direction

Angle

Area

Volume

Curvature

Shading

Color
saturation

FIGURE 7.8 Cleveland and McGill's elementary perceptual tasks.
Credit to Alberto Cairo for arranging these on a continuum.

The lesson from all this is that some visual elements are better suited than others for representing precise information. Go ahead and use elements such as color intensity or circles to represent information—but only for *generic* judgments. For data that needs to be represented accurately, forgo these aesthetic preferences (and that's why things like circles and shades are often chosen) and choose the visual properties best suited for accurate judgments.

Let's apply this perspective then to another example: the pie chart.

DEFENDING THE OFT-MALIGNED PIE CHART

If you've worked in a business environment or with charting tools, you may have heard someone state that "pie charts are bad."

Let's clear the record. Pie charts are not bad. Pie charts are bad for representing *precise, quantitative information.*

For example, in the image in Figure 7.9, which representation makes it easier to see that red outperformed green?

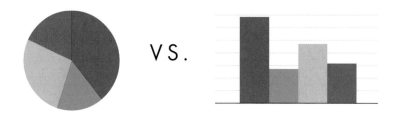

FIGURE 7.9 The same statistical information, represented with a pie chart (left) and a bar chart (right). Notice how the bar chart makes it easier to make precise, comparative judgments.

Pie charts would be a poor choice where you needed to make precise comparisons, especially where the differences were small. We get a sense of this simply by assessing the two representations side by side. But, if we look back at the chart from Cleveland and McGill, we see that for precise judgements, comparing *angles* (and perhaps *area*) is more difficult than comparing *position* and *length.*

So then, when might a pie chart be really useful?

TRACKING TIME WITH A PIE CHART

In the crowded world of time-tracking applications, one tool stands out for its visual dashboard: Noko. Among other pleasantries, Noko offers a brilliant and simple dashboard for time tracking (see Figure 7.10).

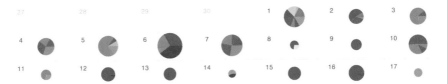

FIGURE 7.10 The time-tracking app Noko uses a combination of pie charts and a calendar to represent time spent on different projects.

Each calendar day contains a pie chart. The relative size of each circle correlates to the total hours worked that day. Each slice of the pie shows time spent on different projects. At a glance, you quickly get a *sense* of where all your (tracked) time went, as well as an *idea* of how much time you're putting in per day. Organizing these pie charts on a calendar view allows you to spot interesting patterns, such as where and how you spent your time on particular days of the week.

A pie chart, in this case, seems to work very well. As with our birthday heatmap, the primary function of this dashboard is to help you recognize patterns: general, qualitative information. If you do need a deeper dive, then specific, detailed information, is available on hover (see Figure 7.11); for even more detailed analysis (precise, quantitative information), Noko also offers traditional reporting.

FIGURE 7.11 With Noko, more precise time-tracking information is available through a hover interaction.

Debating pie charts vs. bar charts misses the point: Is it more appropriate to make accurate or generic judgments? What is good then depends upon the problem you are solving.

Table 7.1 lists a few visual encodings and what they're best suited for.

TABLE 7.1 VISUAL ENCODINGS FOR QUANTITATIVE INFORMATION

THINGS THAT ARE GOOD FOR SHOWING PRECISE QUANTITATIVE DATA	NOT VERY PRECISE QUANTITATIVE PERCEPTION	NO QUANTITATIVE PERCEPTION
Length	Width	Shape
Spatial Position	Size /Area	Enclosure
Direction	Color: Intensity	

Showing Ordered, Ordinal, or Sequenced Data

What about information that needs to also represent a sequence or progression? This might be identifying top, mid, and low performers in a group setting. Or perhaps identifying different temperatures. Maybe it's different severity of bugs and issues in a software app. Or relative ages of students. Relative difficulty. Required level of proficiency. Pricing tiers. Star ratings. All sorts of visualization problems will require you to visually represent some kind of *ordered* data.

For showing sequence, the visual encoding of scale (or size), color intensity, line thickness, and orientation are commonly used. Let's run through a few, quick examples where visual encodings are used to show ordered information.

You may recall this example from earlier where we discussed the concept of "thicker means stronger," where the line thickness connecting different avatars suggested the strengths of each relationship. Instead of line thickness, the example in Figure 7.12 uses size (and shading) of a circle to communicate similar information. The size of the circles, each containing more precise numeric information, makes it easy to scan and find patterns in the professional relationship.

In Common with JD

2 Groups

7 Skills & Expertise

1 Location

FIGURE 7.12 LinkedIn uses circles to indicate the strength of a relationship between two individuals, as suggested by shared groups, skills and expertise, and location(s).

Bing Travel uses orientation and color coding to indicate buying confidence, as shown in Figure 7.13.

SHOULD YOU STAY?
OR
SHOULD YOU GO?

PRICE PREDICTOR
bing.com/travel

FIGURE 7.13 Bing Travel uses a combination of orientation and color coding to indicate buying confidence.

Iconography can also be used, as we most commonly see in star ratings of all kinds.

None of these examples should be surprising. The takeaway here is how specific visual encodings are used to show ordered information. If we return to our heatmap example, in addition to showing general, qualitative information, the use of color intensity also represented ordered information, the average number of birthdays for a given calendar date.

Visual encodings to show ordered information can show up in clever and fascinating ways, as with the example in Figure 7.14.

FIGURE 7.14 This clever sticker, showing common colors for different degrees of ripeness, supports a comparison between the visual information on the sticker and the avocado on which it was placed.

With a simple sticker, *color* is used to assess the ripeness of an avocado. By comparing the sticker color—ordered information representing ripeness—with that of the avocado, we can determine ripeness.

Rotation is another encoding that can be used to show order, or things on a continuum. We could easily point at how the hands on a clockface use rotation to show the precise progress of time (also precise quantitative information). But how else might rotation be used? With card games, we typically think about information on the card itself, or collecting sets of cards. Here's a card game that uses the full rotation of a card (over several turns) to indicate that card's *status*.[9] The card's orientation indicates whether the card is ready to be used, or if it (representing a creature) is "exhausted" and needs to recover before it can be played again. Each turn then, you rotate the card by 90°, until it is completely recharged and ready to play again (see Figure 7.15).

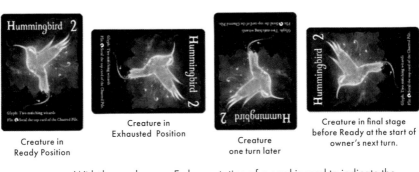

Creature in
Ready Position

Creature in
Exhausted Position

Creature
one turn later

Creature in final stage
before Ready at the start of
owner's next turn.

FIGURE 7.15 With the card game, Ember, rotation of a card is used to indicate the present status of that card.

HOW SCALABLE IS YOUR ENCODING?

As we discuss using visual encodings to show sequenced data and categories (next), it's important to anticipate how *scalable* a particular encoding might be. For example, discerning the differences between line thicknesses would be difficult after more than four or five line weights. If orientation were used with a shape, such as a pointer, you might easily get 12 different orientations (think of the hour hand on a clock); any more orientations, and it would be challenging to spot these nuanced differences. If you used orientation with a shape like an equilateral triangle, you'd only get through a third of your 360-degree rotation, before the shape began repeating itself.

9. "Ember: The Magical Card Game." 2017. Kickstarter. District 31. October 23, 2017.
   www.kickstarter.com/projects/1118172895/ember-ultimate-collection-limited-edition
   -wood-dec

Representing Categories, Types, or Classifications

Similar to ordered data are *categories*. Whereas ordered data includes a sequence or progression, categories don't necessarily have this continuity. For example, if you want to show degrees of mastery for a subject (ordered data), it is common to use tint or saturation to create a range, say a light blue to deep green:

These degrees would be *ordinal* information (what we just covered). But, if you also wanted to represent different subjects or skills, you might assign each an associated icon, shape, discernible texture, explicit label, or some other unique identifier. In the example below, we've combined an ordinal assessment of mastery, with the categorical information (iconography) to indicate a particular subject.

Let's turn to a more complicated instance of categorical information, using several encodings in combination. In the "End of the Line" infographic by Camden Asay (see Figure 7.16), color is used to broadly classify the *application* of natural resources (for Fuel, Technology, or Weapons). Then within these colored bands, iconography and labels are used to further distinguish *types* of natural resources (Oil, Gas, and Coal).

The writing app *Hemingway* uses unique colors to highlight different areas to improve your writing. In the example in Figure 7.17, you can see red and yellow highlighting used to indicate sentences that are very hard or hard to read. Purple highlighting is used where phrases might have simpler alternatives. In all, *Hemingway* offers five kinds of color coding to highlight potential areas for improvement.

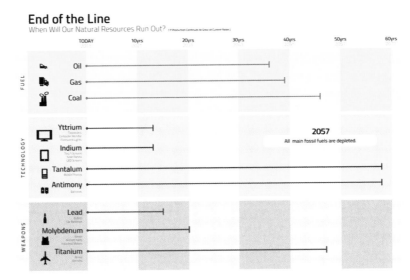

End of the Line
When Will Our Natural Resources Run Out? (If Production Continues to Grow at Current Rates)

FIGURE 7.16 An infographic indicating when various natural resources are estimated to run out.

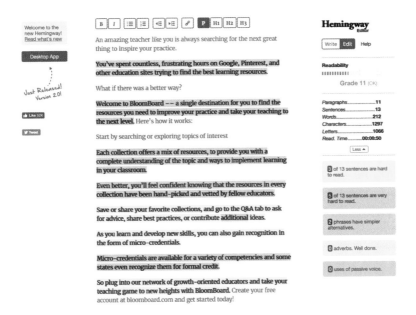

FIGURE 7.17 The writing app *Hemingway* uses five categories of color coding to
highlight potential areas for improvement.

As a reminder, these visual properties show up in all areas of life—not just in screen and paper visualizations. For anyone who plays or knows a bit about guitars, it's not uncommon to recognize a guitar from some distance based solely on the *shape* of the headstock, as shown in Figure 7.18.

FIGURE 7.18 The headstock shapes used by different brands of guitars are instantly recognizable to many guitarists and guitar enthusiasts.

Hotel listings, both online and in the printed directories commonly found at rest stops, are infamous for using dozens of icons to represent everything from hotel services to types of attractions.

☕ Free breakfast   🅿 Free parking

🏊 Pool   📶 Free WiFi

🐕 Pet-friendly   🚆 Airport transfer

🚭 Non-smoking   ❄ Air Conditioning

Of course, this abundance of icons leads us to the topic of *scalability*. Were we to use color coding or shapes, these might be a bit fast to scan (visually), but we'd quickly run out of options, and there's a lag in comprehension when we have to learn or relearn the associated meaning (often through legends) of these colors and shapes. Precise labels, on the other hand, are clear and accurate, but difficult to scan visually, and certainly not as space efficient. For these reasons, iconography is often used to represent categories where efficiency is required, as are colors and shapes where the categorical association is fairly obvious (green = good in many Western countries, star = top performers, etc.). In Figure 7.19, we've illustrated this trade-off between easy to scan and clearly understood, by placing the various kinds of encodings commonly used to represent categories along a continuum.

"Cat" "Dog"
"Elephant"

Easy to scan, but requires learned, contextual associations; space efficient

Clearly understood, not as easily scanned, and less space efficient

FIGURE 7.19 Some visual encodings commonly used to represent categories, and the relative benefits and trade-offs of each.

The goal here is to help you understand the different *functional* properties of various visual elements and how to combine them to serve different purposes. For example, you might start with iconography to represent categories, but depending on the context, reinforce these icons with either use of color or labels.

Working with Visual Properties

Let's put all this into practice, with an exercise we've used in our workshops. The exercise is fictional, but we've found it useful as it has broad relevance to a number of different business situations, and is a great way to explore visual encodings in isolation.

Imagine that you work at a super-secret government organization, tasked with tracking and monitoring mutant superheroes (and villains) around the world. What kind of system might you use to track the geolocation of mutants around the world?

You might represent each mutant with a point or marker placed on a map. But more than a mere location on the map, you might want to know a bit more, such as:

- **Mutant Power Level Classification:** 1–5 (A classification of 5 is a rare and serious threat to humanity—someone who can control people or elements such as metal with their mind; a classification of 1 is something like the benign ability to glow in the dark or make your hair dance.)

- **Whether this mutant is viewed as Good, Bad, or Unknown:** Going back to our visual properties, the 1–5 classification could be sequenced data, or general qualitative information, while the good/bad/unknown affiliation could be considered either categories or sequenced data.

A clear and simple way to design the marker might be to color code the good, bad, unknown affiliation, and then label each pin with a number to represent the 1–5 classification.

(Note how the green to red colors go from a light green saturation to something stronger. We'll talk more about this when we talk about accessibility and color blindness.)

Given that you may be scanning dozens or hundreds of these pins on a map, it's probably a better choice to represent the 1–5 rating using the visual property of scale. Using larger pins rather than labeling in this case will allow you to easily spot those mutants whom you should be most concerned about!

You could still include the 1–5 label, but given the small number in this sequence, and given that you're mostly concerned with relative (vs. precise) threats, you can omit this detail. This decision then allows use of the center area for other purposes, such as a photo or perhaps additional points of information, such as mentions in the media.

You could stop here, but it's a good practice not to rely on color. While it is very powerful, color should be used sparingly and with very specific intent, typically to represent outlier information that needs attention. You could easily reinforce the color by using the additional visual property of shape. While you could introduce common shapes such as a triangle, square, or circle, these would require learning a meaning specific to this map (probably using a legend). Alternatively, you could use some shapes that might be a recognizable concept for many people: a devil and an angel.

In addition to being easily recognizable and distinguishable, these associations add a bit of emotional engagement and humor, without requiring much additional space. Note, these are culturally specific references, common to Western culture. For such associations, you'd want to be certain the concept is familiar to your audience.

So far, so good. But suppose that you needed to add one more bit of information, perhaps a mutant's ability to travel great distances quickly. The hero who can fly. The villain who can teleport to any location he can see. This would be useful information to evaluate when assessing a potential mutant threat!

For this additional data point about travel, let's use the visual property of line length. Again, there are many ways you could represent this piece of information. Line length seems to correspond with distance traveled. (The longer the line, the great the distance that can be traveled in the same time frame.)

In this first version, the suggestion of a mouth is a bit fun and functional.

Both line length and curvature represent the relative distance that our mutants can travel.

But this mouth is only good at representing general qualitative information. What if you needed to represent more precise, quantitative information? As an alternative, you could curve the line around the inner circle and use length to give a more precise indication of speed that can be traveled. You could even add ruled markings for precision.

Much like reading the second hand on a clock, you could get precise information about distance traveling capabilities. With this variation, you could also use color thickness or texture to represent additional information.

Of course, you could certainly go on layering on more and more pieces of information, but with each additional piece of information, you also increase the complexity and time needed to understand what's being represented. Your humble marker that should make information easier to understand becomes itself an inscrutable puzzle to sort out! In a case where people will infrequently encounter such a representation, you'd want the marker to be simple and direct, such as this example from travel booking site Hotels.com, where markers are used to indicate if a hotel (a) matches your selection criteria, (b) doesn't match, or (c) is unavailable for the dates you selected (see Figure 7.20).

However, if you know your audience will spend a great deal of time—perhaps working on a daily basis with this map—you could do something more complex that requires a steeper learning curve. Perhaps the most ambitious example of what you can do with a marker on a map is in the "Megacities" visualization,[10] shown in Figure 7.21.

10. Blickle, Paul, ed. 2010. "Megacities." *IN GRAPHICS*, December 2010.

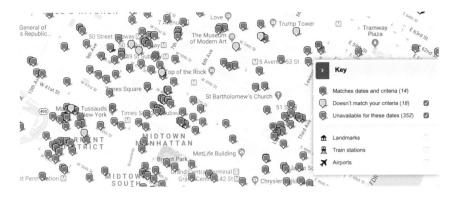

FIGURE 7.20 Simple legend and markers used by Hotels.com.

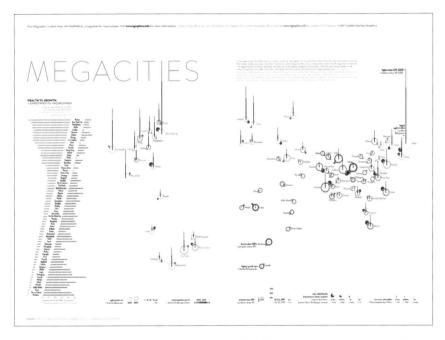

FIGURE 7.21 This visualization, created for *IN GRAPHICS* magazine, is an ambitious visual representation of present and predicted statistics for dozens of megacities worldwide.

Like the map examples above, you have markers on a map. However, each of these markers represents an impressive amount of information, from expected population growth to water supply levels to estimated urban GDP—nearly one dozen points of data in all! See Figure 7.22.

FIGURE 7.22 A close-up of the marker treatment used for each city in the "Megacities" visualization.

Of course, for this to be readily useful requires working with this visualization, for a sustained period of time. Nonetheless, it's an impressive demonstration of how much information can be packed into a dense space—in this case, the marker on a map.

With this fictional example, we've focused specifically on a map marker, but only because it's a narrowly focused way to walk through the visual properties presented in this chapter. (We'll talk more about the map itself in Chapter 9, "Ways We Use Space to Hold and Convey Meaning.") There are, of course, few limits to how you can combine and play with different visual properties— whether it's pins on a map or sticky notes on a wall or gathering employees for a team offsite. In some cases, it may be very clear when there is a "right" solution. In other cases, such as with this example, there may be many good ways to represent this information. What you see from this exercise is that how you choose to represent information is both an art and a science.

A Couple of Issues to Consider

At this point, we've discussed how visual encodings can be used to represent quantitative—or qualitative—information, to represent sequence, and to represent categories. Let's call out a few issues to consider when mixing and matching different visual encodings.

Issue #1: Color and Scalability

Discerning the different functional properties of these visual elements is one challenge. The other challenge is scalability.

We've mentioned the topic of scalability once already, but it's worth mentioning once more, with a focus on color scalability. Color is the encoding that most people grab when creating visual representations. Colored sticky notes. Color coding for just about everything. And yet, colors, like shapes, are very limited, especially for those who are color-blind. Yes, the human eye can perceive about one million different colors, but discerning the difference between one shade of blue and another—especially where many people are looking at the same thing—proves very difficult. We're left with maybe a dozen shared color options. Be thoughtful about how and when you decide to use color to convey information. (Note: This is such a critical topic, and oft misunderstood, that we've dedicated the next chapter to color).

Issue #2: Mixing and Matching Encodings

When mixing visual encodings, be clear about when you are reinforcing existing information vs. representing additional information. Depending on the complexity of your visual representation (how much information you need to represent), you may want to combine multiple visual encodings to reinforce the *same* attribute, for example, combining colors with icons to represent categories, or using scale and numbering to represent quantity. See Figure 7.23. Where you're not constrained to allocate different visual encodings to represent different information, using different encodings to reinforce and represent the same information is a good thing!

FIGURE 7.23 This dashboard from the issue-tracking software *GitHub* combines labels and color coding to classify different issues.

Visual encodings can be used to: show *quantitative* (or *qualitative*) *information*, to represent *sequence*, and to represent *categories*. There's one final topic to cover related to our sense of vision: how we see and perceive *relationships* between things. How we think about this topic requires us to pull out a bit, as relationships aren't created in quite the same way through specific visual encodings. Whereas visual encodings help us think critically about the treatment of very specific, discrete *objects*, to understand relationships requires us to take a step back and examine how we perceive and process these discrete objects as a *whole*. In Chapter 9, we'll examine the use of spatial arrangement to hold and convey meaning. But for this final section, we'll limit our focus to how our brain tries to find patterns in visual information. For this, we'll look at Gestalt psychology.

Using Gestalt Psychology to Show Relationships

Gestalt psychology is concerned with how people perceive and process visual information. Gestalt principles give us a language for describing the *perception* of *relationships* between different objects.

For example, we could talk about the three black Pac-Man-like shapes in the image below, but you probably see what looks like a white triangle. This is your brain's attempt to simplify and reconcile discrete pieces into a whole. The same goes for the collection of random black shapes on the right; it's far easier to recognize this as a panda bear.

These common examples (both demonstrating the law of closure) show how "the whole is other than the sum of the parts" (Kurt Koffka), which is the central idea of Gestalt psychology. Indeed, if we recall the lessons of earlier chapters on perception, this attempt by our brain to find the (familiar) pattern and reconcile the information makes complete sense.

For a complete list of the Gestalt Principles, see the spread on pages 166–167.

The Application of Gestalt Principles

Rather than dedicating a space explaining each Gestalt principle in detail (plenty of online articles do a great job of this), let's focus on why these principles are relevant to our topic of understanding. If you're using visuals to convey information, how you go about doing so can either clarify or confuse. Used with intent, Gestalt principles will help you reduce the cost of understanding; ignored, and you're likely to create confusing situations. Here are a few cases where ignoring these principles creates confusion.

SIMILARITY

Things that are similar in color, shape, or size are perceived to be more related than things that are dissimilar.

PROXIMITY

Things that are close to one another are perceived to be more related than things that are spaced farther apart.

FIGURE GROUND RELATIONSHIP

We tend to perceive things as either the element of focus in the foreground or as part of the background on which the figures rest.

LAW OF PRÄGNANZ/ SIMPLICITY

We tend to perceive ambiguous or complex images as the simplest form possible.

COMMON FATE

We tend to perceive elements moving in the same direction as being more related than elements that are stationary or that move in different directions.

LAW OF SYMMETRY

Things that are symmetrical to each other tend to be perceived as a unified group.

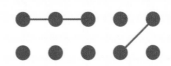

COMMON REGION/ ENCLOSURE

Things which are grouped together within a region will be understood as a group.

UNIFORM CONNECTEDNESS

Things that are visually connected are perceived as more related than elements with no connection.

CLOSURE

We tend to fill in the missing details when an image is incomplete or appears to be missing information.

GOOD CONTINUATION

Things arranged on a line or curve are perceived to be more related than things not on the line or curve.

LAW OF ISOMORPHIC CORRESPONDENCE

We respond to some images based on prior associations in the physical world or another context.

LAW OF FOCAL POINT

A point of interest, emphasis, or difference will capture and hold our attention.

Gestalt Anti-Pattern #1

Let's start with a poor use of proximity, that, unfortunately is all too common on the internet. The Gestalt Law of Proximity states that "things that are close to one another are perceived to be more related than things that are spaced farther apart." So imagine this scenario: you're on a website, maybe it's a list of the top movies from last year, most of which you aren't familiar with. You're about halfway down the page when you realize you're not sure whether the picture goes with the text above or the text below (see Figure 7.24). From the movie still, it looks like an interesting movie, but now you have a small understanding problem: *Is the caption above or below the image?*

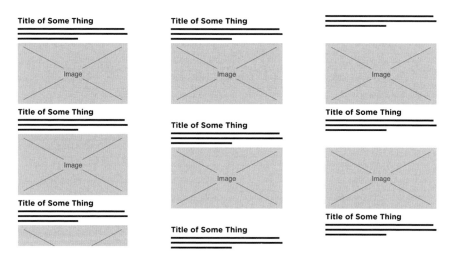

FIGURE 7.24 Abstraction of a common scenario: With the example on the left, you're unsure if the headline and associated text go with the image above or the image below. With the center and right examples, adding a bit of space eliminates any such confusion.

To solve for this confusion, you could add a line to separate the picture-text groupings, but simply adding space accomplishes the same thing—without adding more design elements to the page. We perceive things that are close together as related.

Gestalt Anti-Pattern #2

Let's consider another "anti-example," one that demonstrates how our brains work overtime to find a pattern in things, even when there may not be one.

This same principle of proximity is incredibly useful for finding patterns in large sets of data. But what if, unlike our movie example, there is no pattern? Cluster analysis is a useful tool for grouping things based on similarities (see Figure 7.25). In doing so, everyone from scientists to engineers to school principals can find patterns in the data.

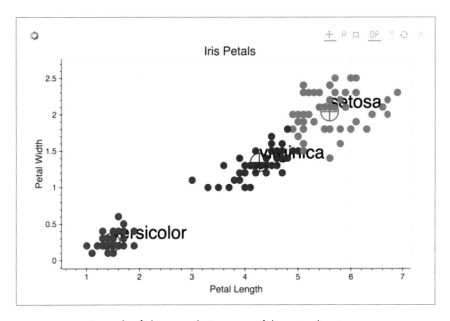

FIGURE 7.25 Example of cluster analysis, a type of data visualization.

In the data viz above, it's easy to spot patterns in the data that would have been difficult to spot in a spreadsheet. Our human ability to see patterns in things is incredibly valuable. But this ability to spot patterns is also fallible. With something like proximity, we have to be on guard against what Cornell psychologist Tom Gilovich describes as the "clustering illusion." In Figure 7.26, you see a map of London showing V-1 rocket strikes during World War II.

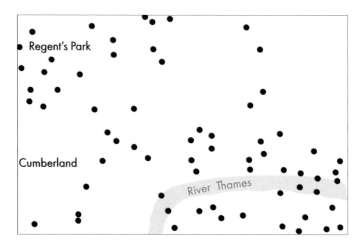

FIGURE 7.26 Map of central London showing 67 V-1 rocket strikes. *Adapted from How We Know What Isn't So by Thomas Gilovich.*

Just glancing at this, it appears there is a heavier concentration of bombings in the lower-right and upper-left quadrants. Don't see it? Let's overlay the map with a grid.

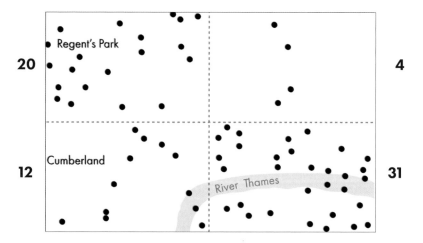

Now it certainly looks like there is a pattern—that German bombers were getting more precise and targeted with their strikes. But this grouping is statistically random. To show this, let's overlay the same map with a diagonal grid:

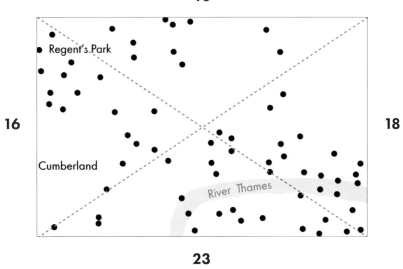

A simple change in framing how we look at this map makes things appear more random.

The lesson? We want to simplify things. We want to find a pattern that makes things more understandable. This is the crux of Gestalt psychology. Being aware of how we all naturally look for visual relationships can help to avoid confusing situations.

So how can we design *for* the mind's affinity to perceive patterns, whether present or not? What are some *good* examples of Gestalt psychology?

Good Examples of Gestalt Principles

If you've ever organized your bills or other paperwork by carefully arranging piles and stacks of papers, you're following the Gestalt principle of proximity. You practice this very same skill when you pack for a trip, by laying things out on the bed before packing them into the suitcase. We'll revisit these same examples when we talk about categorical arrangement and chunking as an interaction pattern, but core to both of these lenses is the simple principle of proximity, which is: "Things that are close to one another are perceived to be more related than things that are spaced farther apart."

Speaking of travel, hotels will often arrange toiletries in a box or on a platform—a form of *enclosure* or *common region*. Why? To make several objects seem like one; this creates the perception of simplicity by suggesting these things are all related and part of a larger whole (see Figure 7.27). This is about managing the perception of organization, and it makes things feel simpler.

FIGURE 7.27 Toiletries arranged in a box employ the Gestalt principle of enclosure, creating unity between the items.

Remove the box (sometimes just a slab of wood or glass), and this organized space might feel less organized, unless also ordered in a line, an example of the Gestalt principle of *good continuation*. Moreover, notice in the photo how the shampoo, conditioner, and body wash are in consistently shaped and styled containers. This is employing the Gestalt principle of similarity. Things that are similar (color, shape, size, etc.) are perceived to be more related than things that are dissimilar. The net effect of all this is the perception of wholeness and simplicity.

If these principles seem like common sense, or natural things, that's great! The point is that you learn to recognize these principles of visual perception and be intentional with their use. This isn't about specialized graphic design skills, but rather visual perception.

Visual Doesn't Mean Pictures

It's easy to think this chapter is all about *pictorial* representations. Graphic design. Illustrations. Sketches. Images. No, it's about visual perception. This is about how understanding comes from what we see, and how our sense of vision can facilitate, or confound, what is perceived.

To show just how blurry the line between pictures and text is, let's pause for a moment and think about these words you're reading.

These words are made up of individual letters.

But these letters, what are they, really? Unless you've traveled to a foreign country that uses an entirely different writing system, it's easy to forget that letters and punctuation are all essentially pictorial, symbolic representations of information, symbols combined into words and sentences and paragraphs and books.

When you read, you're scanning symbols, symbols whose meaning comes through careful arrangement, through the use of spacing, punctuation, breaks between paragraphs, and so on. These cues let you know which of these words should be considered together as a set.

Quite literally, arranging words in a line and adding punctuation between words suggests a kind of visual relationship between different sets of information.

Consider the words you just read without continuity or punctuation:

words

words

relationship   between

adding

between   of   suggests

a

punctuation

literally

Quite

information

visual   sets   line   in

arranging

of   and   kind

different   a

Your ability to understand meaning in words is as much about word choices as it is about *visual perception.*

You perceive things arranged in a line as related (continuation) …

…and the symbolic meanings of punctuation are explicit indications that words belong together in a set (contained region).

And this is where our analogy—comparing the written word with Gestalt principles—converges. The *visual* principles that apply to text also apply to shapes and visuals.

The whole is other than the sum of the parts. That is the simple point of this final section. In the chapter on spatial arrangement, we'll revisit this topic, but with a different perspective—noting that how things are placed in space can hold or convey meaning. But for this short introduction, we wanted to direct your attention to how, when presented with a collection of parts, you naturally look for how these parts fit together and relate.

What We Know About How We See Things

In writing this chapter, we wanted to draw attention to how we see things. Since vision is such a vital part of how we understand and make sense of the world, our goal has been to place a spotlight on how visual properties (such as color, shape, or orientation) directly influence all that is perceived.

Here's a recap of everything we've discussed so far about our sense of vision:

- External representations extend our limited thinking space.
- Our sense of vision is the most sophisticated of our senses, able to pick out patterns and very subtle differences quickly.
- Not all visual encodings function in the same way; we should choose visual encodings based on how well they satisfy our goals.
- We naturally perceive holistic relationships in visual information.

Let's move on to a very special topic—color!

ANSWERS TO THE QUIZ

A. 2.18

B. 18

C. 5.9

D. 111

E. 231

F. 141

G. 330

H. 7,400

8

An Intelligent Understanding of Color

Who in the rainbow can draw the line where the violet tint ends and the orange tint begins? Distinctly we see the difference of the colors, but where exactly does the one first blendingly enter into the other? So with sanity and insanity.

—HERMAN MELVILLE, *BILLY BUDD*

Color is, without a doubt, the visual element that is most often misunderstood and misused.

As mentioned earlier, when designing visual representations, color is often the first visual encoding that people use. It's also quite limited to about a dozen, distinguishable colors. It's a potent visual element, but one fraught with accessibility and perceptual problems. A general rule of thumb: *Save color for things you want to draw people's attention to.* Start with grayscale representations. Add in color only later, where it might be really, really useful. That's it. We can move along.

Except …

We need to dispel some popular beliefs about colors, beliefs that are often held up as truth, when, in fact, this is not the case. What's presented in this short chapter is more foundational knowledge than tips for immediate application. But also, this understanding of color is—we found in retrospect—a powerful lens for understanding the concepts shared throughout this book. We see in our exploration of color this pattern: while many of the absolutes we cling to are social constructs (varying across cultures and over time), behind these changing constructs we also find some universal human constants.

How Many Colors Are in the Rainbow?

Let's begin by unpacking the statement above, suggesting that we only see about a dozen colors. Actually, the human eye can perceive many more colors, perhaps a million or so. Of this million, it's estimated that each of us—individually—can distinguish somewhere between 130 to 300 colors.[1] But within a cultural group, we can only share about a dozen such colors. These limitations have little to do with personal visual acuity, but rather with language: a group's ability to see and perceive a specific color is determined by language. Do we—as a society—share the same named color value associations?

We can talk about something being "*red*" and feel confident in what we all see. From both a developmental perspective and an anthropological perspective, red is the first color (after white and black) that most cultures are aware of. But if I describe something as *magenta*, do we have a shared agreement as to what that named concept refers to? Perhaps you see hot pink where I see a vibrant, purply-reddish color? Another example of this language-color dependency: the Russian language has a specific word for the color that we (English speakers) perceive as light blue.

To put this shared vocabulary into perspective, let's start with something that is constant and beyond our language: the visible spectrum of light that is a rainbow.

When Colors Are Constant

Around the world, the meteorological phenomenon we describe as a rainbow is a constant thing. Light refracts across water droplets to create a spectrum

---

1. "Bob Myers's Answer to What Are the Colors of the Rainbow?" May 4, 2018. Quora. www.quora.com/What-are-the-colors-of-the-rainbow/answers/82150378

visible to humans. What we see as colors are the wavelengths of light visible to the human eye (see Figure 8.1). On either end of this visible spectrum are ultraviolet and infrared waves, which while invisible to human eyes, we know they *are* visible—that is, seen—by cameras and some nonhuman creatures (cats can see certain infrared frequencies, for example). Beyond this visible spectrum, we have things like gamma rays, X-rays, and radio waves, which all make up the entire spectrum of white light from the sun.

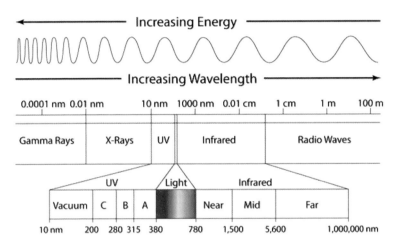

FIGURE 8.1 The visible light spectrum is a small part of the broader electromagnetic spectrum. Starting from this perspective helps us recognize the subjectivity of what is "seen" and how this might vary with different creatures and devices.

But let's stay focused on the portion of this light spectrum that is visible to humans, the part that allows us to see. Within this spectrum, the rainbow possesses millions of color combinations, as there are no clearly defined boundaries between the colors.

Why then, should diverse cultures over thousands of years arrive at the same set of color language definitions? Are colors an absolute thing? Not exactly.

The Subjectivity of Color Identification

Consider "ROYGBIV," which is the acronym we all learned to name the colors of the rainbow. How did we conclude, at least in Western cultures, that a rainbow has seven colors? Why not five, or six, or eleven? We have Sir Isaac Newton to thank for this.

These seven colors—red, orange, yellow, green, blue, indigo, and violet—were not the result of any serious scientific inquiry. Rather, Newton was fond of the number seven. Just as there are seven musical notes in a scale, Newton believed that colors should follow a similar pattern. He might have connected this with seven days in the week or the seven known planets (at the time) in our universe. In other words, ROYGBIV was an arbitrary choice based on mystical superstition.

Understanding how we arrived at these seven colors sheds light on the subjective nature of color identification. This may also explain a bit about the challenge that so many people have with indigo—that odd color that sits somewhere between blue and violet—as a separate color!

But here is where we have to be careful, as we are stepping into a decades old debate: Do the number of basic color terms and the location of color category boundaries vary across languages? Or might there be a universal pattern to the color naming systems of all cultures?

This Wikipedia entry sums up the debate rather nicely:

> There are two formal sides to the color debate, the universalist and the relativist. The universalist side claims that the biology of all human beings is all the same, so the development of color terminology has absolute universal constraints. The relativist side claims that the variability of color terms cross-linguistically (from language to language) points to more culture-specific phenomena. Because color exhibits both biological and linguistic aspects, it has become a deeply studied domain that addresses the relationship between language and thought.[2]

An Argument for Relative Linguistics

We can characterize what Newton did as imposing an arbitrary number of colors upon the color spectrum. And we might conclude the same thing has happened throughout history as different people groups formed words to describe the world around them.

2. "Linguistic Relativity and the Color Naming Debate." 2020. Wikipedia. Wikimedia Foundation. January 20, 2020. https://en.wikipedia.org/wiki/Linguistic_relativity_and_the_color _naming_debate

Indeed, various studies of diverse cultures reveal that "although the physiological basis of color vision is essentially the same for all humans with normal trichromatic color vision, there is considerable diversity in the way that different languages segment the continuum of visible colors."[3] In other words, the rainbow has no natural boundaries; how we slice it up into colors is a subjective thing that varies across different cultures and time. (See Figure 8.2 for an illustration of this concept.) From one research paper, we learned that "some languages have been reported to use as few as two terms to describe all visible colors (Rosch Heider, 1972). Others have been reported to use between three and eleven (Berlin & Kay, 1969), while some (e.g., Russian; Davies and Corbett, 1997) may have twelve."[4]

Specific examples in support of this argument:

- In Russian culture, there is no generic concept of blue. Rather, Russian makes an obligatory distinction between lighter blues (*goluboy*) and darker blues (*siniy*).

- The Japanese language (before the modern period) had just one word, *Ao*, for both blue and green. It wouldn't be until the year 1,000 that the word *midori* would be introduced to distinguish a greenish shade of blue.

- The Himba tribe from Namibia recognizes five basic colors.

- The Berinmo of Papua New Guinea has also reached a different conclusion as to the number of colors they recognize. While they draw no distinction between blue and green, they do "draw a distinction within what English speakers would consider yellow, with the word *nol* on one side and *wor* on the other."

From this, we might conclude that the colors of the rainbow do seem to be arbitrary and dependent upon language. (Connect this with earlier points we made about thoughts and cognition as layers upon layers of prior associations.)

But surely, you may be thinking, color identification isn't entirely subjective? Here's where the research gets interesting: despite these regional differences, a fascinating and consistent pattern begins to emerge.

3. Roberson, Debi, Jules Davidoff, Ian R. L. Davies, and Laura R. Shapiro. 2004. "The Development of Color Categories in Two Languages: A Longitudinal Study." *Journal of Experimental Psychology: General* 133 (4): 554–71. https://doi.org/10.1037/0096-3445.133.4.554
4. Roberson, Debi, Jules Davidoff, Ian R. L. Davies, and Laura R. Shapiro. 2005. "Color Categories: Evidence for the Cultural Relativity Hypothesis." *Cognitive Psychology* 50 (4): 378–411. https://doi.org/10.1016/j.cogpsych.2004.10.001

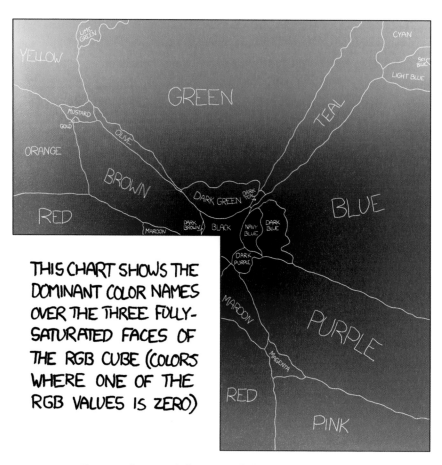

FIGURE 8.2 This comic from Randall Munroe of xkcd nicely illustrates the subjectivity of the shared color language for English speakers.[5]

An Argument for the Universal

In the late 1960s, after studying color terms across many different languages, researchers Berlin and Kay introduced the idea that there were eleven possible basic color categories: white, black, red, green, yellow, blue, brown, purple, pink, orange, and gray. They argued a universalist theory: that color cognition is *an innate, physiological process rather than a cultural one.*

5. Munroe, Randall. 2010. "Color Survey Results." Xkcd. May 3, 2010. https://blog.xkcd.com /2010/05/03/color-survey-results/

While their research has been challenged on different grounds, what has since followed is some agreement that for all noted language differences, there is a fixed order in which color names arise. The ways in which color language evolves across cultures suggest maybe there is a universal pattern governing the direction of patterns in the evolution of colors. All cultures start with the ability to distinguish dark things from light things. This is followed by the recognition of red. After that, it might be the addition of yellow or green. And blue always seems to come last. Not every language follows the exact same path, but they adhere to this same general pattern.

While the broader debate is not necessarily concluded, the general consensus seems to be that "in color, relativism appears to overlay a universalist foundation."

Why All the Fuss over Color?

While this is certainly fascinating, how is this useful? We include this as a mirror to challenge assumptions. If we turn a critical eye to the commonly accepted color wheel, this was likely influenced by Newton's original color wheel sketch. But is this the "right" way to think about colors? *Primary colors combine to make secondary colors, which in turn allow us to describe tertiary colors.* We learn this from an early age and accept this way of thinking about color as absolute. But this is just one frame. This is just *a way* of thinking about visible light. And this singular perspective has limitations, especially when used in medical, scientific, and engineering visualizations. Research papers such as "Rainbow Color Map (Still) Considered Harmful"[6] question the value of the rainbow color spectrum in data visualization applications. The point is simple: there are other ways we might think about color. We can look at alternatives such as perceptually ordered color spectrums, an *isoluminant* color map, or simply use representations of color that aren't derived from a wheel. Tools such as ColorBrewer 2.0[7] or the NASA Ames Color Tool[8] are incredibly useful for choosing a palette more suitable for visualizing data.

Since this book is concerned with how human creatures understand information, and because we so often use color to clarify, we felt it worth calling out that color and color recognition are not necessarily universal things,

6. Borland, David, and Russell Taylor Ii. 2007. "Rainbow Color Map (Still) Considered Harmful." *IEEE Computer Graphics and Applications* 27 (2): 14–17. https://doi.org/10.1109/mcg.2007.323435
7. http://colorbrewer2.org
8. "Color Usage Site Home Page." NASA. https://colorusage.arc.nasa.gov/

but are dependent on cognition, language, and biology. Understanding this allows us to challenge common assumptions about what is "true" about color and perception.

Which leads us to …

Color, Cultures, and Universal Associations

Red means stop. Green means go. These concepts are universal, right? Not so fast. Across cultures, colors do not necessarily convey the same concept. And where we may have the same ability to identify a color, the associated meaning is just that—a learned association. Concluding that red means passion, vitality, or energy, because blood and fire are red things is *not* a universal idea. Neither is associating green with growth, just because nature involves so much green. (In some Chinese cultures, green can be associated with death.) At this point, please throw away those blog posts and posters about colors to choose for different cultures. While we're keen to seek out human universals, color has proven to be something that does not have consistent meaning across cultures, or even within a culture group. Rather, the concepts we associate with particular colors are highly contextual and local, not just to a particular culture, but sometimes to smaller social groups. The meanings we point to—blue as a safe, corporate color, for example—are highly generalized assumptions, highly contextual, and mostly learned associations.

The Color Purple

Let's take purple, as an example. For many centuries, purple dye was expensive and rare. Procuring purple dye was labor intensive and required collecting a secretion from sea snails. Historian David Jacoby remarked that "twelve thousand snails of Murex brandaris yield no more than 1.4 g of pure dye, enough to colour only the trim of a single garment."[9] As a result of this laborious process, the high cost of producing purple clothing made this color a status symbol among kings, queens, and other rulers. If you could afford to wear purple, you were quite wealthy. The conceptual association then is one

---

9. Jacoby, David. 2004. "Silk Economics and Cross-Cultural Artistic Interaction: Byzantium, the Muslim World, and the Christian West." *Dumbarton Oaks Papers* 58: 197–240. https://doi.org /10.2307/3591386

of scarcity (in this case of a particular dye), signaling something to be valued above other things. While we may still see the lingering effects of this history (the Purple Heart is among the highest honors awarded for U.S. military service), the constraint of purple as a scarce color is no longer true. As such, this color is able to take on new meanings.

"Pink Is for Girls, Blue Is for Boys"

To put this into perspective, let's investigate the idea that "pink is for girls, blue is for boys." From clothing choices to marketing toys to how we decorate bedrooms, most of us grow up believing there's some inherent gender association built into the colors pink and blue. But, were we to travel back in time—just over 100 years—we'd find no such distinction. Or we might find the opposite association.

According to University of Maryland historian Jo B. Paoletti, author of *Pink and Blue: Telling the Girls from the Boys in America*, pink and blue weren't always gender-specific colors. For centuries, young children mostly wore a functional white dress, and then in the early 20th century, things began to change. Consider this quote, pulled from the June 1918 issue of Earnshaw's Infants' Department, a trade publication:

> The generally accepted rule is pink for the boys, and blue for the girls. The reason is that pink, being a more decided and stronger color, is more suitable for the boy, while blue, which is more delicate and dainty, is prettier for the girl.

A Smithsonian review of Paoletti's book,[10] goes on to add:

> Other sources said blue was flattering for blonds, pink for brunettes; or blue was for blue-eyed babies, pink for brown-eyed babies, according to Paoletti.

> In 1927, *Time* magazine printed a chart showing sex-appropriate colors for girls and boys according to leading U.S. stores. In Boston, Filene's told parents to dress boys in pink. So did Best & Co. in New York City, Halle's in Cleveland, and Marshall Field in Chicago.

---

10. Smithsonian Institution. "When Did Girls Start Wearing Pink?" 2011. Smithsonian.com. April 7, 2011. www.smithsonianmag.com/arts-culture/when-did-girls-start-wearing-pink-1370097/

By the 1940s, this association had flipped. Manufacturers had settled on pink for girls and blue for boys (see Figure 8.3 as an example of this association). Baby Boomers were raised with wearing the two colors. The point of this narrative? Color associations are learned things and can change over time. Even something as seemingly strong as the pink/blue binary was a manufactured association. To be clear, this doesn't mean a color association is any less powerful in the moment, at a particular point in history, but these color associations do not represent any universal truths.

FIGURE 8.3 The "blue is for boys and pink is for girls" concept was a manufactured one, originating in the first half of the 20th century.

Accordingly, it's good to be wary of generalizations such as "blue is a safe, corporate color." In the case of corporate associations, one generation's "safe" may—depending on the media and actions—signal stuffy, inauthentic, or distrustful to the next generation. It all depends on the learned associations embraced—for a time—by a particular culture.

Not All Colors Are Created Equal

We tend to treat our color palettes like interchangeable parts. Just pick a color. Or pick some colors we all find pleasing. Consider how many of us use the default color palettes built into software tools like Excel or PowerPoint. We usually choose a pleasing color palette, with the sentiment being "as long as you can distinguish one color from another, it's okay, right?"

Not exactly. Not all colors are created equal. In terms of visual perception, some colors jump out at you while others recede into the background (see Figure 8.4). This is because of variances in hue and saturation.

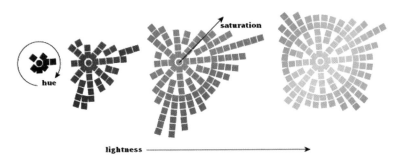

FIGURE 8.4 The range of colors perceived by humans is uneven.
Equiluminant colors from the NASA Ames Color Tool

A very bright color is going to draw more visual attention than a more desaturated color. This makes sense if we consider how things farther away from us tend to be hazier and desaturated. If something in the distance is noticed, it's likely because it's moving or contrasts with the surroundings.

This same disparity applies to color hues. We tend to look at color charts like this one and assume that the extreme ends of red, green, and blue are on equal footing.

However, because of the wavelengths of these colors and how our eyes perceive color, we see green as brighter than red, which itself is brighter than blue.

How Is This Knowledge Useful?

While it's nice to think that precise color values are interchangeable (setting aside any cultural associations), your perception doesn't work that way. In the same way that certain frequencies on the radio come in clearer than others, certain colors do the same. You need to account for, or at least consider, the unevenness of color perception.

In the example in Figure 8.5, you see the same eight-segment pie chart. The example on the right uses all high-saturation colors while the example on the left mixes high- and low-saturation colors.

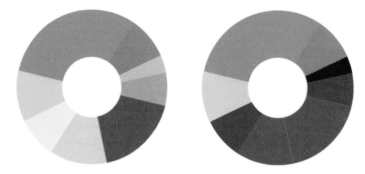

FIGURE 8.5 Two pie charts showing identical information. The chart on the left uses colors of mixed saturation, meaning some colors will naturally stand out more than others, making this an uneven representation.

Functionally, these both communicate the same thing. But consider how you *perceive* each. With the example on the right, use of high saturation is consistent; no color should be more prominent than another. But when you mix high and low saturation, as with the example on the left, the higher saturation colors tend to "pop" more—drawing you to these segments. While this chart is more aesthetically pleasing (as it uses half as many colors), it's also a bit misleading—notice how your eye is drawn to the orange segment in the upper right. The lesson? Assuming the goal is objectivity and truthfulness, you'd want to avoid mixing saturations and hues that are unevenly perceived. If the goal were the opposite, to draw attention away from or toward a particular bit of data, you could manipulate perception by adjusting saturation and hue (not that this is being recommended!). This ability to direct attention by using bolder colors is something that everyone should be aware of and intentional about.

Color Blindness

Because of my work with school systems (Stephen), I frequently encounter some sort of visual representation indicating performance or mastery on a subject. The default representation in these cases is typically a range of colors progressing from red to gray (or yellow) to green (see Figure 8.6).

FIGURE 8.6 A range of colors progressing from red to yellow to green, as seen by those with no form of color blindness.

The problem with this color selection is that a good percentage (7% of males, .5% of females) of the population have some form of color blindness. These people see something quite different, as shown in Figure 8.7.

protanopia (red/green color blindness; no red cones)

deutanopia (red/green color blindness; no green cones)

FIGURE 8.7 The same colors shown in Figure 8.6, but shown as seen by those with two different kinds of color blindness.

What to most of the population looks like a transition from red to yellow to green looks like a transition from greenish brown to yellow (or cantaloupe) back to greenish-brown. For this, the most common type of color blindness, red and green are virtually indistinguishable.

A Few Solutions

One solution to this problem is to change your color spectrum. Rather than going from one dark color (red) to another dark color (green), try going from light, *de*saturated colors to bright, saturated colors. This contrast in both hue *and* brightness increases contrast for all people. This approach is a net-win for both the color-blind and others, as shown in Figure 8.8.

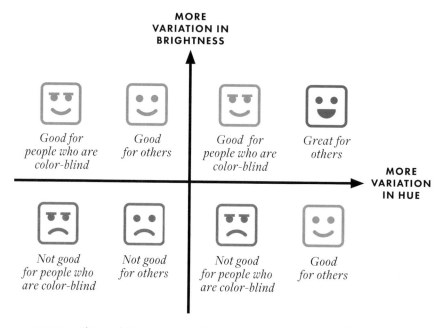

FIGURE 8.8 This model (based on an illustration by Samantha Zhang[11]) shows how using variation in both brightness and hue will satisfy everyone, color-blind and noncolor-blind alike.

Figure 8.9 shows how to modify the color swatch shown in Figure 8.6.

FIGURE 8.9 An alternative color palette to use in place of the one shown in Figure 8.6.

11. Zhang, Samantha. 2015. "Finding the Right Color Palettes for Data Visualizations." Medium. Graphiq Blog. November 23, 2015. https://blog.graphiq.com/finding-the-right-color-palettes -for-data-visualizations-fcd4e707a283?gi=5b050f767cc9

If you must use red and green together—perhaps you need the "bad" association of red (a learned association, mind you)—then you should also use the light to dark continuum, as this would be distinguishable.

Never Rely Solely on Color

Another solution of sorts is to never rely solely on color for distinguishing things. Modern board games are generally good at reinforcing color differences with additional icons or illustrations. Figure 8.10 shows a sample of cards used from the game Lanterns: The Harvest Festival. Notice how the shape of the lanterns varies for each of the seven colors. Also notice how this iconography—the lantern shape—is then carried over into the game's tiles. Whether iconography or labels or some other treatment, reinforcing colors with a secondary visual encoding is a good practice.

FIGURE 8.10 Cards from the board game Lanterns: The Harvest Festival. Notice how the color of each card is reinforced with unique iconography; the game is never dependent upon color.

Color Is Contextual

Below is an exercise commonly practiced in undergraduate design classes. Using yellow, orange, and red markers, students are asked to draw something like the image below, an orange square situated within a larger yellow or red square.

While the orange color in each box is identical, they appear lighter or darker, depending upon the surrounding color. This is an example of *simultaneous contrast*, a visual phenomenon that shifts the appearance of colors and shades based on their surroundings.

For a more pronounced example of this and potential consequence, consider the example shown in Figure 8.11.

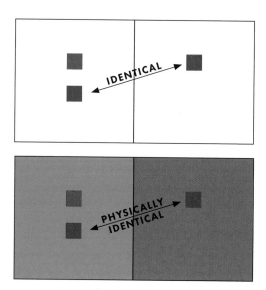

FIGURE 8.11 Examples of simultaneous contrast. Notice how the purple box appears to be a different color, based on the surrounding colors.

In all cases, the purples are physically identical. However, in the lower-right example, by simply changing the background colors, not only does the color of the purple shift, but it also more closely resembles the blue box to the left.

A Challenge to Be Color Conscious

What we're challenging here are several widespread beliefs: that colors are functionally interchangeable (they're not); that color associations are widespread (not necessarily true); or that color meanings are absolute (no, associations are learned and changed over time). Color perceptions, like hue and saturation, are rooted in biology; color associations are learned and shaped by culture.

The most widespread application of all this is in the area of corporate branding. No doubt, you've worked for a company that has some kind of corporate branding guidelines which specify approved or "on brand" colors. Or maybe you've been part of a software project that specified an exact hex color that must be used. While well-intended, a slavish adherence to these laws can actually backfire, producing colors that appear inconsistent, despite being technically correct. The most vulnerable place for this effect is when corporate logos are placed onto contrasting colors—such as the colored logo embroidered onto a colored shirt. But this is drifting into legibility and similar topics.

What about our topic of understanding? How do these distinctions aid or hinder understanding? That depends on how you apply this knowledge. Data visualizations or other visual representations of information are certainly going to be affected by a knowledgeable use of colors. But the application of this knowledge shows up in subtler ways, such as choosing the colored sticky notes to be used in an exercise. For example, if you know that the bright magenta sticky note will draw more attention than the desaturated yellow sticky notes, you should be intentional about when different colored sticky-notes are permitted. Choosing colors that don't exclude a significant percentage of the population should also be widespread knowledge. But more than anything else, we wanted to pause and draw attention to one of the single most used visual properties—and a powerful visual property at that—in hopes that we might all deepen our understanding and use of color. How color affects perception is frequently overlooked or misunderstood, so hopefully, this chapter can begin to change that.

9

Ways We Use Space to Hold and Convey Meaning

The problems are solved, not by giving new information, but by arranging what we have known since long.

—LUDWIG WITTGENSTEIN, *PHILOSOPHICAL INVESTIGATIONS*

You're at lunch, catching up with a friend who now works in a very complex industry—let's say health care and pharmaceuticals. As she starts to explain the industry (patient-provider transactions, behind-the-scenes payments, affiliate partnerships, government regulations, and so on), it's clear that she's losing you. Sensing this, she grabs the salt-and-pepper shakers, a few sugar packets, an empty straw wrapper—stand-ins for different entities. She moves them around the table and gestures between them, maybe even adding in a spoon to indicate direction.

So "this" she grabs the salt shaker, is "the health care provider." "And these …" she grabs the pepper shaker "… are the five biggest businesses that no one has ever heard of. They do all of the behind-the-scenes payment processing." She pushes a sugar packet between these two pillars to represent the flow of money from one organization to another.

This friend has created a *visual representation* that makes an otherwise abstract idea concrete. It's not a fancy infographic. There's no sketching on napkins or graphic design talent involved. But this is every bit as much a visual explanation. This ad hoc visual representation arranges *things* (the selection of salt-and-pepper shakers, sugar packets, spoons) in *space* to aid in understanding.

Let's examine what's going on here: using available objects, we're able to *hold information in the world*. Information has a materiality. This holding of information includes discrete things—when you point to the pepper shaker and ask your friend to "tell me more about this group, here," the pepper shaker has become a physical stand-in for an otherwise abstract concept, an aid to memory and recall. Here you've formed an association between these material objects and the abstract ideas they represent. But more than just persistent markers, information also resides in the *arrangement* of these things. Through grouping or sequencing these physical entities, or perhaps by rearranging them, your friend has exposed otherwise abstract *relationships* such as processes, flows, approvals, influence, and so on.

Thinking Extended into Our External Environment

Indeed, this example gets to the heart of why industries have formed around mapmaking, data visualization, and similar visual representations: these are all tools that extend thinking into the external environment. These tools help us see relationships and patterns. When a topic becomes just complex enough that it's too difficult to explain using words alone, or we have trouble making sense of a subject, we expand our cognitive abilities by bringing ideas into the world. It's not uncommon to sketch ideas, take notes, use sticky notes, or even create crude models involving condiments. We also use data to create computer simulations, all to extend our capacity to understand. We create these external representations to hold and organize our understanding, whether the understanding is for ourselves or others. And for as long as we've organized things into stacks ("my pile, your pile") or arranged things into some continuum (letterforms carved into a clay tablet, sorting children by height), we've used the spatial *arrangement* of things to hold meaning. Stanford researcher Barbara Tversky, whose work helped clarify many of the ideas presented in this chapter, remarks that: "Before the page, there was space itself. Perhaps the simplest way to use space to communicate is to arrange or rearrange things in it."[1]

Consider some of the common ways we use space around us:

- **Packing for a trip.** When packing for a vacation, how many of us arrange our clothes, books, toiletries, electronics, and other items on our beds or a big table before packing?

- **Cooking in the kitchen.** If we're making chocolate chip cookies, or a recipe with a complex series of steps and ingredients, it's common to arrange these things (flour, sugar, spices, butter, and so on) into groups or change their position as each is used, as a way to recognize what step we're on.

- **Prioritizing tasks.** In team spaces everywhere, it's not uncommon to have a wall plastered with dozens of sticky notes, of varying sizes and colors. The color and size of each sticky often represents a task or project competing for attention; the arrangement of sticky notes (often into

1. Tversky, Barbara. 2010. "Visualizing Thought." *Topics in Cognitive Science* 3 (3): 499–535. https://doi.org/10.1111/j.1756-8765.2010.01113.x

various status and backlog columns) helps teams to assess and prioritize where to devote their time.

How do you arrange the clothes in your closet? How do you sort dirty laundry? How do you organize (or not!) the papers on your desk? What about the books on your bookshelf?

Whether or not you've applied some organizing principle in all these examples, the point is simple: we all *naturally* use space to hold and convey meaning. This doesn't mean we always do this well or understand how this is in support of our thinking—this is a skill to develop, like any other skill. But we do—all of us—naturally think in spatial terms.

A Natural Orientation

From the time we're infants, aware that we have joints and limbs in space (proprioception), we start to assign meaning to spatial movements, interactions, and orientations. The knowledge of one's self in space becomes an early building block for other types of knowledge. By nature of being embodied creatures who move through and interact with environments, we can't help but associate specific spatial concepts with meaning. Things revered get placed high up, whether it's a prized possession or the judge's seat. In school, we line up in order, with a leader at the front. On the playground, we create symmetry by organizing into teams, and we tend to equate height with better athletic performance. We learn about division as we cut a pie into slices.

Given that spatial thinking is a natural skill, why aren't we better at this? Why don't we see more sketches, models, and so on? Why aren't more people so-called *visual thinkers*? The world is filled with essays, books, emails, and other written information that could be made so much clearer with a simple visual explanation. And to be clear, we're not talking about decorative illustrations, but tactics as straightforward as arranging text on a continuum, into a grid, or into a cluster. If you look back at our simple model for making sense of embodied cognition (Figure 2.4), it's all text, but arranged in a way that reveals relationships. This is about using space—in often subtle ways—to hold and convey meaning. So what keeps all of us from making this a norm for everyone? And more to the point, how might we get better at using space to facilitate understanding?

To answer these questions, we've spent years trying to understand the thought process—conscious or not—used to create visual models. Our belief?

If we can identify the "grammar" that underlies all visual thinking, especially with how we use space to hold meaning, then we can—all of us—be more intentional about how and when we arrange things.

Cooking in the Kitchen

To illustrate this approach—to expose the visual grammar at use in an everyday activity—let's return to a cooking example. For anything more than a simple recipe, consider how you *might* manage space within your kitchen to aid with food preparation.

Let's imagine you're preparing a curry dish, complete with vegetables to chop, spices to add, and a stovetop where things will be assembled and cooked. Let's go through a few of the activities you might do, with a nod to the visual grammar being used.

- For starters, you'd probably place things into zones—a zone for chopping and prepping vegetables, a zone for assembling the spices you might use, a zone for the liquids and creams that go into your final zone, which is the pan on the stove. All the while, you may have an entirely different zone set up for a completely different recipe. Grouping like things together into these zones is known as a *categorical arrangement*. (Note: sorting things into zones, stacks, or piles is probably the most oft-used strategy for taming a lot of information.)

- How are the zones themselves organized? The placement and sequencing of the zones within the kitchen also suggests a *precedent-antecedent relationship*, such as the food prep area being placed to the left side of the cooktop while the spice zone is placed closest to the burner where the cooking pan is, to the right of the stovetop.

- By using the stovetop as a dividing line, you employ a *solid boundary* between zones.

- As you cut and add veggies into a mixing bowl, you're creating a *contained relationship*.

- Consider the placement of objects *within* each zone. You use *ordinal arrangement* (sorting things based on a rule) if you arrange spices in the order they'll be added, according to the recipe.

- As the spices are probably lined up along the kitchen counter, we could discuss how this uses a *horizontal sequence*.

- Perhaps you push the spice jars away as they're added to the pan, to indicate a change in state, that these spices have already been added. Pushing things away from your immediate line of sight follows the logic of *central-peripheral arrangement*, where things less important are placed farther away from your focal point.

A Shared Grammar

The point of this deconstruction is to highlight the kinds of things we naturally do, every day, to facilitate understanding—and *label* these patterns. As with written or verbal communication, the grammar is there, whether we're aware of it or not. The labels we use to describe how we use the space around us may not be shared or even agreed upon, but the patterns exist, regardless. The fact that we are embodied creatures, and that much of our thinking is rooted in language (which itself is embodied), suggests we can start to identify cultural, if not universal, patterns for how we use the space around us for understanding.

Consider the ubiquitous "bulls-eye" diagram. The fact that the most important things should go in the center seems obvious. But why? This center-outward organization is consistent with our sense of vision and how we see the world. Things at the center of our visual field are given attention and focus; things in the periphery are less important. As with the "taller things are stronger/better/greater" concept, this association is biological in nature.

But how we use space is also *culturally* dependent. Consider a horizontal line. The direction in which information increases tends to be culturally dependent, showing correlation with reading order (reading words left to right in Western cultures, or vice versa in Arabic cultures). When an abstract concept such as time is presented horizontally, Western cultures agree that we move into the future as we move to the right.

Still other concepts—abstractions with no literal mapping—may have no constant. When we ask folks to place time on a vertical line, the responses are inconsistent, and entirely dependent on prior associations. With something like Apple's Time Machine backup, the past is "up" or in the background, like going back through files in a file cabinet. But if we're reading a newsfeed, the newest stories get placed at the top, with older things getting pushed down. Worse yet, the newest comments on that same article get added to the bottom of the page! (And even these observations overlook the dynamic rules that

sort things based on algorithms, which consider recency as only one of a constellation of inputs.) This inconsistency in no way undermines our grammar
perspective, but merely reminds us that all meaning is based on prior associations (the entirety of Part 2, "How We Understand by Associations") and
abstract concepts will often have no clear or consistent match with literal
representations.

Does this all mean that there's no point in understanding the visual language
used to arrange things in space? No. As we learned with colors, many things
we think of as absolute are socially constructed. Just as different cultures may
arrive at a different vocabulary for describing colors, we may—within a social
group—end up with a slightly different way to think about how we use space.
But within our social group, except for the entirely new or abstract concepts,
there's a high likelihood we all share the same visual language.

An Exploration of Time

Because time is an abstraction, it can be represented in many different ways.
Consequently, it's a useful concept to explore *different* ways to apply the visual
grammar we're suggesting in this chapter.

A CRITICAL LOOK AT THE COMMON CLOCK

Consider the common clock, the kind that hangs on the walls of many schools
and offices:

When you reduce a clock to its fundamental visual elements, there are two elements at play: *interval sequencing* and *circular arrangement*.

With interval sequencing, things are arranged on an ordered scale, with meaningful uniform spacing. The resulting scale will have fixed and defined intervals. Tracking time is essentially about placing a marker somewhere along a ruled line (interval sequence).

Actually, we've done this twice: once for hours and once for minutes. Sometimes a third time, if we include seconds. It just so happens that these scales are overlaid on top of each other.

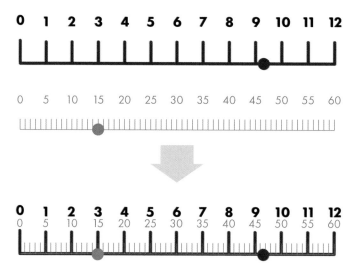

That's the ruler part of representing time.

So why then are these scales wrapped in a circular pattern?

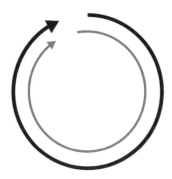

What is the significance of folding these scales into a continuous, never-ending circle? Simple. *Circular arrangement* is good for representing continuous, repetitive cycles. Time. Seasons. Anything that repeats in essentially the same way—with little to no fundamental changes. (For things that are ever-changing, such as a repetitive, creative process that eventually has a conclusion, we'd opt for a *spiral* representation.) In a flat, 2D space, this circular arrangement manifests as a watch face or a clock on the wall.

But the concept presented here, that time repeats itself in a circular arrangement or repeating loop, could also lead us to imagine a futuristic wristband where "time" is continuously orbiting around your wrist (see Figure 9.1).

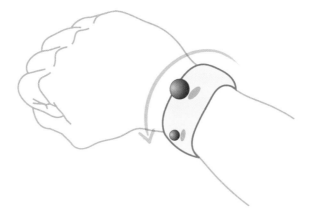

FIGURE 9.1 A concept sketch for an imagined watch, where balls magnetically orbit the circumference of the wristband.

While the final form might be different, the underlying visual concepts are fundamentally the same.

WHEN TIME STOPS AND STARTS

We've learned that a flat, ruler-like representation of time would feel odd. Having time reach the "end" of a scale, to then return to the beginning, like the carriage return of an old typewriter, is conceptually challenging. A ruler-like representation of time might suggest specific "start" and "end" points, where none were intended. For a clock then, with an unspecified use, you'd want a representation that was continuous and never-ending. Generally speaking, time is a concept with no universally defined start and stop point.

And yet …

When a social group agrees upon defined start-and-stop points, such as the "9 to 5" work hours held by many organizations, then arranging things in a noncircular pattern suddenly makes sense. Consider the normative workweek calendar, where even the software comes with defaults that discourage scheduling meetings outside of "normal" work hours.

THE REDESIGNED CALENDAR

This stop-start view of time seems to work in context when planning a week. But let's use this same logic to examine—critically—how we commonly break out months in calendars. When planning our calendar at this high level (say planning a team meeting), we naturally think in terms of "the next several days or weeks." We look out ahead into the distance. Time races out in front of us. And yet, if it's the end of the month, we've somehow become accustomed to arbitrary splitting of things up by months. It could be the 29th of a month, but we're somehow okay with flipping back and forth between "this month" and "next month," whether it's a paper calendar or different screens in an interface. Is there an alternative? For this kind of high-level planning, consider the *continuous* year-long calendar, as shown in Figure 9.2.

Sometime around 2015, out of sheer necessity, I (Stephen) started planning my time using a continuous, yearlong calendar view. This view helped me gain a significantly better sense of time, travel plans, and potential issues. By removing the arbitrary breaks at the end of a month, I'm no longer surprised by events that are a lot closer together than I might think. Another notable feature here is how my weeks start on a Monday and end on a Sunday. As most family events—like a weekend campout—would naturally span Saturday and Sunday, shifting my weeks such that these two days were neighbors, helped me see a single event represented once, rather than broken into two units, one at the end of a row, the other at the beginning. At the time of this screenshot, my attention was roughly split between work, professional (nonwork) events, and family commitments. The color coding of each allows me to quickly assess the nature of different events. All in all, these kinds of subtle shifts have made this a preferable planning tool for high-level commitments.

	Mon	Tue	Wed	Thu	Fri	Sat	Sun	
	8	9	10	11	12	13	14	
	15	16	17	18	19	**20**	21	World IA Day (2/20)
	22	23	24	25	26	27	28	
	29	1	2	3	4	5	6	
March	7	8	9	**10**	11	12	13	UIE Virtual Seminar (3/10; out part of day)
	14	**15**	**16**	**17**	**18**	19	20	GDC - Training (3/13 — 3/19)
	21	22	23	24	25	26	27	
	28	29	30	31	1	2	3	
April	4	5	6	7	8	9	10	
	11	**12**	13	14	15	16	17	Dallas Startup Week (4/12; out part of day)
	18	19	20	21	22	23	24	
	25	26	27	28	29	30	1	Mike's 40th Bday party (April 30)
May	2	3	4	5	6	7	8	IA Summit (5/4 — 5/9)
	9	10	11	12	13	14	15	Court of Honor (5/10) / Erin gone Th 5/12 — M 5/16
	16	17	18	19	20	21	22	Travel to Palo Alto (5/17 — 5/20)
	23	24	25	26	27	28	29	
	30	31	1	2	3	4	5	
June	6	7	8	9	10	11	12	UX Sofia — Bulgaria (6/6 — 6/14)
	13	14	15	16	17	18	19	
	20	21	22	23	24	25	26	
	27	28	29	30	1	2	3	
July	4	5	6	7	8	9	10	
	11	12	13	14	15	16	17	
	18	19	20	21	22	23	24	
	25	26	27	28	29	30	31	
August	1	2	3	4	5	6	7	
	8	9	10	11	12	13	14	UX Week — San Francisco (8/8 — 8/12)
	15	16	17	18	19	20	21	
	22	23	24	25	26	27	28	
	29	30	31	1	2	3	4	
September	5	6	7	8	9	10	11	Big Design Conference — Dallas (9/8 — 9/10)
	12	13	14	15	16	17	18	Creative Mornings (9/16)
	19	20	21	22	23	24	25	
	26	27	28	29	30	1	2	Delight Conference, Seattle - Not confirmed
October	3	4	5	6	7	8	9	
	10	11	12	13	**14**	15	16	Creative Mornings Oct 14

FIGURE 9.2 A continuous year-long calendar for long-range planning.

At this point, you could point out that ending in December and starting over in January violates this continuous flow of time. Bravo! You're correct. In a digital format, we'd make this flat, one-year calendar continuous and never-ending. But planning in terms of a calendar *year* has not been problematic, mostly due to winter holidays that form a natural stop-start point, which is generally agreed upon by Western culture. Stopping and starting once a year is acceptable; doing this twelve times a year, not so much! If you're really paying attention, you might point out that time is broken at the end of every Mon-Sun week. Yes. But this has been an acceptable trade-off, given the infrequent number of events that span from a Sunday into the next, new week.

If we can begin to look at our world through the lens of these kinds of spatial elements, then we see not only how things function, but also how they might be improved. In short, we become critical of how space is used to hold or convey meaning.

And that's the point of all this, to think critically and be intentional about how we use space to facilitate understanding. To put a fine point on this, let's return to the kitchen …

Up-Leveling Our Use of Space (A Return to the Kitchen)

As with an understanding of a language's grammar, these natural skills at using space can be improved. Experts in the kitchen become more skilled than nonexperts; this is true of many skills, including the effective use of immediate surroundings. Professional chefs, who must be intentional about cooking, will talk about the importance of mise en place, a French phrase meaning "to put in place." Great care is taken to gather and arrange all the tools and ingredients needed for cooking. But it's more than just food prep. According to *The New Professional Chef*, a textbook from the Culinary Institute of America:

> Mise en place means far more than simply assembling all the ingredients, pots and pans, plates, and serving pieces needed for a particular period. Mise en place is also a state of mind. Someone who has truly grasped the concept is able to keep many tasks in mind simultaneously, weighing and assigning each its proper value and priority.[2]

2. Donovan, Mary Deirdre. 1996. *The New Professional Chef*. New York: Wiley.

This ability to "keep many tasks in mind simultaneously" correlates with research into the use of immediate surroundings as a cognitive space. The thread throughout this book has been about the cost of understanding, who bears that cost, and how to shift that cost around. When we extend information into our immediate surroundings, the space around us becomes a structure for holding information, which, in turn, reduces the individual cost of understanding. By using space in an intelligent way, we extend our cognitive abilities. This is true whether we're making marks on a cave wall, stacking piles of bills to be paid by the door, or pivoting between views in a complex computer simulation.

This use of space to hold meaning and aid in performing tasks is a topic that researcher David Kirsh has been investigating, with research that, coincidentally, extends into the kitchen. In his classic paper "The Intelligent Use of Space,"[3] Kirsh shares a study where he asked subjects to prepare a veggie platter.

> The placement problem our cook faced was to apportion ingredients in a uniform manner. This required either elaborate planning beforehand, recall of similar case experience, or online tracking of the relative number of remaining slices.

What Kirsh called out throughout this particular paper were the differences between how experts and novices approach a task, with comments on how they structure the space around them to support each task. With examples ranging from chopping vegetables to playing chess, a pattern emerges.

When faced with a complicated challenge, subjects responded with either elaborate planning, a recall of similar experiences, or an intelligent use of space. With the subjects who were asked to prepare a veggie tray, the addition of an elliptical platter made this a new challenge. According to Kirsh:

> Having never worked with an elliptical platter this size, our cook had no ready case knowledge to call on. Nor was she eager to count items and measure the circumference of the platter, a step she would perform if planning. Instead she relied on tracking the remaining slices and her moment by moment adaptive skills.

Where novices tend to arrange veggies into piles, before transferring them to the platter, the expert did something different: she arranged the slices

---

3. Kirsh, David. 1995. "The Intelligent Use of Space." *Artificial Intelligence* 73 (1–2): 31–68. https://doi.org/10.1016/0004-3702(94)00017-u

into "well ordered, neatly separated rows." Rows are easier to estimate and compare than piles, something we saw in the previous chapters with visual encodings. This approach made it easier to figure out how to distribute things when making the platter. The key piece of understanding here is this: *estimation of length is easier and more reliable than estimation of area or volume.* This example should bring to mind our earlier examples of how we're better and worse at different kinds of visual estimations. With this example, you may notice that we're expanding our visual grammar to include the "visual encodings" described in Chapter 7. Visual encodings and the use of space to hold meaning all fit together, as we'll demonstrate next.

Before we show how all this fits together (including a structured way to think about the use of space), let's address some beliefs and mindsets that prevent many folks from practicing the kind of visual thinking we're exploring here.

Three Barriers That Hold Back Visual Thinking

In our experience, we've observed three barriers that keep most people from practicing this kind of widespread visual thinking. None of these barriers stem from a lack of understanding, but rather a struggle to translate existing skills that are natural in one domain (say, organizing a closet or pantry) to another domain, such as sketching an abstract concept. This, and a simple lack of practice and acute awareness. The three barriers we've observed are as follows:

- **Barrier #1:** Transferring skills at sorting things into sorting abstractions
- **Barrier #2:** An over-reliance on a few, existing models
- **Barrier #3:** Recognizing how visual models reveal information

Barrier #1: Transferring Skills at Sorting Things into Sorting Abstractions

While the ability to use space in meaningful ways is a natural skill, we (the authors) have discovered an interesting disconnect: most of us have no problem organizing *physical* objects, such as clothing or books. However, ask most people to apply these very same skills to abstract concepts, such as health insurance or theological worldviews, and it's a struggle. It's difficult for most people to make the connection between how they organize laundry and how they organize their thoughts. People are somewhat better with *quantified* concepts such as calories burned during a physical activity, or budgets and spending, but this is likely because numbers themselves are perceived as more tangible. But we (people) struggle to represent ideas. *We struggle with abstractions.*

Scott Berinato, an editor at *Harvard Business Review* and author of *Good Charts* illustrates this distinction with a model of, well … models!

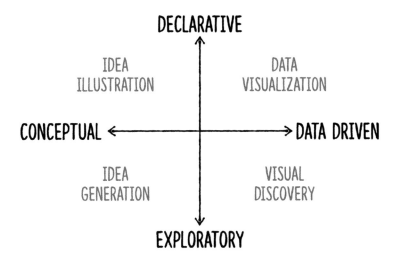

In this X-Y matrix, representations can be understood based on two dimensions:

- Is this more declarative or exploratory?
- Is this more conceptual or data-driven?

This simple graph highlights one of the fundamental holes when it comes to much of the literature on charts, diagrams, visualizations, and so on: most of the literature and online tutorials are concerned with things that are data-driven. *Grab your numeric data. Plug this into one of these charts. Voilà!* Far fewer books are dedicated to models that are conceptual in nature. For these matters, books such as Dan Roam's *Back of the Napkin* or Sunni Brown's *The Doodle Revolution* are helpful in this respect.

That said, if we pause and look around, we are surrounded by concept models of all types.

In Berinato's model, things are sorted based on two dimensions. Depending on the specific scenario, this kind of two-dimensional model can be represented in a few different ways:

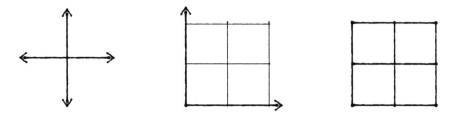

Specific instances of this two-dimensional model show up in everything from Gartner Groups' Magic Quadrant to marketing tools such as the SWOT (Strengths, Weaknesses, Opportunities, Threats) analysis. And it's not just two dimensions. The business world is rich with visual tools that have been created to help leaders organize and evaluate otherwise abstract concepts (see Figure 9.3). PowerPoint decks and analyst reports are brimming with matrices, continuums, swim lanes, "fishbone" diagrams, and more—all intended to convey a lot of information in a way that facilitates understanding.

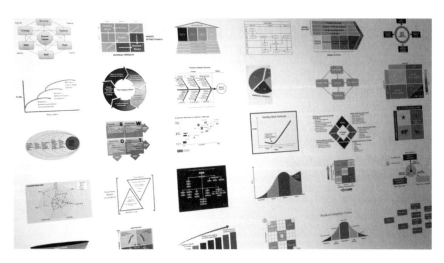

FIGURE 9.3 A collage of many different models, diagrams, and charts commonly used in business settings.

Indeed, hybrid models exist as well. If the two dimensions of a matrix are too simplistic for analysis, representations such as the Strategy Canvas allow you to compare a small number of competitors along a longer list of differentia-tors. This mixes qualitative attributes (identified competitive differentiators) with a quantitative assessment (ranking on a numeric scale).

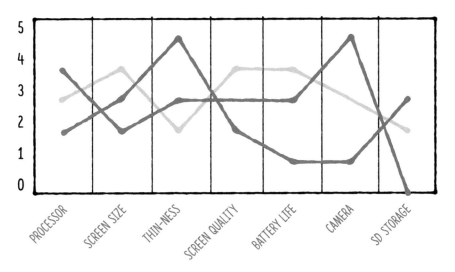

VISUAL THINKING FOR PERSONAL MATTERS

But it's not just the business world that uses visual models. In school, we're given tools to help us think more clearly. From grade school, we're all familiar with the classic Venn diagram:

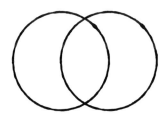

We also pick up simple tools to help us make difficult choices, like drawing two columns and listing pros/cons in each.

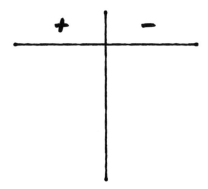

It's also becoming more common to teach young students how to create bubble diagrams (also known as *concept maps*) as a pre-research way of exploring what they know and might learn about a subject:

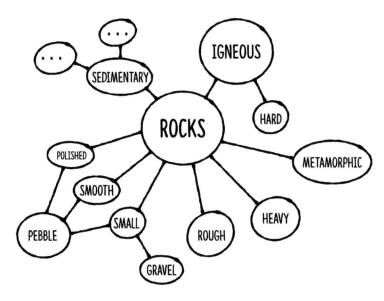

We could go on naming more models that we use. We could even spend some time classifying these models: charts and diagrams, data visualizations, abstract patterns, models, templates, frameworks, concept models, canvases, etc. The bigger takeaway here is how these models each use space to hold and clarify *concepts* (vs. numeric data).

So how can we become more comfortable using models to represent concepts?

1. **Curate models.** Simply by surrounding ourselves with a small collection of these ready-to-use models, and by becoming aware of the conceptual models we already use, this is a great way to begin thinking in a more structured way about abstractions.

2. **Use analogies.** Analogies are useful in that they connect the abstract to the familiar, often tangible, objects and experiences. Simple questions such as *How is this like _____?* (especially when repeated with multiple comparisons) help us see an idea from different vantage points. Play this out, and something like a company's org chart becomes little more than a branching tree-like structure. What if we asked other questions, such as *How is an organization like our body's cell structure?* or *How is our maintaining a company similar to surfing?*

3. **Identify the information units.** For any problem of understanding, we typically start by identifying our units of information. When working with numbers, this step has already been done for us. If anything, we only have to ensure that we're comparing like numbers (currency with currency, for example). With concepts, the added step of translating fuzzy and immaterial ideas into a material unit of information we can then work with is often where people falter. We've seen success simply by calling out that this is a step that can't be skipped.

Once you see that you can represent abstract ideas as easily as concrete things, you are empowered to do so.

Barrier #2: An Over-Reliance on a Few, Existing Models

In presenting all these concept models, there's a catch that is rarely articulated. Look back and see if you can spot what all of these examples share in common.

The examples listed previously are all tools *we use.* They exist. We use them. We employ a pre-existing visual model to help us with a complex or complicated topic. This is the level of comfort most people have with visual thinking. *Did you encounter a challenging idea? Try organizing your thoughts with one of these templates!* To be clear, there is nothing wrong with this approach, and it may be all you ever need. Not everything needs to be built from scratch. But consider how you learn to cook by following a recipe, or write adhering to a rigid five-paragraph essay format. These are fine to start with, but as you get better at cooking and writing (or using visual models), you should begin to recognize patterns and feel free to experiment and try out your own ideas.

We see a great number of young professionals eager to know the "right way" to do things, whether that *thing* is creating an artifact such as a customer journey map or defining the ideal process for their product team. While there are certainly nuanced details and best practices to follow, we must never forget that many of the artifacts and tools we use are simply inventions that originated within a particular set of circumstances, inventions that can and should be adjusted when used elsewhere. Even authors who publish books or share their ideas in training courses will continue to iterate and improve what they're sharing, as they discover new things.

This learning mindset then, when applied to how you use space, is what empowers you to do things like grab salt-and-pepper shakers to create an ad hoc visual representation. With our opening example, there wasn't a model already in place, waiting to be filled with information. Instead, that was a visual model created in the moment, to support that particular conversation.

This kind of thinking also paves the way for all kinds of visual models that aren't intended as templates (or even based on templates), but rather are one-off explanations for otherwise difficult topics. Consider this illustration in Figure 9.4, which was created by New York designer Chris Fahey.

It's easy to imagine Fahey at a bar with friends, and the perennial question comes up: "So, what is the difference between rye, bourbon, and Scotch whisky?" With an intimate knowledge of the subject, Chris goes on to explain things as simply as possible, with a crude but effective visual model that reveals similarities and crucial differences in the distillation and fermentation process. Again, no fancy graphic design skills were required. Rather, by identifying the different kinds of whiskey, and lining up the process of producing each, we can quite literally "see" similarities and differences in the processes that produce each drink. Fahey has, in the moment, created a visual explanation, to answer a very specific question; the ability to do so stemmed from deep expertise with the topic and experience using and creating models of all sorts.

We can use the tools given to us, but creating an original visual model, whether to explain whiskies or translate street signs (as you'll see in Chapter 14, "A Critical Look at Tools and Technologies for Understanding"), doesn't come naturally for most people. We're impressed by these visual models because we didn't come up with them, and we marvel at the skills required to think in this visual way. But here's the truth: the skills required to think in this visual way are in no way mystical or beyond mere mortals. It is a learned skill, like any other, that may come naturally for some people, while still others require practice and instruction. But make no mistake: visual thinking is a literacy. We can all think in this way, if we understand the language being used. And once you recognize existing models as recipes, you are empowered to create your own new models.

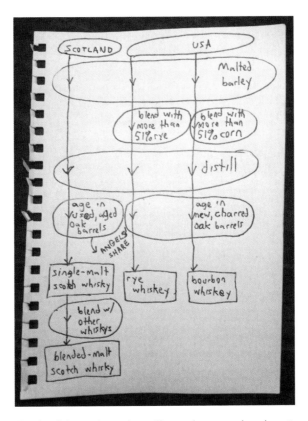

FIGURE 9.4 This sketch from Chris Fahey offers a clear, visual explanation of the similarities and differences between blended-malt Scotch whisky, rye whiskey, and bourbon whiskey.[4]

4. Note the whisky/whiskey difference in spelling. *Whisky* usually denotes Scotch whisky and Scotch-inspired liquors, and *whiskey* denotes the Irish and American liquors. We'll use the "whiskey" spelling (with an "e") to refer to all these liquors.

Barrier #3: Recognizing How Visual Models Reveal Information

From sticky notes on the wall to better street signs, what all of these examples have in common is that they arrange information in order to *reveal patterns*.

When we off-load information into the world, there's less we have to retain in memory; we create something others can respond to. But much of the understanding depends on how exactly we represent this information in the world. Are we comparing things? Showing a sequence? Representing relationships in a system?[5] In short: Are we *revealing patterns* that would otherwise go unnoticed? Simply off-loading information out of our heads and into the world is immensely helpful. But this chapter is about more than externalizing information—it's also about arranging that information to reveal patterns. (Note, it's not just the final arrangement, the thing seen or shared, that reveals patterns; the process of getting there—the act of arranging and rearranging information—is also a way to reveal patterns. The next section is devoted to interactions, such as these.)

To illustrate this point, that these visual models reveal patterns, let's return once more to our concept of time. In Figure 9.5, you see two different renderings of the same conference schedule.

The information in each visual is identical, save for one critical difference: the first example uses ordinal arrangement (sorting things on a rule, in this case *time*) to list out events, whereas the second example uses interval arrangement to line up events on a schedule. Look at what's different in each representation. The first version lists the information, but we're left to sort out overlaps and durations between sessions; the second version makes this information explicit, freeing us up to make judgments about which sessions we'd like to attend.

By arranging information in a very intentional way, we reveal patterns that might otherwise go unseen or require extra work to sort out and then hold in memory.

To drive this point home, we (the authors) often open our workshops with a simple game, drawn from Don Norman's book *Things That Make Us Smart*.

---

5. Gray, Dave. 2017. "Organizing Things." Medium. The XPLANE Collection. April 12, 2017. https://medium.com/the-xplane-collection/organizing-things-1dbc6faf5d79

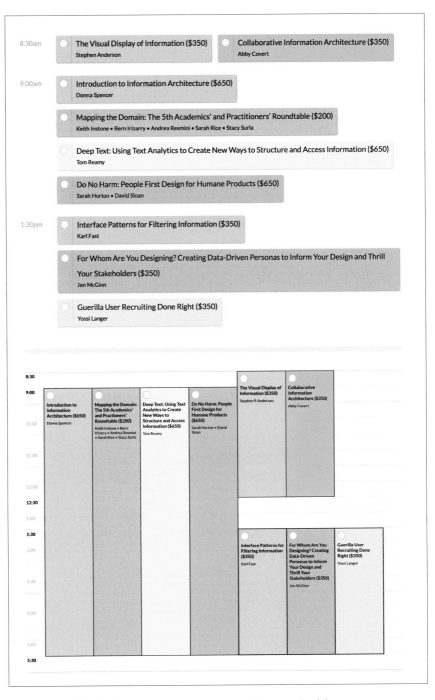

FIGURE 9.5 Two different ways to represent a conference schedule.

Participants are instructed to pair up with a partner, before being handed a sheet of paper with the numbers 1 through 9 *listed* on a sheet of paper. They are then instructed to take turns selecting numbers from the list (crossing off each number once it has been selected). The winner is the first person to have chosen exactly three numbers that add up to 15. For example, if player A selected 9, 6, 2 and player B selected 3, 8, 4 then player B would win because 3 + 8 + 4 = 15.

Typically, there's a wee bit of confusion over the instructions and a lot of hilarity playing the game. And almost always, there's a winner in this first version of the game.

We then tell participants that they are going to play a second game, for which we provide a board known as the "3 x 3 magic square" (see Figure 9.6). What's remarkable about this square is how the rows, columns, and diagonals all add up to 15; moreover, every way of writing 15 as the sum of three numbers from 1 to 9 is represented. This game plays exactly like the first game—the winner is the first person to have chosen exactly three numbers that add up to 15— except when one player chooses a number, they draw an X over it; when the other player chooses a number, they circle it.

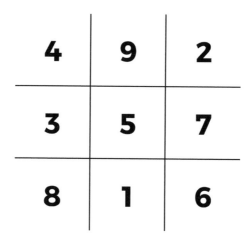

FIGURE 9.6 The "magic square" where the rows, columns, and diagonals all add up to 15.

This second game should be familiar: it's essentially *tic-tac-toe* (also known as *noughts and crosses* or *Xs and Os*). Not surprising, folks always find this second game much easier to play (with far more "draws" where there is no winner!). Why is this? Why is this game of identifying three numbers that add up to 15 so much easier to play when the numbers are arranged into a magic square? Simply stated: tic-tac-toe is *a model that reveals patterns more easily*. This is known as an *isomorph*, where the information presented in each case is equivalent; however, as we pointed out, the representation of the magic square affords greater perceptual understanding.

At this point, we've written a lot about information in the head, as opposed to information in the world, but this simple example with tic-tac-toe makes the value of this distinction abundantly clear. Arranging information into an external representation—one that supports the perceptual recognition of patterns—helps us create understanding more efficiently and effectively.

The first step is getting information onto the page—writing out the numbers one through nine was helpful to relieve our limited, working memory. Imagine having to play the first game without the visual aid of paper, with each player mentally tracking which numbers they had selected! Writing down the numbers one through nine is an external representation (and an incredibly helpful way to track which numbers have been selected), but it is only by *arranging* those numbers in a way that adds up to 15 that we are able to spot a *pattern* that otherwise would remain unseen.

> *Solving a problem simply means representing a problem so as to make the solution transparent.*
>
> —HERBERT SIMON

We off-load information out of our heads and into the world all the time, scribbling notes in a journal being a prime example. But the kind of off-loading we're concerned with in this chapter is the kind where we use spatial arrangement and rearrangement to reveal new patterns, discover relationships, and create insights. Once you see models as revealing patterns, you'll be looking for instances where there are relationships that are not being shown.

Of course, each of these barriers points the way to what's next: the underlying patterns behind all visual representations and the elemental pieces that—in various combinations—make these models unique. Given the grounding we've established thus far, let's turn our attention to how we might begin developing our visual literacy.

A Universal Pattern Behind All Visual Models

At this point, we've mentioned everything from sticky notes on a wall to a simple model for understanding hard spirits to the ways we arrange ingredients on our countertops. While these examples are all quite different from each other, they all draw upon *a common set of visual elements*. Much like the written language has letters, sounds, and grammar, so does our visual language.

In Figure 9.7, we've provided a list of the 30 or so identified spatial elements, grouped into their respective categories. That said, the goal of this section is not to go over each and every element—that's content better suited for a workshop or a toolkit than a book format. Rather, we want to focus on the overall organizing structure. It's a bit overwhelming at first, but by the end of this chapter, this diagram should make complete sense. And once understood at this broad level, you'll have the mental scaffolding to begin recognizing a universal pattern common to all visual representations, and perhaps just enough guidance to begin arranging things in space with intention.

From Substrate to Placement and Territories

The best place to begin is with a simple illustration. Let's suppose that you have a map of the world. On this map, you've placed pushpins in all the places you'd like to visit or perhaps have already visited.

Objects

The things, concepts, or
objects being arranged

Placement

How objects are placed or arranged
relative to other objects

ARRANGMENT

- Categorical Arrangement
- Ordinal Sequencing
- Interval Sequencing
- Ratio Sequencing

SEQUENCE

- Direction: Vertical
- Direction: Horizontal
- Central-Peripheral
- Circular
- Spiral
- Diagonal

Territory

How to define the places represented
by this arrangement

BOUNDARIES:

- Bounded Set
- Fuzzy Set
- Centered Set

SHAPES

- Geometric
- Literal-Symbolic
- Figurative

RELATIONSHIPS

- Connected
- Contained
- Adjacent
- Common / Overlap
- Precedent/Antecedent

VISUAL TREATMENTS

- Implied Similarity
- Connection Strength
- Implied Direction
- Symmetry

- Evolution/ Transformation
- Distortion / Fisheye
- Magnify
- Relative Size

- Depth/Form
- Distance
- Distortion
- Curvature

FIGURE 9.7 A simple way to organize many different visual elements.

The pushpins in this illustration are *objects* and the map itself is the *substrate*. Phrased another way, a substrate is the base layer upon which objects are placed. Venn diagrams, scatter plots, geographic maps, and so forth are all substrates. This object-substrate approach is well documented in the information visualization world. However, for what follows, we're going to take things a bit further: let's split the concept of a substrate in two. Let's talk instead about the *placement* of objects in relation to each other and the resulting *territories* suggested or clarified by our arrangement.

Distinguishing Between Objects, Placement, and Territory

For any spatial representation, we can discuss these three core concepts:

- **Objects:** The things, concepts, or objects being arranged
- **Placement:** How these objects are placed or arranged relative to other objects
- **Territory:** How to define the places represented by this arrangement

This distinction between object, placement, and territory is important, because not everything is as simple as a pin on a map, not everything starts with an existing substrate onto which you place an object. In the process of creating a map or diagram (especially if doing so from scratch), you may need to do the work of arranging objects in order to arrive at the resulting map.

To make this distinction clear, and to show how this model shows up in all manner of cases, let's explore six examples, each chosen to highlight a different aspect of this three-part model.

TIC-TAC-TOE

Let's return to our tic-tac-toe example.

When we place marks on a page (our X's and O's) each of these marks is an *object* in an imaginary game space. An X or an O is a symbolic representation, indicating which player made that mark. (In terms of visual encodings, we are using iconography to indicator players.)

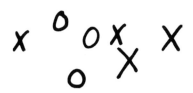

We arrange these marks relative to each other, in a way that has meaning. This is called *placement*. Within the game space that is tic-tac-toe, these objects are arranged into a row in any direction (vertical, horizontal, or diagonal), along an understood grid, in order to win the game.

We could certainly play this game without this grid drawn beforehand, but that would present challenges. To clarify this placement within the game space, we define *territory* by adding clear boundaries.

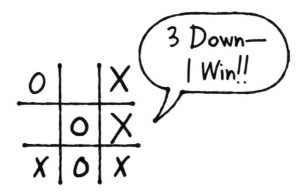

For a typical game of tic-tac-toe, we place our respective marks into a pre-existing game board. *Objects Placed into Territories.*

A DIRTY EXAMPLE

If you're sorting a pile of dirty laundry to be washed, each clothing item—socks, underwear, t-shirts, jeans, and so on—is an "object." These objects all have different attributes: size, color, material, etc. How dirty are they? Do they have any stains? What are the brand names? Writing on the tag might indicate to whom these shorts belong. We could go on. As this is not an exhaustive taxonomy project, most of these attributes are irrelevant for the purpose of washing clothes. In practice, these "objects" are typically arranged in one of two ways: we either organize into piles based on the owner ("I'm not washing *his* clothes!"), or to prevent stains, we separate things into lights, darks, and colors. When we create three piles of clothing—one for lights, one for darks, and one for colors—we're using spatial arrangement (specifically *categorical groupings*) or *placement*; each *place* is defined by one of the three piles, and hopefully the unique reason for each pile is self-evident.

Note, there is no predefined territory. The groupings are a result of how things are organized—there is no visible substrate. The spatial meaning goes away when the piles are removed. That said, if we wanted this organizational structure to *persist*, we might introduce laundry hampers, one for lights, one for darks, and one for colors.

Whether empty or full, these laundry hampers now form a substrate. We've defined "placement" in an otherwise open space where forms with a certain attribute should be placed; the laundry hampers are labeled "territories" waiting to be filled with "objects" (dirty laundry!).

It's a simple example, but it's this perspective that empowers us to later pick up a pen and explain more complicated topics. From how we use space to hold meaning, there's very little difference between three laundry bins and more complicated matrices and concept models.

ORGANIZING PEOPLE

Let's take on a topic much more nuanced and complex, if only to show how this simple pattern persists. If we pull way out and take a broader view of how societies and nations have formed throughout history, we see these same visual components and patterns: people (objects) gather or grow into tribal groups (placement) who later define natural or agreed-upon boundaries (territory).

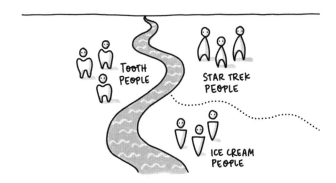

If we stick with this people as "objects" association, there are many other ways to think about placement and territories.

We can organize people based on something *literal*, such as sorting people by height. Or we can sort people by something *conceptual*, like student grades, emotional well-being, or employee performance. The popular 9-Boxes model assesses employees based on potential and performance, before placing people into one of nine boxes.

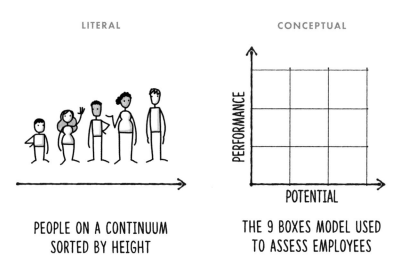

Whether we're talking about laundry or civilizations, the fundamental concepts are the same: *objects, placement, territory.*

ORGANIZING PROJECTS

Let's turn to something more familiar and tactical: *visual management.* If we look at how we use sticky notes to manage a team or project, we see the same concepts, as shown in Figure 9.8.

FIGURE 9.8 A basic Kanban board with columns for things To-Do, Doing, and Done.

The sticky notes, each having a task scribbled on them, are the *objects.* We use *placement* to cluster tasks, by things like type, urgency, completion status, assignee, and so on. And finally, we define *territory* by the addition of lines and labels. This is, in many respects, like our game of tic-tac-toe. We have a predefined territory waiting to hold objects. However, a key difference here would be that the rows and columns are endowed with meaning: which box you place something into indicates something—usually status and project. These project boards can be very simple, or very complex, like the one in Figure 9.9.

Regardless of the complexity, in all cases we see the pattern of objects, placement, and territory.

FIGURE 9.9 A much more complex project board.

VISUALIZING DATA

Even with something more complex like a data visualization, you can identify these same components. Consider the popular Gapminder visualization, pioneered by Swedish physician, academic, and public speaker Hans Rosling (see Figure 9.10).

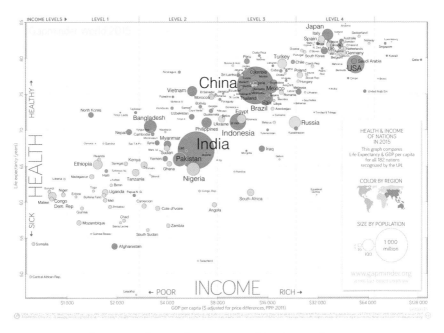

FIGURE 9.10 The Gapminder visualization created by Hans Rosling.

Each of the circles (here representing a nation) is an object. You might notice how the visual encodings of size and scale are applied to each circle, to convey additional information. In this case, placement isn't within an *area* (as with all of the previous examples), but rather at a specific *point* along an X-Y matrix. Territory is defined along a very precise scale. If we wanted to add predefined areas, we could add in shaded regions to define different areas.

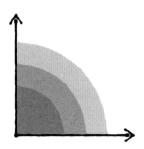

PATTERNS IN GAMES

Finally, to keep things interesting, let's turn our attention to board games. Board games, in particular, make rich use of visual information. From the iconography that adorns many cards to the affordances suggested by the bits and pieces, these games are wonderful little puzzles to figure out. If you happen upon two people playing a card game you've never seen before, it will be difficult to figure out exactly what's going on, if only because you don't know the rules. However, if you watch people play long enough, you can learn a bit about the game based solely on how things are placed and the meaning this holds for the players (see Figure 9.11).

Which cards belong to which player? Why are some cards rotated 90º? What does the color coding mean? Why are some cards in stacks while others aren't? To the uninitiated, it can be quite confusing. However, watch long enough or learn the rules of the game, and it all makes sense. Some of the games we (the authors) have played have a visual language that rivals the most elegant data visualization.

FIGURE 9.11 A game of Star Realms.

To link this example back to our three-part concept, look at the photo in Figure 9.11. Each individual card is an object, with unique identifying properties. These cards can be played in specified areas, implicitly understood by the experienced players (placement). And while territory is often understood by players, it's become more common in recent years to supplement these kinds of card games with playmats, which make the playing areas explicit.

OBJECTS	PLACEMENT	TERRITORIES
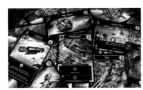		
INDIVIDUAL PLAYING CARDS EACH HAVE UNIQUE PROPERTIES	CARDS ARE PLAYED IN SPECIFIC AREAS, IMPLICITLY UNDERSTOOD BY PLAYERS	PLAYMATS CAN BE USED TO MAKE THE PLAYING AREAS EXPLICIT

It is worth noting a difference between this card game example and that of tic-tac-toe. With a game like tic-tac-toe, the game begins with a predefined territory, into which players place their objects. With this card example, territory is implicitly understood by players without needing to be explicitly defined. In all cases, the same three components are present, even if some components aren't readily seen.

What the Objects, Placement, Territories Model Unlocks

This simple idea of *Objects Placed into Territories* is universal to all the ways we organize information in space. Whether our organization involves sorting laundry or looking for patterns in the human genome, our representations will be some combination of objects, placement, and territory.

Okay, so what? Why is this structure useful?

First, we start to see things—everything—a bit differently. (Will you ever look at laundry in the same way?)

Two, this paves the way for a more nuanced discourse about specific visual elements. With language, we learn about nouns and verbs so that we can move onto things like adjectives and transitive verbs. So, too, with this visual grammar. The simple idea of *Objects Placed into Territories* provides the mental scaffolding needed to consider the 30 or so specific elements related to spatial arrangement (at this point, it might be useful to refer back to Figure 9.7).

From a distance, this may all seem easy. However, once you get into the details of things, you'll encounter questions such as these:

How do you sort information on a scale? Is there a difference between using a vertical or horizontal line? What kinds of shapes should we use in order to define our territory? How should we represent boundaries between different regions? How might distorting our representation change the intended meaning?

This is where the structure—and understanding of all the elements— becomes helpful.

When we talk about placement, there are diverse ways to both *arrange* and *sequence* things. A discussion of territories presents us with *boundaries*, *shapes*, *relationships*, and the use of *visual properties*.

Let's go a bit deeper on each of these fundamental concepts:

OBJECTS

In the simplest terms, objects are the things—concepts or literal objects— being arranged. If we're shopping for a camera, the objects are represented by different makes and models of cameras. If we're planning a project, the objects are the individual tasks written on a sticky note. If we're assessing the population of countries over time, the objects are countries. In these problems of *comparison*, identifying the objects is a fairly straightforward task—it's the similar things arranged on a map of some kind. In Figure 9.12, the "objects" being compared are a variety of coffee bean options.

FIGURE 9.12 Shopping for coffee is a problem of comparison, where you are comparing "like" objects.

Identifying objects can be a bit more elusive when they are *parts* of a whole. In these cases, objects are dissimilar rather than similar. For example, comparing different roasts and blends of coffee beans is a very different problem than understanding how to brew the perfect cup of pour-over coffee (see Figure 9.13). These are both understanding problems that can benefit from a visual-spatial explanation. However, with this latter example, your objects are dissimilar things: the beans, water, brew method, time, grind size, and so on. This isn't a problem of comparison. Rather, this is a problem of *comprehension*, where you're arranging these objects in a system or flow to show how all the elementary parts relate to each other.

What you'll notice with the objects in most representations are the visual properties that differentiate them. Scale. Color. Size. Treatments. You may have noticed how in a previous chapter we used the treatment of a pin on a map to explain visual encodings. For instructional reasons, we (the authors) have found an easy mapping between objects and visual encodings.

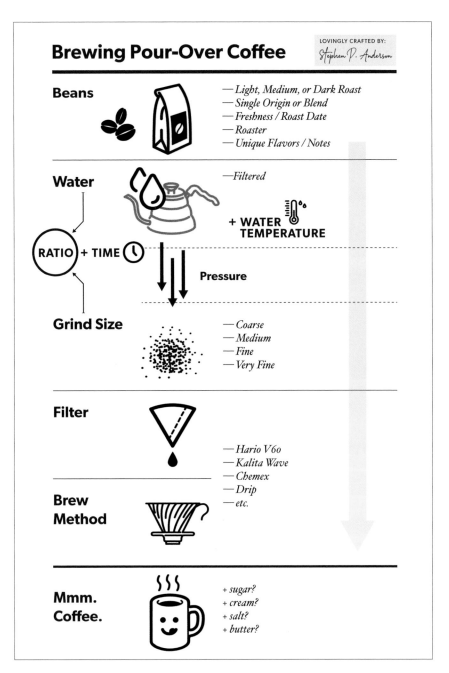

FIGURE 9.13 Understanding the coffee-brewing process is a problem of comprehension, where the objects in this case are dissimilar things. *Infographic by Stephen P. Anderson*

PLACEMENT

Placement is the arrangement of objects in relationship to each other. We often single out a particular attribute—the *colors* of our dirty laundry or the *age* of our children, for example—and we use this dimension to sort accordingly into groups, rows, stacks, grids, and so on. The cards in our poker hand. The pile of mail by the door. The stuff in our kitchen drawers. We use spatial *positioning* to hold and convey meaning. We arrange things. We sequence things. We place things in space. Remove the things themselves, and we're left with maps, timelines, categories, flows, scales, and other visual models— models waiting to hold information. And whether we're conscious of it or not, how we place things in space reflects our understanding (our internal representation) of the concepts we're organizing.

So then, how might we describe the way we place things in space? Broadly speaking, we can talk about two ideas: how we organize objects and how those objects are sequenced.

You've already seen some examples of how we can organize things, but for completeness, things can be organized in four ways:

- Into categories
- Based on a simple rule ("sort by price" or "closest to me")
- Placed onto a scale with fixed intervals (a ruler, temperature, time)
- Placed on a scale with ratio sequencing (with cases such as age or weight where there is an absolute zero start-or-end point).

In addition to different ways of arranging and sequencing things, we can also talk about *how* those things are sequenced—the shape of the sequence. We've seen a few of these, from the circular arrangement of the clock to the horizontal arrangement of spices on the kitchen counter. There are at least six ways we can sequence things, each with different associated meanings. These are: horizontally, vertically, in a spiral, in a circle, radiating out from a central focal point, and diagonally.

TERRITORY

Territory is how we define the places in space. We can arrange objects, which, in turn, suggests place, as with sorting dirty piles of laundry. We can also do the opposite: use territory to predefine the places, which may or may not be filled with objects, as with the labeled laundry bins that suggest where particular kinds of laundry should go. This last point is vital: the territory may be the result of placing things in space, or may be predefined places ready to hold different ideas. Many of the models, canvases, and diagrams we fill with specific information were first arrived at through the sorting and arrangement of many objects, which were later removed to create an empty container.

An exploration of territories presents us with four, broad kinds of considerations. They are, in no intended sequence: shape, boundaries, relationships, and the use of visual treatments. Each of these considerations in turn has any number of elements, which you can see listed in Figure 9.7.

"But Wait, What About …"

Throughout countless workshops and years of scrutiny, we've road-tested this Objects, Placement, Territories model, and it has held up with few to no exceptions. However, we have encountered a few things that might seem to break the pattern and do need clarification.

CLARIFICATION #1: CONCEPT MODELS

Concept models are a specific type of visual representation that varies widely in form but shares a common essential purpose: making difficult concepts and ideas easier to understand. We mention concept models specifically, as many of these seem to break the Objects-Placement-Territory pattern. A common question we hear concerning concept models, is "where are the objects?" Here are a few such examples shown in Figure 9.14 that have prompted this question.

With concept models, objects are often the bits and pieces—the mental scaffolding—used to arrive at a model; once the model is defined, those specific objects are removed, allowing other people to place their experiences onto the model. What's most important in the concept model is the resulting structure or system, which is tested and proven by placing different objects. Our whiskey example didn't need to identify every brand and type of liquor—it's a model (or classification system) upon which we could now place any specific brand of whiskey (or Scotch whisky!) that we are considering.

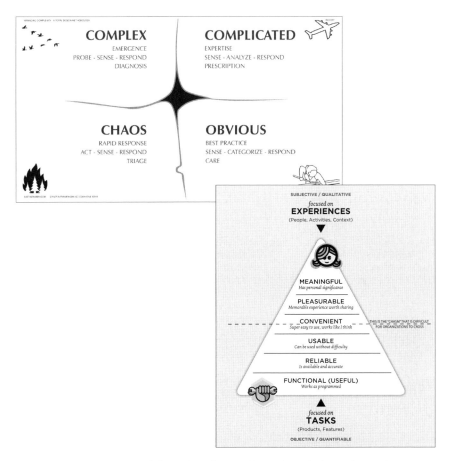

FIGURE 9.14 Concept models, such as the two shown, have led people to ask "where are the objects?" With concept models, objects are used to arrive at a model and then removed to reveal the underlying structure. *Top: Cynefin Framework (visual by Justin Tauber); bottom: User Experience Hierarchy of Needs by Stephen P. Anderson.*

CLARIFICATION #2: SMALL MULTIPLES AND CHARTS

We've mentioned that most concept models are essentially territories minus the objects. We also find the reverse to be true. Most of our simplest charting tools (pie charts, a single bar chart) are simply stand-alone objects. Where things get a bit tricky is with small multiples, where we repeat a series of simple charts or graphs (all using the same scale and axes), to enable an easy comparison of differences. This coffee infographic in Figure 9.15 is a great example of small multiples.

FIGURE 9.15 This infographic, created by Lokesh Dhakar, uses small multiples to illustrate the differences between various espresso drinks.

We are able to quickly distinguish between different espresso drinks because of subtle variations in how the designer represented each drink's composition. Note however, that the 3 x 3 arrangement of the different kinds of espresso drinks holds no meaning. We could rearrange these into other layouts—say a vertical 1 x 9 column—and no meaning would be lost. If we were to arrange these coffee illustrations by some rule: price, difficulty to make, historical creation—then (and only then) we'd be introducing a substrate upon which things were organized.

CLARIFICATION #3: RECURSION—OBJECTS CAN BE SUBSTRATES FOR OTHER OBJECTS

For purposes of explanation, we've simplified things into *Objects Placed into Territories*. A pin on a map. Students placed into a gradebook. But these are building blocks. Things can get more complicated and *recursive*, where the object on a substrate is itself a substrate with ever more narrowly defined objects. In other words, some objects function *recursively* as substrates for other objects. A situation in which you see sets and subsets of things might be an example of this recursive pattern. We often see this with more complicated Gantt and project planning charts, where you might have projects within projects, or a row per team that is then subdivided into more rows per team member or task. When booking a flight online (see Figure 9.16), each flight option is an object on a very straightforward substrate—one that sorts flights into a vertical list based on one or more rules. However, given the number of items contained within a single flight option box, that area itself might be considered a substrate for the specific flight details, such as carrier, duration, and departure time.

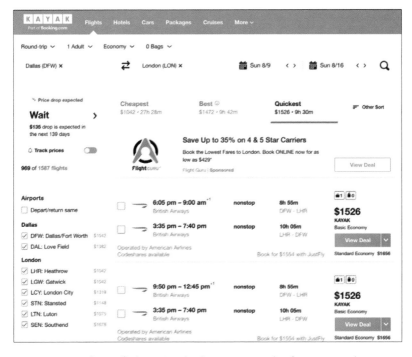

FIGURE 9.16 Booking a flight at Kayak. This is an example of recursion, where an object is itself the substrate for more objects.

CLARIFICATION #4: PRETTY PICTURES ARE NOT THE SAME AS INFORMATIVE VISUALS

Pictures that seem like visual representations of information may actually make no use of spatial arrangement. (More accurately, they do use spatial arrangement, just not in a way that adds any meaning.) In these cases, things could be rearranged and no meaning would be lost. A nearly ubiquitous example of this are sketchnotes, as shown in Figure 9.17.

FIGURE 9.17 Sketchnotes use visual encodings to aid in recall and to clarify meanings, but there is rarely any significance to the spatial arrangement of different information clusters.

While highly visual, sketchnotes mostly use visual encodings and illustrations to reinforce the most interesting ideas. There is rarely any kind of significance to the overall structure or arrangement of the notes themselves. In fact, some sketchnoting tutorials are clear on this point: to take and capture notes (in a way that aids with recall), not organize them in any meaningful, structured way.

Place These Thoughts into Memory

- We are concerned with representations that use spatial arrangement to hold meaning.

- We all *naturally* arrange physical things in space to hold meaning, but this is a skill that must be developed.

- Things and numbers are far easier to organize than abstract concepts.

- To organize abstract concepts, we tend to look for pre-existing models and templates. But …

- We're all fully capable of modifying or creating original visual representations, *if* we can learn to see the patterns in how things are arranged.

- All visual models use some form of the *Objects Placed into Territories* framework.

- Once understood, this model helps us understand a more robust visual grammar.

PRIOR ASSOCIATIONS

EXTERNAL REPRESENTATIONS

INTERACTIONS

COGNITION

4

How We Understand Through Interactions

It is through interactions that we connect what's in the head with what's in
the world. Even when stacking bills, it's
not just the resulting piles, but the act
itself of sorting and stacking that is part
of the knowledge construction process.
Think about playing a game of Scrabble.
Why do we rearrange scrabble tiles?
Because we're able to see more possible
combinations of letters than we could by
just thinking about it.

By interacting with tangible thoughts, we reveal more possibilities, patterns, and ways of understanding. But interactions are more than a solitary activity. By drawing an idea on the whiteboard, someone else can now grab a marker and say, "Mmm, not quite right. What if we …?" We can then cut, add, alter, and otherwise do things—together—with that information. Through different tools and methods, we interact with information in a manner that is more powerful than trying to work it out "in our heads."

In this section of the book, we explore how interactions are not the *result* of thinking (our brain telling our hands to grab something), but rather an integral *part of* thinking. We then identify the different kinds of interaction patterns we use to create understanding from information.

10

Interacting with Information

The interaction is the inquiry ... not just the manipulation of interface controls.

—WILLIAM A. PIKE ET AL., *THE SCIENCE OF INTERACTION*[1]

Imagine you are seated at a table littered with a few dozen coins. The surface is a jumble of pennies, nickels, dimes, and quarters. It looks like the picture in Figure 10.1. Your task is to establish, quickly and accurately, how much money is on the table. There's just one catch: you can't use your hands.

We have done this activity in classrooms and workshops with hundreds of people, and it always plays out the same way. We show the picture, silence descends, and the clock ticks until someone calls out the wrong answer. More wrong answers follow, along with a few anxious chuckles. The task seems easy. Yet it always takes several minutes, and many mistakes, before anyone arrives at the correct answer.

1. Pike, William A., John Stasko, Remco Chang, and Theresa A. O'Connell. 2009. "The Science of Interaction." *Information Visualization* 8 (4): 273. https://doi.org/10.1057/ivs.2009.22

FIGURE 10.1 How quickly can you add up the amount of money in this picture without using your hands? Try doing this by sitting as still as possible, not even nodding your head or counting aloud.

More Than Visual Information

If our brain is so adept at making sense of visual information, as we saw in previous chapters, why is adding up a handful of coins by sight alone such a formidable task? The information is plainly visible, and the math is simple addition, yet people stumble to come up with the right answer. Part of the reason, of course, is that the coins are in disarray. They're not in neat and tidy piles ready for counting. The addition is arduous because the information hasn't been structured to make it easy. It doesn't take advantage of our perceptual superpowers.

Enter visual—*spatial*—representations. The preceding chapter explored all the ways that a good spatial representation can be used to transform the messy and cluttered into the tidy and organized, and through that, render the information in our lives more understandable.

Yet our everyday world is often just like the coins: a little bit messy and not quite right for our needs. We often have to tinker with, organize, and adjust the information we encounter. And we're doing this with information that someone else—writers, designers, marketers, filmmakers, and more—has crafted to communicate clearly. And yet we are constantly interacting with information. We cut, copy, and paste. We sort search results, clip pages from magazines, and scribble in notebooks. We point, gesture, and mutter quietly to ourselves. Why do we do these things? Why don't we just sit still, look at the information, and "think?" The answer, as we shall see, is that interaction is an integral part of how we create understanding.

Interactions Are Pervasive

These interactions don't need to be grandiose or depend on powerful technology. Often, they are small and seem insignificant. The coins are much easier to count if you point at them one at a time and say the running total out loud: ten, twenty, twenty-five, fifty, and so forth. If these were real coins on a real table, you might put them in equal-sized piles, count the piles, and multiply. No matter what strategy you adopted, using your hands would smooth the whole process. Even moving your body as you counted would improve things. When researchers asked people to count objects on a screen without pointing, those who nodded their head while counting—one (nod), two (nod), three (nod), etc.—were faster and more accurate.

We rely on our hands and bodies when we think. We also tend to overlook how pervasive and useful this behavior is. In an experiment similar to our coin example, college students were given a series of pictures, each with 20 to 30 coins, and asked to calculate the sum.[2] They were asked to count under one of three conditions: without pointing or touching the coins, pointing at the coins but not touching them, and lastly, both pointing and touching the coins. The students were 50 percent slower when they couldn't point at the coins or touch them. The fastest way to finish the job was to use their hands, even if only for pointing. The benefits weren't just about speed. When people could use their hands, the number of wrong answers also fell, by up to 80 percent. In a study that used real coins, rather than pictures, people were allowed to move and rearrange the coins. While this didn't always speed things up, it significantly increased the chance of getting the right answer. The researchers concluded that since it was better to be right than quick, the time spent

2. Kirsh, David. 1995. "Complementary Strategies: Why We Use Our Hands When We Think." Edited by Johanna D. Moore and Jill Fain Lehman. *Proceedings of the Seventeenth Annual Conference of the Cognitive Science Society*, 212–17. http://adrenaline.ucsd.edu/kirsh/Articles/Cogsci95/cogsci95.html; Kirsh, David. 1997. "Interactivity and Multimedia Interfaces." *Instructional Science* 25 (2): 79–96. https://doi.org/10.1023/a:1002915430871

organizing the coins was "a smart investment" because it broke the "task into more manageable steps."[3]

Even simple interactions help us think. That's the lesson of the coin-counting studies. Adding up some loose change is vastly simpler than differential calculus. It shouldn't make our neurons sweat and yet it does—until we bring our body into it, until we start using the table to create piles, until we start interacting with the world. If using our hands makes it easier to tally a handful of coins, surely it has benefits for more complex problems as well.

Why interaction helps us think is a complex story. We've explored the foundational elements of this story at the start of this book, when we learned about embodied cognition. In this chapter, and the one that follows, we'll go further and zoom in to how interacting with information plays an inextricable role in how we solve problems, analyze information, reason through situations, and make sense of the world. But before we delve into these details, let's briefly return to the topic of external visual representations.

Doing, Not Just Seeing

When it comes to the power of visual representations, one of the towering, classic works is Edward Tufte's *Envisioning Information*. He writes:

> We thrive in information-thick worlds because of *our marvelous and everyday capacities* to select, edit, single out, structure, highlight, group, pair, merge, harmonize, synthesize, focus, organize, condense, reduce, boil down, choose, categorize, catalog, classify, list, abstract, scan, look into, idealize, isolate, discriminate, screen, pigeonhole, pick over, sort, integrate, blend, inspect, filter, lump, skip, smooth, chunk, average, approximate, cluster, aggregate, outline, summarize, itemize, review, dip into, flip through, browse, glance into, leaf through, skim, refine, enumerate, glean, synopsize, winnow the wheat from the chaff, and separate the sheep from the goats. (emphasis added)[4]

3. Neth, Hansjörg, and Stephen J. Payne. 2011. "Interactive Coin Addition: How Hands Can Help Us Think." *Proceedings of the 33rd Annual Conference of the Cognitive Science Society*, 279–84. http://csjarchive.cogsci.rpi.edu/proceedings/2011/papers/0054/paper0054.pdf
4. Tufte, Edward R. 1990. *Envisioning Information*, 50. Cheshire, CT: Graphics.

Although Tufte is writing about what makes for a good visual representation on a plain, motionless piece of paper, this passage is a catalog of dynamic processes. Read the paragraph again, and you will realize that everything, all those "marvelous and everyday capacities," are things we do *to* and *with* information. To live in a world thick with information, Tufte is saying, even when we follow his guidance for creating visual representations, the understanding comes from *doing*, not just *seeing*.

Doing is powerful. We opened the last chapter with the story about explaining a niche area of the American healthcare and pharmaceutical industry by constructing a visual representation on the fly from salt shakers, sugar packets, and other table detritus. The point was that spatial arrangements encode meaning and shape our ability to understand.

But this example also illustrates the role of human action: *grabbing* objects, *rearranging* them, *pointing* to them, *gesturing* with the hands, *asking* questions, and more. The end result of these actions was a visual representation, but the understanding came from the interactive process of creating the spatial arrangement. It was a process that depended on many of the everyday capacities from Tufte's catalog: select, structure, pair, merge, focus, organize, discriminate, integrate, chunk, cluster, summarize, refine, synopsize, and so much more. It's a *long* list.

This chapter marks a turning point in our understanding of understanding. This is where we start drawing a stronger connection between the body and the mind, action and cognition, as well as doing and understanding. So far, we have learned how we perceive information, make associations, and interpret visual objects. We've identified principles and concepts for designing information to be more understandable, with special attention given to visual encodings. Now we turn more directly to concepts from embodiment, a turn which the Tufte passage brings into sharp relief: understanding is a deeply dynamic process. And this dynamism goes well beyond electrical signals bouncing around the gray goo in our skull.

We have already encountered one of the most fundamental reasons that interaction matters: it doesn't always come to us in the form we need. We come into contact with information that is somewhat unorganized, not quite the way we want, and structured in a way that doesn't take good advantage of our visual superpowers. When that's the case, the art of understanding needs to draw on an interactive strategy.

Everyday Interactions

We don't need to look far to find examples of how we interact with and adapt information to our needs. We highlight passages in a book, we slap Post-it Notes on our monitor, and we rotate jigsaw puzzle pieces to fill the empty spot that's making us go bonkers. We create piles of coins, piles of papers, and bookmark favorite websites. We make to-do lists, cross them out when complete, and hang inspirational posters on the wall. Architects create building mock-ups, carpenters construct jigs, chefs prepare their mise en place, and designers depend on prototypes and walls of sticky notes. In these and countless other examples, we don't experience the world in a passive way. We are forever tweaking an information-thick world to our needs, abilities, and situations.

That's what happened with the coins. Counting them in your head was hard. Nodding your head made it easier. Pointing made it faster and more accurate. Moving and grouping them would yield additional benefits. The coin example is trivial at first glance, yet it exposes an important truth: we think better when we interact with the world, even when those interactions are small and seemingly insignificant. To understand why this is so, let's look at how people play *Tetris*.

How People Play *Tetris*

As one of the most popular video games in history, you are, in all likelihood, quite familiar with *Tetris* (see Figure 10.2). But just in case, here is a quick reminder. Assorted geometric shapes appear at the top of the screen, one at a time, and as they drift down, players fit them into odd-shaped spaces at the bottom. The game is so simple that it has only four actions: move the piece one space left, move the piece one space right, rotate the piece by 90 degrees clockwise, or drop the piece into position.

You make a lot of mistakes learning to play *Tetris*, as when you learn anything new. A typical mistake is inefficient moves. For instance, new players might move a piece three spaces to the left only to realize they should have moved it two spaces. So they backtrack one space and drop the piece into position. This requires five actions—three left, one right, then drop—when they could have used just three—two left, then drop. That's a 67 percent increase over the minimum number of actions.

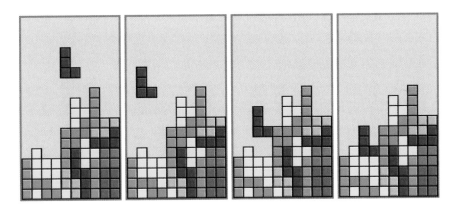

FIGURE 10.2 Playing *Tetris*.

Why would you ever do more actions than absolutely necessary? The obvious explanation is that mistakes are part of learning. We try, we fail, we learn from the experience, and we steadily improve. As a beginner, we are defined by our lack of experience. It's normal, as we get started, to bungle things and take unproductive detours. But as we gain experience, we also expect to correct these miscues, whether we are learning to ride a bike, prepare an omelet, or play *Tetris*.

Or maybe not. When two cognitive scientists, David Kirsh and Paul Maglio, studied *Tetris*, they found that even skilled players made a lot of mistakes.[5] They had people play *Tetris* and recorded every keystroke, which gave them timing data down to the millisecond. The computational theory of mind, which we encountered in Chapter 2, "Understanding as a Function of the Brain, Body, and Environment," predicts that new players would make a lot of mistakes early, and fewer mistakes as they improved. That isn't what happened. Kirsh and Maglio found that all players, no matter their experience level, made unnecessary movements and rotations. Moreover, in some situations, people made *more* mistakes as they became better players.

This is a puzzling result. Why would players do more work than necessary and make more mistakes? More importantly, why would *better* players do this more often? Take these results at face value, and it's a bit like saying the best quarterbacks throw more interceptions, or the best mountaineers fall off higher cliffs. There must be something else going on.

5. Kirsh, David, and Paul Maglio. 1994. "On Distinguishing Epistemic from Pragmatic Action." *Cognitive Science* 18 (4): 513–49. https://doi.org/10.1207/s15516709cog1804_1

Kirsh and Maglio argued that actions come in different forms, and are done for different reasons, even when the actions are physically identical. To move a *Tetris* block left, players have to press the left arrow key. If they press the key two times, those are two identical actions. They're equal, right? Not quite. After each key press, the *Tetris* block moves and the world is just a wee bit different. Because players can see this difference on the screen, they now have information they didn't have before. While they could have imagined this change in their head, now they can see it in the world. The two key presses may be *physically* identical, but they are not *informationally* identical. Press the key once and the world changes, and that change can influence your next action.

Imagine you are playing chess instead of *Tetris*. You examine the board and think you see a good move. You lift the bishop and move it three spaces, but keep your finger on it just in case. Once you see the board in this new configuration, you realize, suddenly, that it would be a terrible move, so you move the bishop back. You have just performed two actions—moving the bishop, then moving it back—and the world is unchanged. It's as though you pressed *undo*. But moving the bishop wasn't wasted effort because it allowed you to see the move *in the world* rather than imagine it *in your head*.

Tetris players use the same trick to become better players. Take the case of rotation. The game lets players rotate pieces in 90-degree increments, clockwise only. Players can do this rotation in their head, something that has been investigated in umpteen psychology studies. But Kirsh and Maglio found that *Tetris* players routinely rotated pieces on the screen more than they needed to. Not only that, but the better players were more likely to do these seemingly extraneous rotations.

Only when the researchers looked carefully at the data did this behavior make any kind of sense. It takes 800 to 1200ms to rotate a block in the head, yet as little as 100ms to rotate it in the world.[6] Extra rotations weren't a mistake; they were essential to good play. It's just like moving the bishop. You could have moved it in your head, but players gained an advantage by doing it in the world instead.

---

6. Kirsh and Maglio describe how they measured rotation speeds, and, while there are many nuances, they note that no matter how you add it up "the time saving benefits of physical over mental rotation are obvious." (1994, p. 532).

What about experts? Serious chess players, after all, *do* make all their moves in their head. Only novices make moves and then take them back. This only underscores the benefits from interaction. It takes years of practice to make good chess moves just by looking at the board. Nobody is an expert in everything. At some point, our cognitive needs outstrip what we can do in the head alone. Grand masters can play chess at the highest levels, without moving the bishop and taking it back, only because they have trained their brain through years and years of intense training.

Even smart people externalize, even world experts. Take this example with Richard Feynman, one of the great physicists of the twentieth century. Toward the end of his life, Feynman worked with the historian Charles Weiner, to document—in a series of biographical interviews—his contributions to theoretical physics. At one point, they were reviewing some of his scientific notes and papers. Weiner casually described the papers as "a record of [Feynman's] day-to-day work." Feynman disagreed:

> "I actually did the work on the paper," he said.
>
> "Well," Weiner said, "the work was done in your head, but the record of it is still here."
>
> "No, it's not a *record*. It's *working*. You have to work on paper, and this is the paper. Okay?"[7]

Today we have much more to work with than paper. We have a whole host of tools at our disposal. Thinking, in this sense, becomes an act of interactive bricolage: a dynamic assembly of different resources, all brought together through interaction.

The Light Bulb Moment

Of course, the real world, which has information everywhere and options galore, is more complex than the game worlds of *Tetris* and chess (and simpler than particle physics). Take, for example, the task of choosing a light bulb. It's a surprisingly tricky business. To peruse the lighting aisle of your local hardware store is to become mired in the quicksand of consumer choices. Yet it's not meant to be that way. Each box of bulbs is crafted to be eye-catching

---

7.   Gleick, James. 1992. *Genius: The Life and Science of Richard Feynman (1st Edition)*, 409. New York: Pantheon Books.

and informative. Each package declares the bulb size, brand name, and energy efficiency. Everyday bulbs are clumped together, flood lights have their own section, and specialty bulbs are off to the side. It's an information space quite unlike the coins scattered on the table. Where the coins were random and disorganized, the lighting section is curated and well structured. The light bulb display is, in effect, a sprawling visual representation of the lighting choices. In theory, it shouldn't require much interaction: just scan shelves and choose.

Yet, deciding depends on interaction. You start by scanning, left and right, to locate the right section. You pick up a box, turn it over to read the fine print, grab a second box, and compare it with the first. Realizing the second box won't work with a dimmer switch, you place it back on the shelf and begin looking for an alternative. At that point, your eyes might be drawn to a display explaining light bulb temperatures. It has a chart, which explains that 2700K bulbs produce yellowish-white light, while the light from 5000K bulbs is a bluish-white. The display includes actual bulbs, all lit up, and invites you to put your hand under each one. Doing so makes it easier to understand that 2700K bulbs—softer and warmer—would be best for the living room and 5000K bulbs—brighter yet harsher—will be best in the garage. This process continues: scanning for bulbs, reaching out to inspect the box, comparing different items, and steadily working towards a decision.

There's a lot going on as you stand in the aisle. Except you aren't just standing and perceiving information. You're picking things up, moving them around, reading the product descriptions, and considering options. All this action is helping you build up an internal representation of the light bulb decision space. To pick out a light bulb is to enter Tufte's information-thick world and engage in his long list of our marvelous and everyday capacities, which we can roll up into a single world: *interaction*.

Now imagine looking for light bulbs in an online store. How would it be different? At one level, you are doing exactly the same thing: comparing similar bulbs, searching for specific brands, eliminating bulbs that don't work with a dimmer, and working toward a decision. But when it comes to the physical actions—how your body interacts with the information—it's wildly different. In the physical store, your whole body is involved, and in the digital one, it's mostly your fingertips going point, click, tap.

When we change the technological setting, in this case from shelves to screens, we change how our bodies engage with the environment. It looks like we're doing two completely different things, yet the information hasn't changed and neither has the outcome we seek. The physical store and its digital counterpart may be different worlds, but they're not worlds apart. This suggests there should be a universal way of describing, at least at some level, how people use interaction to figure things out, no matter what the medium.

Epistemic Interactions Are Universal Across Mediums

We take this kind of universality for granted when it comes to perception.[8] For example, a bowl of *blue* spaghetti (we'll spare you the image!) demonstrates how one perceptual system (sight) can influence another (taste). Just seeing a picture of the spaghetti is enough to judge that it will taste disgusting. Note that the material form of the spaghetti is irrelevant. We would make the same judgment if the blue pasta appeared in a magazine, on a screen, or on our dinner plate. We don't expect our perceptual powers to be fundamentally different between print images, digital images, or physical objects. So then, why should we expect interaction to also vary across worlds?

The main reason is that interaction is rooted in physical movement, and those movements vary with technology. Walking through a forest in a 3D game is analogous to walking through a real forest, but in the game, we use fingers to manipulate controls and in the real world, we use our feet. This difference naturally leads us to treat these as different, even as we know they're connected because they are both means of navigating through space.

While the answer might seem obvious, all this raises another question: What are we talking about when we talk about interaction?

What Is Interaction?

What are the *ways* we interact with the world? Interaction, from an evolutionary perspective, has given us just three ways, each of which arises from our physical bodies.

The first comes from how we move through the world, often by walking, but also by turning our head to gaze in a new direction or adjusting our

---

8. *"Socially constructed"* universality! (See Chapter 8)

orientation to the world in some fashion. The world doesn't change, only where we are in the world and what we can perceive from it. Let's call this class of interactions *navigating*: moving on around the world, changing our position and perspective relative to the information it contains.

We also interact with the world by *manipulating* objects, such as flipping pages in a book or taking a sip of tea. We manipulate the world by touching it, or grasping objects, and handling those objects in various ways. In the early days of personal computers, the only way to use them was by typing in commands. Computers became an everyday technology only with the widespread adoption of windows, icons, and mice for controlling the cursor. Being visual was important, but the big shift was being able to directly manipulate information through our hands.

A third major class of interaction is *conversing*, which means language. We tend to associate language with speaking aloud, in Finnish or Swahili for instance. But the general case is far broader: think of sign language, or Braille, or emojis. As a broad form of interaction, conversing is how we use symbols to communicate our ideas and intentions.

Navigating suggests walking with our feet, *manipulating* implies working with our hands, and *conversing* reminds us of talking with our mouth. Every way that we have of interacting with the world comes back to, broadly speaking, one of these three classes of interaction. This is the legacy of being physical creatures, dependent on bodies evolved over millennia in a three-dimensional universe.

Our technology, however, has allowed us to transcend the associations between these ways of interacting and our natural bodies. Walking doesn't have to be done with the feet, manipulating doesn't always require hands, and conversing isn't restricted to moving our lips. We converse through messaging apps by using our hands to select letters and symbols. We walk through the world of *Minecraft* or run down the football field in *Madden NFL* by manipulating controls with our fingers. When we need to set an alarm, we might talk to a digital assistant, a task that used to be done by manipulating toggles on a clock. Even though our bodies provide us, at a metaphorical level, only three basic ways of interacting with the world, our technology allows us to mix and match these approaches, changing and improving our ability to interact with information.

One way to define interaction, no matter how it happens, is something we do to the world. But in our discussion of embodiment, we saw how there is a deeper connection between mind and world. Recall Clark's idea of the extended mind, with cognitive processes leaking out into the world.

This gives us another way of thinking about interaction. Not as a one-way flow from brain to world, but as a dynamic back-and-forth between a person and something in the world, something outside the person. This could be a computer or a phone or a whiteboard. It could be the controls in an airplane, or LEGO bricks, or the kitchen sink. And it certainly includes both other people and artificial agents, be it Google or Siri or anything that reacts and responds to human behavior. The *Oxford English Dictionary* defines interaction as "reciprocal action" or the "action or influence of persons or things on each other." The key words are *reciprocal* and *influence*—the dynamic back-and-forth between people and things. Interaction modifies the world and this, in turn, modifies us and our understanding of the world.

Interaction is an action-reaction pair: acting on the world *coupled* with the reaction. We tend to think of interaction as action, *then* reaction. Viewed on a timeline, that's a fair description, and it can be a useful way to analyze behavior. Yet when it comes to how interaction helps us make sense of information, it's more useful to think of it as action-reaction coupled together.

Consider the difference between your hand and your arm. It makes intuitive sense to describe them as separate objects. At the same time, your hand doesn't dangle from your wrist. It's *coupled* to your arm—joined at the wrist in a deep and meaningful way. Thinking of your arm as a bundle of separate parts is helpful when picking out some winter gloves, but chop off your hand, and it no longer works. When it comes to how your hand functions, you have no choice but to consider hand, wrist, arm, elbow, and shoulder as connected together and part of the whole body.

Interaction, as we use the term here, is similar. It refers to the action *and* the response, rather than action and *then* the response. This is sometimes called *tight coupling*: the senses, the brain, the body, and the world in close connection with each other.[9]

---

9. See: Ahlberg, Christopher, and Ben Shneiderman. 1994. "Visual Information Seeking: Tight Coupling of Dynamic Query Filters with Starfield Displays." *Proceedings of the SIGCHI Conference on Human Factors in Computing Systems Celebrating Interdependence - CHI 94*, 313–17. https://doi.org/10.1145/191666.191775; Clark, Andy. 2001. "Reasons, Robots and the Extended Mind." *Mind & Language* 16 (2): 121–45. https://doi.org/10.1111/1468-0017.00162

Modeling Interaction

Let's return to *Tetris*, taking with us this idea of interaction as tightly coupled, action-reaction phenomenon. When Kirsh and Maglio studied *Tetris* players, they didn't just track how humans played the game. They also wrote a program to play *Tetris*. They called it *RoboTetris*, and it was developed around a cognitive model based on the same assumptions as EPIC and the Model Human Processor, which we explored back in Chapter 2. Like those models, which followed from the computational theory of mind, *RoboTetris* worked on a serialized feedback-loop mode: perception, cognition, action, and then back to perception.

As each new *Tetris* piece appeared, *RoboTetris* would visually examine it by creating an image in its "head" and determining the shape. Then it would encode the shape in working memory, compute the optimal place to put it, and plan a sequence of movements and keystrokes to get the shape in place. The final step was to carry out this plan by tapping the necessary keys. It was a straightforward model based on the leading science of the day.

Yet *RoboTetris* didn't play like a human. One of the most striking differences was that it didn't move or rotate a piece until after it had decided where to place it. In this way, it was completely unlike human players. Humans moved and rotated pieces as early as possible, even when they could see only part of it. Early rotation gave human players an edge by exposing hidden parts of the piece, a trick that let them suss out the whole shape a few hundred milliseconds early. *RoboTetris*, however, waited until it could perceive the whole shape before doing anything. The human players did a lot of seemingly extraneous rotations and movements. *RoboTetris* did none. Even though it was modeled after humans, it played like—well, like a robot.

If cognition is no more than brain-based computation, how do we explain what the human players were doing? The problem wasn't that they were doing extraneous rotations and movements. The problem was that they *kept* doing these extraneous rotations and movements, even as they got better at the game. That result didn't line up with the predictions of standard cognitive theory, which viewed these actions as mistakes. These unnecessary actions should go down, not up, as skill increased. In their analysis, Kirsh and Maglio proposed a novel explanation: action isn't something that happens *after* cognition; it's part and parcel of our cognitive apparatus.

They write:

> In our view, the failure of classical [cognitive models] to explain the data of extra rotations is a direct consequence of the assumption that the point of action is always pragmatic: that the only reason to act is for advancement in the physical world. This creates an undesirable separation between action and cognition. If one's theory of the agent assumes that thinking precedes action, and that, at best, action can lead one to re-evaluate one's conclusions, then action can never be undertaken in order to alter the way cognition proceeds … On this [classical] view, cognition is logically prior: Cognition is necessary for intelligent action, but action is never *necessary for intelligent cognition*. (Emphasis added)[10]

Models are, by definition, a simplification of reality built on assumptions and generalizations. The better the model, the less these simplifications matter. All models are wrong, in the end, but good models are useful. Scientists build climate models, for example, because that's the only way to simulate the long-term effect of atmospheric changes. In a good model, minor deviations from the real world are a rounding error, like the difference between 32 and 31.9999973—insignificant in most cases. But in their analysis of *RoboTetris*, Kirsh and Maglio argued that assuming cognition is distinct from action is a large deviation from reality.

Traditional cognitive models assumed that action was "never necessary for intelligent cognition." Kirsh and Maglio showed that this was a deeply false assumption. It is naive to think that interaction is merely mental computation leading to changes in the world. A truer picture is that action is a dynamic coupling between brain, body, and world. Imagine the mind as a collection of interacting parts. Traditionally, we have assumed all those parts were in the head, with information flowing in and action flowing out. Now we have a new notion of the mind, one where the parts are distributed everywhere and interaction is binding them together.

---

10. Kirsh & Maglio (1994), p. 526

Two Kinds of Action

To explain why people do so many seemingly superfluous movements and rotations, Kirsh and Maglio distinguished between two types of action, which they dubbed *pragmatic action* and *epistemic action*. Let's start with the first of these.[11]

The purpose of pragmatic action is to move closer to a desired physical goal. We change the world, that is, to bring about a specific change in the world. Suppose that you are painting a sunset and want to redden the sky. You dip your brush and dab red paint on the canvas. Your actions move you closer to your desired goal state for the world: a redder sky. But dip your brush in blue paint, and you'll change the world in an undesired way. Pragmatic actions either move you closer to your desired goal, or they move you farther away. Dipping your brush in blue paint when you wanted red moves you away from the goal, so it is a true mistake.

If humans only performed pragmatic actions, there would be only two ways to interpret everything we did: either it was the right action (because it moved us closer to our goal), or it was a mistake (because it moved us farther from our goal). It's a mistake to swallow the blue pill when you meant to swallow the red one. Similarly, it's a mistake to rotate the *Tetris* piece twice when once will do. If all actions worked this way, then we would either bring about our intended changes (good), or we wouldn't (bad). Furthermore, it would mean that we would always learn to correct these mistakes by eliminating extraneous actions. But the *Tetris* study provided compelling evidence that we don't always act on the world for pragmatic reasons.

The purpose of epistemic actions, on the other hand, is to "uncover information that is hidden or hard to compute" in our brains.[12] The term is derived from *epistemology*, the branch of philosophy concerned with knowledge and how we create it. The phrase *epistemic action* is scholarly shorthand for creating knowledge through interaction. As the name implies, this class of action has special relevance for understanding problems.

---

11. See: Kirsh (1997); Pike et al. (2009); also, Yi, Ji Soo, Youn Ah Kang, and John Stasko. 2007. "Toward a Deeper Understanding of the Role of Interaction in Information Visualization." *IEEE Transactions on Visualization and Computer Graphics* 13 (6): 1224–31. https://doi.org/10.1109/tvcg.2007.70515

12. Kirsh & Maglio (1994), p. 513

Kirsh and Maglio define epistemic actions as ones that make "mental computation easier, faster, or more reliable" than doing the work just in your head.[13] The *Tetris* players intuited this as they played. These extra actions may seem unnecessary and inefficient on the surface, yet closer inspection reveals that they improve overall cognitive performance. Epistemic actions provide an advantage when our biological brain falters.

Take loading the car for a family vacation. Making everything fit can be quite a challenge. Imagine that you have the luggage on the ground and are about to pack the trunk. How do you decide what goes where? One option is to look at all the pieces, estimate their size and shape, mentally consider how the pieces all fit together, and then determine an optimized plan of action: first the big suitcase on the left, then the duffle bag on top, then the small roller bag tipped sideways, and so forth. But nobody packs a car by planning it in their head and then executing the plan. Instead, you would add a piece that seems like a good starting point, then another, make some adjustments, add a third piece, and continue tweaking and shuffling things around until you have a workable arrangement. Packing the trunk is entirely epistemic actions from top to bottom. And then, inevitably, just as all the luggage has finally been tucked away and the trunk closed, somebody comes out of the house and hands you another suitcase.

Thinking of interaction in this way means adopting a holistic perspective on human behavior. Interaction is not merely pragmatic movements toward a goal. It's a way of establishing a partnership between what happens in the head with everything in the world. Interaction works as a kind of glue for understanding. It takes all the pieces of an understanding problem—representations in the world, the tools we work with, the space around us, and the computations in our head—and weaves them together.

Why Epistemic Actions Matter

We tend to think of interaction in simplistic terms: click a button, grab the coffee cup, twist the key, swipe the screen, open the menu, and so forth. We interact with the world to bring about some desired change in the world around us. But interaction can also have a significant impact upon ourselves, as when moving a bishop makes it easier to see the consequences of that move.

13. Kirsh & Maglio (1994), pp. 513-14

When it has an epistemic component, interaction runs in two directions at the same time: some is directed outward toward whatever we are interacting with in the world, and some is directed inward.

Epistemic actions are not merely a useful concept for interaction design. They can fundamentally alter the way we interpret human behavior. Action takes on more nuance and power. It becomes a way to incorporate representations, physical objects, and the environment itself into our thinking. It turns action from something that happens after we think, to an integral part of thinking. Without interaction, we struggle to understand.

11

A Pattern Language for Talking About Interactions

It's very easy to confuse the essence of what you're doing with the tools that you use.

—DR. HAROLD ABELSON, OVERVIEW AND INTRODUCTION TO LISP

Life is interactive. Much of this interaction is pragmatic in nature, or at the least has a pragmatic component. But if epistemic actions are so helpful when faced with the accelerating frenzy of *Tetris*, we should expect to find them everywhere. And we do. They are a mechanism for spreading cognitive processes across brain, body, and the world. They allow us to see wildly different behaviors as serving the same cognitive purpose. Consider, again, the light bulb example. Joe goes to the hardware store, picks up a box of light bulbs, and reads the fine print. Mary goes to lightbulbs.com, scans the search results, and clicks through to a product page with all the gory details. Each of them searches for information and then probes for more details. This latter action, *probing*, is one of the epistemic actions we will encounter in this chapter. Probing is a means of acting on the world to reveal more detailed information.

As *physical* actions, Joe and Mary are doing different things, but as *epistemic* actions they are doing the same thing.

In this chapter, we are going to describe a suite of epistemic interactions that people use to create meaning, solve problems, make decisions, establish plans, analyze information, and do other cognitively complex tasks. Taken together, they serve as a versatile vocabulary for describing how people figure things out. In effect, we're going to take Tufte's long list of dynamic and "marvelous everyday capacities" and collapse them down into a small set of terms that can be used to describe a wide range of understanding behaviors, across any technology. In our own work, we, your authors, have found this vocabulary to be an invaluable framework for pinpointing the underlying cognitive work that drives the understanding process.

We opened this chapter with a quotation from Dr. Harold Abelson, a computer science professor at MIT, who warns against confusing the essence of what you're doing with the tools that you use.[1] Computer science isn't about transistors and compilers, Abelson is arguing, any more than mathematics is about calculators and chalkboards. We must distinguish our tools from the underlying concepts and principles. That's what our interaction vocabulary will do. It provides a way to separate the visual trappings of our digital world—windows, menus, and scrollbars—from the essence of how we interact to figure things out. Moreover, these interactions are not tied, in any way, to a particular technology. They can also be used to describe how we create understanding with paper-based technologies, or virtual reality, or any other technology—even ones that have yet to be invented.

The cognitive act is a partnership between brain, body, and world—a partnership forged through evolution. While technology keeps changing, and changing our world, it cannot overwrite the fundamental ways in which understanding happens. There are deep-seated aspects of how we understand that remain true, and will remain true, even in the face of relentless innovation and disruption. This has been the case throughout this book, from perception to associations and representations and, now, interactions. Earlier

---

1. From the first lecture in an MIT course called *The Structure and Interpretation of Computer Programs*. Video and transcripts are available from the MIT Open Courseware website. Abelson, Hal, and Gerald Jay Sussman. 1986. Overview and Introduction to LISP. https://ocw.mit.edu/courses/electrical-engineering-and-computer-science/6-001 -structure-and-interpretation-of-computer-programs-spring-2005/video-lectures/

chapters pursued a timeless approach to creating understandable visual representations. This chapter aims to do the same for interaction.

Four Interaction Themes

Our interaction vocabulary is comprised of fifteen epistemic actions. They are divided across four major themes and, taken as a whole, these nineteen terms (four themes; fifteen interactions) constitute a broad vocabulary to describe how we create understanding from information.[2] The four themes are:

- **Foraging:** Locating resources that will lead to understanding
- **Tuning:** Adjusting resources to align with desired understanding
- **Externalizing:** Moving resources out of the head and into the world
- **Constructing:** Forming new knowledge structures in the world

The interactions are organized into general themes, rather than narrow categories, because each interaction can fall under multiple themes. For example, rearranging refers to changing the spatial position and orientation of a resource. When rearranging is directed at small-scale change—sorting search results to make the cheapest flights appear at the top—it is more about tuning. When rearranging creates substantial change and plays a central role in understanding, such as when a hiring manager divides résumés into different piles to reflect a preliminary assessment of job candidates, it fits better under constructing.

Note also the word *resource* instead of *information*. We described information as a resource in the opening chapter. While we have tended to use the word *information* here, in this and subsequent chapters, we are going to lean more heavily on this notion of information as a resource. This is because embodiment forces us to consider the physical world and, especially, our habit of recruiting objects as props and scaffolds to power thinking. That's what happened in the restaurant, where sugar packets and coffee cups were used to explain the complexity of a niche area of the American healthcare and pharmaceutical industry. The sugar packet was just a sugar packet, until it was co-opted into the understanding process and took on a representational role.

---

2. A version of this vocabulary was first developed in relation to digital libraries. Fast, Karl V., and Kamran Sedig. 2010. "Interaction and the Epistemic Potential of Digital Libraries." *International Journal on Digital Libraries* 11 (3): 169–207. https://doi.org/10.1007/s00799-011-0066-8

The term *information* tends to make us think of words, numbers, and documents. *Representation* makes us think of images and pictures. The word *resource*, however, reminds us that anything in the world, including what's in our heads, can help with understanding.

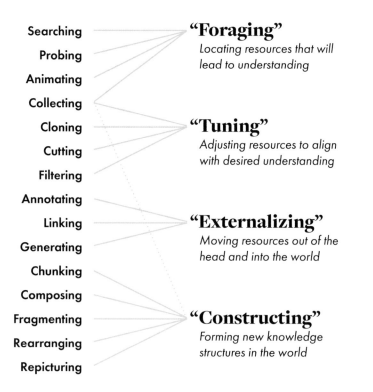

15 INTERACTIONS *organized into* **4 INTERACTION THEMES**

Searching
Probing
Animating
Collecting
Cloning
Cutting
Filtering
Annotating
Linking
Generating
Chunking
Composing
Fragmenting
Rearranging
Repicturing

"Foraging"
Locating resources that will lead to understanding

"Tuning"
Adjusting resources to align with desired understanding

"Externalizing"
Moving resources out of the head and into the world

"Constructing"
Forming new knowledge structures in the world

Foraging for Resources

When you hear the word *foraging*, you likely picture someone scrounging around the forest for berries, firewood, or mushrooms. Today, we forage for information more than berries or anything else. We are always on the lookout for information. It's the essential resource of civilization. If aliens visited earth, their anthropologists would conclude that information foraging is what humans do most. Even our own scientists have long described our species as *informavores*—biological organisms that consume information.[3] There is even a theory of information foraging, which posits that how early humans learned to find food was the evolutionary basis for how modern humans look for information.[4]

We forage for information everywhere. We tap on our glowing screens, select avocados in the grocery store, and scan the parking lot for empty spots. Foraging happens anytime we need information from the world, in any form, to accomplish a task. We can distinguish between at least four types of foraging interactions: *searching*, *probing*, *animating*, and *collecting*.

Searching

Let's start with the prototypical foraging interaction: *searching*. Searching is what happens when you set out to find resources in the world. You might search for a known fact, such as how many times Robert Redford won an Oscar for his acting work, or something more vague, such as when you need to fix a leaking dishwasher.[5] No matter what you're looking for, searching happens when you need information and believe it exists somewhere.

While the web has forged an association between searching and typing words into a box, this is just one way to search. Searching means to look for and locate information in the world. On our screens, we search by typing words, scanning results, and clicking through options. But we also search by scanning our screens for facts and figures and tweets and buttons to press. Beyond our screens, we routinely search with our body. When you need a replacement light bulb, you search the hardware store for clues that will guide you to the lighting section and then, once there, you search by adjusting your body to scan the shelves for the right kind of bulb. You don't need Google to search.

Searching, no matter what form it takes, depends on how we articulate our information needs. With the search box, we use words. With our body, we rely on spatial positioning and orientation. When it comes to visual representations, we scan with our eyes to locate important features, elements, and patterns. All searching.

3. Miller, George A. 1983. "Informavores." In *The Study of Information: Interdisciplinary Messages*, edited by Fritz Machlup and Una Mansfield, 111–13. Chichester: Wiley-Interscience.
4. Pirolli, Peter, and Stuart K. Card. 1997. "The Evolutionary Ecology of Information Foraging." Technical Report, UIR-R97-0l. Palo Alto, CA: Xerox PARCo.
5. Robert Redford never did win, although he was nominated in 1974 for his role in *The Sting*.

Probing

Probing is a constant companion to search, and is summed up by the phrase "tell me more." You probe when you follow links to the next page, zoom in for a closer look, and scroll down to the next paragraph. Probing happens when the information you have isn't quite enough. You are probing when you take the next step, move to the next level, and obtain more salient specifics. Probing isn't about switching direction or following a tangent. It's about drilling down and saying to the world "show, explain, and reveal more about *this*."

Probing is a relentless feature of everyday life. If, while reading this book, you pause to read a footnote, you're probing. If you're listening to some music and ask Alexa to name the song, that's probing, too. If your child asks why the sky is blue, they are searching for information, and when they question you on the finer points of your explanation, they are probing *you*. Searching locates information; probing pursues that information one step further.

As technology delivers more and more information to our fingertips, it feels as if we should be able to probe anything. The technology writer Kevin Kelly tells the story of a mother in a grocery store. When she stopped to examine a product label, her son suggested she "just click on it."[6] The kid had the right idea. When you point your smartphone camera at a soup can or desk lamp, image recognition apps (Google Lens, for example) will display details about the object including brand, price, and purchase options. These apps can identify artwork, plants, buildings, people, and eventually almost any person or thing. The technology feels magical, yet as an interaction for gaining knowledge, it's probing all the way down.

We probe because we suspect there is useful information just around the corner. It happens when the information at hand isn't enough, and we go looking to evaporate our dissatisfaction. But probing give us more than info-nuggets. We can probe to reveal new patterns, structures, and relationships. It brings to light new information that helps us reconsider what we already know and, from that, we can build more robust mental representations.

6. Kelly, Kevin. 2016. *The Inevitable: Understanding the 12 Technological Forces That Will Shape Our Future*, 223. New York: Penguin.

INTERACTION PATTERNS VS. INTERACTION TECHNIQUES

Let's pause to emphasize a feature of both searching and probing and every other interaction in this vocabulary: there is no one, single, ideal way to accomplish them. They take many shapes or forms. You can search for kale salad recipes by typing terms into Google, flipping through a recipe book, or recalling one from your brainbound memory. It's all searching.

The same is true for each and every interaction in this chapter. There is never just one way to search, or probe, or collect (an interaction we'll consider shortly). Consequently, we can distinguish between the *interaction* in the cognitive work and the *interaction technique* we use to achieve the interaction. The interaction is a conceptual construct that describes what cognitive benefits the interaction provides. The interaction technique, however, describes one of many ways the interaction could be accomplished. Separating interactions from techniques—from the infinite ways each interaction could play out—is a critical step for describing interaction in a timeless way.

To introduce a highfalutin word, interaction is *polymorphic*. That just means an interaction can take many different shapes. An *interaction technique* is specific to a particular technology or environment. The *interaction* is the generalized, conceptual form, one that describes all techniques, across all technologies, in any environment.

To see how polymorphism is a desirable feature of our interaction vocabulary, imagine people working for the CIA, doing their analysis, in the weeks leading up to the Cuban missile crisis. You would see them working with desks and paper and chalkboards and no computers. Study the same people today, and they'd still be using paper, but all mixed in with computers and tablets and powerful visualization tools. Now jump fifty years into the future and the analysts might use a 3D holographic, virtual reality system much like Tony Stark in the *Iron Man* movies. It was polymorphism at work when we compared finding light bulbs in a hardware store and an online store. Polymorphism lets all of us see through the same lens and describe critical features of the understanding process with the same vocabulary, no matter how simple or futuristic the technology.

Animating

Do we forage in ways other than searching and probing? Consider a study where people learned to tie knots from video clips instead of diagrams. For some knots, people could only watch the videos from beginning to end, although they could watch it as many times as they wanted. For other knots, they could control the video—pause, rewind, slow it down, and so forth. When people had this type of control, they learned to tie the knot in less time and needed less practice.

Thanks to the controls, the learner was able to focus their attention on troublesome and confusing parts of the knot. It let them "adapt the pace and density of the visual information presentation to their cognitive processing needs."[7] The controls made it possible for each person to focus on what mattered *to them*. When learning the bowline, for example, some people paused on the opening step while others slowed down the latter stages where the rope passed through a loop, around the main line, and back through the loop.

This is *animating*. It means to initiate and control motion in an information resource. When you learn knots from a book, you follow a sequence of images. You need to infer what happens between each step and how to twist and turn the rope. Animating brings this information to the surface and, as a result, it's a kind of foraging. Animating is similar to probing, but where probing increases the level of detail, animating makes information more comprehensible by showing how it changes over time. Every interaction happens over time, by definition, but the benefits of animating exist in relation to time. This is especially helpful for understanding transitions and transformations.

Movement can clarify, and it can also confuse. If static images are good, then dynamic, moving, animated ones must be better. But this assumption is not born out by the research: animating is beneficial in some situations, but not

7. Schwan, Stephan, and Roland Riempp. 2004. "The Cognitive Benefits of Interactive Videos: Learning to Tie Nautical Knots." *Learning and Instruction* 14 (3): 293–305. https://doi.org /10.1016/j.learninstruc.2004.06.005

all.[8] While each successive frame reveals new information, it also removes the previous frame. This puts a new burden on working memory. Pausing, rewinding, changing speed—this reduces the problem. Other times, it's better to show information as a series of individual images so they can be examined carefully, a method known as *small multiples*.[9] But when time and motion are central to understanding, animating can be powerful.

Collecting

Foraging creates a new problem: too much information. Information appears on the scene, and then we forage for more and the prior information flutters away. Our brainbound memory is rapidly overwhelmed. *Collecting* is how we gather foraged information and tuck it away for future use. Until we invented writing, this meant storing information in our head. Since the days of clay tablets, we have sought to invent ever new ways of amassing information like squirrels gathering nuts for the winter.

If your web browser has a lot of open tabs or windows, each showing a different page, that is collecting. If your desk has piles of articles or magazines or other papers, that is also collecting. Have items in your Amazon shopping cart that have been lingering there for weeks or months? Again, collecting.

In the era before the web, electronic search systems were designed entirely around keyword searching. The information scholar Marcia Bates proposed an alternative model that she called *berrypicking*.[10] While her metaphor evokes our broader notion of foraging, it also raises a critical question: What happens to the "berries" that are picked? You gulp down some of them on the spot, but quite a few more are collected.

8. See: Lowe, Richard. 2004. "Interrogation of a Dynamic Visualization During Learning." *Learning and Instruction* 14 (3): 257–74. https://doi.org/10.1016/j.learninstruc.2004.06.003; Robertson, George, Roland Fernandez, Danyel Fisher, Bongshin Lee, and John Stasko. 2008. "Effectiveness of Animation in Trend Visualization." *IEEE Transactions on Visualization and Computer Graphics* 14 (6): 1325–32. https://doi.org/10.1109/tvcg.2008.125; Tversky, Barbara, Julie Bauer Morrison, and Mireille Betrancourt. 2002. "Animation: Can It Facilitate?" *International Journal of Human-Computer Studies* 57 (4): 247–62. https://doi.org/10.1006/ijhc.2002.1017
9. You may recall the espresso drink poster in Chapter 9 as an example of small multiples. That poster highlighted differences between similar things, whereas in this case we're describing tiny changes to the same thing, seen "snapshots" over time.
10. Bates, Marcia J. 1989. "The Design of Browsing and Berrypicking Techniques for the Online Search Interface." *Online Review* 13 (5): 407–24. https://doi.org/10.1108/eb024320

We collect and clip for all kinds of reasons, including as a trigger for future work, to capture and evoke certain memories, and to share with others.[11] Collecting is rampant and essential in a world of cheap, abundant, easily accessible information. Apps such as Evernote, Pocket, OneNote, and many others all exist to solve this problem. Even so, our homes and cubicles and kitchens are filled with scraps of information captured on sticky notes, scribbled in notebooks, and stuck on the fridge door.[12] We collect incessantly.

Foraging Interactions, Summarized

Let's summarize our foraging interactions with some concise definitions.

- **Searching:** To look for, or locate the position of, resources in the world
- **Probing:** To acquire more detailed information from the world
- **Animating:** To initiate, and optionally, control motion in a resource
- **Collecting:** To gather resources for future use

Understanding problems often begins with foraging. We search for data, then analyze. We spot a new flavor of granola on the grocery shelf, then flip over the box and probe for the calorie count. We collect items in the cart, then compare. Once we have information, then other interactions come to the fore. Foraging never disappears, but as understanding proceeds, it often downshifts to take on a supporting role. Probing, in particular, is something that happens so frequently it's hard to put in just one category. But when the situation shifts from researching to analyzing, exploring to sense-making, and preparation to problem-solving, then foraging goes from being the melody to the bass line.

11. Marshall, Catherine C., and Sara Bly. 2005. "Saving and Using Encountered Information." *Proceedings of the SIGCHI Conference on Human Factors in Computing Systems - CHI 05*, 111–20. https://doi.org /10.1145/1054972.1054989; Sellen, Abigail J., Rachel Murphy, and Kate L. Shaw. 2002. "How Knowledge Workers Use the Web." *Proceedings of the SIGCHI Conference on Human Factors in Computing Systems CHI 02*, 227–34. https://doi.org/10.1145/503376.503418
12. Bernstein, Michael, Max Van Kleek, David Karger, and M. C. Schraefel. 2008. "Information Scraps: How and Why Information Eludes Our Personal Information Management Tools." *ACM Transactions on Information Systems* 26 (4): 1–46. https://doi.org/10.1145/1402256.1402263; Kirsh, David. 2001. "The Context of Work." *Human–Computer Interaction* 16 (2–4): 305–22. https://doi.org/10.1207/s15327051hci16234_12

Tuning the World

Tuning modifies, adjusts, and tweaks the resources we use to understand. Tuning happens whenever you adapt a resource to your own needs. You tune when you snip an article from a magazine, or when you search for a new sweater and filter out the cashmere ones. Tuning means tinkering with information. Foraging treats the world as an environment with resources to aid understanding; the job is to uncover them. Tuning is how you align foraged information with your needs and goals.

There are three primary tuning interactions: *cutting*, *cloning*, and *filtering*. Collecting can also work as tuning, not just foraging, and we'll consider why that's so. Tuning interactions tend to result in modest, temporary, or reversible changes. Think of a musician preparing to play. Tuning doesn't change the guitar into a saxophone or a basketball. It brings the guitar into a harmonious state, literally in tune, which is a precursor for making music. Tuning information is similar. The idea is to tweak, alter, and customize a cognitive resource to support the understanding we seek.

Cutting

Foraging leads to clutter, and *cutting* reduces clutter by trimming, pruning, or slicing away some parts to focus on other parts. No matter the metaphor, the primary work of cutting is to hack off what's in the way of the essential, useful, and interesting.

When you think of cutting, you probably think of the cut-and-paste feature on your laptop. But cutting is more than a mechanical operation. When researchers have studied how people use paper documents, for example, they routinely find cutting is pervasive.[13] Cutting is a way of saying "this matters" and "I need this part, but not the rest." Summarizing more than a decade of research on how people interact with paper and digital materials, the scholar Catherine Marshall concluded that three interactions were pivotal above all else: cutting,

---

13. Bishop, Ann Peterson. 1999. "Document Structure and Digital Libraries: How Researchers Mobilize Information in Journal Articles." *Information Processing & Management* 35 (3): 255–79. https://doi.org/10.1016/s0306-4573(98)00061-2; Sellen, Abigail J., and Richard H. R. Harper. 2002. *The Myth of the Paperless Office.* Cambridge, MA: MIT Press.

collecting, and annotating (the latter an interaction we will encounter under externalizing).[14]

Most of the time, cutting is directed at the information we're interested in, such as when we clip an article from a magazine or when we grab an image from a web page. In other situations, cutting is the inverse: removing parts we *don't* want because they're hiding the parts we do. When approached this way, cutting is like peeling away the skin of an orange and discarding it to get at the fruit underneath. With paper, we use scissors to literally cut away what we don't want or clip out what we do. Think back to our light bulb example. We picked up an individual bulb and, upon realizing it could not be dimmed, put it back on the shelf. The bulb won't work, so we physically return it and mentally cut it away, blotting it from memory, even as it remains visible.

Cloning

A close cousin to cutting is *cloning*, an interaction so pedestrian that it hardly seems worth mentioning, and so pragmatic that it hardly seems essential to understanding. Yet cloning supports every kind of cognitive work. Whatever name it goes by—*copying* or *duplicating* or *replicating*—cloning lets us take information from one situation and use it in another while leaving the original intact. Scholars of the ancient world, to cite just one example, have come to depend on precise digital clones of antique vases, clay tablets, and illuminated manuscripts.[15] This not only preserves the originals but also allows for new kinds of analysis.

But set aside the scholar, at her desk, scrutinizing ancient runes, and imagine your life without cloning. What would your day be like, just today, if it were impossible to clone information. No photocopies, no cut-and-paste, no downloading files or printing reports. To share that great *New York Times* piece

14. Marshall calls them clipping (cutting to us), gathering (collecting), and annotating. See: Marshall, Catherine C. 2005. "Reading and Interactivity in the Digital Library: Creating an Experience That Transcends Paper." *Proceedings of CLIR/Kanazawa Institute of Technology Roundtable* 5: 1–20. https://citeseerx.ist.psu.edu/viewdoc/summary?doi=10.1.1.76.7532

15. Cubaud, Pierre, Jérôme Dupire, and Alexandre Topol. 2005. "Digitization and 3D Modeling of Movable Books." *Proceedings of the 5th ACM/IEEE-CS Joint Conference on Digital Libraries - JCDL 05*, 244. https://doi.org/10.1145/1065385.1065440; Hunt, Leta, Marilyn Lundberg, and Bruce Zuckerman. 2005. "InscriptiFact: A Virtual Archive of Ancient Inscriptions from the Near East." *International Journal on Digital Libraries* 5 (3): 153–66. https://doi.org/10.1007/s00799-004 -0102-z; Shiaw, Horn-Yeu, Robert J. K. Jacob, and Gregory R. Crane. 2004. "The 3D Vase Museum." *Proceedings of the 2004 Joint ACM/IEEE Conference on Digital Libraries - JCDL 04*. https://doi.org/10.1145/996350.996381

with a friend, you couldn't copy the link, and would have to resort to typing it out by hand. But even that involves cloning: you read the link, store each letter in your memory, then type it out—that's copying, too, from the screen to your brain and back through the keyboard.

Cloning used to be expensive and time-consuming. Digital tools make it cheap, a recurring theme with epistemic actions, not to mention perfect. But cloning also paves the way for generating new variations from information, comparing different scenarios, and testing hypotheses. And among the most transformative inventions in history, who among us would not rank the printing press in the top ten, if not first. We are now so used to cloning, so dependent on its everyday nature, that we can miss how it drives the desire to understand.

Collecting as a Tuning Action

Now that cutting and cloning is so quick and easy, it accelerates collecting, and that creates clutter. Life is filled with stacks of papers, tweets flagged as favorites, and files tagged *#readlater*. We previously encountered collecting as a foraging interaction, but we also collect as we tune our information environment. It's an interaction that is at home in both roles, and it's not alone. Every interaction can take on dimensions of all four themes, depending on context. Our interaction vocabulary organizes interactions into themes—foraging, tuning, externalizing, and constructing—to capture their *primary* role, which makes it easier to grasp their similarities and differences. But these themes are not hard categories, and each interaction carries some traits from other themes.

As part of tuning, collecting is largely a choice between piling and filing.[16] Piles are a feature of every home and every office. We have piles of books, magazines, and letters. Piles are the cockroaches of the information world: a structure that you find everywhere and that technology never eliminates. Adding to a pile requires almost no effort, so piles proliferate. Filing, on the other hand, requires more work, first to establish the categories, and then to decide which categories apply. Both paths lead to new arrangements of

16. Malone, Thomas W. 1983. "How Do People Organize Their Desks?" *ACM Transactions on Information Systems (TOIS)* 1 (1): 99–112. https://doi.org/10.1145/357423.357430

information and so collecting, because it produces new kinds of structures, is also an interaction for tuning our information landscape.

Where does cloning end (or cutting) and collecting begin? The distinction is clear enough in theory, but when you watch someone working with information, it's not always obvious how to separate these interactions.

Suppose that your washing machine is broken. The washer starts to rumble but then gives a thunk, stops, and displays an error code. You write down the code along with the model number and head for your laptop. Let's pause there: Was writing down the model number an example of cloning or collecting? It's cloning, because the information is now in two places. It's also collecting since you needed it for typing into Google. You might think we have only dodged the question, but consider the idea that it's both at the same time.

Think of Interactions Like Atoms

As an analogy, think of each interaction in this vocabulary like an atom. Atoms are the building blocks of the physical universe, yet they rarely exist independently. Most of the time, they bond with other atoms to form molecules. Hydrogen is the most abundant element in the universe, but here on earth, hydrogen gas is quite rare. It exists mostly as a component of hydrocarbons and water. While hydrogen is definitely an atom, unique and distinct from other atoms, it is almost always linked to other atoms.

The interactions in this chapter work in much the same way. We can define, describe, and conceptualize an interaction called *collecting*. We can list its cognitive benefits and give examples. But when it comes to how collecting happens in the wild, it routinely co-occurs with other interactions. Often, as with the washing machine, they are difficult to tease apart. Observe someone making a photo album from their summer vacation, and you might, now and then, be able to unambiguously observe discrete interactions: some searching, then probing, a bit of collecting, and some rearranging. But other times, these interactions will occur so fused together that it makes little sense to worry about where one ends and another begins.

This is a feature, not a bug, of our vocabulary. In chemistry, the periodic table defines each individual chemical element and this leads to a massive number of molecular combinations. These interactions work the same way. Human interaction is extraordinarily complex and subtle and takes on an immense number of forms. By condensing this infinite variety down to a handful of interactions that combine, and recombine, and take on different forms, we can begin to describe interaction for understanding with a smaller and more manageable set of terms.

Moving forward, let's consider another example to illustrate how our vocabulary can be used to break down an everyday understanding problem. Imagine you're at a restaurant, flipping through a menu that runs a dozen pages, trying to decide among hundreds of choices. A salad might be good, but you're allergic to walnuts, which means finding the ones to avoid (searching) and removing them (cutting), though only in your mind's eye. Perhaps a burger instead, so you flip through the menu (searching), scan the offerings (searching again), and read the descriptions for anything that sounds especially delicious (probing). You run your finger down the list (searching). The blue cheese burger looks amazing, as you tap your finger on the description (annotating, we'll get to this soon enough), but you keep reading (searching and probing) and identify two more burgers for your short list (collecting).

All this interaction, yet note that none of it changes the menu. You can't physically pull out scissors and cut out any dish with walnuts, or alternately, snip out three different burgers and collect them in a pile. The cognitive work has to rely on memory and brainbound processes. But you can also see all the foraging and tuning, which leads to possibilities for doing some of the work in the world, as with *Tetris*.

Tuning simplifies perception and choice. Once we locate the information we need, we often discover that we don't need all of it. So we cut, clone, and collect, simplifying the world to the information we do need, right now, and setting aside the rest. There is, however, another important interaction for tuning: filtering.

Filtering

Filtering reduces complexity, like cutting, by reducing visual clutter to expose salient details. But where cutting is directed at a specific element—remove this object from the picture, delete that paragraph—filtering applies to anything that matches specified criteria. Take online shopping. Search for winter gloves, and you get options for hiding the expensive ones and, of those remaining, deciding to show only the black ones from Patagonia and North Face. From there, it's all about adding a filter, removing a filter, probing for details, and so forth. Filtering is expedient and not strictly necessary. You could sift through *all* the gloves, one by one, pulling out any that seem promising, either collecting them in brainbound memory, or more likely, saving them to a shopping cart or opening up a new tab. But filtering speeds this up dramatically: of all the options, just show gloves made of leather, size large, in black, from these brands.

Of the interactions we've encountered thus far, filtering is perhaps the most dramatic example of how technology enhances our perceptual powers. In the hardware store, you have to mentally filter out the bulbs that don't match. There is no way to physically change the shelf to only show 2700K bulbs, with E12 sockets, providing at least 400 lumens. In the online store, we expect this capability. One promise of augmented reality is making this kind of filtering a feature of everyday life. If Google Lens can recognize real-world objects, like a glove, and let us probe for details, the next step is having it recognize *all* the gloves in a store, provide on-screen filters, and then highlight the most likely matches. In a world overflowing with options, the possibilities are enticing.

Tuning Interactions, Summarized

Tuning interactions cover a wide range of small changes to the world, and we can define them as follows:

- **Cloning:** To create an identical copy of a resource
- **Collecting:** To gather resources for future use
- **Cutting:** To remove unwanted resources
- **Filtering:** To expose, conceal, or transform parts of a resource that have certain characteristics

Tuning happens throughout the understanding process. Quite often, we dismiss these interactions as trivial and insignificant since each change tends to be small. But think of the chef, sipping the soup, then adding a pinch of salt, or the woodworker who sands the chair just a wee bit more in the quest for perfection. The differences may be small, but they're not insignificant. The benefits of each adjustment takes us, step by small step, closer to understanding.

Externalizing Thought

Externalizing actions are how we move information from our head into the world. We have already explored externalizing earlier in our discussion of external representations. But there, the emphasis was on the representations themselves. Here, we will revisit the topic from the perspective of externalizing.

The point of externalizing, as an interaction, is to add information to the world. In contrast, foraging and tuning deal with the world *in situ*. As a result, externalizing is a more direct means of shifting cognitive work from brain-based processes to perceptual ones. Consider calendars and day planners. In theory, you could remember to pick up the dry cleaning on Friday afternoon. In practice, it's easy to forget. Hence the calendar, the day planner, the check-list, and the task management apps.

Externalizing is fundamental to any kind of cognitive work. Writers dump words on the page. Mathematicians scribble equations onto whiteboards. We write on sticky notes, in notebooks, and highlight important passages. We have a vast repertoire of ways to externalize our thoughts. This is not just about the markings we make in the world. It's *why* we create these marks that matters: to adjust the balance between internal and external representations.

We can identify three main types of externalizing actions: *annotating, generating*, and *linking*. Annotating is adding meta-information to the world, like comments or labels. The new information augments the information that already exists. Generating, on the other hand, happens when we add completely new information to the world. It's pure creation. The third form of externalizing is linking, which establishes the relationship between different pieces of information.

The term *externalizing* conveys the characteristic feature of these interactions: information flowing from the head into the world. Other words that could describe this interaction theme include articulating, expressing, or off-loading, among others. While these are all in the same spirit, externalizing best captures the underlying cognitive imperative: get this outta my head.

Annotating

Annotating is how we add information to the world, extra information to augment and amplify what is already there. Think of the red ink on your freshman history essay or the forceful note, scrawled in bold letters, beside a plate of freshly baked cookies, reading "Do not eat! *This means YOU!*" Annotations are informative marks, clarifying or enhancing or directing attention to other information.

While the forms that annotations can take are vast, the most familiar forms are scribbles, highlights, and other markings. When people annotate for themselves, highlighting passages in a textbook for example, they are "often embarrassed by [the annotations] and what they reveal about their understanding of the text," even when they also say the annotations helped them understand.[17] The mark may not be useful once on the page, in other words, but the act of *creating* the mark is essential. It also matters how the marks get made. Annotating works best as a fluid interaction, as effortless as possible, and without diverting your attention. Annotation is a detour, flagging the important or notable, while staying on course to the primary destination.

Paper remains a fabulous annotation medium. It's simple and flexible, adaptable to almost any situation. At the same time, working on paper means some tasks, such as editing and revising, are tedious. Jane Austen wrote her books longhand, almost a century before the typewriter, and curtailed the drudgery of revision by co-opting an everyday object to speed things along: straight pins. Faced with a full page of script, and no space for anything but the smallest changes, Austen would scribble out her changes on paper scraps, attaching them to the draft with straight pins.[18]

Today, we use other techniques for introducing small, useful bits of information to the world, techniques that are faster and easier. The straight pin has given way to paperclips, sticky notes, and highlighters. We have digital stickers and stamps, and merrily flag items with hearts, stars, and tiny thumbs pointing up or down. Austen could have done the revisions in her head, or written out a new draft, but she developed her annotation strategy because it afforded rapid tinkering. Making things easier reflects a common theme in epistemic actions: reducing the interaction cost. In annotation and other interactions, it's important for things to be fast, easy, and fluid.[19]

17. Marshall (2005)
18. "Jane Austen Fiction Manuscripts: The Watsons." n.d. https://janeausten.ac.uk/edition/ms/WatsonsHeadNote.html
19. Learning is a notable exception. When things are too easy, learning is shallow. If too hard though, learning may not happen at all.

Linking

Another way we externalize is by *linking*, an interaction for connecting bits and pieces together. While the idea can be traced to 1945, the term *hyperlink* was only coined in the mid 1960s, and hyperlinks didn't appear in their modern form until the early 1980s. Today, hyperlinks are like oxygen, so familiar that to remember a world without them is like imagining a world without light bulbs—primitive and undesirable. And yet, connecting one piece of information to another, whether we make the link explicit or not, gives us undeniable epistemic benefits. Consider the footnotes on these pages, which give you the title of a research paper, cite more research, etc. The hyperlink didn't make the World Wide Web possible so much as made the invisible connections and joints of the information world into something visual, perceptual, and tangible. The links have always been there. The hyperlink just made it easier to follow the thread.

Mind-mapping tools, such as *MindJet* or *TheBrain*, are built on linking. It's more than a feature. It's the pivotal interaction. While other tools provide ways to externalize thoughts and ideas, mind-mapping tools emphasize how to create links between different ideas. But whether it's about drawing a line between two items on a whiteboard, or building a massive mind map, linking is how we formally express patterns, relationships, and connections. By putting that connection in the world, the relationship can be referenced visually and no longer needs to be remembered.

Generating

Generating is the most generic externalizing action. Annotating and linking create new information, always relative to information already in the world. Generating is different. It introduces new information into the world, on its own, without needing any clear connection to what was previously there.

Imagine finishing the first draft of a report for your boss. You prefer to revise on paper, so you print it out and grab a pen. You read through, striking some words, adding others, and marking where one paragraph should be split. This is annotating since each mark is spawned as a reaction to the original text. In another paragraph, you circle a sentence, then draw a line to the start of the paragraph, indicating where you plan on moving the sentence when you get back to the keyboard. This is linking—you're defining a relationship. But then, midway through the report, you have an idea, and jot some notes about a new paragraph that will clarify your point. This is generating: adding new information, but without an explicit connection to what is already present.

A key benefit of generating, as with all externalizing actions, concerns memory. Shifting information into the world means not having to keep it in the head. Generating, however, is rooted in the acknowledgment that thoughts and ideas come to mind and, when we recognize them as valuable, we want to do something with them. If you have ever tried meditation or mindfulness techniques, you have firsthand experience with how the brain is always generating ideas, always producing new thoughts, even when you don't want them. Focusing attention and quieting those thoughts is difficult. Where mindfulness methods are designed to calm the mind and let go of thoughts, generating is how we capture them.

But more than this, generating is also about the benefits of articulating our thoughts. We have all had the experience of having an idea and then, upon writing it down, realizing that it wasn't quite right, and so we had to revise and elaborate. The act of writing changes ideas. Writing techniques that emphasize stream of consciousness, such as free writing and morning pages, derive their power by acknowledging that ideas in the head are partial. We develop them by writing them down, sketching them out, and speaking them aloud. Externalizing gives us distance and perspective and new ways to explore, shape, and modify the ideas. Generating is a precondition for understanding.

Externalizing Interactions, Summarized

To summarize, we can define our externalizing interactions in this way:

- **Annotating:** To add useful markings and meta-information to a resource
- **Linking:** To establish relationships between resources
- **Generating:** To create new information structures in the world

Young children love to share. They burst with insights and ideas and need, often desperate, to talk about it. Even as adults, we can feel a similar drive to share. Externalizing actions, in a narrower way, describes three major ways in which we satisfy this drive, by moving information into the world where it can find fertile ground. Then we can organize, break it apart, and use it to create new structures. This is the essence of our next and final theme, constructing interactions.

Constructing Knowledge

The shape of information matters. *Constructing* is how we assemble new shapes, using the information at hand to fashion meaningful structure. Constructing fills the gap between what we know and what we want to know, between what we can see and what we want to understand. Any number of words, not just constructing, could describe this process: assembling, forming, building, making, and more. We'll use constructing because the world offers so many ways to combine information, bit by bit, piece by piece, like LEGO bricks, into new shapes.

Constructing is tuning on a more ambitious scale. Where tuning makes small tweaks, constructing goes further, leading to substantial change, treating resources as building blocks, props, and scaffolds for higher level thinking. When your browser has dozens of tabs, tuning happens when you close the useless one (cutting) or save them all into a folder (collecting). Constructing happens when you work through the tabs, culling the irrelevant items, dividing the rest into groups, giving the groups memorable labels, and introducing other meaningful structure. In this, the final theme in our vocabulary of interactions for understanding, we will discuss six interactions: *chunking, composing, collecting* (again; it's versatile), *fragmenting, rearranging,* and *repicturing.*

Let's begin by differentiating between three similar interactions: collecting, chunking, and composing. We have encountered *collecting* twice before, first for how it helps us forage, and again for how we use it to tune information to our needs. Collecting naturally leads to new structures. We put files into folders, add papers to piles, and move sticky notes into clusters. This often produces a spatial arrangement and, as we saw in Chapter 9 on spatial representations, the way we structure information in space has special powers.

Chunking

Chunking groups independent yet related information together. It's the strategy our brains use to extend the severe limits of working memory, similar to when we remember ten-digit phone numbers by creating chunks of three digits, three more digits, and then four digits. We also create chunks in the world. Chunking explains why we can read a sequence of ten digits as a large sum of money when chunked as triples (5,557,283,118), and as a phone number when the same numbers are chunked in a three-three-four pattern (555-728-3118).

As an interaction, chunking is the epistemic process of grouping independent yet related information. No matter where the chunked information is found, head or world, it's all chunking.

Composing

Chunking and collecting have strong similarities. They both take different pieces of information and pull them together. But before we tease out the distinction, let's consider a third interaction. *Composing* produces a new, separate structure that has its own meaning and purpose. Where collecting and chunking take separate pieces of information and group them together, they don't introduce deep structure. Composing does. You compose an email. You don't just collect words from a dictionary or arrange those words into chunks. You assemble the words into a coherent sequence, complete with punctuation and spacing. Composing produces information with a high degree of organization and meaning.

Here's a simple way to grasp the difference between collecting, chunking, and composing. Suppose that you want to build a house from LEGO bricks. Collecting happens when you forage for useful bricks and set them aside. Chunking happens when you organize the collected bricks into useful groups: these for the walls, those for the roof, and windows in a separate pile. Composing happens when you take all of the bricks and build the house.

Fragmenting

Fragmenting runs in the opposite direction, taking information and breaking it apart. You might read books, or watch videos, to understand how a combustion engine works, but those are weak substitutes for disassembling your lawnmower or getting grease under your fingernails. Information is the same. When scholars read scientific papers, for example, they don't gloss their eyes over the words. They decompose the paper into pieces "to access and manipulate individual components of a document, such as its figures, conclusions, or references."[20] Breaking information apart, and stitching it together in new ways, is how knowledge is born.

20. Bishop (1999), p. 255

Fragmenting serves two major purposes. The obvious reason is gaining access to the individual pieces—a movie divided into scenes; a book partitioned into chapters; a recipe into ingredients. The other purpose is figuring out how the parts are related, identifying patterns, and grasping the overall structure. Fragmenting is less about breaking and more about creating opportunities for more interaction, bit by bit, piece by piece. Viewed as breaking, fragmenting is the opposite of composing and chunking, and in the opposite sense, fragmenting enables such interactions, and more besides.

Rearranging

Rearranging sounds simple enough: to adjust the spatial position of a resource or the elements within it. Simple, yet with a tremendous boon to understanding. Rearranging is what made it easier to count coins and play *Tetris*. Or consider a study of Scrabble, which found that players who rearranged their letter tiles found more word combinations, in less time, than players who could only look at the tiles.[21] Putting two letters beside each other was an effective way of triggering new words, and more effective than doing a brain-bound word search.

If arranging is the art of creating order, rearranging is the art of creating *meaningful* order for ourselves. Libraries are highly organized and librarians are experts in organizing information. The work of librarians has been called "order-making in the large": structuring vast swaths of information so that *other* people could find what they needed.[22] When it comes to how we create understanding for ourselves, arranging is key: it's order-making in the small. While all these interactions, from the beginning of this chapter through the end, play a role in understanding, there is a strong case to be made that rearranging is the essential one (which is why we dedicated an entire chapter to spatial understanding). There is an enormous amount to be gained by taking matters into our own hands, quite literally, and moving things around to explore possibilities, reveal new patterns, and simplify problems.

21. Kirsh, David, Paul Maglio, Teenie Matlock, Dorth Raphaely, and Brian Chernicky. 1999. "Interactive Skill in Scrabble." *Proceedings of the Twenty-First Annual Conference of the Cognitive Science Society*. http://adrenaline.ucsd.edu/kirsh/Articles/cogsci-final2/cogsci-final2.html
22. Marshall, Catherine. 2000. "The Future of Annotation in a Digital (Paper) World." In *Successes and Failures of Digital Libraries*, edited by Susan Harum and Michael Twidale, 97–117. Urbana-Champaign: Graduate School of Library and Information Science, University of Illinois.

Repicturing

Repicturing, the last of our fifteen interactions, changes the way that information is represented without changing the information itself. Think back to the numbers game, where the goal was to pick numbers until they summed to fifteen, and how it became vastly easier when we switched from numbers to the 3 x 3 magic grid. That's repicturing. The game was a chore when represented as numbers, and a breeze once repictured as the tic-tac-toe grid. Similarly, with the revised diabetes chart, information was neither added nor removed in the visual transformation. The revision was more understandable, thanks to repicturing.

Repicturing, like any of these interactions, isn't just for diabetes charts and everyday information in everyday life. Richard Feynman, the Nobel Prize winning physicist, developed diagrams that visually describe the interaction between different subatomic particles. These interactions are complex and, even for theoretical physicists, difficult to understand when represented in abstract mathematical equations. Known today as *Feynman diagrams*, they carry the same information as the equations, but are so much easier to use in their repictured form that they "have revolutionized nearly every aspect of theoretical physics."[23]

Collaborative work often uses repicturing to create understanding. You're at work, in a conference room, and the discussion is going nowhere. Then someone goes to the whiteboard, diagrams the options, converts words into pictures, and reframes the debate. Sometimes, changes to the representation are all it takes to trigger insight, agreement, and move the conversation forward. Sometimes, a different way of representing information is the key to understanding something as complicated as the subatomic world. Repicturing can also occur in a nonvisual sense, such as the conceptual frame or narrative that allows someone to see something in a different way.

Constructing Interactions, Summarized

Tuning interactions fiddle at the edges. Constructing is directed at the center, leading to new structures, putting information into new forms. It happens whenever understanding is driven by the need to create, build, and assemble.

- **Chunking:** To group independent yet related resources into a unified structure

---

23. Kaiser, David. 2005. "Physics and Feynman's Diagrams." *American Scientist* 93 (2): 156.

- **Composing:** To create a new resource by assembling other resources into a meaningful structure
- **Fragmenting:** To dismantle a resource into its component parts
- **Rearranging:** To alter the position of a resource or the elements within
- **Repicturing:** To convert a resource from one form, or shape, into another

By this point, after four themes and fifteen interactions, you may be wondering how this all works in practice. As our numerous examples suggest, these interactions can be somewhat slippery, overlapping in places, making them tricky to separate. Yet they also describe a wide range of ways that interaction aids understanding, and not just with digital information. So let's take another step and try using these interactions, the full arsenal, to describe a more complete scenario.

Putting It All Together: How Tony Stark Understands

In the movie *Iron Man 3*, the hero, Tony Stark, grapples with a series of terrorist bombings, one of which has seriously injured Happy Hogan, his security chief. Being Iron Man, and being a movie, Stark has fantastic technology, which includes J.A.R.V.I.S., his AI assistant, and an interactive 3D holographic data visualization system (see Figure 11.1). While the system is Hollywood magic, it's instructive to watch the scene through the lens of our interaction vocabulary.

The scene opens with Stark holding a holographic blob of reports, videos, and forensic data about the explosion. He throws this all into the room, splaying the information into space, *composing* the data into a structure akin to detectives pinning photographic evidence on a corkboard. Stark wanders into the data, asking himself "what have we got here?" scanning for information that will unravel the mystery. He's *searching*, with his body, looking this way and that, without a Google search box, yet constantly searching. When he finds nothing he says "close," *cutting* the information away, and switches analytical gears.

FIGURE 11.1 Stills from the movie *Iron Man 3*, depicting Tony Stark doing a bit of detective work, assisted by J.A.R.V.I.S., his AI assistant.

As Stark struggles to understand, he asks J.A.R.V.I.S. to *construct* a 3D representation of the blast site. Stark studies it, gets an idea, and flips through a holographic book of the forensic evidence, *searching* for something. He finds military dog tags, mangled and burned, and *repictures* them with an algorithm that brings the imprinted text into sharp relief. The tag reads "Taggart"—a clue. This leads him to consider other explosions, not just the one that injured Happy, so he asks J.A.R.V.I.S. to *compose* the data on a map. Stark *filters* the results, *searches* the remaining items, and *cuts* away some irrelevant ones until a single bombing catches his eye. "Bring it around" he tells J.A.R.V.I.S., so he can *probe* deeper. His suspicions growing stronger, and realizing the data can take him no further, Stark plans a trip to the site of the explosion.

Despite the digital wizardry, we can break down Stark's path to understanding as epistemic actions. Of course, the vocabulary we developed in this chapter isn't complete. It can't describe every gesture or turn of the head. What it does do, however, is provide a way to see the essential features of understanding in action. When we watch the scene in the theatre, we see Hollywood wizardry. When we watch through the lens of our interaction vocabulary, we see Stark composing, filtering, and searching. Moreover, we could see this just as easily if Stark were using laptops, whiteboards, and whatever else was available to us common folk outside the superhero class. That's what the interaction vocabulary does: serves as a tool for identifying what people are doing in a way that helps us unpack why they are doing it. It's a tool for understanding understanding.

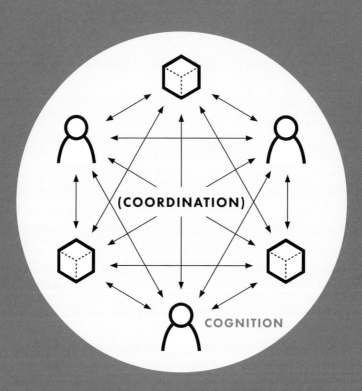

5

Coordinating
for
Understanding

Understanding isn't solely about what happens in the head, what we bring into the world, or how we interact with resources. It is also about the coordination of these things. To repeat a key phrase: understanding is about a system of resources distributed across the environment and then dynamically assembled to perform the activity and achieve a goal.

In this section, we'll examine the coordination as an activity, first challenging you to see a system of cognitive resources, before considering the many ways you might coordinate these resources. We'll look at the coordination of information at the level of the individual, reflecting on the kinds of understanding challenges you've seen thus far, before extending our focus to cases where there are many other people in the environment, each with their own set of experiences and viewpoints.

In short, we need to appreciate the complex interplay between prior associations, things we bring into and manipulate in the world, and also how we figure things out by collaborating and cooperating with others.

12

Seeing the System of Cognitive Resources

Perspective is worth 80 IQ points.

—ALAN KAY, COMPUTER SCIENTIST

It was the early days of the great depression when Malcolm McLean graduated from high school. Lacking the money for college, he got a job pumping gas, saved up the then-substantial sum of $120, and bought a used truck to start his own trucking company.[1] McLean was ambitious, and by the early fifties, despite the occasional setback, his fleet had almost 1,800 trucks. It was the largest trucking operation in the southern states and fifth largest in the country. But this success was merely a warm-up act, for Malcolm McLean had an idea that would change the world.

The genesis of his big idea came in 1937 when McLean delivered cotton bales to the port in Hoboken, New Jersey. He pulled up to the docks and waited for the longshoreman to heave the bales off the truck, carry them onto the ship, and pack them in the hold. The job took most of the day, leaving McLean

---

1. Mayo, Anthony J., and Nitin Nohria. 2005. "The Truck Driver Who Reinvented Shipping." HBS Working Knowledge. October 3, 2005. https://hbswk.hbs.edu/item/the-truck-driver-who-reinvented-shipping

waiting around, paralyzed with inaction, and frustrated—a parked truck was a truck not moving, and a truck not moving was a truck losing money.

In those days, cargo was loaded onto ships item by item: each box, crate, barrel, and sack was individually stowed in the hold. Known as *break bulk cargo*, this method of loading was so laborious that a ship could spend more time dockside than on the water. This was fine in the age of sailing ships, when voyages might take months, but by the 1930s, the inefficiencies had become a costly impediment. "There has to be a better way," McLean mused, "than loading cargo aboard ship piece by piece."

McLean's idea, which we know today as *container shipping*, would obliterate this impediment. Instead of dealing with cargo piece-by-piece, McLean wanted to pack cargo, long before it arrived at the docks, into a truck-sized box. The box would be loaded at the warehouse, lifted onto a truck, driven to the harbor, and lifted off. The truck could drive away, and the just-delivered container could be loaded onto the ship, when convenient, at a fractional cost. There was only one question: How small a fraction?

McLean first tested his big idea with beer.[2] First, analysts calculated the cost of sending beer from New York to Miami as break bulk cargo. They estimated it cost four dollars per ton to load the truck at the factory, drive it to the warehouse, unload the beer into a storage shed, move the beer from the shed to the docks, wrap the beer in netting, hoist the netting onto the ship, and finally unwrap the beer and stow it in the hold. When the bean counters ran the numbers, the loading cost—from warehouse to loaded ship—for McLean's container idea was a measly twenty-five cents per ton. Even including the cost of the container, McLean's method was 94 percent cheaper. Clearly, the container was a promising idea. Even so, the analysts were wrong: container shipping would turn out to be even cheaper.

Two years after selling his trucking company, in the spring of 1956, McLean launched the first modern container ship. He purchased an old tanker, rigged it with a special decking to hold containers, and constructed a dockside crane to lift his big metal boxes onto the ship (see Figure 12.1). For its maiden run, the revamped tanker was loaded with 56 containers in less than eight hours and sailed for Houston later that day. In those days, loading that much break

---

2. Levinson, Marc. 2016. *The Box: How the Shipping Container Made the World Smaller and the World Economy Bigger.* Princeton: Princeton University Press.

bulk cargo would have cost $5.83 a ton. Loading the *Ideal-X* came in at 15.8 cents per ton.

FIGURE 12.1 Shipping container entrepreneur Malcom McLean with his Sea-Land shipping containers. *Photo courtesy of Maersk Line.*

Container shipping did more than reduce the cost of loading and unloading: it made the entire process of global shipping laughably cheap. In the late 1950s, well before containers became the norm, the cost of importing goods via ocean freight into the United States was 10 percent of a product's value. Exporting was higher, about 12 percent on average, and when you accounted for the trip from overseas factory to domestic warehouse—trucking, railways, storage fees, port fees, and more—the cost of ocean shipping could be 25 percent of a product's cost. The container didn't reduce costs—it demolished them. Container historian Marc Levinson notes that by the early 2000s, it cost more money to fly between Ohio and Malaysia, first-class, than shipping a 25-ton container of coffeemakers between the same destinations.

But McLean's real insight, and the reason his idea is relevant here, wasn't about the container. That big metal box, so ubiquitous today, was still just a big metal box. McLean's idea came about because he saw something deeper and more fundamental. Levinson summed up McLean's achievement this way:

> Malcom McLean's fundamental insight, commonplace today, but quite radical in the 1950s, was that the shipping industry's business was moving cargo, not sailing ships. That insight led

him to a concept of containerization quite different than anything that had come before. McLean understood that reducing the cost of shipping goods required not just a metal box but an entire new way of handling freight. *Every part of the system—ports, ships, cranes, storage facilities, trucks, trains, and the operations of the systems—would have to change.* In that understanding, he was years ahead of almost everyone else in the transportation industry."[3] (emphasis added)

Mark that phrase—*every part of the system would have to change*—for it captures both the essence of McLean's insight and the implications. He didn't see a truck, or a ship, or even a container. He saw a *system*. Everyone in the industry saw the same pieces and everyone knew these pieces were connected, but they only paid attention to their piece of the puzzle, be it trucks or ships or warehouses or tariffs. McLean wasn't interested in the pieces, only how fitting them together led to seeing something bigger. He took a step back, took a different stance on the problem, and saw a global system for moving cargo.

Until this point, we have explored understanding problems in much the same way as the world thought about cargo before containers: as a series of related yet separate pieces—the brain, perception, representations, and interaction. What we haven't done, until now, is pull a McLean: step back to see *a system of understanding*. That's what we'll do in this chapter. Let's begin by looking at how people fly airplanes.

Seeing a System of Understanding

It was 1929 when pilot Jimmy Doolittle did the impossible. He covered the windows of his Husky training plane, blinding himself to the outside world, then took off, circled the airfield, and touched down in a smooth landing. Doolittle had flown by instruments alone, the first person to ever do this, unable to see anything but the knobs and levers and dials in his cockpit. It was a critical step toward modern aviation. Before Doolittle, flying in anything other than clear skies was a treacherous business. Flying through clouds left pilots confused, often to their peril, even their death. Instrument flying made it possible to head into the clouds, or fog, even total darkness, and be confident you would come out alive.

---

3. Levinson (2016), p. 53

Pilots need to rapidly interpret a ceaseless flow of information, which makes flying an understanding problem that, without the necessary skills, has life-or-death consequences. The pilot and copilot need to know where the aircraft is heading, how fast it's flying, the current altitude, the position of flaps, if the landing gear are raised, how much fuel remains, if the plane is on course, and more. Before Doolittle, pilots gathered most of this information by looking out the window. Today, they get it from instruments. An airplane cockpit is an environment loaded with external representations that make flying easier and safer.

If you want to study how pilots fly, where would you focus your analysis? Would you look at the instruments? Would you look at the controls in the cockpit? If you had a portable real-time brain scanner, would you monitor the pilot's neural patterns? Or perhaps you would observe how pilots interact with the instruments? While each of these could reveal something of interest, none would give you a complete and robust picture of how flying actually happens. But McLean points to the alternative: stop looking at the pieces, step back, and see the system.

This is exactly what the cognitive scientist Ed Hutchins did when he asked the question "How does a cockpit remember its speed?"[4] Note the subtle yet critical shift. Hutchins focused on the cockpit's memory, not the pilot's.

Speed is an indispensable piece of information for pilots. They need to fly fast enough to keep the plane aloft and prevent stalling. But landing requires the pilot to *reduce* speed so that, once on the ground, the plane can brake safely before the runway ends. In this situation, the speed has to be as slow as possible without stalling. Landing is almost the opposite of flying: instead of making the plane go fast and high, you have to keep it slow and close to the ground. As a result, remembering the speed is essential for a safe landing.

When Hutchins looked at how pilots land their planes, he didn't look at the pilot, or even the instruments. Instead, he viewed the pilot as part of a system that includes the instruments, the copilot, the plane, and the surrounding environment. In other words, Hutchins changed his *unit of analysis* from the mind of an individual pilot to the system of the whole cockpit. McLean did the same thing by adjusting his perspective from a single mode of transport (whether it was trucks or ships or trains) to an interconnected system for moving cargo.

---

4. Hutchins, Edwin. 1995. "How a Cockpit Remembers Its Speeds." *Cognitive Science* 19 (3): 265–88. https://doi.org/10.1207/s15516709cog1903_1

This puts a novel twist on the idea of the cockpit as a representation-rich environment. Yes, each instrument is a representation. But there are also mental representations in the head of the pilot and the copilot. Even what can be seen through the window, such as the lights on the runway, can be thought of as representing information used to fly the plane. In the standard view, which was centered on the pilot, landing the plane meant reading instruments, mental computation, and adjusting controls. In Hutchins's analysis, the plane landed when these representations worked together as a coherent system.

Consider the representations needed to safely land a passenger jet: flap positions, current airspeed, rate of descent, aircraft weight, and the safe landing speed for the approaching runway. Then there are messages from the control tower, chatter from the copilot, and whatever can be seen out the window. In smaller aircraft, there may not be a copilot. In older aircraft, the safe landing speed might be calculated from a booklet prior to landing, while other aircraft might display this automatically on a computer. In an emergency situation, some instruments may fail. But in each case, looking at the cockpit as a whole, rather than at an individual pilot, provides a dramatically different perspective. For the plane to land safely, all this information needs to flow smoothly around the cockpit.

The cockpit, in this view, is a system for doing the cognitive work of flying and landing the plane. This system is comprised of myriad representations working in lockstep. The pilots store the airspeed in working memory, to be sure, but speed is also tracked and measured and recorded through other instruments and information sources. The pilot is obviously doing cognitive work. But when we change the unit of analysis—pulling a McLean—we can see the whole cockpit doing cognitive work. Viewed this way, the plane doesn't land because of what the pilot does. The landing happens because the pilot, the copilot, the instruments, the control tower, and the flight controls function as a *distributed* cognitive system.

Admittedly, it feels strange to say that a cockpit, or anything that isn't purely biological, does cognitive work. But forget not—the brain is not the mind. If you multiply 32 by 11 in your head, the cognitive work happens in your brain. Where does it happen when you use pencil and paper? Not in your brain and not in the pencil either. It happens everywhere, spread across brain, hand, pencil, and graphite symbols etched on the page.

This shift in perspective, away from objects and representations and inter-actions, and toward distributed cognitive systems, is a necessary step if we want to take on the most complex of understanding problems. It changes what we look at and how we interpret what we see. When we narrow our atten-tion to a single brain, an isolated representation, or a solitary interaction, we block ourselves from seeing the whole story. This broader vantage point is what illuminates thorny and multifaceted problems, especially when there is a strong social dimension. Quite often, the primary unit of analysis should be, as Hutchins puts it, "a socio-technical system, rather than an individual mind,"[5] or, we would add, an individual object, screen, or app. With the phrase "socio-technical system," Hutchins was simply saying that cognition is distrib-uted across other people (the *socio-* part) as well as things, artifacts, materials, and technology (the *technical* part).

5. Hutchins, Edwin. 2010. "Cognitive Ecology." *Topics in Cognitive Science* 2 (4): 705–15.
    https://doi.org/10.1111/j.1756-8765.2010.01089.x

The Locus of Understanding

To say that cognition is distributed across people and things doesn't mean we're talking about a new kind of cognition.[6] It's about seeing how all forms of cognitive activity—remembering, planning, reasoning, deciding, analyzing—depend on the ways that people use their available resources. Moreover, these cognitive resources can include everything from neurons and whiteboards to laptops and airspeed indicators. Figuring it out is the art of bringing all this to bear.

While changing the unit of analysis seems obvious, even trivial, it's a tough leap to make. When the leap does happen, it can produce powerful insights, which is what happened for Malcolm McLean. He saw how containers would stitch trucks, ships, and trains together into a globally distributed set of transportation resources. Other people had tried putting cargo in boxes, but McLean made the bigger leap, recognizing that the benefit wasn't the box; it was how the box could integrate multiple modes of transport. When Hutchins analyzed pilot landings, he made a similar leap, seeing a smooth flow of information across pilots, instruments, and cockpit controls. Expanding the unit of analysis revealed a system with "cognitive properties that differ radically from the cognitive properties of the components alone, no matter how much we know about the details of those components."[7]

Should we always adopt this perspective? Frankly, no. Think of a microscope from your high school biology class. You must choose the right level of magnification (20x, 50x, 100x, or higher) and then adjust the lens until a clear image emerges. We're doing the same kind of thing here. Sometimes, you need a high-powered lens so that you can zoom in on a single representation. Other times you need to zoom out to see how the person is interacting with a representation. And sometimes, you need to zoom out, even way out, to see everything.

This is the *locus of understanding*. *Locus* is Latin for place, and we introduce this phrase to mean *where* understanding happens. It refers to the position we must adopt to see how understanding is created as part of a system. Adopting

6. Halverson, Christine A. 2002. "Activity Theory and Distributed Cognition: Or What Does CSCW Need to DO with Theories?" *Computer Supported Cooperative Work (CSCW)* 11 (1–2): 243–67. https://doi.org/10.1023/a:1015298005381

7. Zhang, Jiajie, and Vimla L. Patel. 2006. "Distributed Cognition, Representation, and Affordance." *Pragmatics & Cognition* 14 (2): 333–41. https://doi.org/10.1075/pc.14.2.12zha

the word *locus* carries echoes of Andy Clark on embodiment: "It is increasingly clear that, in a wide variety of cases, the individual brain should not be the sole locus of cognitive scientific interest. Cognition is not a phenomenon that can be successfully studied while marginalizing the roles of body, world and action."[8]

The locus varies with the understanding problem, like adjusting the zoom on a metaphorical microscope. Fix the locus to the airspeed indicator, and we miss the chatter between pilot and copilot. But set the locus on the human verbal chatter, and we also miss the airspeed indicator. Sometimes, we need a narrower locus, yet more often we need to consciously pull back until everything is in view. When our locus includes more than one part of the system—one representation, one app, one device, or one person—then it becomes a matter of recognizing how the pieces fit together. Let's explore some examples where the locus of understanding is spread wide.

Everyday Understanding with Everyday Things

Adjusting the locus of understanding provides deep insight into everyday systems of understanding, not just cockpits and global transportation systems. Let's consider a few examples.

Assembling furniture. Buy shelving from IKEA, and they throw in a puzzle for free: you open the box, lay out pieces, grab bolts, skim instructions, and solve the puzzle. You might group identical pieces in a stack. If two pieces look similar, you might need to hold them up and compare them to the picture in the manual. Shelves are big, and you might need a second person. Understanding how to assemble the furniture is more than reading the manual.

Ordering a meal. Going to your favorite restaurant means stepping into a well-ordered cognitive system. Consider everything that happens when you order your meal: choosing items from the menu, communicating your choice to the waiter, the waiter writing it down (or storing it in their head), the waiter accurately getting the order to the kitchen, the cooks matching the order to the ingredients and cooking equipment, checking temperature and doneness,

---

8. Clark, Andy. 1999. "An Embodied Cognitive Science?" *Trends in Cognitive Sciences* 3 (9): 345–51. https://doi.org/10.1016/s1364-6613(99)01361-3

arranging things on the plate, signaling when the food is ready, and so forth. Ordering food is more than reading the menu and making a choice.

Managing family life. Family life is chaotic with going to work, walking the dog, driving to swimming lessons, and shopping for groceries. Families use calendars and fridge doors to stay on track, but it's a messy process none-theless. It's so messy that some families have adopted techniques from agile software development, complete with kanban boards and daily family standup meetings.[9] One technique, familiar even to those for whom agile means that which fades with age, is using checklists as a scaffold to help children do their chores and complete all the steps. The secret, however, lies not in kanban boards and checklists, but in thinking of families as a distributed, cognitive system that includes parents, children, whiteboards, sticky notes, and other resources. Managing family life is more than maintaining a calendar.

Each of these examples *could* be boiled down and tackled as a problem of per-ception, or external representations, or interactions. Indeed, over the previous chapters we have shown why, and how, each of these provides useful lenses for thinking about understanding problems. Consider again the diabetes chart Stephen created for his son: it worked because it represented information so well. Powerful as these lenses can be, they eventually reach a breaking point in much the same way that walking won't always get you where you want to go; sometimes, you need a bike, a car, or a bus. Whenever we hit that breaking point, it's time to step back, pull a McLean, and adjust the locus of understanding.

When we use the phrase "distributed cognitive resources," we mean anything that contributes to the cognitive work being done. Suppose that you're head-ing out to the grocery store and need ingredients for making a big Sunday dinner featuring a savory roasted chicken. If you tried to remember your gro-cery list—the chicken, seasoning, vegetables, and other items—the cognitive resources would include memory and other brainbound processes. Of course, these days you're more likely to make a list of ingredients on your phone. Adjusting the locus of understanding means that you can, and should, treat the phone as a cognitive resource. Some of the memory is in your head, and

9. Feiler, Bruce S. 2013. *The Secrets of Happy Families: Improve Your Mornings, Tell Your Family History, Fight Smarter, Go Out and Play, and Much More.* New York, NY: William Morrow, an imprint of HarperCollinsPublishers; Starr, David, and Eleanor Starr. 2009. "Agile Practices for Families: Iterating with Children and Parents." *2009 Agile Conference*, 344–49. Chicago, USA: IEEE. https://doi.org/10.1109/agile.2009.53

some is on your phone. When you're in the store, see a fresh loaf of bread, and think "Oh, yes, we need bread, too," then the physical store becomes another resource. Open a text on cognitive science, and you will find pages and pages about human memory, but only as something in the head. In everyday life, memory is a cognitive resource that we distribute, routinely and casually, across the brain and world.

The cognitive scientist Donald Norman once conducted a memory experiment that elucidated how much depends on our perspective. Norman had subjects listen to a sequence of numbers (say, 9, 8, 1, 4, 3, 5, 7). Then he told them one of the numbers (say, 4) and asked them to remember which number came next. During the experiment, Norman realized that one woman was writing down the numbers and, as a result, always got the correct answer. In his view, she was cheating, so he asked her to leave the experiment. She was puzzled by his request, and upset, because she was doing so well.

Was she cheating? That's a matter of perspective. The woman was participating in a scientific study about how the brain remembers information. In that context, yes, most definitely, she was cheating. But in the context of how people go about their everyday lives, the woman was doing what comes normally to us all—using the external world to improve what her mind could do alone, but not do well. Reflecting on the experience years later, Norman realized that, from her perspective, what he'd asked her to do was counter to how humans actually think: "Who but an experimental psychologist would expect anyone to remember anything as silly as unrelated digits without the aid of paper and pencil?"[10]

Who, indeed? Imagine a scientist who studies human locomotion by taking volunteers, putting their legs in a cast, and asking them to walk across burning coals. Such a study, if well designed, could reveal insights into the motor mechanics of the human leg. The study also seems bizarre (not to mention cruel), given how disconnected it is from how people actually walk. Yet this is how cognitive science is often done: studying how people think under artificial conditions and then extrapolating to everyday experience. Done well, this approach is how good science tends to work, even though everyday experience rarely includes traversing burning hot coals.

10. Norman, Donald A. 1993. *Things That Make Us Smart: Defending Human Attributes in the Age of the Machine*. Reading, MA: Addison-Wesley.

Despite these examples, speaking of your smartphone as a cognitive resource can feel a touch odd. We have a deep association between the terms *cognition* and *brain*. Andy Clark has proposed a useful way to overcome this association, which he calls the *parity principle*.

> If, as we confront some task, a part of the world functions as a process which, were it to go on in the head, we would have no hesitation in accepting as part of the cognitive process, then that part of the world is (for that time) part of the cognitive process.[11]

Need to calculate the square root of 1,369? You have a lot of cognitive resources at your disposal. If you answer the question in your head, you'd have "no hesitation" in accepting that as cognitive. So why should it be any different if you work it out on paper, punch it into a calculator, ask a mathematically capable colleague, or say "Hey Google, what's the square root of 1,369?" The parity principle says that we can, and should, treat each of these alternatives as part of the cognitive system.

The parity principles show how our tools, especially well-designed tools, can profoundly enhance our capabilities to understand. If we define the mind as the brain, we must also admit to its limitations. There is much we cannot remember or learn or analyze or make sense of, until we extend the mind outward. This is why we make tools and technologies, not for their own sake, but to overcome the inherent limitations of our innate cognitive capabilities. This is the work of design.

Cognitive Resources as Material Objects

When we adjust the locus of understanding and combine it with the parity principle, the world becomes a place where *anything* can serve as a resource for understanding. We've already seen examples of everyday objects, such as sticky notes and calculators. Now let's consider another everyday object, the whiteboard, in a particular environment: trauma centers.

Hospitals exist in a state of constant flux, with perpetual and unpredictable changes to the operating schedule. When researchers studied a large trauma

11. Clark, Andy, and David Chalmers. 1998. "The Extended Mind." *Analysis* 58 (1): 7–19. https://doi.org/10.1093/analys/58.1.7

center, one with six operating rooms (ORs) and 6,000 admissions per year, they found the humble whiteboard was more than helpful—it was critical.[12]

The whiteboard was large, about 12 feet by 4 feet, and had been divided into sections for scheduled surgeries, unscheduled surgeries, names of OR staff, and important announcements. Magnetic strips made it easy to move and adjust the schedule, assign people to particular schedules, and make other ad hoc changes. Extra information about a patient or the status of a surgery was added by special magnets, such as smiley faces, or slips of paper tucked under a magnet. Being a whiteboard, critical information was often added to the board as needed. Each of these elements served as a cognitive resource.

The real value, however, was in the social processes and routines that were connected to the whiteboard. Being large, it was easy for many people to gather around the board to consider new schedules, update the status of patients, assign staff to a surgery, consider new plans, and debate critical decisions. Taking the trauma center as the locus of understanding, rather than just the whiteboard, meant seeing the people as resources in the cognitive system, too. The whiteboard didn't do cognitive work on its own any more than the people managed everything in their heads.

The trauma center was a "joint human-board cognitive system."[13] It's easy to see the humans as doing cognitive work. They remember details about patients, consider alternative operating schedules, take in new information, suggest treatments, juggle priorities, and make decisions. But the people can't do all this without some external aids, and the whiteboard is especially powerful because it can play so many roles. It's the critical link.

People routinely enlist everyday objects as cognitive resources. The whiteboard is an example of a formal system created by a group, but individuals do the same thing in less formal, but no less useful ways. Continuing in the healthcare domain, consider the problem of taking medications at the proper dosage and the correct times. This can be a vexing problem, especially when faced with multiple medications, each of which has its own requirements. Small bottles, small type, and written instructions require patients to do a lot of cognitive work. The obvious solution is to design a better pill bottle with a

12. Xiao, Yan, Caterina Lasome, Jacqueline Moss, Colin F. Mackenzie, and Samer Faraj. 2001. "Cognitive Properties of a Whiteboard: A Case Study in a Trauma Centre." *ECSCW 2001*, 259–78. https://doi.org/10.1007/0-306-48019-0_14

13. Xiao et al. (2001), p. 268

better external representation showing when to take the medication and how much. PillPack, for instance, promises "your medication, made easy" by sending your pills in a roll of packets organized by time and date. The first packet might be for Sunday at 9 a.m., and once you pull it off the roll, you'll see the next packet, which could be that same day at 2 p.m.

While better labels and services like PillPack are an improvement, it's not the only way to organize medications. A study of Danish seniors, for example, found that people created effective strategies by distributing their medications throughout their home.[14] One patient kept her pill bottles in the kitchen cabinet and laid them out, from left to right, in the order it was to be taken. This spatial arrangement encoded the sequence directly in the world, making the bottles function as a kind of physical checklist. Another patient used a similar technique for her medications, except for one prescription. She had a heart condition and only needed to take the pills if she deemed it necessary. To mark this pill as special, she kept it on a separate shelf, away from anything else, clearly visible, and easy to reach. This is a kind of annotation through spatial positioning, rather than adding a special mark to the object.

Other people organized their treatment around time instead of space. One woman, who viewed her medical life as deeply private, kept her pills in a piano bench. All her medication was to be taken at mealtimes, so every day at breakfast, lunch, and dinner, she first made her way to the piano. The time of day

14. Palen, Leysia, and Stinne Aaløkke. 2006. "Of Pill Boxes and Piano Benches." *Proceedings of the 2006 20th Anniversary Conference on Computer Supported Cooperative Work - CSCW 06*, 77–89. https://doi.org/10.1145/1180875.1180888

was the cue for action, a strategy that worked extremely well, until her prescriptions changed to include medicines to be taken outside of meal times, at which time she had to adapt new strategies.

Time and space are powerful principles for understanding how people distribute cognitive resources. We've seen this before in our work on external representations. But now we're seeing it in the light of pulling a McLean. In the case of medications at home, it's typical for people to construct their own cognitive system. Do you have a pill to be taken every night before bed? How about keeping it in the nightstand or putting it right next to your toothbrush. Take something daily with breakfast? Maybe keep it on the kitchen table or tuck it next to the cereal boxes.

Or consider the art of bartending, which looks to be a problem of simple memorization: learn the recipes, mix the drinks. And indeed this is where novice bartenders begin. But when the psychologist King Beach enrolled in bartending school, he found that skilled bartenders made extensive use of the physical world as a memory device.[15]

Photo by Helena Yankovska on Unsplash

15. Beach, King. 1993. "Becoming a Bartender: The Role of External Memory Cues in a Work-Directed Educational Activity." *Applied Cognitive Psychology* 7 (3): 191–204. https://doi.org/10.1002/acp.2350070304

Bartending students learn at least a hundred recipes. They are judged on speed and accuracy and, even as they take additional orders, must be able to mix multiple drinks simultaneously. With no time for reading recipes, they must do all this from memory, but what counts as memory? In the first few weeks, students memorize drink recipes and use a strategy that Beach called *verbal mnemonic systems* (VMS). These verbal mnemonics were names of drinks, ingredients, and steps in the process, which students often spoke aloud as they mixed: get a shot glass, then vermouth, and so forth. This worked for mixing one drink at a time and when they could focus. But bars are noisy places, distractions abound, and the art of bartending also means multitasking. The VMS strategy, when plunked into the real world, is slow and leads to many mistakes.

Skilled bartenders used an alternative strategy, which Beach called *material mnemonic systems* (MMS). This approach distributed objects in space to constrain choices and sequence operations. For example, if asked to produce a whiskey sour, a vodka martini, and a white Russian the bartender would start by choosing the glasses, which varied with drink type, and arranging them on the bar rail, in order. The shape of the glass, its location, and the contents were a *material* form of memory. They triggered which drinks to mix, the ingredients required, and who ordered which drink. Eventually, novice bartenders adopted the same strategy.

Whiteboards, piano benches, and martini glasses are not normally treated as cognitive resources. They are things that exist out there, beyond the head. But they are not beyond the *mind*. These examples illustrate, in their own way, how cognition is linked to place and that there is a material aspect of how we think. Separating mental activity from physical reality leads to an impoverished description of how understanding happens. Only when we adjust the locus of understanding does a martini glass become a cognitive resource, and doing so reveals the glass not as James Bond's preferred drinking vessel, but a tool for thought.

Expanding the Locus of Understanding

When we adjust the locus of understanding, there is always a question of how much to include. In the airplane example, we changed the locus from the instrument panel to the cockpit as a whole, but we don't need to stop there. We could expand further to include the air traffic control system. While Hutchins was rethinking how a cockpit does cognitive work, another researcher, Wendy MacKay, was studying airport control towers. Her research drew attention to a particular technology in common use at the time: paper flight strips.[16]

The flight strip is a long narrow piece of paper, about one-inch wide and eight inches long, that concisely captures all the essential data about a flight: airline, flight number, location, heading, and more. It might seem low-tech, but paper flight strips are a critical tool for understanding what is happening at the airport and directing traffic. Search YouTube for air traffic control towers, and you can see this in action: people wearing headsets, watching radar, big screens, and looking out of the tower. And right there, central to the entire operation, are racks and racks of flight strips.

Each flight strip is slotted into a frame, which can be slid into a rack that holds dozens of flight strips. Once in the rack, strips can be quickly rearranged to reflect the sequence of incoming flights. Controllers can pull a strip partly out of the rack, a lightweight method to draw attention to a flight. Being paper, it's easy to add status updates right on the strip without going through menus or learning arcane features of an interface. Strips can be rapidly moved to another rack, a simple and intuitive way to assign responsibility of a flight to other people in the control tower.

This description should have a familiar ring about it. These are our epistemic actions from the previous chapter, such as rearranging, annotating, composing, fragmenting, and searching. While there have been many efforts to replace these paper strips with electronic ones, usually under the banner of modernization, the benefits of these easily manipulated paper representations are so substantial that they remain a feature in air traffic control towers the world over.

Flight strips endure for several reasons. The most obvious is that they're a cheap, effective medium for representing flight data, while also affording fluid epistemic interactions. The more powerful reason is how they smooth the cognitive work of the entire control tower by distributing that work across a team of people and the tools they are using. In their book on why paper remains such a persistent feature of knowledge-work, even in the digital era,

---

16. MacKay, Wendy E. 1999. "Is Paper Safer? The Role of Paper Flight Strips in Air Traffic Control." *ACM Transactions on Computer-Human Interaction* (*TOCHI*) 6 (4): 311–40. https://doi.org/10.1145/331490.331491

Abigail Sellen and Richard Harper summarized the value of flight strips this way: "Attempts to introduce electronic alternatives to paper flight strips have turned out to be fraught with very profound problems because it is not just the flight progress data tools—the strips themselves—that need to be changed but also the teamwork in those settings and the air traffic movement processes they allow."[17] Flight strips are the linchpin of a functional air traffic control *system*, and much of their utility is overlooked when the locus of understanding is placed on the strips or the interactions they enable. Being paper is not even what matters. It's how the flight strips integrate the parts of the air traffic control system together: flight data, radar signals, radio chatter, and the people in the room.

Putting the locus at the entire control tower allows us to see that flight data isn't just in the flight strips—it's everywhere. Some of it's on the radar screens, some is on the flight strips, some is visible out the window, and a lot of it is in the heads of the people in the room. The people are a vital part of the system. As individuals, they are engaged in an understanding problem, but viewing them as individuals only gets us so far. Adjust the locus of understanding and the entire air traffic control tower can be understood as a giant distributed cognitive system for tackling the same problem at a larger scale.

But why stop at the tower? The entire air traffic system—flight decks, control centers, pilots, and all communication—can also be viewed as a part of a single distributed cognitive system.

> A cognitive system is one that performs cognitive work via cognitive functions such as communicating, deciding, planning, and problem solving … as, for example, in military command and control, transportation, health care, and air traffic management. These sorts of cognitive functions are supported by cognitive processes such as perceiving, analyzing, exchanging information, and manipulating. The characterization of the airspace as a cognitive system represents a claim that the airspace is an entity that does cognitive work.[18]

---

17. Sellen, Abigail J., and Richard H. R. Harper. 2002. *The Myth of the Paperless Office.* Cambridge, MA: MIT Press, 111.
18. Lintern, Gavan. 2011. "The Airspace as a Cognitive System." *The International Journal of Aviation Psychology* 21 (1): 3–15. https://doi.org/10.1080/10508414.2011.537556

Once again, we have this idea that adjusting the locus of understanding to something beyond the brain is often to our benefit. But that adjustment is more than a single step. We can set the dial at one of several levels—from the airspeed indicator, to the cockpit, to the control tower, to the airspace—and with each new locus, different patterns and connections between the constituent parts are revealed.

Can a Horse Do Math?

Name a famous horse, and you will likely think of a racehorse, perhaps Seabiscuit or Secretariat. But across Europe, early in the twentieth century, the most well-known horse was famous not for his speed, but for his math skills. His name was Clever Hans and according to his owner, Wilhelm von Osten, Hans could add, subtract, multiply, divide, and tell time (see Figure 12.2). He even learned to calculate square roots and work with fractions. Von Osten would ask Hans a question, such as "What is 2 times 6?" and the clever equine would tap his hoof twelve times. Hans was so famous that news of him spread across Europe and even the Atlantic Ocean. In 1904, he was featured in *The New York Times*, which proclaimed that Hans "can do almost everything but talk."[19]

Hans was so amazing that some grew suspicious. There had to be a trick, though von Osten refuted all accusations. Eventually, a commission was established to investigate. The Hans Commission, as it was known, found no evidence of trickery, subterfuge, or wrong-doing. Hans could indeed, the commission concluded, do math.

Then a psychologist named Oskar Pfungst got involved, and here the story takes an important turn. Pfungst devised a series of experiments and found that, no matter who asked the questions, Hans still got the correct answer. While this proved that von Osten was not conspiring with his horse, Pfungst also found that when von Osten didn't know the answer, Hans didn't either. Von Osten was on the level, yet there was still a mysterious force at play.

19. Heyn, Edward T. 1904. "Berlin's Wonderful Horse." *The New York Times*, September 4, 1904.

FIGURE 12.2 Wilhelm von Osten and Clever Hans.

Pfungst kept digging and devised a series of experiments that showed Hans was picking up on subtle cues from von Osten. Hans would tap out his answer and, as he approached the correct number, von Osten would tense his shoulders, or raise his head, or give a slight smile. Hans interpreted these as a cue to stop tapping his hoof. Von Osten wasn't doing this deliberately. The experiments showed that Hans responded to cues from anyone, including Pfungst, and these cues could be incredibly subtle. Even after he had solved the riddle, Pfungst, too, when in the same room as Hans, was unable to prevent himself from sending these signals.[20]

Clever Hans lives on in psychology courses, where the story is told as a warning against poorly designed experiments. The experimenter must not influence the participant in any way that students learn, and that influence can be so delicate that it might not even be consciously detectable. Pfungst's careful work led to the double-blind experiment, where the subject cannot see, or hear, or influence the experimenter in any way—and vice versa. Research done this way is now the gold standard for any research that involves humans or animals.

This is where the story usually ends. But when Pfungst ran his double-blind experiments, he also narrowed the locus of understanding down to Hans, all alone, stripped of any connection to the outside world. That's great for the experimenter, who wants to isolate the phenomenon under investigation, but

20. Pfungst, Oskar. 1911. *Clever Hans (the Horse of Mr. von Osten): A Contribution to Experimental Animal and Human Psychology.* Translated by Carl L. Rahn. New York: Henry Holt and Company.

it doesn't reflect how people use the world around them to think, whether it's landing a plane or mixing a whiskey sour.

Let's return to our original question: Does Hans do math? The answer depends on our locus of understanding. If the locus is Hans's brain in isolation, then no, he doesn't do math. But if we expand the locus to include Hans and von Osten, then yes, he very much does. Hans all alone, double-blind, is the same as you in a dark room, without a calculator or even an abacus. But Hans *plus* von Osten is also like you with a calculator in hand—or these days, a smartphone. Strip the externalities away, and your cognitive capability is radically diminished.

To adjust the locus of understanding is to cross boundaries, and boundaries are where things get interesting. Do we draw the boundary at the instrument or the cockpit, the flight strip or the control tower, the bartender or the bar? The question itself can mislead us, for it suggests there is a single best place, always, to draw this boundary. There isn't. Where we put this boundary depends on what we are trying to see in the system.

Think back to Gregory Bateson's thought experiment of the blind man with a stick going tap, tap, tap. Where, Bateson asked us to consider, does the man's mental system end? At his skin, at the handle of the stick, partway down the stick, or at the end? All nonsense questions, Bateson argued. You need everything working together. The way to see everything is to pull a McLean, adjust the locus of understanding, and see von Osten and Clever Hans as part of the same cognitive system. It's all a matter of perspective.

A Shifting Coalition of Resources

Changing the locus of understanding can have enormous consequences. Malcolm McLean changed his locus and invented the shipping container, which, eventually, gave rise to global supply chains. When James Doolittle flew by instruments, he started a chain reaction that set off decades of innovation to simplify and automate air travel. But it is also naive to think that introducing automation did no more than off-load work from the pilot's brain into a device in the cockpit. The story is *much* more complicated. Consider the following description of cockpit automation from John Lauber, an aviation safety engineer, who also sits on the National Transportation Safety Board (NTSB):

Cockpit automation increases, decreases, and redistributes workload. It enhances situational awareness, takes pilots out of the loop, increases head-down time, frees the pilot to scan more often, reduces training requirements, increases training requirements, makes a pilot's job easier, increases fatigue, changes the role of the pilot, has not changed the role, makes things less expensive, more expensive, is highly reliable, minimizes human error, leads to error, changes the nature of human error, tunes out small errors, raises likelihood of gross errors, is desired by pilots, is not trusted, leads to boredom, frees pilot from the mundane, and finally increases air safety and has an adverse effect on safety.[21]

This remarkable paragraph highlights just how dramatic the ripple effects can be. This is why paper flight strips have retained their place well into the digital era. As a representation, flight strips are easily digitized, but this also discounts their central role in the cognitive work of air traffic control towers. In some systems, small changes create minor ripples. But in other systems, small changes create a cascade of unexpected change, some of which might be disastrous.

This reflects the reality of adjusting our locus of understanding to see a distributed system. When information is distributed around, it is also *re*distributed around, which turns our expanded cognitive apparatus into a "shifting coalition of resources and constraints, some physical, some social, some cultural, some computational (involving both internal and external computational resources)."[22] That's what we saw with the emergency room, and the bartender, and the air traffic control room. This is what happens when we assemble IKEA furniture and order a meal at a restaurant. The cognitive resources at our disposal, whether in the head or out in the world, function within this "shifting coalition." The first step is to pull a McLean and see the system. The next step is to see how the pieces work together. That requires coordination.

---

21. Mindell, David A. 2015. *Our Robots, Ourselves: Robotics and the Myths of Autonomy*. New York: Viking, 73-74.
22. Kirsh, David. 1999. "Distributed Cognition, Coordination and Environment Design." *Proceedings of the European Conference on Cognitive Science*, 1-11.

CHAPTER

13

Coordinating a System of Resources

You think that because you understand "one" that you must there-
fore understand "two" because one and one make two. But you forget
that you must also understand "and."

—SUFI TEACHING STORY

So then, *how* do we coordinate information for understanding? We shared the importance of seeing the broader system of cognitive resources. Now what? Once we've identified a system of resources, *how* do we coordinate these things for the purpose of understanding?

A nice segue from the last chapter, then, would be to determine what level of analysis we should use. Let's draw an artificial distinction between *local-* and *macro*-level coordination. Local coordination, for our purposes, will be at the level of the individual or small group of folks figuring things out; most of the examples referenced thus far would be at the level of local coordination. The redesigned diabetes chart. The various solutions to our confusing terms of service. Tony Stark playing detective. The pilot in the cockpit. We'd even argue that arriving at a model for DNA, even though many people were involved, was treated as a local coordination problem. By contrast, mapping the human genome, some decades later, we'd label a macro-level problem of coordination. As you'll soon see, these kinds of challenges involve working at a much larger scale, where *people* (rather than *information*) become the *primary* resource to coordinate. Prime examples then of challenges requiring macro-scale coordination would be: open-source research projects, coordinating the connected work of many small teams throughout an organization, or addressing a global challenge such as sustainable energy. Macro-level coordination challenges require many more people to participate and will involve working with changing, dynamic information.

The distinction we're drawing is a blurry one. But as we walk through each of these levels of analysis, you should get a better *sense* of how to best approach a particular problem of understanding.

Local Coordination

At the local level, coordination can be unconscious, implicit, and unintentional. We see this in how people study, prepare for a talk, and other activities, where a variety of skills have been acquired over time. But those who take the time to learn how to coordinate information—in the form of study tips, facilitation techniques, orchestrating experiences, and so on—benefit from a more thoughtful approach to managing information.

Everyday Coordination Practices

For small problems of understanding, say working out a math problem or evaluating health plans, coordination is often an unconscious process. We may recall from grade school the requirement to *show your work* or *get ideas out on paper*, but it's highly unlikely these activities were framed as *coordinating a system of cognitive resources*, as is suggested in this book. We can quite easily go about our daily routines researching new topics or preparing a presentation without ever thinking about coordination as an explicit activity.

Consider these everyday examples:

- The student taking notes on index cards so that ideas can later be remixed, sorted, cut, edited, and so on. You can see in the index cards the fundamental concepts of external representation and interactions.

- The college student who asks her roommate for help with an essay. *I want to run something by you* ... In reaching out to the roommate, that person becomes an additional cognitive resource, and the ensuing dialogue is a form of interaction.

- The designer who uses a creativity tool such as SCAMPER[1] to see other possibilities. The SCAMPER exercise hearkens back to our chapters on associations and changing frames.

Fundamentally, these are ways to expand a system of cognitive resources. While normally labeled as *studying tips* or *creativity exercises*, these are tactical ways we've been taught to extend our thinking space, and in doing so, enable better understanding. When we reframe these local problems as a coordination exercise, we see these as *intentional* coordination activities, and in so doing, we see why these practices work (and perhaps how to improve upon these practices). For the student taking notes on index cards, this shift in perspective helps move this exercise from that of a tedious requirement (*Why can't we just write the paper!*) to that of an invaluable exercise for capturing, exploring, and playing with information. Indeed, we used just such an approach in writing this book, and this practice is also quite common when preparing a talk (see Figure 13.1).

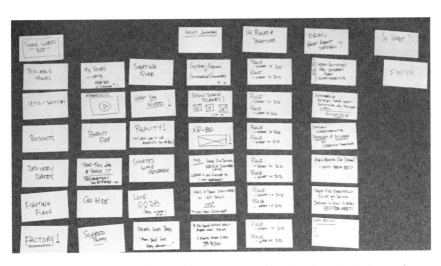

FIGURE 13.1 It's common for speakers to organize their thoughts using index cards or sticky notes. *Image courtesy of Russ Unger.*

---

1. SCAMPER is a creativity tool to help generate ideas for *new* products and services by thinking about how you could improve *existing* ones, in any of seven ways: S = Substitute, C = Combine, A = Adapt, M = Magnify, P = Put to Other Uses, E = Eliminate (or Minify), R = Rearrange (or Reverse).

By putting thoughts into the world—onto pieces of paper—we can see and shuffle our thoughts around, structuring and restructuring until we arrive at something that feels appropriate.

So here, we have practices that are routinely taught, passed down, or learned, that are—even if we're unaware of it—fundamentally about coordinating our system of resources to shift the cost of understanding.

Facilitation as a Form of Coordination

For more explicit examples of coordination at the local level, we only need to look at skilled facilitators and coaches. These are professions where people are trained to think about activities and situations that encourage understanding. For the coach, understanding shows up for the individual as reflection; for the facilitator, understanding shows up in the group as collaboration. People in these roles have been trained to think about subtle phrases, tools and techniques, mannerisms, expressions, activities, and more that all bring the individual or group on a learning and discovery journey. These folks have been trained to *coordinate* for understanding. That understanding might be a personal realization for the person being coached, or it could be the group arriving upon an exciting idea, *together*, in the case of a workshop. And these people who coordinate need not be experts in the subject matter—that's what the individuals bring into the room. Coaches and facilitators are, in our view, experts in coordinating for understanding.

If we look at the kinds of things these facilitators (and also good managers) routinely do, it looks like our list from Chapter 2, "Understanding as a Function of the Brain, Body, and Environment."

1. Attend to every association.
2. Make learning active.
3. See learning as a communal activity.
4. Make concepts tangible.
5. Make concepts visible.
6. Design the environment.
7. Explore multiple frames.
8. Use the whole body.

These are the kinds of things that facilitators are trained to do.

As a facilitator, you're constantly reading body language to see when people are confused or becoming disengaged. You carefully phrase your questions to invite participation. "What questions do you have?" is far better than "any questions," because it assumes that people should have questions, and that speaking up is expected. You create the space for active learning, by bringing structure in the form of group activities, toolkits, and improvisational exercises. You work hard to create an inclusive environment where everyone contributes.

There are many, many ways to think about coordination at this local level. We'd recommend looking at books on facilitation, coaching, training, education, and more, as these things—while not directly about understanding—run a parallel path to our own. That said, let's examine this kind of local coordination with a couple of familiar examples.

Situation 1: Kicking Off a New Project

You pull up in a meeting to kick off a new project. One colleague is prepared to get you up to speed with information she's collected in a PowerPoint deck.

Pause.

Survey the room.

What are the cognitive resources?

There are three people, including yourself. Is there a whiteboard in the room? Are there sticky notes? Blank paper? What about markers? What about pens and sharpies? The table you're sitting at—is it a normal height or a bar height table? Behind each of these items is a deeper consideration. You know that bar-height tables invite more impromptu collaboration and make it easier to shift between sitting down and standing up. With the pens, the decision to have people use a Sharpie marker or something with a finer tip will affect not only how much can be written on a sticky note, but also how visible that note is from a distance. Picking a room with a whiteboard is critical for impromptu drawings, which are so often needed to facilitate conversations.

Consider the content. Is a prepared deck appropriate? Would a question-and-answer format work better? Or, as has proven useful in these orientation meetings, why not invoke a prior association: *What is this project like, that's already in the marketplace? How will this be different?* Starting from a shared prior association is a powerful way to make sense of or provide context for all the minutiae to follow.

Consider your peers. How well do you know them? Do you feel "safe" asking questions that may reveal your ignorance? What's been done to "warm up" the room and build some initial rapport?

And what happens during the meeting? Do you interrupt a long-winded —and frankly, confusing—explanation and ask that person to draw what they're sharing? More than ask, do you pick up a marker and hand it to them? Notice by handing them a marker, rather than a pen, you're inviting (perhaps nudging) that person to get up out of their seat and stand in front of the whiteboard. By joining their side, the situational dynamics have changed, from people sitting across from each other, or someone at the head of the table, to a more egalitarian stance, where everyone is gathered around the whiteboard. You've shifted from a mostly one-way exchange of knowledge to active participation in the exchange of that knowledge.

What we're exposing here are the kinds of thoughts and considerations that might come from someone coordinating a system of resources, for the purposes of understanding. We saw a version of this meeting in the opening chapter. But that was what was seen and observed. Here, we're turning that story inside out, to consider how to bring all that you've learned into action— how that kind of meeting is designed. These are the kinds of subtle interactions, assessments, preparations, decisions, and so on that bring *intentional* coordination into the meeting. You are treating information as a resource, as opposed to content to be received. Everyone and everything in that room, including things seen and unseen, are part of a system of resources. By coordinating this system of resources—the people, the content, the supplies, the interactions—you have actively adjusted the balance between the available information and the understanding you (and frankly everyone in the room) needs from this meeting.

Situation 2: The Retail Shopping Experience

For a completely different way to think about coordinating a system of resources, let's turn to retail shopping in the near future. You'll see parallels to our first situation, although what our information looks like in this scenario is very different.

Early on in the book writing process, I (Stephen) put a question to Karl: "How do you design a data visualization for the limited screen size of a mobile device?" This is a tough question, to be sure. After reviewing hundreds of diverse examples of data visualizations, infographics, concept models, and the like, they all share in common the use of space (screen or paper) to hold information. Think about the Mission(s) to Mars infographic or the redesigned diabetes chart. So much of the understanding comes from seeing the arrangement of things relative to each other; understanding comes from the ability to see *across* all this information. Attempts then to cram this information onto a small screen seem at odds with the ability to see relationships when we spread information out in space. Even if we were to add the ability to zoom in or out on an image, or pan back and forth, these interaction controls are small consolation—it's still difficult to see all the information at once. It's as if we're trying to look out a tiny window onto a much bigger landscape.

Karl surprised me by reframing the question. "Why," he asked, "is your visualization limited to what is shown on the screen?" He was challenging me to rethink the information environment, to expand what I viewed as the system of resources. What if instead of constraining the information needed to that of a screen, we also considered the physical environment we're presently occupying as part of the information space? The device, in this instance, becomes *an* information resource—and a powerful one—inside of a much broader system of resources. Now we can ask a different question: *What can this device do or bring to the broader information space?* This is a powerful, generative, way of thinking.

When Karl challenged me with this question, he was thinking about the future of retail shopping. At the time, he was teaching at Kent State, where one of his students, Jonathan Morgan, was researching computationally-enhanced retail environments.[2] Here's the gist of that thinking: today, smartphones are transforming the in-store shopping experience. People use their phones to learn more about specific products, compare related items, and check competitor pricing. Where the web replaced the traditional shopping experience—you no longer needed to visit the store—the smartphone is augmenting it. Computation is creating new reasons to visit the mall.

This is merely the beginning. A wave of emerging technologies will embed computation deeply into the retail environment. This means new kinds of in-store devices. It means new ways of understanding how people shop. It means technologies that communicate with smartphones, tablets, and other personal devices. But what it really means is that stores will be designed with computation as an integral part of their shopping experience (see Figure 13.2).

FIGURE 13.2 Shifting our locus of understanding from a mobile device to that of the in-store retail experience enables us to include and play with many more information resources.

2. http://pervasiveretaildesign.com/

By changing our locus of understanding from the level of the mobile device to that of the in-store experience, we're able to see new possibilities. Rather than asking how to fit a visualization onto a screen, we could ask what task(s) the visualization would support, and how other in-store information resources might be used to support this task.

If we assess what's in the store already, we have a number of information resources. The merchandise (potentially recognizable via image recognition). The physical space. The store layout. Sensors built into the environment. Store cameras. Signage. Kiosks and other in-store devices. Staff, ready to assist. We could even consider other shoppers as part of the information environment, opening up all kinds of social possibilities. And what about the invisible information? Through digital devices, we have access to just about every conceivable bit of information we might want, from pricing trends to reviews to who in a specific social group has also purchased this item. In this way, the entire store and everything in it become part of the system of cognitive resources.

Combine all these potential information *resources* with the identified *tasks*— whether that's comparing similar laptops or trying to determine if a fitness band has a specific feature—and we have all sorts of new, possible ways to facilitate understanding. Many of our options might never require a visual representation. And if a visual representation is still deemed useful, we can think about the retail space itself as being a canvas for overlaying digital information. Advances in augmented reality are transforming our mobile devices from an end point for information to that of a window through which we see things anew. And as store owners, we might consider embedding projectors into the ceiling that interact with consumer devices.

By reframing and redefining what the information space is, we unlock new possibilities.

Touchpoints and Integrations

This is the kind of reframing that has become more commonplace as companies increasingly focus on the customer experience. Organizations are learning that it's never about their mobile app or the retail store or the website—alone. Rather, it's about how these things integrate and fit into a broader system of resources (see Figure 13.3). Internal artifacts such as *customer journeys* and *service blueprints* are becoming more commonplace to align different groups around these experiences. But it's not just to support better experiences. With an increasing number of digital devices, along with the seamless flow of information between people, devices, and environments, comes a vital need to identify and coordinate these interactions.

FIGURE 13.3 A patient experience journey map. Artifacts like this one are useful for aligning many people around a shared experience, especially where there are many moving parts to be considered.
Image courtesy of Mad*Pow.

Tips for Coordination at the Local Level

Both of these situations highlight what coordination might look like at the local level. While very different from each other—in one case, we're facilitating dialogue in a room, the other supporting an individual shopping experience—both of these situations fit with how we're thinking about coordination at the local level. What can we learn from both of these examples?

If nothing else, simply pausing to reframe things as a coordination exercise, redefine the boundaries of the system, and see everything within our boundaries as a cognitive resource should get you much of the way there. While there are no hard-and-fast rules for coordinating understanding at this local level, here are some tips we've collected to help you coordinate cognitive resources for the purposes of understanding. Because the nature of coordination activities varies so much, the relevancy of these will vary with context. Accordingly, these are in no way intended as a checklist, but rather examples to spur your own thinking.

- **Plan for the flow of information.** Think about paths, relationships, seams, edges, and other hand-offs between information. This could be device to device (sharing a photo from a mobile phone to a laptop) or between people and devices. Focusing on this *flow* of information will help you see the system of resources.

- **See *everything* as a potential cognitive resource.** This could be the teacher who incorporates classroom ceiling tiles into a class project or the public speaker who creates live "body polls" by having attendees align themselves along a room-sized scale. No whiteboard in the room? Use the windows—they also work with whiteboard markers.

- **Break information down into pieces.** With the diabetes chart, every element was treated like a piece of information and broken apart, which allowed for remixing until patterns began to emerge. Think of information in this way, like a LEGO brick construction, waiting to be broken down and assembled into new and varied configurations.

- **Think deeply about context.** When hanging paper on a wall, think about what is at eye level for other participants. Observe how you work differently under different conditions: at the office, at home, at a public café. Even standing up, leaning back in a recliner, or leaning forward at a desk caters to different kinds of work activities. Place your work—especially work in progress—in public spaces, say an office hallway through which many people pass.

- **Encourage participation.** Hand people markers or pens when they start to explain something. If you're trying to get feedback on a visual artifact (like a blueprint), be the first person to "defile" your own work by marking on it—this signals to others that there is nothing sacred about this work artifact. Everyone staring at their devices? Ask everyone to gather and stand in front of the whiteboard.

- **Set the stage to encourage participation.** This could be social engineering by arranging chairs in a room for an intended behavior or by forcing an even number of chairs to make it easy for people to pair up. Stock a room with sticky notes, markers, whiteboards, flipcharts, and other tools to help externalize thinking. Think about the furniture and how the desk height—sitting, countertop, and bar height—can affect moving between sitting and standing.

- **Think deeply about information structures.** Structures prepared ahead of time can help facilitate clearer thinking. This applies to frameworks, maps, and models that drive an activity (think *Business Model Canvas* or *empathy maps*). If you're going to use an activity such as dot-voting, apply some rigor to the things to be voted on, in order to avoid split votes or other problems.

- **Be mindful of unseen power structures.** For group activities, it's important to recognize and manage invisible power structures that influence collaboration. For example, high-order cultures might defer to the highest ranking individual in the room or at the table. If your goal is open sharing and collaboration, ask these people to go last or use activities where people go around the table sharing.

- **Be conscientious about the digital and physical divide.** Look for opportunities to integrate or connect these two worlds. New tools from companies like Mural allow teams to transform a photo of sticky notes into a digital version, further eroding this distinction between physical and digital worlds. Even the concept of "bridging the divide" is one to be mindful of, as this division is an increasingly artificial one, as the friction between these two kinds of environments becomes more enmeshed.

To be candid, it's hard to stop sharing these tips for local coordination without bleeding into a discussion of macro-level coordination, where we have a *structured* way to think about coordination. While there is no hard boundary between local and macro levels of analysis, we have made one observation. Whereas coordination at the local level will certainly improve understanding, it is not a requirement; by contrast, coordination at the macro level—at the level of communities, organizations, and globally distributed teams—is a necessary and critical requirement. With many more people involved, and with information distributed across locales, we must be intentional about how we structure the information space. For problems involving more than a few people or other cognitive resources, we must shift our thinking to begin attending to coordination of cognitive resources as an *explicit* activity.

Macro-Level Coordination

Let's think about this shift from local to macro level as the shift from coordinating *information* for understanding to the coordination of *people* for understanding.

Much of this book has been written from the perspective of the individual figuring it out. We've referenced the objects and representations and interactions in a cognitive system. We've also referenced the interactions with other people. But our own locus of understanding for this book has (implicitly) been at the level of an individual looking out, treating other people as cognitive resources in the system.

With the diabetes chart, all the information was there, waiting to be sorted out.

With the story of the bartender, tracking drink requests, he was using information in the world to facilitate his own understanding.

With our confusing terms of service, we have a variety of solutions, but they're all between a person that the artifact created to communicate the information.

These are local problems of understanding. What, then, defines a macro-level coordination problem?

A Puzzling Problem

Let's revisit the jigsaw puzzle analogy we made in the opening chapter. We compared getting from information to understanding to that of assembling the pieces of a jigsaw puzzle. The jigsaw pieces are information; understanding comes through assembling these pieces into a coherent picture. We treat information as a resource that can be managed and transformed.

But this kind of simplicity, with all the pieces already laid out before, waiting to be assembled, is increasingly not the case with more complex problems. What happens when there are many people in a distributed cognitive system and coordinating information is synonymous with coordinating people?

This is increasingly true of 21st century workplaces, where rather than trade in things, we trade in information. Within most large organizations, we hear the familiar refrains of "How do we respond to competitive disruption?" and "How do we do business in an increasingly interconnected world?" And for the startup trying to disrupt the status quo, things are equally complex, although in different ways. Between critical partnerships, risky bets, short funding runways, attracting and retaining talent, navigating regulations and established systems—there is no end to the web of challenges.

This is also true of the increasingly complex, societal concerns. If we drill into the rising costs of higher education, we quickly discover seemingly irreconcilable tensions between faculty, students, alumni, donors, administration, state and federal governments, credentialing boards, and other interested parties. Rising healthcare costs (in the U.S.) indicate a systemic breakdown between patients, physicians, insurers, government, medical-device manufacturers, pharmaceutical companies, researchers, vendors, and so on. Rather than working together, these entities have become understandably defensive, entrenching themselves in self-serving practices that only exacerbate a growing problem.

And finally, this need to coordinate people in a distributed cognitive system is also true of science and medicine, where everything from genetic research to space exploration to climate studies increasingly requires the coordination of many scientists and researchers, working as one cognitive system on a global scale.

These are all cases where individuals need to work and learn together.

In these cases, people are much more than additional cognitive resources for a local or personal understanding challenge. Instead, people are both players and pieces in a complex information puzzle. We—each of us—contain pieces to not one, but many jigsaw puzzles: "sorting things out" is a much more complex activity, as there are so many more pieces, we're not sure which pieces should be shared with whom for which puzzle, and we don't even know if all the pieces exist—at best, we may only arrive at an incomplete puzzle.

None of this invalidates or diminishes the critical importance of everything we've shared about managing information as a resource. Rather, it begs a new set of questions, mostly around how we coordinate "people"—lots of people—for understanding. More specifically, how do we coordinate people for *learning*, in a space where things are dynamic and emergent?

A Framework to Coordinate People for Understanding

Everything we shared about coordinating information still applies, only now we have the added complexity of coordinating people as information resources. How do we get large groups of people to gain traction and make progress—as one entity—when there is no "right" answer? To effectively coordinate people for understanding in these cases, we propose that teams and organizations be intentional about shaping each of the following five items:

1. Shared Standards—*Ways we communicate*

2. Invisible Environments—*Ways we align, conceptually*

3. Visible Environments—*Ways we collaborate*

4. Psychological Safety—*Ways we behave*

5. Perspectives—*Ways we see (and see differently)*

1. SHARED STANDARDS—WAYS WE COMMUNICATE

When we talk about *standards*, we're talking about establishing the fundamental units by which we exchange information. More simply: *Do we speak a common language?* Not just in what we—as humans—say to each other, but also how we communicate with machines, and how machines communicate with other machines. This may seem like an overly obvious thing to address, yet it is one of the most common and easily overlooked challenges to coordinating groups of people.

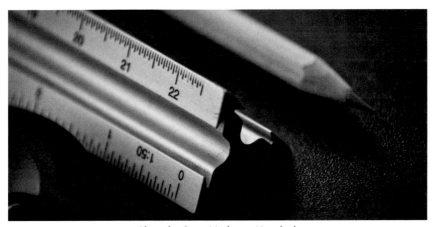

Photo by Sven Mieke on Unsplash

While we're keenly aware if someone doesn't speak the same geographic language (English, French, Mandarin), we tend to overlook more subtle kinds of language differences. A simple word like "customer" might mean wildly different things for different members of the same team; the product team might be thinking about who uses a piece of software while the sales team is thinking about who writes the checks. Functional groups, such as software engineers and designers, might use the same word—"design" or "interface" for example—but the meaning is different for each group. There's also jargon that creeps into a group's vocabulary, as well as cultural nuances and connotations that can endow words with additional meanings not shared by all.

It's not just the language we speak with each other, it's also the standards we've agreed upon. Time. Currency. How we measure things like distance, volume, or space. Physics. Geometry. Programming languages. Protocols for exchanging data. And while this may seem like a black-and-white topic, it's often not. Two data scientists are unable to exchange raw data, because protocols are incompatible. Within a company, there are different factions that have chosen to document and share knowledge within different software tools, preventing the exchange of information between these groups. NASA once lost a $125 million weather satellite because of an engineering team that used English (imperial) units of measurement instead of the metric units specified by the agency!

2. INVISIBLE ENVIRONMENTS—WAYS WE ALIGN, CONCEPTUALLY

Where standards create a common *unit* of understanding (enabling people to exchange ideas), invisible environments create the shared conceptual space in which people exchange ideas. More succinctly: where standards let us *communicate*, invisible environments let us *cooperate*. Knowing why you are coming together and how you will work together is as critical to coordination as speaking a common language. Throughout organizations we see attempts at all kinds of invisible environments: Team norms. Goals. Vision statements. Mission statements. KPIs, OKRs, and other metrics. Quarterly initiatives. These are all elements of an invisible environment constructed to align people around a shared concept. But these business examples of invisible environments can mislead us, as there are more bad than good examples; for example, every company has a mission statement, but few companies live their mission.

To really understand what we mean by "invisible environments" and why this is so vital, let's consider team sports: players on a basketball team know the rules and the goal of the game. Each player is an autonomous being, who at every moment is making their own choices. But to play *together*, players enter into a shared concept of what it is they are doing and why (see Figure 13.4). This shared conceptual space is the invisible environment. While there is a visible environment in the form of a basketball court, the critical environment is the one not seen: the implicit agreement that to play together, we also agree that this is the goal and these are the rules.

FIGURE 13.4 While the basketball court is a visible structure, players are bound together by an invisible structure in the form of rules and a shared goal. *Photo by Max Winkler on Unsplash.*

Invisible environments let us know where and what "here" is, why we're even here, and what we hope to accomplish.

With the basketball example, players implicitly agree upon rules and the goal of the game. Imagine if these concepts weren't shared; imagine the player who chooses to believe in a different scoring system or follows different rules about walking or dribbling. There would be no cooperation. For people to play as part of a team in a team sport, they have to agree upon some core tenets. *To play together*, we agree upon the imaginary game space in which we will play; players must have a shared understanding of the game they are playing. This is also true of coordinating people for understanding. *To work and learn together*, participants must have a shared understanding of the problem space in which they are working.

3. VISIBLE ENVIRONMENTS—WAYS WE COLLABORATE

Visible environments are, quite simply, the *seen* places in which we work and think. These can be obvious, such as war rooms, command centers, and similar *physical* group spaces. These could be *virtual*, as with the software we use to collaborate. Perhaps a visible environment is a *hybrid* of the physical and the virtual, as with teleconferencing systems. We can also think of visible environments being *temporary* (as with a conference or webinar) or *distributed* across many physical and virtual spaces, as with the experience of traveling from one city to another. It's rare to see people design—and maintain—these environments with the explicit goal of creating a shared space for learning. The results of this inattention? Lack of participation, coordination, or any sort of useful, organic, ongoing knowledge construction.

Think of forums and Slack channels where conversations are either dead or the opposite—so much activity that information has become noise (often filled with animated GIFs!). Think of command centers with information on the walls that hasn't been updated in months. Think of conferences where by cramming the day so full of speakers and short breaks, we unintentionally discourage conversation and participation among attendees. (As a counterpoint, some of our favorite conferences have built in extra-long morning and afternoon tea breaks and plenty of open spaces to encourage hallway conversations.)

This effect of the designed (or undesigned) environment on behaviors and outcomes is a critical one. I (Stephen) have begun using language like "create the *conditions* for …" and "design a *sandbox* learning environment where …"—the idea being that to encourage learning and coordination at scale, we need to attend to the environments (visible and invisible) that encourage play, discovery, and sharing. In the digital realm, this is seen in everything from how Wikipedia enables collective knowledge sharing to how players in *Minecraft* learn from each other. In the physical, this is as much about strategic intent as it is the workspaces we occupy: open spaces, closed spaces, private spaces, breakout rooms, high ceilings, low ceilings, desks for standing, desks for sitting—all of these decisions have an effect on how people work and learn together.

4. PSYCHOLOGICAL SAFETY—WAYS WE BEHAVE

These first three items are about external conditions needed for coordination. Standards let us *communicate*. Invisible environments let us *cooperate*. And visible environments affect how we *collaborate*. But we still have to address the people in this equation. Systems and structures are one thing. But people—with our biases, beliefs, hang-ups, hot buttons, and egos are something else altogether. What enables us—as complex human creatures—to actually work and play and learn together?

Much of the literature seems to point to the same direction: we need *psychological safety*.

While the concept isn't new, research into psychological safety has recently come into the spotlight due to a large-scale research study from Google.

In 2012, researchers at Google launched a multiyear study[3] looking across hundreds of teams to determine why some teams soar while other teams stumble. The hope? Answer this question, and you can consistently engineer the perfect team. Researchers hoped to uncover "the perfect mix of individual traits and skills." Instead, the behaviors and norms they observed seemed to vary from team to team, with no consistent pattern. Strong management or flat structure? Strangers or friends outside of work? No conclusive pattern emerged. More frustrating, the traits that made one team successful didn't also make another team successful. So much for solving this riddle. But when researchers dug deeper into the data, they did find one, fundamental thing in common: while norms and traits and skills and processes might vary, the highest performing teams shared a common belief *that you won't be punished when you make a mistake*.

This eureka moment led the team to more formal research into *psychological safety*, a topic that has been described as "the most studied enabling condition in group dynamics and team learning."[4] Studies go back several decades, most notably associated with Harvard Business School professor Amy Edmondson and before her William A. Kahn. Why is psychological safety such an important topic?

---

3. Duhigg, Charles. 2016. "What Google Learned from Its Quest to Build the Perfect Team." *New York Times Magazine*, February 25, 2016. https://www.nytimes.com/2016/02/28/magazine/what-google-learned-from-its-quest-to-build-the-perfect-team.html
4. "Psychological Safety." 2019. Wikipedia. Wikimedia Foundation. December 5, 2019. https://en.wikipedia.org/wiki/Psychological_safety

For biological reasons related to safety and self-preservation, we create the images of how we want to be seen and perceived by others. In caring for this image, we then avoid actions that might make us seem ignorant, incompetent, negative, or disruptive. This is natural and healthy, but follows from a place of fear. We might think of these survival instincts as the modern equivalents of our evolutionary fight-or-flight response and life vs. death instincts. As with the protection from physical danger that being part of a tribe might afford us, we are—in modern terms—at our best when we can let our guard down and speak freely among our peers. It's in these moments that we're less likely to be argumentative and more likely to engage in productive conversations.

A safe environment then creates space for a more beneficial set of behaviors. When people feel safe to disagree or ask the "dumb" questions, everyone benefits. When people feel safe taking risks and experiments, knowing that failure will be viewed not as a reason for reprimand, but as a learning opportunity, everyone benefits. By creating psychological safety, you create a climate where it is okay to be fully present and engaged, vulnerable, and challenge or build upon the ideas of others. Everyone benefits. For problems of understanding, at the kind of distributed scale we are discussing, this is exactly the kind of learning (and innovation) culture you want to instill. This is true for complex topics, but even more so where there is vicious disagreement. How else can we possibly start to entertain unfamiliar, frightening, or foreign ideas if we can never let our guard down, so to speak? In game terms, psychological safety is akin to the shift from a competitive game, where in order to win someone must lose, to a cooperative game, where we all win or lose together.

The thread that runs throughout the literature on psychological safety— and why we found this so relevant for the intent of this book and chapter, coordinating people for understanding—is the focus on *learning*. In Amy Edmondson's research into this topic, she is concerned with "collective learning" and how groups of individuals might come together "to help themselves, their teams and their organizations to learn."[5] Quotes like these, from Edmondson's research, get into the heart of what we are discussing:

5. Edmondson, Amy C. 2008. "Managing the Risk of Learning: Psychological Safety in Work Teams." *International Handbook of Organizational Teamwork and Cooperative Working*, 255–75. https://doi.org/10.1002/9780470696712.ch13

Learning as a team also requires coordination and some degree of structure, to ensure that insights are gained from members' collective experience and also used to guide subsequent action.

And:

Although human beings are endowed with both desire and ability for learning, collections of interdependent individuals, whether small groups or large organizations, do not learn automatically.

Where most of this book has focused on understanding at the individual level, we've escalated that focus to include understanding where many people are involved. Psychological safety is a natural fit for this topic. If you're working in a space where there is both uncertainty and interdependence, then it's absolutely vital that you have psychological safety. For more on this topic, we recommend checking out Amy Edmondson's book *The Fearless Organization: Creating Psychological Safety in the Workplace for Learning, Innovation, and Growth*.

5. PERSPECTIVES—WAYS WE SEE (AND SEE DIFFERENTLY)

Finally, we must become aware of how we see things differently and how to shift this way of seeing for ourselves and for others.

It's amazing how two people, having both observed the same event, can walk away with two very different narratives about what happened. This is as true of ethnographic research as it is recalling a tragedy on the witness stand. We don't all see—nor recall—things in the same way.

Facts get filtered through a mix of emotions and beliefs. How I see the world is different from how you see the world, which leads us to see and recall a different set of things. As Obi-Wan clarified in the *Star Wars* movie *Empire Strikes Back*, "Many of the truths we cling to depend greatly on our own point of view."

It is okay that few of us see things the same way. Great, actually. A diversity of perspectives and viewpoints is a healthy thing—so long as we learn to be aware of our perspectives and when they help or hinder a situation.

For large-scale problems of understanding, where information is distributed across many people, it's critical that we all—as individuals and groups—learn to move fluidly between many different perspectives. This will be a challenge for most of us, as we're hardwired to develop our mental model, or view of the world, and then assess how well things do or do not fit into this model. We see the patterns we've trained our brains—from an early age—to see. While it's uncomfortable to *accommodate* new information, it's also vital for coordinating the efforts of many people working toward a shared goal. Failing to develop this "liquid" thinking ability prevents us from seeing possibilities.

We've touched on this already. In the section on prior associations, we discussed the importance of activating different prior associations in order to see a thing in different ways. In the last chapter, we shared a few ways to shift our locus of understanding—to change how we see a system of resources. What else can be done? Indeed, making things—or getting hands-on experience whether through drawing or sculpting—is a great way to change perspectives, as these activities afford more experimentation and serendipitous discovery. Trying on different hats, whether that's Edward de Bono's six thinking hats or the imagined hat of how a famous brand or personality might see things, can be a fun and provocative way to see things differently. Exposing the personal narrative that fuels our behaviors, then challenging this narrative, is a powerful (if elusive) way to see our present circumstances anew.

What of shifting the perspective of the group? In a way, everything described up to this point has been a way of seeing together. Drawing a picture. Using a choice analogy. Enabling interactions with a difficult concept. Whether we seek to understand a thing for ourselves or with others—the tools are the same. When we externalize our thoughts, our thinking becomes something that can be shared among a group.

For more about shifting your perspective, we recommend the book *Liminal Thinking* by Dave Gray.

Macro-Level Coordination and 21st Century Knowledge Work

Where we largely coordinated for performance in the 19th and 20th centuries, the organizational challenge of the 21st century is coordinating for understanding—that is, transitioning from how we organize people to make *stuff* to how we organize people to work and learn together to solve wicked problems. While the need for routine and predictable processes doesn't go away, we also know that information work requires more dynamic and collaborative ways of working. This is nothing new. In his 1959 book *The Landmarks of Tomorrow*, management consultant Peter Drucker coined the term "knowledge worker" to refer to a new class of workers who would be the most valuable assets of a 21st-century organization. He was looking ahead to a time when hiring people for their minds would be more critical than hiring for muscle. Think about how this statement from Drucker connects with our topic of coordinating people for understanding:

> Every knowledge worker in modern organization is an "executive" if, by virtue of his position or knowledge, he is responsible for a contribution that materially affects the capacity of the organization to perform and to obtain results.[6]

This hearkens back to our analogy of people as pieces in the information puzzle, waiting to be sorted out.

Fast-forward several decades, and we're presently grappling with what all this means. While organizations do—by and large—treat people as their most valuable asset (and *not* as "cogs in the machine"), our prevailing organizational structures still hearken back to that of the industrial systems. Recognizing this tension, between celebrating people while preserving old structures, gives a perspective on many issues faced by today's organizations. When agile product teams lament not having autonomy to make decisions based on learnings, we see a disconnect between decades of hierarchal top-down decision-making and an agile mindset that is about decentralized power. When managers are challenged to become more like coaches, we see an acknowledgment of dynamic, changing times, and a recognition that what worked yesterday won't necessarily work today. When companies train workers on topics such as emotional intelligence, we see a desire to create healthier collaborative organizations. We could go on.

The five items listed in this last section may have felt a bit like something from a book on business management. Indeed, when *people* are keepers of information, we see an overlap between information as a resource to be managed (our focus) and that of creating the learning organization. For this reason, we see a number of conversations within the business world as the logical extension of our topic, understanding.

---

6. Drucker, Peter. 2018. *The Effective Executive*. Saint Louis: Routledge.

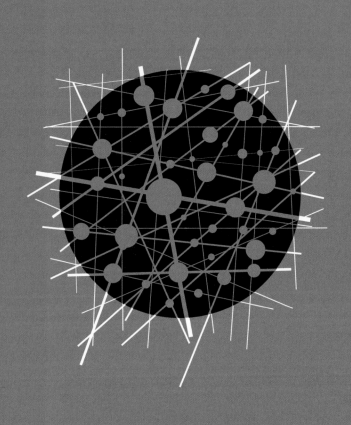

6

Tools and Technologies for Understanding

U p to this point, we've focused on what doesn't change, or changes very slowly over thousands of years: how we, as humans, adjust the balance between the information we have and the understanding we need. We've explored the timeless ways we adapt, modify, and transform information to suit our needs. And while previous chapters have certainly mentioned a number of tools (maps and stories, diagrams, sticky notes, and so on), our focus has been on what the tools do to us and change for us. Intentionally, our focus has been on the humans at the center of it all.

In this final section, we can now direct our attention to the tools and technologies we create to extend our cognitive abilities, as well as the tools and technologies that help us think better, understand more, and solve bigger problems. While our focus on human understanding doesn't change, we now have a solid lens by which to assess the value of these present and potential future tools. We can think critically about what they do—and don't do—for us. And while emerging technologies promise amazing new possibilities, they also don't radically reconfigure anything we've written about in this book. We always have and always are creating the means to increase our human *capacity* for understanding.

14

A Critical Look at Tools and Technologies for Understanding

These miraculous machines!
Do we shape them
Or do they shape us?
Or reshape us from our decent, far designs?

But we are learning.
We are learning to build for the future
From the ground up.

— ROBERT J. FLAHERTY (FROM THE FILM, *THE LAND*)

When things are too complex to work out "in our heads," we bring information into the world; we employ or engage with other cognitive resources in
the environment, be these other people, tools, time, and so on. Whether it's
writing (a technology) in the margins of this book (also a kind of technology)
or building a giant supercomputer to answer our hardest questions, we have

a rich history of inventing new ways to help adjust the balance between the information we have and the understanding we need. While humans change very slowly, technologies change all the time.

In this chapter, let's take a critical look at the present technologies we use to facilitate understanding, to figure things out. What digital tools do we commonly use to transform information into understanding? And what are some of the invisible limitations these tools impose upon us? We'd like everyone to be more thoughtful about the current state of tools, what they allow us to do (and not do), and what they do to us, in turn.

Tools for Understanding and Their Limitations

Consider, for a moment, all the information we might work with on a regular basis. Performance reviews. Contract negotiations. Customer feedback. To-do lists. Grocery lists. Tracking the kids' homework. Tracking movies to watch. Evaluating a new major purchase. What digital tools do you use to work with this information?

Topping the list is probably some form of a text editor. It could be a robust writing tool such as MS Word or Google Docs. Or a way of drafting and composing your thoughts in a lengthy email. It could be taking notes in a simple notes app. Or something as simple and convenient as text messaging. And these are all great tools—for *capturing* information, for communication now or recall later. But what if you need to work with this information, to work out some difficult understanding problem? You can certainly cut and paste text, as well as edit and undo. These are valuable interaction patterns. Indeed, writing much of this book was an internal dialogue, mediated by thoughts held in place on the page. But holding concepts in place on a page is not the same as, say, writing things out by hand.

With pen and paper, you're free to add words and marks anywhere on the page. You can circle and underline things. While taking notes as expected, you can also keep separate notes at the bottom of the page and in the margins. And if you want to write down three words, arranged in a circular fashion, and then draw connecting lines between a few of these (as shown in Figure 14.1), you can do so, effortlessly. And as a *thinking* activity, you might do something like this several times over in the course of a few minutes, each version a refinement of your previous thoughts.

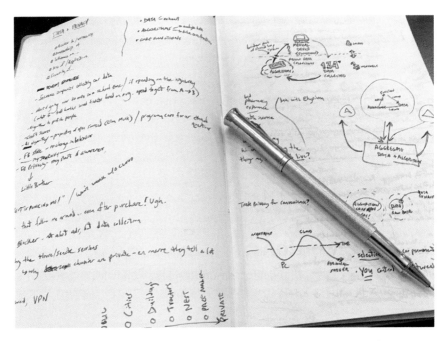

FIGURE 14.1 Writing on paper affords many possibilities for interacting with written words.

But this kind of flexibility—quickly arranging words in a pattern—is inhibited by text editors.

While it's possible to *render* something like this with the drawing tools built into more robust text editors, the friction of doing so leaves these features useful only as a way to *express* the idea you've already explored elsewhere.

A text editor forces a linear, sequential kind of thinking. As with the typewriter that text editors are based upon, these tools encourage you to think a line at a time. Top to bottom. Bullets and lists. This kind of thinking is fine, for certain types of problems. When you need to analyze simple cause and effect, rank order items in a list, or outline a topic, this format is fine. But what about other ways you need to work with information?

Complex understanding problems tend to be problems of comparison or comprehension, which call for a tool that supports *associative* thinking. As we showed earlier, visual and spatial representations do exactly this. By arranging things into Venn diagrams, matrixes, timelines, and so on, we expose relationships between concepts. Being able to arrange words on the page (using good old pen and paper, shapes and lines) can be superior to taking notes in a scripted, linear fashion, where the relationships between entities are hidden, left to the imagination, or left to subjective inference. With most text editors, it is difficult (if not impossible as with composing an email) to use space freely—placing text anywhere on the page—to hold meaning.

None of this is to say that you should stop using text editors and switch back to paper—paper has its own limitations. Tools are tools. And tools are suited for different purposes. The danger is in not recognizing the limits of a preferred—or nearly ubiquitous—tool. The callout here is to recognize the effect that these text editors have on how we think.

We could level a similar critique on something like the card-based format popularized by a site such as Pinterest, a popular place to collect ideas and information. While this tool is great for visual bookmarking, it affords none of the interaction patterns you'd get if your saved "pins" were physical cards on a table; beyond adding cards to boards and subdividing them into groups, there are no meaningful ways to organize information. You can't chunk things into piles, move things closer or farther away, turn cards sideways as a form of annotation, etc. If these were physical cards, you could sort, stack, annotate, arrange, remove, and otherwise manipulate them to derive meaning (recall everything we've already covered about *interactions* and *spatial arrangement*). The virtual card *styling* that is so popular affords none of the actual properties you would get if these were physical cards (see Figure 14.2).

FIGURE 14.2 Consider how many more interactions you can do with a physical set of cards, compared to the "digital" card style commonly seen across many websites.

While these two examples may seem like praise for analog tools, it's not that. From earliest PCs through our modern ability to access all the world's knowledge on mobile devices, technology tools allow us to do things that previous generations could not do, at least not without bearing serious costs. Our goal here is simply to recognize what is good, or not so good, about a particular tool—analog or digital. *How well does a particular tool support transforming information into understanding?* That's all we're calling out. For all the benefits of digital technologies, our current wave of tools could also be improved in many ways. Recognizing this allows us to be better thinkers and move fluidly between different tools, and if we're in such a position, to challenge the status quo and push for better tools.

Bret Victor and Dynamic Drawing Tools

This push for better tools is precisely what pervades the work of inventor and visionary Bret Victor. In a lecture to HCI students at Stanford University, he opened with this scenario: "Say you're a scientist, you need to understand this data, and you know that one of the best ways to understand anything is to turn it into a picture, today you have three options …"[1]

Victor begins with the assertion that being able to see data is vital. He then calls out the three most common tools for visualizing scientific data: you can use a chart generator, draw pictures (whether on paper or with drawing tools), or write code that renders your drawing. He then goes on to critique each of these tools. We've summarized his critique in Table 14.1 on the next page.

With a chart generator, you can easily render graphs and charts, but you're limited by what's built into the tool.

With drawing, you have enormous freedom, but drawing (whether on paper or with a piece of software) is not a dynamic medium—a single change in data means redrawing the entire picture.

And with software, while coding can be a powerful medium for expressing dynamic data, there is a learning curve and the process of coding is that of "blindly manipulating symbols." The code isn't the picture, so there's no direct manipulation, no real-time feedback loop between changes made and the results of those changes.

---

1. Victor, Bret. Feb 1, 2013. "Drawing Dynamic Visualizations." https://vimeo.com/66085662

TABLE 14.1 COMMON TOOLS FOR VISUALIZING SCIENTIFIC DATA

	USE A CHART GENERATOR	DRAW A PICTURE	WRITE CODE
	Charting tools built into Excel	Illustrator	R, Python, D3.js
+	Easy rendering of data.	Drawing is a direct manipulation tool that affords freedom and directness.	Powerful tools: you can code up a dynamic picture.
−	Fixed structure with limited options; not expressive enough to let you explore your thoughts.	Not a dynamic medium—you have to draw by hand and create a one-off for that particular data set, and redraw whenever new data is introduced; this limits what you can draw by hand.	Indirect manipulation tool (not manipulating the picture itself); you're blindly manipulating symbols.

Consistent with our criticism of text editors, Victor remarks that "being limited to these three options is limiting the thoughts that our creative scientists can think." This analysis might seem rather bleak, considering these are the options available to most scientists and working professionals.

"What if there was a fourth option?" Victor goes on to ask. "A way to create pictures through direct manipulation, but pictures that were dynamic." He then demonstrates a tool that he's built that is exactly this, a tool that allows anyone to draw dynamic visualizations (see Figure 14.3). In other words, a tool that gives us all the benefits of those mentioned above, with none of the trade-offs.

With this tool, we can draw—freeform—some novel way to represent data, and then hook it up to actual data. Any subsequent changes to the data or the drawing both affect each other. And if you prefer the symbolic language of coding, you can do so, with the benefit of seeing real-time changes. It's a data visualization/drawing/coding/tool rolled into one. This is a new software tool that defies categorization. And it's an exciting tool.

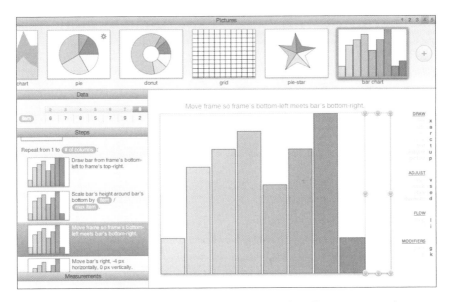

FIGURE 14.3 Bret Victor proposes a new software tool that allows anyone to draw dynamic visualizations.

But the lesson here isn't about a particular tool. It's about how we adapt, modify, and transform information to suit our understanding needs. While this chapter explores current tools and technologies, it's through the lens of how these tools increase (or hamper) our natural human capabilities. On the surface, it looks like Bret Victor is challenging conventions about what computing might look like, but it's more than that. Victor is interested, as we are, in human *capabilities*. What people *can do*. By starting with the humans at the center of it all, we have a new lens by which to assess these tools. Interactive visualizations and dynamic drawing tools are powerful because they allow us to extend our capabilities, to, in Victor's words "think powerfully about systems."[2]

Let's turn this lens to the workhorse of information management: the spreadsheet.

2. Victor, Bret. 2013. "An Ill-Advised Personal Note About 'Media for Thinking the Unthinkable.'" Bret Victor, Beast of Burden. May 28, 2013. http://worrydream.com/#!/MediaForThinkingThe Unthinkable/note.html

Critiquing Spreadsheets, Tables, and Similar Representations

Spreadsheets—think Excel or Google Sheets—are amazing for a great many things. And they are especially great for the things they were designed for: storing, processing, and manipulating small or large sets of numerical data. A brief foray into the origins of spreadsheets reveals this exemplar use: financial accounting. For this reason, we do consider spreadsheets to be a great leap forward in information understanding, after the invention of log tables, engineering rulers, and calculators. A plaque at Harvard even commemorates VisiCalc (the earliest spreadsheet) as the "original 'killer app' of the information age [that] forever changed how people use computers in business."[3] Spreadsheets are amazing tools—for their intended purpose: accounting and financial calculations (and similar quantitative uses).

Fast forward to the present. Spreadsheets are used for nearly everything: tracking job applications. Creating team "scorecards." Tracking contracts. Billing and invoicing. Reviewing survey results.

And yet …

Spreadsheets aren't great for non-numeric content. A friend commented that "half of doing business expenses is attaching the actual receipts—which don't have a place in the spreadsheet." And they're not all that useful for showing relationships, revealing patterns, and other things we routinely need from information. We wouldn't use a spreadsheet to show a family tree any more than we'd use a genealogy tool to make a budget.

Our concern then isn't with spreadsheets per se, it's that rows and columns are poorly suited to represent much of the information being forced into this format.

As with our comments on text editors, card layouts, chart generators, drawing, and coding, the refrain is the same: *use the right tool for the right job*. We're singling out spreadsheets because we see an overuse and abuse of an otherwise great tool.

What we see in abundance is the *thoughtless* use of spreadsheets, data grids, tables, and similar "rows and columns" representations. This abuse is

---

3. Karaian, Jason. 2015. "Dan Bricklin Invented the Spreadsheet—but Don't Hold That Against Him." *Quartz*, December 22, 2015. https://qz.com/578661/dan-bricklin-invented-the-spreadsheet-but-dont-hold-that-against-him/

widespread throughout many businesses, where tools such as Excel are the bread-and-butter for many people. But this way of representing information—in a tabular format—has also spilled over into the building of many software applications—especially business software.

USING A SPREADSHEET TO TRACK RECRUITING APPLICANTS

Let's take a fairly common business scenario: tracking job applications. On the surface, a spreadsheet seems like a convenient choice for such a task. We can easily add columns to track who has applied for the job, add a link to their résumé or portfolio, add columns for notes, next steps, current status, etc. But what happens in the weekly recruiting meeting, when we introduce multiple stakeholders, each with a different set of questions they need to have answered? "Have you followed up with …?" "What's the funnel look like?" "Who was that again?" "Is she better for a different position?" "How many people did we interview this month?" Someone may be a bad fit for one position, but great for another.

If the spreadsheet was created by the recruiter, then it was likely organized around open *positions* to be filled. But not everyone in the room is looking at the information with that same lens. We end up with multiple questions to answer that tend to break the *singular* view offered by most spreadsheets (see Figure 14.4).

FIGURE 14.4 A single view of information is insufficient to answer the many different questions associated with recruiting and hiring.

To be fair, the spreadsheet does *contain* all the information—the spreadsheet as database is fine; it's the use of rows and columns as a tool for understanding where we bump up against the limitations of this format. In these cases, there's a real need to look at things through many, different lenses. There is the open roles view, which is different from the view focused on candidates and where they are in the process. There's the "What do I—personally—need to do as a hiring manager" view and the "Where are we at with that specific referral I made?" question. Each of these questions begs that information be represented in a different way. For example, the process question would benefit from something more stage-based, such as the Kanban board.

As it is, a great deal of time is spent in mental gymnastics, trying to answer a range of questions that a singular view (of information contained in a spreadsheet) will never answer.

A bit of context: historically, committing to one piece of software meant committing to how that software chose to represent information. Pick a spreadsheet, get a spreadsheet view. Pick a project planning tool, get a Gantt chart view. Pick a team project management app, get a list view or agile board. Where you stored data dictated how you viewed that same data. But this is changing.

At the time of this writing, we see a rise in tools that are challenging this singular view of information. A new breed of tools such as Airtable, Zenkit, Targetprocess, and Coda all allow you to view the same information in many different ways. This is a pretty big shift forward. If we go back to our applicant tracking spreadsheet, we could create dozens of customized views of the same data set. You can easily pivot between a timeline view that shows how long folks have been in the queue, or a get a dashboard view of overall recruiting metrics.

TABLES IN SOFTWARE

With information technology, it's easy to bring data onto the screen in a way that mirrors how this same data is stored in a database. What you end up with then are visual representations—data displayed in tables—that does little to facilitate understanding. For example, with paying an annual subscription, you might encounter something like this:

Date		Transaction #	Description		Billed	Paid
1/10/2013			Billing info updated to use Credit card *****3007			
1/10/2013			Credit card *****3007 approved			$138.00
1/3/2013			Dropbox premium service - 100GB + "Packrat" unlimited undo history (1/3/2013 to 1/3/2014)		$138.00	
1/3/2012			Credit card *****3007 approved			$138.00
1/3/2012			Dropbox premium service - 50GB + "Packrat" unlimited undo history (1/3/2012 to 1/3/2013)		$138.00	
		Invoice	Payment	Adjustment	Refund	Current balance: $0.00
			All amounts shown are in US dollars.			

We get rows and columns sharing every detail of the behind-the-scenes processing transaction. But, as a user of this service, what did you really need to know? When we ask this question—"What are people trying to do?"—we arrive at something much simpler and direct, like the statement below:

> 1/10/2013
>
> Success!
>
> We've billed $138.00 to your credit card ending in *****3007.
>
> This gets you:
> 1 year Dropbox premium service
> (100GB + "Packrat" unlimited undo history)
>
> Your next bill is due Jan 3rd, 2014.

To be clear, this isn't a complex or even complicated problem of understanding. What this is, however, is a simple example of being handed information (much of it unnecessary) and being left on our own to figure out if a payment was processed. Not hard, but definitely fraught with needless cognitive friction.

What we see in this tiny example—information shoved into a table—is the nearly universal state of most business software: from the software used in call centers to the tools used by sales teams, these groups are commonly given rows and columns of data. It's functional to be sure, but at what cost to understanding?

Yes, a database structure is the workhorse of information management. Yes, the easiest way to output data to a screen is to present it in a table format. No, information doesn't need to be represented this way (unless it's an intentional decision and has been determined to be an appropriate way to work with the information).

So, we can be more conscientious about the tools we choose to *organize* information. Whether it's a spreadsheet, a text editor, or simply drawing on a sheet of paper, these are all tools we've invented to transform information into something we can see and work with. And while all these tools do extend our thinking abilities in some way, they can also limit how we think.

What the tools identified here all have in common is that they enable us to extend our own abilities to figure it out. What happens when we hire tools to off-load or outsource understanding?

When Easy Access to Information Keeps Us in the Dark

For more than simple queries, access to information is insufficient for understanding. In these cases, we adapt, modify, and transform information to suit our needs. This is often done using tools, whether it's the pencil-and-paper sketch on a napkin or using a chart generator to transform data into a visualization. In these cases, the tools augment our human capabilities. But what about tools that do the work of understanding for us?

Increasingly, the technologies meant to advance civilization and extend our human abilities are doing precisely the opposite. We've increasingly outsourced understanding to complex algorithms. When we don't know something, we "Google it." We joke about asking voice-activated AI assistants, like Siri or Alexa, to answer our questions, but this behavior is becoming the norm. And as useful as this tech is, there's a dark side to our unquestioning acceptance of these technologies. The deeper question we should we discussing is this: *Do we use technology to off-load understanding, or do we use technology to help us become better thinkers?*

Deciding to Work at Understanding

To frame this dilemma, let's evaluate two different solutions to the problem of confusing parking signs (see Figure 14.5). Confusion around unclear parking signs is a mundane example, to be sure, but one that is useful to expose and explain this deeper concern about our relationship with technology.

Here's our scenario: you're in a hurry, rushing to that meeting. You just need to park your car on the street, and ... The Sign. *Can I park here? Will I get a ticket?* you wonder ... You do the mental gymnastics needed to decipher this information. And if you're correct, you might avoid a ticket. And here's the theme of this book again: we've been given all the information we need, but we haven't been given understanding.

FIGURE 14.5 An extreme example of a confusing parking sign, but one we can all relate to!

SOLUTION 1

Frustrated by the difficulty of deciphering these confusing parking signs (and more than a few parking tickets), designer Nikki Sylianteng took matters into her own hands. In an act that's been described as "guerilla civic design," she started posting "better" versions of these street signs throughout various NYC neighborhoods (see Figure 14.6).[4]

4. Sylianteng, Nikki. "To Park or Not to Park?" n.d. https://nikkisylianteng.com/v2/project /parking-sign-redesign/

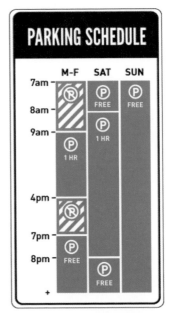

FIGURE 14.6 Designer Nikki Sylianteng took matters into her own hands and began posting "better" versions of confusing street signs throughout the city.

Her version draws inspiration from a week-view calendar, with blocks of green and red that clearly answer the question: *Can I park here now? And for how long?* She effectively reframed the problem from information to be communicated (through text) to information that could be understood. Anyone who glances at this should quickly understand the parking rules.

This is a solution that facilitates understanding. It also reveals the patterns in the information. A glance at this representation allows us to not only answer our immediate question about parking now, but actually *see* generally when we can or cannot park at this location.

SOLUTION 2

An even simpler, more direct solution to our parking confusion has been proposed:[5] a mobile app that uses machine learning to unscramble the information mess to answer our *Can I park here or not?* question with a simple *Yes* or *No* (see Figure 14.7).

FIGURE 14.7 This mobile app solution to the confusing parking sign problem uses image recognition and machine learning to answer the question *Can I park here or not?*

5. Concept by product designer Tara Mann; link to original tweet has since been deleted.

While we applaud the efficiency and inventiveness of this solution, it is also concerning. Yes, this solution efficiently solves the task, but we don't walk away with a mental model of the problem. If we return tomorrow, at a different time, we won't recall the parking rules, because we didn't learn anything—we just needed an answer in the moment, and our device gave us one. Just like "Googling it," just like asking a voice assistant, we've hired a tool to do the work of understanding for us.

WHY THIS MATTERS

This example may seem like a small, silly thing to write about. But these two solutions highlight the serious distinction between *understanding the answer* versus *getting the answer*. In the case of a confusing parking sign, many of us may decide we don't need to understand the rules—ever. While we may be fine with simply getting an answer when it comes to parking rules, what about when it comes to choosing healthcare options, finding a babysitter, or purchasing a vehicle? What is our relationship with technology in these cases, and do we use tools to become more informed, or to get an answer—an answer which, depending on the circumstances, may not be in our best interest?

We have to make a decision about when to accept an easy answer and when to work at understanding. With the parking sign, it's a non-issue. But if we return to the privacy policy solutions from the opening chapter, we're presented with the very same choice. We can trust a group like ToS;DR to transform the information for us, or we can use a tool like Polisis to figure things out for ourselves. These are both viable options to shift the costs of understanding. And while we can probably trust a third-party such as ToS;DR, what happens when we can't trust the entity figuring out what's "best" for us? What happens when it's a corporation—motivated by profits—telling us there is nothing to worry about?

Moreover, what happens when we've become so dependent on the easy (trusted) answer that we struggle to figure it out for ourselves? Visual literacy, critical thinking, active listening—these understanding skills are—like muscles—things we need to exercise. Again, the deeper issue is this: Do we use technology to off-load understanding, or do we use technology to help us— and others—become better thinkers?

When Technology Keeps Us in the Dark

On one hand, *we* keep ourselves in the dark, so to speak, by choosing what's worth figuring out for ourselves, or not. And to be fair, choosing to outsource the cost of understanding is perfectly fine in many cases—societies and civilizations are built upon trusting the conclusions of other, more knowledgeable people. We just need to be aware of it when we're making this choice. But making this choice is even more critical as new technologies appear to offer an easy answer to all our questions. The choice to accept an easy answer—to what may be a very complex or complicated question—also means we're in the

A SPECIAL NOTE FOR DESIGNERS

A note for designers reading this book, I (Stephen) worry that we've conflated making things "user-centered" with always making things easy, and in the process, we risk dumbing down people. There's a kind of bad friction that should be removed from all interactions, but there's also the good kind of friction that gets us into a flow state and leads to understanding. Game designers distinguish between games that disorient players and games that frustrate players: a video game should never be disorienting, that is, needlessly confusing or difficult to interact with, but *frustration* in a video game is essential. It's only through frustration that players are challenged, learn, and make progress throughout the game. Creating the conditions for this kind of learning—whether in games or product design—is something worth advocating for. As a designer, interested in making things that truly benefit people, you have to be aware of when you are using technology to displace understanding, and when you should use technology to help people become better thinkers.

dark about what produced that answer. Outsourcing the cost of understanding means that we're choosing to let someone or something else do the hard work to adapt, modify, and transform information to our needs.

This is a kind of darkness that we can do something about. But there's another kind of darkness, one that is harder to do something about, which involves the invisible layers of software that increasingly govern our lives.

Think about a maps app you might use to get directions. Using a tool like Waze or Google Maps to get around is pretty great, especially when it can redirect your route home because of a wreck a few miles down the road that you don't know about. But have you stopped to consider who is authoring these algorithms and what their aim is? When I'm told my trip will be 24 minutes, are these algorithms optimizing for my *individual* journey? Are they load balancing for an entire *group* of people—what's best for the whole? Are advertisers able to influence these algorithms to direct my path home such that it passes by their stores? We don't know the answers to these questions. For reasons of intellectual property, businesses do not divulge this information.

We can talk about visibility into these algorithms and the programmatic rules being coded into these systems. We can debate in courts what should be made public—or not. But, even as we're having these debates, what's going on with these technologies is becoming increasingly opaque, even to the businesses and engineering teams writing the code.

MACHINE LEARNING AS A TOOL FOR UNDERSTANDING

At the time of this writing, remarkable things are being done using machine learning. Self-driving cars. Predicting heart disease. Beating championship players at games of *Go*. Even beating humans at games such as poker that rely on bluffing and chance! Without any kind of programmed instruction, we can leave a machine playing an early 1980s game such as Atari's *Breakout*, and the machine will *teach itself* (through an approach called "reinforcement learning") how to play the game. Within a few hours, the machine is playing at an expert level (see Figure 14.8). Given a few days, the machine discovers a clever new way to beat the game that only a few human experts have ever thought of. The technology is very promising—and advancing more quickly than anyone expected.

FIGURE 14.8 After 75 hours of training, DeepMind's machine-learning algorithm taught itself to win at Atari *Breakout* using approaches normally only demonstrated by human experts.

Of course, we've seen spectacular failures, too. Microsoft's AI chatbot Tay that had to be shut down after less than 24 hours. Why? It began mimicking the worst behaviors of people on Twitter, spewing racist, genocidal, and misogynistic messages to users.[6] Or consider Amazon's sexist AI recruiting engine, which learned that male candidates were preferable, as a decade of historical hiring data seemed to indicate this was the desirable pattern.[7] And then there are the fatalities associated with self-driving vehicles.

We mention all of this for one very simple reason: if we understand just a bit about how these technologies work, we can better approach them as a *tool*; we can know how this technology might be useful and under what conditions it might be prone to failure.

To demonstrate this curiosity, let's look more closely at why the same algorithm that taught itself to play and win at dozens of old-school Atari games was successful with some games but struggled with others.

With a game such as *Breakout*, where you're essentially shooting blocks (while avoiding shots back at you), there's an incredibly tight feedback loop between actions taken and consequences. *Get hit, lose a life. Hit a block, it disappears.* This style of game plays to the strengths of a reinforcement-learning algorithm, the kind used to successfully learn and beat the game. But when this same algorithm that won at a game like *Breakout* (and dozens of similar games) took on games like *Montezuma's Revenge* or *Pitfall!*—it didn't fare as well. And here we see the weaknesses of this particular algorithm revealed. The exploratory nature of these last two games required that a player recall and piece together things previously encountered. *That key you picked up in another room—maybe it fits the lock in this one? Maybe that thing that wasn't important before is important now.* This kind of logic requires a memory of past events to support "more sophisticated exploration, planning and complex route-finding."[8] These are things that the human brain—at an early age—quickly figures out, but researchers working on these machine-learning algorithms must look for and address these blind spots, as they are discovered.

Understanding just a bit about how these algorithms work shines a light on why something that excels at one challenge might fail spectacularly at another.

6. "Tay (Bot)." 2020. Wikipedia. Wikimedia Foundation. February 22, 2020. https://en.wikipedia.org /wiki/Tay_(bot)
7. Dastin, Jeffrey. 2018. "Amazon Scraps Secret AI Recruiting Tool That Showed Bias Against Women." *Reuters*. October 9, 2018. www.reuters.com/article/us-amazon-com-jobs-automation -insight-idUSKCN1MK08G
8. Mohan, Geoffrey. 2015. "Is Playing 'Space Invaders' a Milestone in Artificial Intelligence?" *Los Angeles Times*. February 25, 2015. www.latimes.com/science/sciencenow /la-sci-sn-computer-learning-space-invaders-20150224-story.html

And we have to remind ourselves that while a machine might beat humans at poker, machines don't understand concepts, sense intent, or factor in context (at least not until those things are accounted for by additional algorithms).

We mention all this to challenge our implicit "faith in the machine" and to challenge you, the reader, to understand how and why the information tools do what they do. A calculator may be right 100 percent of the time, but if you enter the wrong numbers, you'll get a wrong answer. We can spot the human error in this scenario. In a similar fashion, you get better results from machine-learning algorithms when the data is good and also somewhat structured. But unlike the calculator, ML algorithms increasingly rely on policies and probabilities (rather than straightforward computation rules); at times, the engineers and researchers building these systems aren't entirely sure what's going on or why the machines do some things.

We're building systems whose inner workings are invisible to us. The risk, then, is placing blind faith in a potentially *blind* technology.

SPOTTING COMPUTATIONAL ERRORS WILL BECOME MORE DIFFICULT

While it may be easy for us to spot these obvious errors now—discrimination bias, self-driving cars that hit a pedestrian, racist bots—what happens when we begin to rely on these machines for more complicated questions? When the results aren't obviously flawed, how will we respond? Will we simply act on the recommendation, unchallenged? There's a big difference between asking a verifiable question such as "What's the weather?" and trusting a powerful machine to crunch the numbers and make a recommendation as to which university one should attend. Do we challenge a response that doesn't make any sense, or trust that the machine is right and simply offering up an unconventional answer?

And while this is still in the realm of dystopian speculation, we already know what happens when questionable algorithmic responses are scaled across large organizations: humans suffer. Consider the huge swaths of jobs, routinely measured on efficiency, that follow a defined script, regardless of circumstances. In everything from call centers to pharmacies, we encounter workers instructed to do as they're told, following the on-screen instructions. Even when things don't make sense, front-line workers feel powerless to go against what is displayed on the screen. Computer systems begin to trump common sense. As these systems are scaled throughout large organizations, we lose touch with individuals and humanity.

WORKING WITH MACHINES

While this may come off as critical of technology and the corporations behind this tech, it's not. We're more interested in humans and our *thoughtful* adoption of technology as a society. How might machines make us better? Better at our jobs. Better at making judgment calls. Better as global citizens. Understanding how human creatures adapt, modify, and transform information to suit our needs, that's our focus. This extends to the thoughtful adoption of tools—be that tools that let us manipulate information directly or tools that we employ to do computation (or make predictions) on our behalf.

How then can we work with machines to extend and augment our biological limitations? Use technology for what technology is good for, and recognize the limitations that machine have? In a presentation on conversational design, design leader Erika Hall remarked on what humans and machines are each good at. We've included that list in Table 14.2:

TABLE 14.2 THE RELATIVE STRENGTHS OF HUMANS AND MACHINES

HUMANS ARE GOOD AT	MACHINES ARE GOOD AT
Empathy	Remembering
Persuasion	Calculating
Unstructured solving	Logic
Assessing relevance	Precise repetition

As our technology tools become more robust, having a list such as this is a good, objective way to remind us what machines are good for and how to best use them.

Tools for Taming Complexity

As we take a critical look at tools and technologies for understanding, there's a final perspective we want you to consider, that is: the potential for tools to bring people together around serious and ridiculously complex issues.

Throughout this book, we've explored numerous tools and activities for understanding. Using stories. Drawing things. Moving things around. And while we often discussed this at the level of the individual struggling to make sense of some difficult topic, the beauty of bringing intangible concepts into the world is this: we give ideas a form that *other* people can then adapt, modify, touch, edit, transform and so on. We create the conditions for collaboration.

As a facilitator, one of the things you learn to do is remove yourself from whatever is being discussed. Your job is—to … *facilitate*! And to do this, you pick up all kinds of methods to establish and maintain dialogue between different parties around a given topic. In effect, you learn how to create structures for thinking. Sometimes these are conceptual, such as the *How might we …* question framing. Other times, it's an explicit visual structure, such as the *Business Model Canvas*. You might bring in a game or a toolkit that spurs a deeper discussion, say around how to work better as a team. In effect, you become the neutral third-party, interested only in coordinating interactions around a challenging topic. In other instances, you bring people together not to solve a problem, but to start a healthy dialogue. I (Stephen) believe there's a need for more and better tools that do exactly this, *bring us together* into a meaningful dialogue.

Here's why we need tools to bring us together:

We face serious challenges in the 21st century: climate change, economic growth and sustainable development, globalization and geopolitics, antibiotic resistance, long-term food and water security, human rights, sustainable energy, rapid population increase, the future of work, etc. We could go on. These are serious issues. They're also systemic problems, with no easy solutions. And while these might be a far cry from the medical charts and confusing parking sign examples, what all of these examples share in common is the core need to adjust the balance between the information we have and the understanding we need. Everything discussed up until this point, everything we've discovered about how human creatures figure things out, is relevant to problems of all scale. The question then is where do we apply what we've learned?

Whether it's something personal, like the team conflicts that stem from a lack of self-awareness, or something big, like the tricky, interconnected systems problems that call for the coordination of many parties, we need better ways to work through conflict and come together, as a unified group, to work through these present challenges. This calls for tools suited to these challenges. Tools for thinking through complex, "intertwingled" issues, but also tools that help us work and learn together.

Let's talk about tools for handling the increasing complexity bit, before turning to the potential for tools to bring us together.

Tools for Increasingly Complex Challenges

As we wrestle with increasingly complex challenges, we need tools equally suited to the tasks. Yes, drawing a concept is a powerful way to bring information into the world, but when that same drawing is fueled by real-time dynamic data, and it's not just *a* drawing but dozens of drawings and charts and ways to view the very same data set—that's a powerful tool for understanding a lot of complex information. This is the kind of thinking we see with the dynamic drawing visualization described earlier. This is not to suggest that our present tools for understanding are in any way lacking—that judgment depends upon what needs to be understood. Rather, it's about the right tool for the job. Using pen and paper to work out a complicated math problem is invaluable, but a calculator just happens to be better at efficient computation. But if the job involves working out orbital dynamics, planetary alignment, and thrust velocities to "slingshot" a space craft to Mars, then a computer simulation might be preferable to the calculator.

If we return to more familiar territory, we can present information in a static format, say a poster or slide presentation. We can place things on an X-Y matrix, use boxes and arrows, or spread information across a timeline. These are all valuable ways to extend our thinking capabilities. But how much more powerful might these same visual representations be when augmented through rich interactions, dynamic data, and predictive algorithms? And how much more powerful are these tools when they allow us to pivot and look at things from many perspectives?

This sounds a lot like the kind of tool that Bret Victor is proposing. He talks about dynamic drawing tools to help us "think powerfully about systems,"[9] but what kind of systems might he have in mind? While he's talking generally about a way of seeing and working that many professions—from artists to scientists—would benefit from, he later, in 2015, directs his exploration of better tools to the climate crisis.[10]

Responding to the question *What can a technologist do about climate change*? Victor weighs in with a sharp perspective on the tools for understanding that scientists don't presently have. He offers a reasoned critique of the current tools available to scientists, describes the kinds of tools they need, and

9. Victor, Bret. 2012. "Inventing on Principle." *CUSEC 2012*. https://vimeo.com/36579366
10. Victor, Bret. November, 2015. "What Can a Technologist Do About Climate Change? (A Personal View)" Worrydream. http://worrydream.com/ClimateChange/#tools

suggests that "a sea change in invention and discovery is possible" once scientists can "see what they're doing in realtime, with immediate visual feedback and interactive exploration."

In short, our present—systemic—challenges call for a sort of turbocharged, integrated version of the concepts we've discussed throughout this book. In the next chapter, we'll look at *explorable explanations* and *generative design tools* as examples of this next evolution of tools. But there are also tools we can all use today.

Model Thinking

For the last decade, Scott E. Page has been teaching "Model Thinking" to students at the University of Michigan. His popular class is also available—for free—online.[11] Read the class description (below), and consider all that has been described in this book:

> We see political uprisings, market crashes, and a never ending array of social trends. How do we make sense of it? Models. Evidence shows that people who think with models consistently outperform those who don't. And, moreover people who think with lots of models outperform people who use only one. Why do models make us better thinkers? Models help us to better organize information—to make sense of that fire hose or hairball of data (choose your metaphor) available on the Internet. Models improve our abilities to make accurate forecasts. They help us make better decisions and adopt more effective strategies. They even can improve our ability to design institutions and procedures.

While Page's use of the word *model* has more in common with mathematical models than the visual models we've explored here, everything he explains fits with our call for better tools to think through complex issues. In his class, he walks through all kind of models—Game Theory, Network Models, Distributions, Models of Cooperation—to help us engage critically with complex topics. It's a rich course, with information highly complementary to our focus.

---

11. Page, Scott E. n.d. "Model Thinking." Coursera. https://www.coursera.org/learn/model-thinking

But one theme in particular runs throughout Page's teaching: the need for *many* models. As with the new breed of tools we mentioned earlier (Airtable, Zenkit) that let you pivot between views, and as with comments from Chapter 6, "Closing Thoughts and Cautionary Notes About Associations," about the benefits of many lenses, as the complexity of a problem increases so, too, does the need to see things in many different ways. Commenting on the 2008 global financial market collapse, economist Andrew Lo remarks "Only by collecting a diverse and often mutually contradictory set of narratives can we eventually develop a more complete understanding of the crisis."[12]

We need tools and models and structures to let us and others see a challenge *through many lenses*. Every new toolkit, model, frame, or perspective we bring, helps us break out of our own static mindsets, and helps others do the same. We learn to see things differently, and in doing so, envision unseen opportunities. And we learn to work and learn together. Which leads us to the human side of things.

Social Challenges

In writing this book, we've chosen to focus on mostly *functional* mechanisms for solving understanding problems. What's not included is any sustained focus on the squishy, human side of this equation—cognitive biases, irrational beliefs, political identities and personal motivations, emotions, our attraction to false narratives, and so on. To be clear, these human tendencies are a critical part of the understanding equation. At a minimum, they interfere with good judgment. More often, these tendencies limit our ability to arrive at good or valid conclusions. At worst, these human tendencies divide us along arbitrary lines and prevent us from doing more and more together.

Add to these negative human tendencies the confounding realization that many of our increasingly systemic problems are too multifaceted and controversial for an individual or team to solve in isolation. We need the means to make sense of these issues *together*, to explore possibilities *together*, to align on the critical nuances *together*.

We're hopeful that this will happen.

In his essay explaining "Neuralink and the Brain's Magical Future," writer Tim Urban posed a simple question that gets to the heart of the matter:

---

12. Lo, Andrew W. 2012. "Reading About the Financial Crisis: A Twenty-One-Book Review." *Journal of Economic Literature* 50 (1): 151–78. https://doi.org/10.1257/jel.50.1.151

"Ever wonder why you're so often unimpressed by humans and yet so blown away by the accomplishments of humanity?"[13] Urban goes on to comment on all the biases and beliefs and *human* tendencies. These divide us. They create tribal conflicts. But the great accomplishment—that is humanity; humanity is people working *together* for something bigger. Humanity is "a superintelligent, tremendously-knowledgeable, millennia-old Colossus, with 7.5 billion neurons." The conclusion? Our pressing challenge is to continue nurturing and scaling humanity to come together for increasingly complex, global challenges.

If there's a chance of coming together around these complex issues, we believe—we've seen how—well-designed, playful structures can bring people together to solve contentious issues. Structures that truly facilitate rather than force an agenda are powerful tools for bringing people together. If we go back to the simple, local example (from earlier in this book) of two different ways to run a meeting, we're fairly certain that few of us are eager to listen to another presentation; we naturally crave interaction and active participation in the things we care deeply about.

To this end, we're seeing the emergence of more *cooperation* across different groups.

Liberating Structures

Partly a response to ineffective meetings, and partly a response to the stifling, centralized control structures that discourage collaboration, *Liberating Structures* have emerged as a way to bring workers together, to create the conditions for innovation.

Curated and co-developed by Henri Lipmanowicz and Keith McCandless, the idea of Liberating Structures is a set of 30+ inclusive practices that can be used by anyone, for a range of topics, whether in meetings or conversations. These practices, mostly facilitation activities, can replace or complement conventional ways of working. However, Liberating Structures are firmly rooted in an ethos of inclusion and engagement. *Anyone can play.*

The model shown in Figure 14.9 is a good framework for understanding how Liberating Structures relate to other kinds of activities.

13. Urban, Tim. 2017. "Neuralink and the Brain's Magical Future." Wait But Why. April 20, 2017. https://tompaton.com/blog/cached/waitbutwhy.com/2017/04/neuralink.html

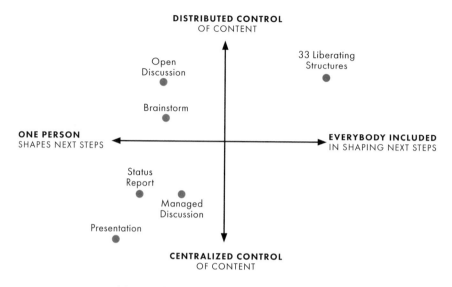

FIGURE 14.9 A useful matrix for understanding how Liberating Structures relate to other kinds of activities.

Unlike conventional ways of working, such as the business presentation or brainstorming session, there's no one person with centralized control over what happens. The criteria are this: distributed control and the inclusion of a fairer, larger number of people. Thus, the "liberating" part of Liberating Structures.

And the structures themselves? They are activities to promote critical thinking, conversation, cooperation, generative thinking, and similar group contributions. To get feedback on a presentation, instead of asking if there are "Any questions?" you might use *"1-2-4-All,"* a simple structure for creating space to reflect alone, then in pairs, then foursomes, and finally as a whole group. To invite people to speak up on a sensitive topic, you can use *TRIZ* to encourage heretical thinking, by asking something like "What must we *stop doing* to make progress on our deepest purpose?" It's a nuanced set of practices that create safe, inclusive spaces to contribute. McCandless comments that they "employ tiny microstructural changes in the way we meet, plan, research, decide and learn together. They quickly foster lively participation in groups of any size, making it possible to truly include and unleash everyone in shaping the future."

These practices are now used around the world, in health care, businesses, and academia. And to use our language, they are tools—facilitation tools—that bring people together to support understanding.

Of course, it's not just tools for collaboration, we also see groups of individuals coming together to collaborate and create new tools, as happened with Pathline.

Pathline

An inspiring story of *interdisciplinary* collaboration comes from computer scientist Miriah Meyer and designer Bang Wong, both of whom are researching how improved visualizations can advance scientific research. A bit of context: historically, scientists relied on available computational and visualization tools to sort through the scientific data; these tools are sufficient, but have not been designed to accommodate any particular research needed.

Working in close collaboration with geneticists, Meyer and Wong developed "Pathline," a visualization tool custom designed for "comparative functional genomics." What had been a customary heatmap visualization, they replaced with a curvemap (Figure. 14.10).

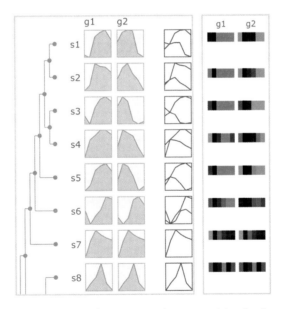

FIGURE 14.10 Two ways to visualize genetic information. A familiar heatmap visualization (right) with a more useful curvemap (left).

In their own words:

> Two main advantages of the new tool were found. First, there
> was a massive gain in efficiency. The study of a heatmap took

up to a half-hour before but can be done at a glance at the cur-vemap now. More importantly, though, the scientists made new discoveries of gene properties they didn't know about before. What was hidden in the data before, is now very clear, even to an untrained eye.[14]

There's more to this visualization, but this is enough to make our point. As with the theme of this book, all the information was there, already. And interactive tools were already being used to work with the information. But, because of a more *thoughtful* representation, scientists are now seeing patterns they didn't see before, making discoveries they may have overlooked previously. This is exciting. The more we, as a culture, learn about the process of understanding and how to collaborate with other groups, the more we can spot opportunities to *improve* understanding, and the better off we'll all be. Were it not for the work of people like Meyer and Wong, these scientists might still be using inadequate tools, not able to make the same discoveries they can now make.

From Marks on Cave Walls to …?

In summary, we look ahead at a near future where the tools and platforms and distributed learning environments help us—collectively—sift through information (and misinformation). Making sense of the most complex challenges requires us to engage with content, to model and simulate possibilities, to explore many explanations, and … that we do all this *together*. In short, we need to understand what it can look like to come *together* to envision unseen possibilities.

Whether it's writing on a cave wall or creating new ways to visualize "invisible" machine-learning algorithms,[15] humans have a long history of creating tools that extend our ability to reason about things. The challenge then is to find or create these *new* tools that are better suited for these increasingly complex challenges.

14. Meyer, M., B. Wong, M. Styczynski, T. Munzner, and H. Pfister. 2010. "Pathline: A Tool for Comparative Functional Genomics." *Computer Graphics Forum* 29 (3): 1043–52. https://doi.org/10.1111/j.1467-8659.2009.01710.x
15. "Cortex 5 AI Platform — Augmented Intelligence for All." Argodesign. www.argodesign.com/work/cognitive-scale.html

15

A Perspective on Future Tools and Technologies for Understanding

Face this world. Learn its ways, watch it, be careful of too hasty guesses at its meaning. In the end you will find clues to it all.

—H. G. WELLS, *THE TIME MACHINE*

If we take a long view of understanding, we notice two things: first, our *natural* human ability to understand has evolved very slowly. We still succumb to base human tendencies and fall prey to cognitive biases suited for an earlier time in our evolution. Second, we are always creating the means to increase our human *capacity* for understanding.

In this final chapter, we want to look ahead at some emerging technologies and how these technologies might further reduce the costs of understanding. Our interest is not on the technology per se, and we certainly have no interest in predicting what's next. Rather, we want to explore how these new technologies might extend (and in some ways integrate) all that we know about how we—as human creatures—adapt, modify, and transform information to suit our needs.

For context, let's consider (just a few of!) the historical technologies we've invented to extend our limited cognitive abilities:

- Written language enabled us to off-load thoughts onto the page, where we could then reflect upon this information, share this information with others, or save this information for later retrieval. Humble additions, such as the bound manuscript (instead of long scrolls) or page numbering, allowed us to *retrieve* information quickly.

- Ancient tools such as astrolabes allowed mariners to chart their way across vast waters.

- The Greek Antikythera Mechanism—the earliest known "computer" built around 150 to 100 BC—was designed to model and predict planetary orbits, as well as the dates and locations of upcoming Olympic games.

- Calculators, both modern and ancient, have allowed us to do computations far more quickly and with far more accuracy than most of us are naturally able to do.

- Microscopes and telescopes have amplified our vision, allowing us to observe things that far exceed our natural human abilities.

- Even simple devices, such as pen and ink, pencils, or the piece of charcoal used to make markings upon a cave wall, have endowed us with the ability to record and render information in a way that extends beyond our short lives, well into the future.

In short, we have a long history of creating tools that extend our natural abilities to make sense of and navigate through the complex world we live in. But it's not just tools for personal or local use.

Tools for Group Cognition

We've also developed means of enabling larger *groups* of people—throughout space and time—to work and learn together. Libraries established formal standards for organizing and retrieving the written word. Over several centuries, researchers, scientists, and academics codified the manner in which knowledge builds upon prior knowledge. We've launched global positioning satellites into space, which allowed us to guide missiles to other continents or direct people to a new restaurant. With the International Space Station, we have command centers, located around the world, where people share the knowledge required to get and keep astronauts in orbit around our planet.

And, of course, there's the internet. More than just increasing the speed of communications, this technology has connected scientists, toppled governments, and placed all manner of knowledge a simple keyword search away, among other things.

We are—as a species—ever extending our ability to compute, to think, to explore, and to understand.

"What's Next?"

To answer the question of "What's next?" let's look to the recent past, going back just a few decades, to the origins of the internet. While we commonly think of the internet as how we share photos, buy stuff, and search for all manner of things, there has always been a bigger, bolder vision. Understanding a bit of this history—and the aspirations—will help us peer into the future.

Origins of the Internet

In 1945, Vannevar Bush published his famous article "As We May Think."[1] The device he conjured up, the memex, was a reaction to a problem that was of pressing concern to Bush: *information overload*.[2] Bush imagined a future device that might capture not just the discrete bits of information, but also the "information trails" between these ideas. Looking to the mind for inspiration, Bush commented:

> The human mind ... operates by association. With one item in its grasp, it snaps instantly to the next that is suggested by the association of thoughts, in accordance with some intricate web of trails carried by the cells of the brain.

More than just a device for recalling information, "the essential feature of the memex" was capturing the information trails that string information together. Bush said, "When the user is building a trail, he names it, inserts the name in his code book, and taps it out on his keyboard."

---

1. Bush, Vannevar. 1945. "As We May Think." *The Atlantic Monthly* 176 (July): 101–8.
2. It seems our modern concern over information overload was not new, even in 1945. For a good look at the historical roots of our information age, we recommend the book *Glut* by Alex Wright.

This concept would go on to inspire the development of early hypertext systems that would eventually become the World Wide Web. Today the mass of information Bush had to work with seems modest compared to our daily flood of tweets, posts, and emails. But here's the underlying concept: *understanding cannot be achieved alone*. It's not just the brain, or the representation, or the interaction, or the tools, etc. The memex (short for *Memory Extension*) was a device for extending our memory and connecting ideas. And it cast a powerful vision for the future.

From 1945, we have a vision—granted, one whose implementation involved microfilm—of technology extending the capabilities of the individual. In the 21st century, we talk about things like data visualizations or computer simulations as a way to help us make sense of complex information. But presenting information behind glass, in a historical context, is just the most recent addition to a long line of tools designed to extend the limits of human reasoning and understanding.

This vision of extending one's own memory was picked up in the early 1960s by two computer pioneers, J. C. R. Licklider in his paper, "Man-Computer Symbiosis," and Douglas Engelbart in his paper, "Augmenting Human Intellect."[3] Where the memex was about off-loading information from the brain into the world, Licklider went further and talked about a symbiotic relationship: humans and machines in concert. Engelbart framed this around augmenting intelligence and, while very much in agreement with Licklider about a symbiotic relationship, worked on the idea of humans working *with other humans* and the role of the machine in that relationship. These ideas, though they date from before the moon landing, are consistent with everything we've discussed, especially where we ended up in our chapters on distribution and coordination (see Figure 15.1).

3. Licklider, J. C. R. 1960. "Man-Computer Symbiosis." *IRE Transactions on Human Factors in Electronics* HFE-1 (1): 4–11. https://doi.org/10.1109/thfe2.1960.4503259; Engelbart, D. C. 1962. "Augmenting Human Intellect: A Conceptual Framework," October. Stanford Research Institute, Menlo Park, CA. https://dougengelbart.org/content/view/138

    Note: Licklider was influenced by Bush. And Engelbart was funded by Licklider. For a good book on this bit of history, see *The Dream Machine* by Mitchell Waldrop. Also, Licklider funded Bob Taylor's research on computer networking that started ARPANET.

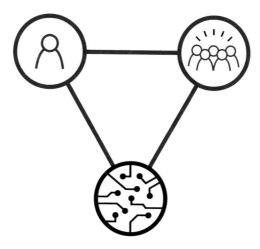

FIGURE 15.1 Individuals, groups, and machines, all working together in a symbiotic relationship.

The point we're trying to make is this: understanding is not solely about the brain, or representations, or interactions. It's not about any one thing, in isolation. There is no magic bullet. Yes, there are times when we can move the needle on understanding by creating a better visual representation. But this is merely a lens appropriate to certain understanding problems or certain slices of problems. The better version of the diabetes chart fixed that *slice* of the understanding problem, but didn't address the broader systems and organizational structures that routinely produce those kinds of artifacts. (And if we really expanded the scope of that understanding problem, the broadest understanding challenge might be that we don't yet understand why we have or how to end these chronic illnesses.)

The ideal perspective is a more holistic one that can address the broader, systemic concerns. In Bush's terms, we need to look for the trails connecting many distinct pieces of information. The act of connecting all this information might then appear as symbiosis, or intelligence augmentation, or distributed cognition (different, though similar ideas). The long arc of all this exploration is this: *increasing connections between humans (plural) and the machines we've built to augment ourselves.*

This matters because there are always new technologies on the horizon. And each of them, we are told, will resolve our understanding problems. Get some AI—and problem solved. Buy a VR system and voilà, you're a cognitive superman. The temptation here, as always, is that a "thing" will increase our understanding capacity. But it's not about a thing by itself. It's about a system in which things and humans are working together. It's all about increasing connections.

The big themes, those that we'll comment on here, are about increasing computation, a shift from tools and devices to environments, and digital and physical realities merging. But behind these observable themes is the more profound shift we should keep in mind: *increasing connectedness*.[4]

Behind the story of the internet is the bigger story of *connecting all the world*. Our knowledge. People. Ideas. All connected.

This historical perspective then changes how we look at audacious projects such as Elon Musk's *Neuralink*, a brain-machine interface that might someday allow humans to communicate directly with each other (like tech-enabled telepaths). While the technology may be nascent (and a bit speculative), the fundamental concept goes back at least to the 1960s, with Douglas Engelbart musing about *how might we bring humans and machines together?* Whether the actual technology implementation is a device in our hands, something embedded in our brains, or simply moving throughout intelligent spaces, the fundamental concept does not change.

With this idea of increasing connectedness as the backdrop, and recognizing that the actual technology implementations are ever changing, we've sifted through tech trends and speculative fiction to identify three technology themes that overlap with our topic of understanding. Again, these themes are:

- Increasing computational abilities
- A shift from tools to spaces
- The merging of digital and physical realities

Theme #1: Increasing Computational Abilities

In the last chapter, we offered a brief consideration of current advances in machine learning, and how this can be used to off-load information or help us engage with more complex topics. This distinction—what machines can do *for* us and what we can do *with* machines—is a useful one.

---

4. Note: Increasing connection doesn't negate keeping space for disconnecting and quiet reflection!

Machines Working *for* Us (the Replacement Narrative)

We can talk about the tedious things machines (and robots) might do *for* us—manage supply inventories, prepare taxes, book flights, move stuff around inside warehouses, etc. In this respect, a great number of tedious or laborious tasks can now be done, and probably done with more precision, by machines. This is also the narrative that frightens those of us working in jobs that might someday be obsolete. Headlines suggest that *Robots are coming for your jobs* and *Workers are no longer necessary*. AI is routinely explained to people with this *replacement narrative*. But this narrative views AI as a zero-sum game. There is a fixed amount of work to be done. AI can do this work better, or faster, or cheaper—so humans get replaced. In economics, we know that zero-sum thinking is incorrect. It says the pie can never be bigger, and the only question is how we divide up the pie. It says there are winners and losers, and the win-win option is off the table.

But AI isn't only about *replacement*. It is also, and often, about *expansion*. It can be about the win-win. We can grow the pie. A lot of people reading this book have jobs that didn't exist before computers. That's growing the pie. That's the *expansion narrative*. History teaches us that whenever a technology killed off one kind of job, entirely *new* jobs were also created. This has been the pattern of every new advance in technology, whether that technology was the printing press, the loom, or personal computers.

A good, concrete example of how workers can redefine their roles and value relative to machines comes from the legal industry and LawGeex, a firm specializing in contract review automation. This group built an AI to review specific kinds of legal contracts and flag problems (NDAs). Then they ran a study to compare human lawyers with the AI. The humans, all with huge experience, took an average of 92 minutes and identified about 85 percent of the problems. The AI took 26 *seconds* and was 94 percent accurate. But this "machine beat human" narrative isn't the takeaway here. Rather, the most useful point of this story is that the lawyers were *happy* about this. They were able to off-load the tedious and boring—but necessary—work they had to do.[5]

---

5. "20 Top Lawyers Were Beaten by Legal AI. Here Are Their Surprising Responses." 2018. LawGeex Blog: Legal Technology. October 23, 2018. https://blog.lawgeex.com/20-top-lawyers-were-beaten-by-legal-ai-here-are-their-surprising-responses/

For these kinds of narratives, where machines take over work that humans have traditionally done, we should take comfort in reminding ourselves what machines do best—and what humans do best. Humans are great at things like empathy, persuasion, solving ill-structured problems, and assessing relevance; machines are better at remembering, calculating, logic, and precise repetition. Embrace this, and we can pave the way for a future where humans do work that is more dignified and more rewarding. Let humans do the stuff we're suited for; let machines do the stuff machines are suited for.

All of which starts to blur the line between machines working *for* us and machines working *with* us.

Humans Working *with* Machines

Less talked about is what we will be able to do *with* machines—how machines might extend or augment our own capabilities. Consider how personal computers allowed us to do calculations and model outcomes that weren't really feasible before such processing power existed. In this respect, what might AI allow us to do, or do differently? In terms of understanding, we're far more interested—and excited—by how we might be better because of machines.

GENERATIVE DESIGN

Projects such as *Dreamcatcher* from software company Autodesk[6] demonstrate a very specific way we might work *with* machines to transform manufacturing. In the time it takes to create one idea, a computer will, according to Autodesk, "generate thousands, along with the data to prove which designs perform best."[7] You set the parameters—materials, manufacturing methods, cost constraints, weight, and so on—and the machine can generate and explore literally every possibility. Out of this kind of exhaustive exploration, you get things such as bridge joints and motorcycle parts that use fewer materials, are lighter, and as strong, if not stronger, than the parts traditionally designed by humans. See Figure 15.2.

6. "Project Dreamcatcher." n.d. Autodesk Research.
   https://autodeskresearch.com/projects/Dreamcatcher
7. "What Is Generative Design: Tools & Software." n.d. Autodesk. www.autodesk.com/solutions/generative-design

FIGURE 15.2 These three structural elements are all designed to carry the same structural loads and forces. The one on the left was designed by a human. The remaining two structures were designed by a machine and can bear the same loads but need fewer raw materials to manufacture and are lighter in the process. *Image by Arup*

Play this out, and the role of a human shifts from that of a hands-on creator using software to *render* an idea to that of a conductor (or curator or cultivator) *working with* software to explore possible options. In a sense, we develop a sort of symbiotic relationship with the machine; the machine generates possibilities that we then direct or tweak until arriving at an optimal solution. We see this playing out in nearly every industry, from manufacturing to the design of websites to health care.

COMPUTER MODELING

While this introduction of "deep learning" algorithms is relatively new, we already depend upon computers to model possibilities in many areas of life. From weather and political projections to searching for natural gas and oil—the calculations required often exceed human capacity; in these cases, we already depend on the advanced computational abilities of machines. We build an abstract model of the world and then run simulations. Through abstraction and computation, we forecast the future. The difference that machine learning brings to traditional "brute force" computing is the ability to take on more complex tasks, juggle more demanding goals, and explore more options.

What is new then is the scope, complexity, and—we hope—accessibility of these tools. Examples such as Polisis, LawGeex, and Dreamcatcher signal to us a future where any of us can explore complex topics in a playful way.

VIDEO GAMES AND EXPLORABLE EXPLANATIONS

From a certain point of view, video games are a kind of computing modeling nearly all of us have played with. With video games—and most games of any kind—we step into a world structured with goals and rules. To win at these games, we have to test many possibilities and develop skills until we can arrive at the win conditions. Whether players realize it or not, this is a highly engaging, distilled form of *learning*. Through trial and error, experimentation, and play, we begin to understand new ideas in a manner that is quite potent.

It is for these reasons that we're excited by the work of Nicky Case and others advocating for "explorable explanations,"[8] where traditionally challenging concepts become accessible through playful interactions. With "The Evolution of Trust,"[9] Case uses game theory to help players explore the very complex topic of social trust and cooperation. After explaining a few basic concepts (based on Robert Axelrod's 1984 book, *The Evolution of Cooperation*), players are asked what choices they might make—"cheat" or "cooperate"— under different conditions.

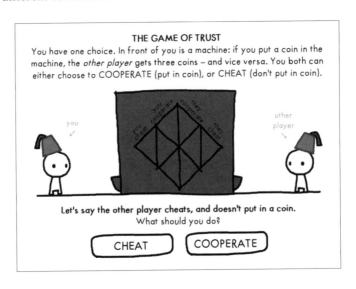

THE GAME OF TRUST
You have one choice. In front of you is a machine: if you put a coin in the machine, the *other player* gets three coins – and vice versa. You both can either choose to COOPERATE (put in coin), or CHEAT (don't put in coin).

Let's say the other player cheats, and doesn't put in a coin.
What should you do?

CHEAT   COOPERATE

8. https://explorabl.es/
9. "The Evolution of Trust." n.d. It's Nicky Case! https://ncase.me/trust/

As the game proceeds, players are given more options and more complicated outcomes. By the end of the game, they have a better sense of likely outcomes based on their individual choices. It's a powerful and stimulating way to bring a difficult topic to life. According to Case, "I think game theory can help explain our epidemic of distrust—and how we can fix it! So, to understand all this … let's play a game!"

With "Parable of the Polygons,"[10] Case transforms a prize-winning research paper on desegregation into a simulation, where through repeated play, you begin to recognize the powerful effects—good and bad—of even small changes to the system.

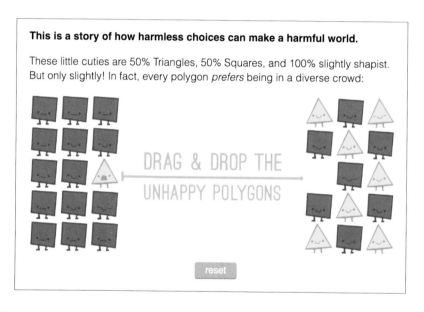

If we evaluate what's going on here, Case has created a powerful combination of nearly everything we've discussed in this book. Using the abstraction of polygon shapes avoids triggering real-world biases and prior associations that we might have around the topic of segregation. Moreover, the animations, illustrations, and typography are all very playful in tone, which also helps us approach a dark subject. And then, of course, learning happens through interactions with visual representations. These explorable explanations are light on text and heavy on cause and effect choices. We can use slides to adjust

10. "Parable of the Polygons: A Playable Post on the Shape of Society." n.d.. https://ncase.me/polygons/

different variables, and fast-forward through time to see what happens. And it's a simulation based on the statistical data collected by researchers.

With topics such as segregation or social trust, these are difficult concepts that many of us struggle to recognize, let alone understand what to do to change things for the better. But through play and simulation, we can explore possibilities and get a deeper understanding of these issues.

Now, imagine where these kinds of "games" might go, as we have the ability to play with more and more complex topics. Might we see explorable explanations that let us "play" through scenarios involving climate change or ending poverty? Might we see more social games where many of us are playing inside the same simulation? What if anyone could load in raw data, maybe even hook up real-time data, to see how that changes the game? We believe it's possible, and likely, that we'll witness more things like this in the near future. And to come full circle round, back to video games, sci-fi novels have—since at least Orson Scott Card's *Ender's Game*—explored blurred lines between reality and games for several decades. The recent novel *United States of Japan*[11] suggests an interesting possibility: governmental agencies using video games as a way to model, assess, and predict complex human behaviors. While this is still speculative, we see this as a natural continuation of present trends.

Theme #2: A Shift from Tools to Spaces

"The computer of the future is not a product, but a place."

This is the bold proclamation made by Dynamicland,[12] a visionary project that shows us another way to think about computing. Forget the notion of personal computers as solitary devices (such as desktops or smartphones) through which we work and connect. Dynamicland shows us how computing can be something altogether different, something we do together, in the open, with no devices, per se, in sight. Visitors to the Oakland-based community center that houses Dynamicland get a glimpse at one possible future, where "computing is done in the real world—on floors and walls, coffee tables, and kitchen counters." See Figure 15.3. Computing is something anyone can do, and do together, using real objects in the real world.

---

11. Tieryas, Peter. 2017. *United States of Japan*. Nottingham, UK: Angry Robot, an imprint of Watkins Media Ltd.
12. https://dynamicland.org/

Compared to traditional computer programming, this vision of computing has more in common with a kindergarten classroom, with people moving about, scribbling on sheets of paper, playing with paper cups, googly eyes, staplers, and other physical objects. It looks like people working together on an arts-and-crafts project, and certainly doesn't resemble our notions of serious programming. But this is the point of the project: to confront and unwind decades' worth of assumptions we've formed as to what computing looks like. Programming need not be something we do alone with virtual objects on screens.

FIGURE 15.3 Images of people "programming" at Dynamicland.

Founder and visionary Bret Victor (the same person who proposed *Dynamic Drawing Visualizations*) describes this as:

> All the possibilities of a personal computer but in a new, communal context in which everyone is capable of authoring their own dynamic media and building on the work of others.

In his post "The 'Next Big Thing' Is a Room,"[13] researcher Steve Krouse offers a brilliant explanation of Dynamicland, using a cooking analogy:

> Dynamicland computing is social like cooking is social. It's also physical like cooking is physical. You're not seated in front of a single-person screen, but walking around an open space, using a range of tools. It's incredibly natural to walk up to someone "cooking" up some code, offering to lend a hand, divvying up tasks, and improvising on the fly. You use your hands in all the myriad ways they're meant to be used …

This excites us, as it brings together many of the timeless themes explored throughout this book: hands-on interactions with physical objects. Arranging things in space (quite literally!). Collaborating with others. Using multiple senses. The coordination of our bodies with the environment …

Not About the Tech!

To make all this possible, Dynamicland currently uses projectors, cameras, and sheets of paper with colored dots (to make objects trackable). But Victor is quick to point out that this implementation is not the point, nor what we should be copying. The interactions enabled by light projections could be replaced by other advances—digital paper, robotics, and so on. Dynamicland is casting a bold vision for computation that pulls technology into new, formative directions.

Smart Dumb Things

Meanwhile, groups such as argodesign[14] are exploring similar possibilities, but with a more narrowly focused premise: *What is possible once projectors and cameras become as cheap and ubiquitous as light bulbs?* This simple question

---

13. Krouse, Steve. 2018. "The 'Next Big Thing' Is a Room." Phenomenal World. October 2, 2018.
    https://phenomenalworld.org/analysis/the-next-big-thing-is-a-room
14. www.argodesign.com/

has unlocked a number of concepts: glass bottles that become volume knobs. Sticky notes that can turn lights off and on. Cutting boards that become culinary coaches. With concept projects such as the "Office of the Future," argo challenges ordinarily solitary activities:

> There's an irony in having open offices filled with personal-computing devices. You have a space designed to encourage collaboration, but it's filled with people who are heads-down, immersed in laptops. We may as well all have blinders on.

In their concepts, they show teams of people, gathered together around ordinarily dumb objects—tables, glasses, sticky notes, that suddenly have smart abilities (see Figure 15.4). Even at the bar, colleagues can play an impromptu game of pong using beer bottles!

FIGURE 15.4 Stills from concept videos produced by argodesign, exploring how the technology of interactive light projections might alter or augment everyday activities. People work at a shared table (left) while recipe directions are projected onto a cutting board (right).

While argo's work is more focused on the technology implementation than that of Dynamicland, what both of these smart environments show us is computing, without computers.

Think of it like this: when you build a house you assume that it will have heat, light, air, water, and electricity. This is basic infrastructure. What happens when *computation*, rather than computers, is simply part of the assumed infrastructure. Computers change from being things in the world to a capacity embedded in our world. Computation is a feature of the environment. This is what projects such as Dynamicland or early experiments with interactive light projections are all about.

Theme #3: The Merging of Digital and Physical Realities

We can also look at these smart spaces through another lens: the merging of digital and physical realities. In many ways, this is what's been happening since PCs became portable laptops, then PDAs, and later smartphones we carry everywhere we go. With every bit of new technology, we remove more of the friction that prevents us from accessing digital information in the real world. At this moment, augmented reality is simply the next step toward this merging. Instead of having to look up reviews or pricing information on a thing, that information comes to you as soon as the thing is identified (see Figure 15.5).

FIGURE 15.5 Augmented reality might overlay the physical world with additional digital information. Here we see online reviews activated after gazing at a specific book cover.

The only bit of friction here is pulling out your phone and opening an app, which itself may also smooth out as AR (augmented reality) technology moves out of our phones into something like glasses or contact lenses. Alternatively, this mixing of digital and physical may come not from anything on our person, but rather through holograms and light projections built into these environments. Imagine the bold retail store that welcomes transparent pricing information and negative reviews, and stops trying or hoping to make information difficult to access!

In terms of making sense of information, this ability to overlay the physical world with additional information unlocks all manner of possibilities. Imagine the house or the used car that can tell you all about its history, or the ability to diagnose or explain a medical procedure without pulling out a book or screen. Less effort spent on knowledge *retrieval* frees up new spaces to actually make sense of—to synthesize and evaluate—the information.

Dumb Objects Become Smart

If we turn our attention then to physical objects, we see a similar trajectory, as ordinarily dumb objects become increasingly embedded with some kind of digital smarts. This shows up in everything from smart watches to thermostats, but also in toys and educational playthings. In a contribution I (Stephen) wrote for the O'Reilly book *Designing for Emerging Technologies*,[15] I speculated about tangible learning objects—things like the traditional counting beads and fraction blocks used in elementary schools—endowed with just a bit of digital smarts. Do this and you get "teaching things" that offer tight feedback loops to the learner, in the same way an app or video game lets us know immediately the result of an action. The benefit of these loops and the collected data are insights in *how* the child arrives at the right answer, which is a better assessment of mastery.

When We Can't Tell Atoms from Bits

That said, all of these trends simply bring digital information into the physical world, or overlay the physical world with digital information. As impressive

---

15. Follett, Jonathan. Ed. 2014. *Designing for Emerging Technologies: UX for Genomics, Robotics, and the Internet of Things,* 1st Edition. Sebastopol, CA: O'Reilly.

as this technology is, especially being able to accurately map and overlay the physical with virtual, the integration need not stop here.

What if physical matter could be altered in the same way that we edit and alter virtual information on a screen? What if you could program a pile of sand to change shape, through software programming? If this conjures up scenes from any number of sci-fi movies or these images from the 2013 movie *Man of Steel*, that's exactly what we're describing (see Figure 15.6).

FIGURE 15.6 In these images from the movie *Man of Steel*, we see physical matter altered in the same way that we currently edit and alter virtual information on a screen.

While still firmly in the realm of science fiction, the Tangible Media Group at MIT[16] has been exploring this very idea. The endgame for much of this integration of digital and physical information is (depending on how you view this merger) what's known as *programmable matter* or *tangible bits*. The vision for this research group spans 200 years, which gives context to early, crude experiments in this direction (see Figure 15.7).

---

16. https://tangible.media.mit.edu/

FIGURE 15.7 "Physical telepresence" allows one location to render a rod-driven approximation of the shapes of people and objects at another location.

In one project, we see how hand gestures filmed in one location can alter the physical surface of a table set up elsewhere. While the text is a table with hundreds of tiny rods that move up and down based on gestural input, it's not hard to imagine this increasing in fidelity over time, the same way pixels on screens have increased from the early, blocky days in the 1970s to our present 4K and 8K screens (see Figure 15.8).

FIGURE 15.8 Self-assembling robots work together in a swarm-like fashion to reorient and reconfigure themselves into new forms.

For a different take on how we might arrive at programmable matter, we can turn to research being done both at MIT's Computer Science and Artificial Intelligence Laboratory[17] and also at Harvard by the Self-Organizing Systems Research Group,[18] where researchers are experimenting with *self-assembling robots*. Using a combination of AI and robotics, the current technologies are little more than small cubes or cylinders, which can arrange themselves in space relative to each other. MIT researchers are focused more on the physical side of the problem developing M-Cubes, small cubes that can "jump, spin, flip, and identify each other." The Harvard group is more focused on the self-organizing nature of systems, and how by "following simple programmed rules, autonomous robots arrange themselves into vast, complex shapes." We mention these in passing, to point out the kinds of experiments demonstrating how something limited to sci-fi films might just be possible in the future.

So what does this technology have to do with information? The ability for physical forms to programmatically take on different shapes, or reconfigure themselves, opens up all kinds of imaginative possibilities. In terms of interaction controls, we can imagine devices and controls rich with sensory possibilities. We could trade in a mouse or tapping on a screen with things that tap into the diverse sensory capabilities built into our hands and bodies. Imagine a game controller that could change temperature, create friction, reshape, resist, give way, and more—all as a way to give feedback to the player. In terms of ideas and concepts, imagine things reshaping to take on different forms. Imagine having access to dynamic, physical models of everything from city maps to brain maps. More than seeing information, we could touch and feel the ideas we're discussing. To put this in perspective, imagine if we traveled back to the 1920s, and asked a similar question of a then fledgling technology, the TV screen: *What might we do with pictures that can reconfigure on a screen?* Really, we're only limited by what we can imagine.

17. Gordon, Rachel. 2019. "Self-Transforming Robot Blocks Jump, Spin, Flip, and Identify Each Other." MIT News. October 30, 2019. https://news.mit.edu/2019/self-transforming-robot-blocks-jump-spin-flip-identify-each-other-1030
18. Perry, Caroline. 2014. "A Self-Organizing Thousand-Robot Swarm." Harvard John A. Paulson School of Engineering and Applied Sciences. August 14, 2014. www.seas.harvard.edu/news/2014/08/self-organizing-thousand-robot-swarm

What's Next?

To be clear, none of what we've shared here is a prediction about the "next, big thing."

And these things—these tools and technologies that facilitate understanding—are part of a broader system of cognitive resources. Our focus is not so much on the tools and technologies, as much as the human at the center of things. While it's easy to get distracted by shiny, new inventions, we've tried to expose those *themes* we see in these things, the themes most relevant to our topic of understanding. The technology examples cited here are meant to provoke and inspire, and provide a different perspective on new technology announcements; we hope you consider any new, exciting technology with this kind of historical perspective.

That said, we are at an interesting point in history—a point where a number of the emerging and speculative technologies seem inseparable from our broader focus on *understanding*. After a period of time where digital meant denying what we know about the rest of the body and interactions, we're seeing the form and shape of technology begin to catch up with our natural human abilities. By considering what is changing, right now, we can speculate as to what understanding might look like in 10, 20, 50, 100 years. But in all this speculation, we consistently return to the timeless things we've always known about humans: we think with the whole body. What we know is based on dozens of sensory inputs. The inputs become electrical signals that we parse into meaning. Chief among our senses is our sense of vision. But it's about more than what we see—it's about interacting with information. And it's not just you, or me—it's us, and the environment we occupy. All of these things work together to help us make sense of the world we live in. Technology changes just give a new expression to these slowly changing abilities.

Perhaps a better question to ask in all of this is "What doesn't change?"

What Doesn't Change?

So what doesn't change (or, more accurately, what only changes *very* slowly, over thousands of years?) The brain doesn't change. The body doesn't change. The importance of representations and interactions doesn't change. What does change—or changes very quickly—is what the artificial externalities are capable of (a smart whiteboard, a voice assistant, ML-assisted tools) and how we stitch these together. These things are, in one view, things: things "out there" in the world, outside our head, outside our bodies. But, if we view them this way, we are saying understanding is something to be outsourced and off-loaded. The more powerful way, and the way we have argued in this book, is that understanding, especially for complex problems, comes through coordinating a system of resources. The things, other people, the spaces we're in, be they virtual or physical, these are all part of a system of resources in which and through which we manage information. Understanding then is rooted in how all these things—and people—integrate and *connect*.

Connecting the Dots

In a sense, this book has been all about connections. While this is a book about how we *understand*, this fine thread of connections has run throughout this book: the connections between neurons that become perception. The connection between prior associations and external representations. The connection with our environment. Connecting with each other. Connecting with and through technology.

We've tried to connect the dots between a broad number of domains and disciplines that—while all circling similar themes—rarely connect. Accordingly, this book covered a lot of ground; there's so much to learn from simply connecting what we already know. As writers, we learned much from researching and organizing this book. As a reader, we hope you experienced a similar transformation, seeing all the ways we might connect bits of information, to create more understanding. Going back to our familiar refrain from the opening chapters: we're given information, but not *understanding*. If, as we've concluded, understanding is a result of making connections, then we look forward to all the connections you will make. The world is filled with problems of understanding, just waiting for us to tip the balance from the information we have to the understanding we need. From confusing parking signs to dynamic, systemic issues, such as our present climate crisis, there is much to be learned, discovered, and understood. And understood not just by individuals or organizations, but by all of us, working together—connecting—in diverse and unpredictable ways. Imagine a world where understanding keeps pace with new information, where we all work and learn and play together. Our sincere hope is that something shared here empowers you to make this kind of understanding possible.

Whatever "it" might be, it's up to all of us to figure it out!

Index

concepts, models to sort abstractions, 208–213

conceptual metaphors, 91–92

conferences

schedules, 216–217

as visible environments, 330

Confucius, 21, 23

connections, 390

between humans and machines, 373–374

mind and body, 27–29, 30, 72–73

constructing knowledge, as interaction theme, 263, 264, 281–285

contained relationship, 199

container shipping, 291–294, 311

continuation, as Gestalt principle, 167, 172, 174

conversing, as interaction, 254

Cookie Monster, 63

cooking example, 197, 199–200, 206–208

cooperation, 378–379

coordination

and cognition as distributed system of resources, 20. See also systems of cognitive resources

of people as resource. See systems of cognitive resources, coordinating

copying, as interaction, 272

corporate branding, and color, 193

corporations, and disruption stories, 114

costs of understanding

extending information into environment, 207

from information to understanding, 13, 14–15, 40

metaphors and, 70

outsourcing to technology, 355–356

reducing with technology, 369

creation of understanding, 8–11

creativity exercises, 315

Crick, Francis, 101–103

crime, and metaphors, 65

Cringely, Robert X., 121

Cron, Lisa, 77, 81

cross-modality anchoring, 75

culture

color identification and, 179–183

social constructions of space, 201

Culture Map, 108

Cunningham, Ward, 64

curvemaps, 367–368

customer journeys, 321–322

cutting, as interaction, 264, 271–272, 276, 285, 287

Cynefin Framework (Tauber), 235

D

"The Dangers of Categorical Thinking," 123–124

data visualization, 227–228, 318–321, 343–345, 367–368

de Bono, Edward, 122, 334

debt, technical and financial, 64

decision framing, 66–67, 68–69

DeepMind, 357

Del-Prete, Sandro, 59

Descartes, René, 30

desegregation simulation, 379–380

design thinking, 121–122

Designing for Emerging Technologies, 385

desktop metaphor, 49

Dhakar, Lokesh, 236

diabetes example, 4–8, 9, 284, 319, 373

direct semantic, 68

disruption story, 114

organization of objects, ways of, 233

orientation, as visual encoding, 153

Oxford English Dictionary, 255

oxytocin, 82

P

Page, Scott E., 121, 363–364

Paoletti, Jo B., 185

paper. *See also* cards

    as annotation medium, 278

    flight strips, 307–308, 312

    index cards, 314–316

    limitations of text editors, 340–342

"Parable of the Polygons" (Case), 379–380

parity principle, 302

parking signs, 350–354

participation, encouragement of, 323–324

Pathline, as tool for complexity, 367–368

pattern-matching process in
    the brain, 56–60

pattern recognition,
    understanding as, 126

patterns

    in board games, 228–229

    information revealed in
        visual models, 216–219

    labeled for grammar, 200

    language of interactions. *See*
        interaction themes

    and principle of proximity, 169–171

    universal, behind visual models.
        See Objects, Placement,
        Territories model

people. *See also* humans

    coordinating people for
        understanding, 327–334

    in narrative associations, 80–82, 86

    organizing as Objects Placed
        into Territories, 225

organizing for 21st century
    knowledge work, 334–335

    as primary resource to coordinate,
        for understanding and for learning,
        314, 325, 326, 327. *See also* systems of
        cognitive resources, coordinating

    roles, in categorizing, 120–121

    technology as person, 47–48, 49

perception. *See also* visual perception

    in the brain. *See* brain, as
        perceptual organ

    in computational theory of mind, 25–26

perception, as process of active
    construction, 56–60

    recognizing letters, 56–57

    recognizing shapes and colors, 57–59

    seeing what we expect to see, 59–60

perceptual tasks, on continuum, 147

personas, 86

perspectives, and ways we
    see, 122, 333–334

Pfungst, Oskar, 309–310

Philosophy in the Flesh (Lakoff
    & Johnson), 91

phones

    as cognitive resource, 301, 302

    coordination of system of resources,
        retail shopping, 318–321

    and human rights, 50

    thought experiment, 41

physical matter, programmable, 385–388

physical telepresence, 387

physics, thinking externalized, 251, 284

pictorial representations, 173, 238

*Picture This: How Pictures
    Work* (Bang), 94–95

pie charts, 148–150, 188

Pike, William A., 243

piling, in collecting, 273–274

repicturing, as interaction, 264, 284, 285, 287

replacement narrative, 375

replicating, as interaction, 272

representations. *See also* external representations; mental representations; visual representation

rows and columns, 346–349

Resmini, Andrea, 113

resources. *See also* cognitive resources; systems of cognitive resources

distributed system of resources, 18–20, 37

information as, 1, 11–14

in interaction themes, 263–264

retail shopping experience, 318–321

RGB color cube, 182

"Rhetoric of the Image" (Barthes), 97

risk aversion and risk taking, 66

Roam, Dan, 99–101, 209

RoboTetris, 256–257

robotic vacuums, 48, 49

robots, self-assembling, 387–388

Rose, Kevin, 116

Rosling, Hans, 227

rotation, as visual encoding, 153

rows and columns representations, 346–349

ROYGBIV, 179–180

rules, in invisible environments, 329

Russian culture, and color, 181

S

safety, psychological, 331–333

saturation, of color, 187, 188, 190

scalable encoding, 153, 163

SCAMPER exercise, 315

"The Science of Interaction" (Pike et al.), 243

scientific method, 117

Scrabble, 241, 283

searching, as interaction, 264, 265, 266, 267, 270, 285, 287

Seductive Interaction Design (Anderson), 47

see-saw metaphor for health care, 99–101

seeing what we expect to see, 59–60

self-assembling robots, 387–388

self-driving cars, 357, 358

Sellen, Abigail, 308

sensory information, and understanding, 53–54

sensory input, and sense of vision, 134–138

sequenced data, 150–153, 233

service blueprints, 321–322

shapes

aesthetic associations and, 94–98

recognizing, 57–59

as visual property, 158–159

shared concepts, and invisible environments, 328–330

shared standards, 327–328

sharing, 280

Sherif, Muzafer, 74

similarity, as Gestalt principle, 166, 172

Simon, Herbert, 219

simplicity/Prägnanz, Gestalt principles, 166

simulations, 83–86

simultaneous contrast, 192–193

Six Thinking Hats (de Bono), 122, 334

sketchnotes, 238

small multiples, 235–236, 269

Smith, Graham, 57

T

tables in software, 348–350

tangible bits, 386

Tauber, Justin, 235

team sports, 328–329

technical debt (tech debt), 64

technologies
framing of, and human rights, 50
historical, 3, 370
and interactions with information, 252–253, 254
parallel evolution with understanding the mind, 39, 41
as person, place, or tool, 47–49
tools and. *See* tools and technologies for understanding

Terms of Service; Didn't Read (ToS;DR), 16–17, 354–355

terms of service documents, 9–11

territory, 221, 222, 233–234. *See also* Objects, Placement, Territories model

Tetris example, 248–251, 256–257, 283

text editors, 340–342. *See also* document editing

theory of mind, 80–82

Thibodeau, Paul H., 65, 119

thick and thin relationships, 89–90

things. *See also* objects
sorting, 208–213
in visual metaphors, 111
in visual representation, 196

Things That Make Us Smart (Norman), 216

thinking. *See also* visual thinking
as associations among concepts, 43, 51–52, 60, 92, 124–125
spread across brain, body, and environment, 2, 32, 35
understanding through interactions, 241–242

thinking extended to external environment, 197–208
cooking example, 197, 199–200, 206–208
embodiment and visual thinkers, 198–199
grammar for, 200–201
time: calendar, 204–206
time: clock, 201–204

thought experiment, blind man and stick, 40–41, 311

three-legged stool metaphor, 104–106

3 x 3 magic square game, 218, 284

tic-tac-toe, 218–219, 222–223, 229, 284

tight coupling, 255

time, 201–206
calendar, continous year-long, 204–206
clocks, 201–203
conference schedule, 216–217
as distributed cognitive resource, 305
start and stop points, 203–204
vertical sequencing, 200

timeline sort, of ideas, 122

Toffler, Alvin, 11

tools
for complexity, 360–368. *See also* complexity, tools for
as distinguished from what we do, 261, 262
technology as, 48, 49
use right tool for the job, 346, 362

tools and technologies for understanding, 339–368
computational errors, 359
in the dark with technology, 355–360
easy access to information, 350–355

W

Wardley, Simon, 120, 121

Watches Tell More Than Time (Coates), 96

Watson, James, 101–103

web browers, 39

Weiner, Charles, 251

Wells, H. G., 369

whiskey/whisky, 54, 214–215, 234

white light spectrum, 179

whiteboards as cognitive resources, 302–303

Wikipedia
    collaboration in environment, 330
    on color theories, 180

Wilkins, Maurice, 101–102

Wired for Story (Cron), 77

Wittgenstein, Ludwig, 195

Wodtke, Christina, 121–122

Wong, Bang, 367–368

World Wide Web, 372

writing
    by hand or with text editor, 340–342
    Hemingway app, 154, 155
    shared document editor, 49
    stream of consciousness writing, 280
    typefaces and associations, 93
    written language, 370

Wurman, Richard Saul, 11

Y

"Your Brain on Fiction," 81

Z

Zak, Paul J., 82

zero-sum game of replacement narrative, 375

Zhang, Samantha, 190

Acknowledgments

STEPHEN WOULD LIKE TO THANK:

While writing a book is a struggle for the authors, those who live with us bear a disproportionate burden. For this, I'm indebted to my wife, Erin. This book would not have been possible without her support, sacrifice, and innumerable gifts of time. For far longer than expected, she generously shared our time— and my attention—with this book. Add to this the precious gift of Saturday mornings for 2+ years (not to mention the many, many evenings) while this book crawled to the finish line, and … Words aren't enough to express my gratitude.

To my co-author, Karl. Thank you for joining me on this journey, and helping to produce something that is so much the better than what I might have written on my own. Your contributions and your critique were invaluable and took this book in new—and better—directions.

Thank you to Lou Rosenfeld and Marta Justak, for believing in this book, and for your incredible patience, year after year. Even as the topic evolved and the page count grew, you continued to have faith in us and gave this book the time and space needed to fully mature.

A big thank you to our early book readers: Jorge Arango, Julie Dirksen, Marsha Haverty, Becca Hummel, Wade Winningham, Ken Starzer, and Samuel Hulick. We listened to what you wrote, and the book is so much better because of you. A special thanks to Marsha and Julie pushing us with some of the hardest questions.

A special thank you to Christina Wodtke, who was the biggest champion, cheerleader, and critic throughout this entire process.

Where we work often goes unacknowledged. And yet, finding a place that welcomes and inspires can be a real challenge. Thank you to Kat and all the crew at Mudleaf, for creating an atmosphere that contributed every bit as much to this book as others listed here.

Both Karl and I would like to thank the unsung heroes who transformed our words into the remarkable thing you're now holding in your hands. The final production team of Marta Justak (editing), Danielle Foster (graphic design and layout), Sue Boshers (proofreading), and Marilyn Augst (indexing) worked long, hard hours on what was an especially challenging book! These individuals are each wizards and masters of their craft.

Dialogue is a critical part of learning. Consequently (and given the breadth of what we've written about here!), much of this book was born out of the conversations and interactions I've had over the past many years. For these everyday experiences, I wish to thank my colleagues, friends, and coworkers. Whether you were aware of it or not, you all contributed in some way. Many of you listened, and some of you read excerpts. While I can't list everyone by name, here are some folks I'd like to call out: Ben Judy, Randy Hoyt, Mike Lee, JD Smith, Rachel Litt, Jason Lange, David "Bru" Brubacher, Jason Cypret, Catherine Reichling, Travis Isaacs, Matt Heard, Ingrid Dahl, Jen Fox, Aaron Hursman, Ben Radcliffe, Kristen Przano, Christine Berglund, Alida Draudt, Piritta van Rijn, Sara Vassar, Kevin Hoffman, Robbert De Haas, Juli Allen, Jason Hoover, Cody Almond, Vitorio Miliano, Dave Malouf, Eva-Lotta Lamm, Martina Mitz, Dave Livingston, Preston McCauley, Candy Bernhardt, Amy Hoy, Ryan Rumsey, Harry Max, Mariana Ivanova, and Noah Iliinsky.

For organizing conferences, podcasts, articles, workshops, or other things that forced me to structure my thoughts and get these ideas put into the world, I'm indebted to the following folks: Andy Budd, Jared Spool, Dirk Knemeyer, Jonathan Follett, Brian Sullivan, Bruno Figueiredo, Wayne Miller, Per Axbom, James Royal-Lawson, Avi Itzkovich, Giles Colborne, Gilles Demarty, Adam Churchill, Haig Armen, Russ Unger, Ryan Carson, Greg Lakloufi, Steve Portugal, Joshua Lowry, Joe Sokohl, Randy Krum, Angelina Ivancheva, Irina Gerdjikova, Jindřich Fáborský, Cornelius Rachieru, Bogi Dufek, Zsuzsa Kovacs, Steve Baty, and Donna Spencer.

KARL WOULD LIKE TO THANK:

My first thank you must be to Stephen for inviting me to become his co-author. This was his book to start. Partway into the project he called to ask if I would consider taking the rest of the journey with him, an invitation that was generous, unexpected, and one I greatly appreciate. I would also like to thank Lou Rosenfeld, our publisher, and Marta Justak, our editor, for their patience and believing in the book, even as the manuscript expanded and took longer to finish than anyone anticipated. Their support, guidance, and experience made a tremendous difference. Thanks also to everyone at Rosenfeld Media for their efforts, large and small, to transition this book from possibility to print.

Many people reviewed this book in various forms while it was being developed and they all deserve thanks. I would particularly like to thank Marsha Haverty, Julie Dirksen, and Jorge Arango, not only for their suggestions, but also for allowing me to pester them with additional questions about the rough draft.

I owe an intellectual debt to many people, even though they had no direct involvement in this manuscript. A decade ago, in serving as my dissertation advisor, Dr. Kamran Sedig helped me open the door to new ways of thinking about the relationship between interaction and cognition. I would also like to thank Dr. Grant Campbell, who has been a vital sounding board and source of encouragement for many years. I am particularly indebted to the writings of Andy Clark, David Kirsh, Yvonne Rogers, Ed Hutchins, Lawrence Shapiro, and Catherine Marshall, along with many other scholars who are investigating how human thinking collides with information, technology, and our physical experience of the world.

It was my great honor to teach many smart, capable, and curious students during my years at Kent State University. Their questions, especially in my seminars on Human-Information Interaction and Information Visualization, helped expand and sharpen my thinking about ideas that made their way into this book. I cannot thank them enough.

Finally, but certainly not least, I would like to thank my wife, Samantha, for her unending patience during this project and all my intellectual expeditions. She has an unerring instinct for when to stay out of the way, how to offer encouragement, and what it takes to pull me out of the research morass and back to the delights of everyday life. She is a far better information architect than I, and the best partner in life that I could imagine.

Rosenfeld

Dear Reader,

Thanks very much for purchasing this book. There's a story behind it and every product we create at Rosenfeld Media.

Since the early 1990s, I've been a User Experience consultant, conference presenter, workshop instructor, and author. (I'm probably best-known for having cowritten *Information Architecture for the Web and Beyond*.) In each of these roles, I've been frustrated by the missed opportunities to apply UX principles and practices.

I started Rosenfeld Media in 2005 with the goal of publishing books whose design and development showed that a publisher could practice what it preached. Since then, we've expanded into producing industry-leading conferences and workshops. In all cases, UX has helped us create better, more successful products—just as you would expect. From employing user research to drive the design of our books and conference programs, to working closely with our conference speakers on their talks, to caring deeply about customer service, we practice what we preach every day.

Please visit **rosenfeldmedia.com** to learn more about our **conferences**, **workshops**, **free communities**, and **other great resources** that we've made for you. And send your ideas, suggestions, and concerns my way: louis@rosenfeldmedia.com

I'd love to hear from you, and I hope you enjoy the book!

Lou Rosenfeld,
Publisher